SLEEPY

Twentieth Century

Dolls

FROM BISQUE TO VINYL

Johana Gast Anderton

Copyright © 1974 Johana Gast Anderton

Twentieth Century Dolls
FROM BISQUE TO VINYL ©

PLATE I

Twentieth Century Dolls

FROM BISQUE TO VINYL

Johana Gast Anderton

Athena
Publishing Company

North Kansas City

Athena
Publishing Company

202 East 18th Avenue
North Kansas City, Missouri
64116

DEDICATION

To my first grade teacher, Miss Bessie Pettit, whom I shall always remember for her lesson, "Never say I can't",

And to my eighth grade teacher, Miss Clara Stockhoff, who graced the position of teacher as only a great lady could,

But most of all,

To my mother, Nellie Blankenship Gast, who gives so much of herself to the divine career of Mother, and to my daughter, Rebekka Suzanne, my passport to the future.

— Johana Gast Anderton

" . . . dolls have a kind of immortality
not granted to humans."

CONTENTS

Plate I   2

Dedication   5

Acknowledgments   7

The Dolls in My Attic   8

Plate II   10

A Brief History of
    Twentieth Century Dolls   11

The Dolls in This Book   13

How to Find Dolls in This Book   14

Plate III   16

Alphabetical Listing of Dolls   17

Plate IV 367

Value of Dolls 443

Bibliography 444

Numerical Index 445

General Index 446

My Dollies' Prayer 464

ACKNOWLEDGMENTS

Anyone who sets out to compile a book of this type learns early in the project that the outcome will depend to a large extent upon the cooperation of many people. A number of generous friends, acquaintances new and old, understanding relatives, and a family willing to walk a wide circle around *Mother and Her Mess;* these are all needed elements in the undertaking.

A bibliography hardly seems sufficient to mention certain important sources, for writers owe a great debt of gratitude to earlier researchers and doll historians. What doll writer today would dare to face her typewriter without having close at hand her copy of the Coleman *Collector's Encyclopedia of Dolls,* or Luela Hart's *Directory of United States Doll Trademarks?* Who would venture into the field of movie star dolls without the exhaustive work of Loraine Burdick for reference? These writers have created important stones in the wall of knowledge upon which future writers may build.

Doll collectors are special people, dedicated to their dolls and to the furtherance of doll research. The following women (and one gentleman) have allowed us to destroy the serenity and order of their homes for whole week-ends at a time in the process of photographing their doll collections: Virginia Battagler, Gwen Bower, Betty Kirtley, Lucie Spalding, Charles and June Vandiver, Josephine Wingfield, Betty Wiseman, Dian Zillner, and Kimport Dolls.

Others have loaned irreplaceable dolls and other items for us to bring home to photograph in our studio: Ruth Baume, Linda and Denise Brink, Dot and Joe's Browse Shop, Carol Glassmire (who shipped her dolls from South Carolina), Mary Lou Highlander, Lois and Sallye's Antiques, Shirley and Cheryl Lynn, Phyllis Odell, Ralph's Antique Dolls, Janice Sanders, and many others whose names are noted at the end of the paragraphs describing their dolls. Last of all, Joseph and Rebekka Anderton routed through toy shelves and trunks in search of the playthings from their own *"childhood".*

Photographs and historic outlines from doll manufacturers and advertisers were of special help. Interested, cooperative librarians at the Mid-Continent Library, Gladstone and Antioch Branches, provided much needed information, found obscure books, and remained cheerful through a long series of telephone calls and requests. L. Rae Walker, immediate past president of the Madame Alexander Fan Club and editor of the doll magazine, *"Milady in Miniature",* answered letters and telephone calls with verifications of several Alexander dolls.

Joseph L. Kallus, founder and owner of Cameo Exclusive Products Company, provided a large assortment of photographs, historic background, and other information pertaining to the work of Rose O'Neill and to the Cameo dolls. He mailed a wealth of valuable and irreplaceable material with complete faith in the United States Postal Department to deliver it in good condition and in me to handle and return it in proper order. All this with only a letter of introduction and several subsequent long distance telephone calls for editorial comment.

The catalog archives of Sears, Roebuck and Company were placed at my complete disposal. The encyclopedic character of these catalogs has long been recognized by researcher and collector alike.

Helen Brink, collector, friend, and secretary, was available at all hours with a ready ear, comments and suggestions, and an oft needed sense of humor. Virginia Groseclose helped type research letters.

Gathering and sorting material, writing picture captions and, finally, the manuscript is a tremendous task, but when typing is finished the big job of proof reading begins. These people worked for hours, reading and re-reading, making corrections and comments: Joe Anderton, Helen Brink, Nellie Gast, Shirley Lynn, and June Vandiver.

To all of these, and to all of you who read this book, my most sincere appreciation is extended.

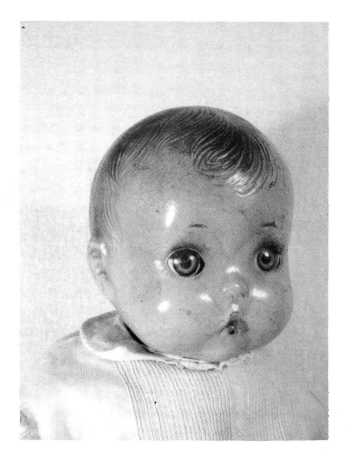

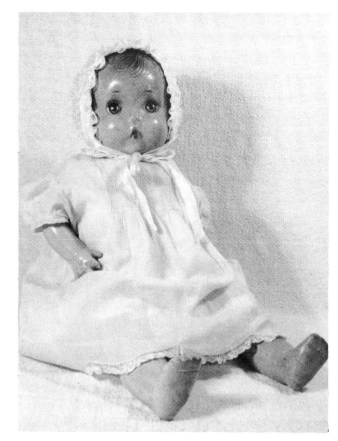

THE DOLLS IN MY ATTIC

These are the dolls I played with as a child, although my first is not shown. It was ruined in a flooded basement when I was seven and the Horsman *Brother* was given me as a replacement. The first time I saw the brown-eyed girl doll, dressed in her white "fur" coat, tam, and muff, she stood on a display stand with dozens of other dolls. I circled the table several times examining all the dolls, but for me there was only one. The coat and tam have been washed unnumbered times yet remain soft and fluffy. I cannot remember when her wig disappeared or how her leg was broken, but it must have been early in her career.

The *Shirley Temple* was our "best" doll shared by the three of us. We took her from the closet shelf, played with her, combed her curls, took her visiting to see the other dolls, but always we returned her carefully to her shelf. As a result of such genteel treatment her body is as perfect as the day it was finished and only a few hairline surface checks may be found on her face and limbs.

One day when her three little girls had grown, our Mother took Shirley from the shelf. "Its time to decide which of you three will keep the *Shirley Temple* doll," our Mother said. We drew white slips of paper from a dish and Shirley Temple came to live with me. She is still wearing a dress our Mother made for her years ago, for even with careful play the original clothes were soon worn out.

My last doll was a fashion mannequin because I dreamed, as so many young girls do, of becoming a fashion designer. This doll is identical in appearance to the store window mannequins of the 1940's and her arms are removeable to facilitate dressing her. She had one of the largest "designer" wardrobes ever seen. Half a dozen dress patterns were included in her box and my imagination provided variations to the original patterns. Many happy hours were spent providing this doll with every conceivable article of wearing apparel.

Along with these larger dolls we always had a peck basket of sewing scraps and a pink celluloid dimestore doll. The same 5c and 10c celluloids now command dollars instead of pennies as collectors add them to their collections, not for their intrinsic value but as representatives of their type.

None of my dolls was particularly expensive. None was splendid except in the eyes of the little girl who loved them. Therein lies the true value of any doll — that it has evoked a loving response or filled a need as an object of love in the life of a child.

PLATE II   10   TWENTIETH CENTURY DOLLS

42   THE LADIES' HOME JOURNAL   December, 1919

Buy American-Made Toys

SANTA CLAUS—the good American that he is—this year has turned to Uncle Sam for his toys. In fact the pair of them have been working together for months and months for our American kiddies.

They have planned and arranged and built really wonderful things. They are original—there is a host of new toy ideas.

They are conceived and built by American men and women —they are not the thoughts or work of foreign countries.

American-made toys are best for the children because each toy is perfect. The design is right, the craftsmanship is careful—there are more to pick and choose from. They are educational—they are amusing.

This Christmas make children happier with American-made toys.

This season—this coming New Year—resolve to support American industries—to protect American trade.

Patronize the toy store that shows the circle of Uncle Sam and the laughing, happy children. You will find there the greatest assortment of Christmas and all-year-round toys— the best ones, too.

AMERICAN TOYS

Patronize the toy store that displays these signs

This space is contributed to the cause of American industries by the Toy Manufacturers of the U. S. A. Flatiron Building, New York

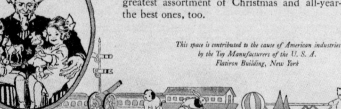

PLATE II

A BRIEF HISTORY OF
TWENTIETH CENTURY DOLLS

Whether a piece of bone wrapped in a bit of fur, a gourd dressed in calico scraps, or a turned wooden bedpost bundled in flannel, children have played with "dolls" through the centuries. On display in the British Museum in London is a tattered rag doll found in the ancient tomb of a Roman child. There is, of course, the scholarly question of whether such an artifact was a funeral effigy or the beloved toy of the deceased child placed in the tomb by a grieving parent. Those of us who love dolls prefer the latter view.

Many volumes have been written to record the history of dolls from ancient times through the first quarter of this century. Most libraries have excellent selections of doll books and librarians willing to obtain what is not readily available. For this reason, we will give only this passing nod to the many hundreds of years of "dolldom" and come swiftly forward to the *Twentieth Century.*

The European doll industry moved into the new century with a great heritage from the past, much promise for the future, and serious economic problems. Newly invented methods of mass production had changed the prospects of the toy merchant from one of catering to the pampered few to that of supplying trinkets and toys to the masses. Often quality was sacrificed to achieve the quantity demanded by the new mass market.

At the same time, the old battle for the market which had long raged between France and Germany had not abated. Several prominent French manufacturers were forced into a consolidation, and war was looming on the horizon. In America, there was a movement to shift a large measure of the toy market from foreign to American manufacturers, but this shift did not actually occur until the advent of World War I.

In old catalogs of 1903 we find the announcement, *"We fill orders in any language. Send in your order; we can read it."* This in a day when immigrants were settling all over the United States. Soon the beautiful German bisques had disappeared completely from the catalogs; the spectre of war was upon the world. Doll manufacturing was so completely disrupted by World War I that Germany was never to regain her command of the world toy market.

Old catalogs of the war years illustrate the efforts of America's manufacturers to fill the needs of her children. Composition dolls lead the lists, most of them with cloth bodies although a portion had jointed, composition bodies. Doughboy dolls, soldier and nurse sets, and nurse dolls in full uniform were very popular.

Following the war German dolls, as well as those from Italy, were gradually added to the offerings in most catalogs until by 1921 the imported dolls were again enjoying prominent display. American manufacturers, who had worked against great odds to supply the market during the war, fought back fiercely. They mounted a campaign aimed at the patriotism of the American people. *"American dolls for Americans,"* and *"Made in America for American boys and girls"* were two of the many slogans fired at a war-weary populace.

Manufacturing methods, design ideas, and price structures were improved to meet and overcome the threat from abroad. For example, in 1928 the Italian Lenci dolls were priced at $1.19 and $1.95 for 11" and 15" dolls, while comparable "domestic" dolls sold for only 49c and 95c.

The American doll and toy industry became an important, if not dominant, factor in the world toy market. World War II completed the ruin of the once-great German industry. There are two notable survivors. The Kathe Kruse Puppen GMBH produces not only the dolls of the late Frau Kathe Kruse, but continues also with the designs of her daughter, Hannah. The Rheinische Gummi and Celluloid Fabrik Company, has given collectors many beautiful celluloid dolls over the years.

The dolls of the early part of the Twentieth Century were most often those with bisque or china heads and with kid, kidalene, cloth or composition bodies. Many had bisque or china forearms and hands; a few had bisque or china legs and feet. The complete range of dollmaking materials was represented, but the bisque and china dolls were most plentiful.

During the 1920's, some of the finest bisque dolls available to collectors today were produced. These were the bisque-head, soft-body babies such as the Bye-lo, the different character babies, the Dream Baby and the other babies issued in competition to the Bye-lo. Not a few of these dolls were designed by Americans and produced in Germany. Several of Rose O'Neill's creations, Grace Storey Putnam's Bye-lo, and the Frank King cartoon character dolls were among those made in Germany in bisque during the 1920's. Bisque-head dolls were not limited to the babies; girl dolls and child or toddler dolls with bisque heads and kid or ball-jointed, composition bodies were available as late as the 1930's. The later ones are often of poor quality and unimaginative modeling, although there are exceptions to every such rule.

The composition doll truly came into its own during

the 1920's and 1930's. There were many beautiful and interesting composition dolls prior to that time, of course. Some excellent examples survive from the nineteenth century to attest to the skill of dollmakers using composition as their medium. Neither can it be said that composition was the *only* material used during the 1920's and 1930's.

During those two decades, dollmakers took advantage of the peculiar properties of many different materials to achieve desired effects with particular dolls. *Popeye* and other cartoon characters were made of wood; *drink and wet* dolls were of rubber and rubber compounds; rag dolls were available in large numbers; even celluloid, bisque, and china were still being used. But the *composition* dolls of the period are outstanding.

The "girl doll" with long, slender legs, soft or composition body, and molded or applied hair, made during the 1920's is among the most collectible of dolls today. In the catalogs of the day these American-made dolls were often given names. *Sally, Patsy, Patsy-Joan, Patsy-Lou* and *Marilee* were popular. Often the manufacturer's name was listed; companies such as *Arranbee, Effanbee, Horsman* and *Ideal* were at the fore. *Mary Ann, Mary Jane* and the *Babies Dimples, Sunshine* and *Bubbles* led a long parade of composition dolls that marched into the 1930's.

War is not the only historical factor which has affected the doll and toy industry. From a peak in the late twenties, the pages devoted to toys and dolls in general catalogs declined in number until about 1935. In that year, only two pages in one large mail-order catalog were given over to displays of such *luxuries* as children's playthings. The Great Depression hung like a plague upon the land; people were hard-pressed to provide the necessities; the dollmaking industry faced one of its darkest hours but continued to produce the *"necessities of childhood"*.

Naming dolls after famous personalities seems always to have assured sales. When the doll bears a resemblance to the personality success is often immediate and profitable. So it is we find composition dolls representing *Baby Sandy* of the movies, *Buttercup* and *Nize Baby* of cartoon strip fame, and *Shirley Temple, Jane Withers, Deanna Durbin* and *Judy Garland,* all movie stars and all very collectible today. The Great Depression appears to have been a factor in the popularity of these movie star dolls.

Several changes in materials used in production of dolls were introduced in the 1940's. *"Magic Skin",* first in natural rubber, then, with the advent of World War II restrictions, in synthetic rubber, was an early innovation. A thin skin of rubber was filled with a combination of cotton, kapok, foam rubber, or other materials. The result was a soft-to-the-touch, life-like doll which was both cuddly and bathable.

When new, these dolls were of a beautiful natural pink "skin" color; too often today the collector finds the skin has darkened or even has mottled unattractively. The only remedy is to dress these babies as completely as possible, covering every square inch of the rubber except perhaps the hands. Usually the heads of *"Magic Skin"* babies were of composition or hard plastic. These are found in varying stages of disrepair today, although the hard plastic has proved the more durable of the two materials.

The hard plastic head of a large *"Brother Coos"* in the author's collection is in beautiful, like-new condition although the composition legs have deteriorated badly. Some of the dolls made of hard plastic were not of such high quality. Often these dolls were of a poor grade plastic or the plastic was thin and has split at the seams or cracked at points of stress. The quality hard plastics, however, are often mistaken for well-finished celluloid.

With the introduction of the soft vinyls, doll production entered a new era. Manufacturers now produce dolls with "rooted" wigs reminiscent of those found on early wax dolls such as the Montanaris. The "hair" may be shampooed, combed, brushed, set, and otherwise styled. In addition, the pliable vinyls and plastics give a soft touch and natural glow to modern dolls. The very nature of the material allows for fine detailing in the modeling and casting.

The variety of today's dolls is seemingly endless; at no time in history have children had so many dolls with which to play and so many costumes in which to dress them. Indeed, the costuming and accessorizing of dolls seems to have attained an all-time peak, surpassing even the marvelous *trousseaux* of the French ladies of fashion of the previous century.

Not only are modern dolls elaborately attired; they seem to be among the most talented in all doll history. There are dolls which walk, skip rope, ride tricycles and "ponies", dance, tumble and flip. There are dolls who sing, tell stories, recite poetry, whisper secrets, or echo the voice of their little "mother". Some are even multilingual. Other dolls blow bubbles, eat from a spoon, shake their heads *no* for spinach, reach for a bottle, and change facial expression with a wave of the hand.

Like people, who keep right on being born, dolls keep right on being created. We need to look around, as collectors, and ask ourselves, *"What is good today that will still be good after many tomorrows?"* The poorly made, gaudy, cheap dolls will not endure, but part of what is being produced today *is* in good taste and *is* well made. From this group will come the antiques and collectibles of the next generations.

THE DOLLS IN THIS BOOK

Although doll collecting is relatively new as a "popular" hobby, the number of collectors has grown in recent years until doll collecting ranks high among collecting hobbies. Doll collectors clubs have been organized even to the national level. As a logical result of the increased demand, prices of antique dolls have been pushed higher and higher.

Anyone with unlimited funds may easily assemble a quality collection of interesting and rare dolls. There are many efficient dealers ready and able to assist the collector in this worthy pursuit. Those of us who are not so fortunate *financially* must find other means of fulfilling our desire for a doll collection.

Although some of the dolls from the first three decades of this century carry price tags beyond the means of many collectors, there *were* many dolls produced during the period 1900 through 1970, in this country and throughout the world, which are both collectible and affordable today. Collectors are now more appreciative of the artistic and intrinsic value of German bisque dolls which had previously been considered unworthy of representation in a truly fine collection.

Some of the German bisques are of poor to average quality; still, many German firms made excellent character faces as well as the finest of infant dolls. The dolls of the French combine, the *S.F.B.J.* (which see), also fall into this category. In addition, some imperfections which often caused collectors to pass by an otherwise desirable doll are now considered less important. The *perfect* doll is still the most desired, of course, but many collectors are willing to make some compromise in this respect.

Many of the dolls in this book are shown just as they were found — wanting a limb, needing a shampoo and set or a new wig, or occasionally an eye operation. Some are *unassembled*. Mussed wigs and smudged features speak of days of play and not-always-loving attention. Most of the dolls found in thrift shops and flea markets are either *wigless* or their original hair-do has been rendered unrecognizable through hard play.

Few of these dolls are dressed; some are merely in remnants of original clothes, but wherever possible dolls are pictured in original costume. This is not to say the illustrated outfit was the *only* original costume in which the doll was released. In some cases, the same doll was available in an assortment of costumes in addition to a wide variety of separate wardrobe items. *Original,* for the purposes of this book, is defined as *that costume(s) or wardrobe in which or with which the doll was sold.*

Often modern dolls have been issued in series, as were their antique counterparts. For example, we find *Tiny Tears, Teeny Tiny Tears,* and finally, *Teeny Weeny Tiny Tears.* A notable exception is the *Chatty Cathy* group from Mattel which includes *Chatty Cathy, Chatty Brother, Chatty Baby,* etc. Each of these dolls was issued in one size only until discontinued. When the line was re-issued in 1969, it had been completely re-designed, new molds were used, and the sizes were different, thus assuring the *original* or *"old" Chatty* dolls a firm position as collectibles. It is to be hoped that Mattel will never re-issue the older dolls. Many of Mattel's latest dolls have first been issued in a large size, then somewhat later a *"baby"* version has been offered. *Dancerina,* then *Baby Dancerina* the following season, is an example of this practice.

Only by studying every available doll and doll book may the collector hope to identify the thrift shop doll. Even so, many of the dolls available in such shops will be of little or no value and will be completely unidentifiable under any circumstance because they are the very cheapest dolls and never had identities in the *new* state.

Identification is simplified when a doll is well-marked, although a few marks remain obscure. Companies which were in business only a few months sometimes left many well-marked dolls to confound collectors and researchers alike. Marks on dolls indicate mold numbers, dates, sizes, manufacturers' names, patent numbers, model numbers, and even sometimes the *"name"* of the doll. On occasion two identical dolls may be found — one unmarked, the other well-marked (see *"Carmen Miranda").* In other cases, portions of the marks may have been deleted accidentally during manufacture. Persistence is often required in authenticating even a "late model" doll.

While those of us who collect dolls have a tendency to believe they were created solely for us, we should remember that doll manufacturers must make a profit or fail. It is, therefore, not surprising to discover that miscellaneous heads have been placed on familiar bodies such as those of the *Shirley Temple, Patsy* or *Anne Shirley* dolls. Economic efficiency required producers to continue use of molds until they were worn out or to use up stocks on hand by uniting them with heads of other design.

Many *Shirley Temple* bodies were used in this way and the marks only slightly smudged out; *Anne Shirley* bodies were used with the Dewees Cochran series of *American Children.* These are but two examples; the collector may find others. Collectors need to be aware, however, that there are those who create *"put-togethers"* from miscellaneous parts and offer them for sale as original. Studying available published material, then seeing as many *original* dolls as possible, will help collectors recognize *put-togethers* when they are offered.

Unmarked dolls are more of a problem. Comparison, or a fortunate find in the original box, is often the only means of identifying these to manufacturer or *personality*. Since early catalogs featured artists illustrations rather than photographs, some non-character dolls are not completely identifiable through such a source. Dolls with definite features are easily recognizable in catalog drawings, however.

Another little-known fact concerning the dolls sold through catalogs is illustrated by the following quotation from the 1926 *Fall and Winter Catalog* of Sears, Roebuck and Company:

"America's best known makers build dolls especially for us, for every doll must be of unusual value to gain a place in this catalog. Such makers as Horsman, Effanbee, Century, American Character (Petite), Ideal, Gem and other well known factories put special value into "Sears Specials" during the quiet months. No one maker, it seems, can supply all of the vast amount we may need on a particular doll, therefore, in most instances we do not mention the maker's name, but you can depend on our sending you a good doll and a big value for your money."

To include *every* doll manufactured in the past seventy years in a single volume would be an impossibility. It is possible, however, to survey *representative* types. Collectors may soon learn to recognize certain characteristics as belonging to certain periods by studying the pictures and descriptions.

Dolls of rubber, composition, rag and wood; dolls of celluloid, metal, bisque and plastic; dolls of nearly every description are available. It is the hope of the author that this book may serve as a guide to *new* collectors, as well as a reminder to *advanced* collectors that there are still many beautiful, interesting, well-made and reasonably priced *younger* dolls waiting to be added to collections. This book is a survey of such dolls.

HOW TO FIND DOLLS IN THIS BOOK

With few exceptions, each individual doll shown in this book has a *number key* shown with the photograph and repeated at the beginning of the descriptive paragraph. An extensive *General Index* lists these dolls in as many different ways as it was possible to consider them. Dolls from larger companies are grouped under the name of the manufacturer and shown in approximate chronological order. Letter marks, ie. **X** or **W** etc., have been included alphabetically in the General Index. *Number marks* are listed separately. In addition, dolls are shown to illustrate types of material from which dolls are made.

Twentieth Century Dolls
FROM BISQUE TO VINYL©

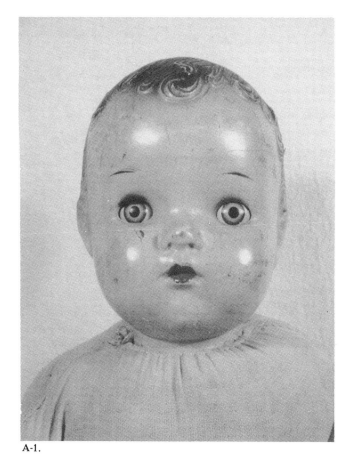

A-1.

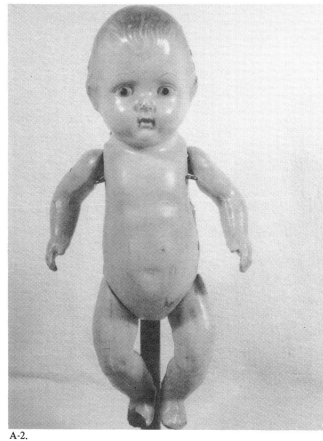

A-2.

A-2

A

A-1. 24" Baby. Composition head and limbs, stuffed body, flange neck, painted hair, cry voice. 1930's. Marks: **A.B.C. / TOYS** on head. *(Courtesy Mrs. Walter Lytle)*

NOTE: ORIGINAL PRICES SHOWN
ARE NOT TODAY'S PRICES.

fig. A-2

A-2. 15" Boy. All composition, strung with metal springs, painted features and hair, possibly original clothing, buttons marked **RAILROAD KING.** Marks: see Fig. A-2 on shoulder. 1910's. *(Courtesy Dot & Joe's Antiques)*

A-5.

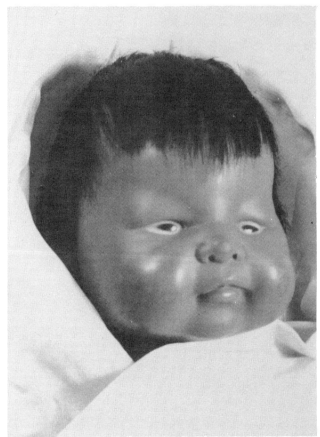

A-3

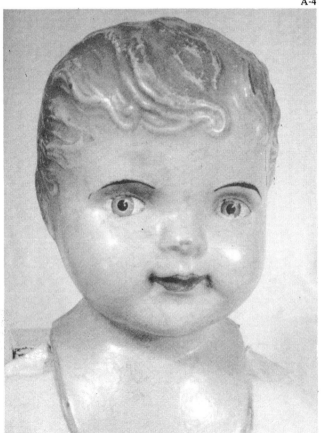

A-4

A-3. 19" Colored Baby. Molded vinyl head and limbs, stuffed cloth body, rooted hair, painted eyes. Marks: © **1961 / ALTER.** *(Kirtley collection)*

A-4. 25" Mama Doll. Composition head and limbs, molded painted features, blue eyes, cloth body, mama voice box. Marks: **AM DOLL CO.** on shoulder plate (probably American Doll Mfg. Co. / American Doll Co.) 1910's-1920's. *(Zillner collection)*

Another example of this doll is excelsior-stuffed and is dressed in a very inexpensive voile trimmed with lace. A sewn-in woven tag reads **"WEATHERBIRD SHOES".** The doll was available for $1.00 with the purchase of a pair of that brand of shoes. The original owner, who receive the doll as a young child, is now about sixty years of age, a fact which aids the researcher in establishing a fairly accurate dating.

A-5. *Amberg Walking Dolls.* 19½", 22½", and 28½" sizes, with painted or sleep eyes, painted or mohair wig, dressed in voille dress and bonnet. Guide by the arm to "walk", no mechanism. Prices from $4.95 for 19½" with painted eyes and hair to $19.95 for 28½" with sleep eyes and wig. *1921 Catalog illustration courtesy Sears, Roebuck & Co.*

A-6

A-6a.

A-7.　　　　　　　　　　　　　　　　　A-8.

A-6. *American Beauty Dolls.* Composition shoulder head and limbs, sleep eyes, mama voice, pink organdy and lace outfit. Sizes 13" at $1.98, 15" at $2.69, 18" at $3.65, 19½" at $4.39. *1924 Catalog illustration courtesy Sears, Roebuck & Co.* In 1920 two sizes of American Beauty Babies with composition heads and forearms, stuffed cloth bodies and shaped legs were listed. 14" size sold for $3.85 and 19" size was $5.95.

A-6a. *American Beauty Dolls.* Ad reads: "New American Beauty dolls with those marvelous eyes; roguish eyes roll, flirt, wink, blink and sleep". Toddles when guided, guaranteed unbreakable head, pink organdy dress; 14", $1.98 and 20", $4.98. Also 15½" and 17". *1925 Catalog illustration courtesy Sears, Roebuck & Co.* 1924 Catalog listed American Beauty "Music Box Doll" with music box in body, played two tunes by turning handle at lower left side of body, also mama voice box.

A-7. 19" Girl. Hard plastic, glued-on synthetic wig, rosy cheeks and knees, flat feet, molded toes, open mouth, four teeth, felt tongue, blue sleep eyes. Original, well-designed clothes: taffeta underpants, nylon organdy petticoat, green taffeta dress with ruffle trim. ca. 1951. Unmarked. *(Charles Vandiver collection)*

A-8. 25" Lady. Hard plastic with soft vinyl head, rooted Saran hair, blue sleep eyes, high-heel feet, swivel waist. Original clothes: beige satin dress, attached nylon petticoat with silver lace trim, large red rose on side of skirt. ca. 1956. Marks: **ARROW PLASTIC,** with arrow in diamond, and numerals **74.** *(Charles Vandiver collection)*

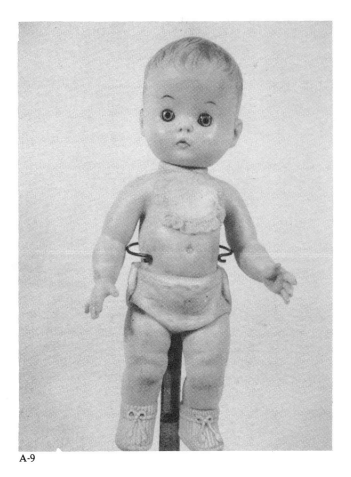

A-9

ADV-A1.

A-9. 10" Baby. Molded vinyl, squeeker, molded on diaper, bib, and booties, body and limbs one piece, inset stationary eyes, molded hair. Marks: © **The Edward Mobley Co. 1959 / Mfd. By / Arrow Rubber & Plastics Corp.** *(Spalding collection)*

ADVERTISING DOLLS

Manufacturers have long been aware of the effectiveness of dolls used in advertising, either as mail-in coupon items or as in-package premiums. These dolls are of two distinct types: regular dolls purchased for the purpose, and specially designed dolls representing the company's trademark.

AUNT JEMIMA DOLLS

The original *Aunt Jemima* was Miss Nancy Green, a former slave who became one of the world's best known women when the product she represented became a staple of modern kitchens. Anna Robinson was the *Aunt Jemima Pancake Flour* representative from about 1933 up to the days of television. Altogether five generations of Negro women have personified *Aunt Jemima,* lending warmth and dignity to one of the most widely known trademarks figures in history.[1]

Keeping abreast of this personification of home-cooking and hospitality, manufacturers have produced an almost continuous line of *Aunt Jemima* dolls. *Effanbee* produced an *Aunt Jemima* doll distributed through Sears' catalogs; rag, oilcloth, and composition were used. Doll collectors may even wish to highlight a collection with examples of the plastic kitchen accessories representing *Aunt Jemima* and *Uncle Mose.*

ADV-A1. 12" *Aunt Jemima.* Oilcloth or plastic-coated fabric, flat-sewn and stuffed, color lithograph. Cartoon approach to the character. Family of four, *Aunt Jemima, Uncle Mose, Wade,* and *Dinah* were issued in this set. Available in stores as well as through a mail-in advertising offer. ca. 1948. *(Courtesy Ralph's Antique Dolls)*

ADV-A2. 15" *Aunt Jemima.* Litho on muslin, yellow dress with black dots, yellow cap with red checks. Distortion in close-up photograph due to lumpy stuffing. Marked **Aunt Jemima** on back. *(Author's collection)*

ADV-A3. *Aunt Jemima* as she appeared in a 1919 Ladies' Home Journal advertisement placed by Aunt Jemima Mills, St. Joseph, Missouri. Miss Nancy Green was Aunt Jemima at this time.

[1] Marquette, Arthur F., "Brands, Trademarks and Good Will", McGraw-Hill, New York, 1967.

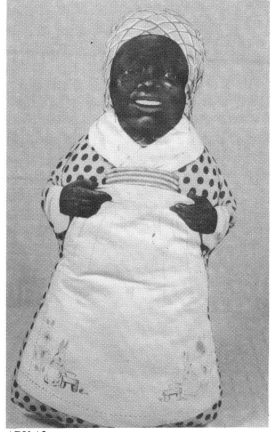

ADV-A2.

ADV-3.

ADV-A4.

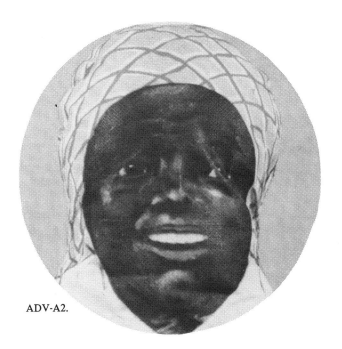

ADV-A2.

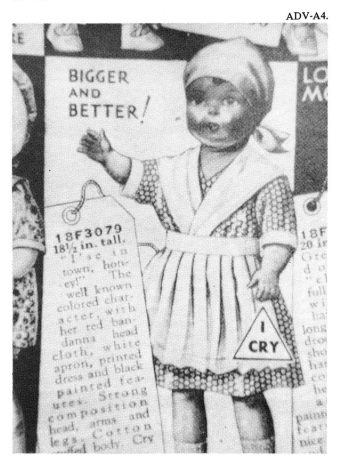

ADV-A4. 18½" *Aunt Jemima.* "Mama" doll of composition and stuffed cloth, featuring the slogan which made Aunt Jemima famous: "I'se in town, honey." *1931 Catalog illustration courtesy Sears, Roebuck & Co.*

ADV-A5.

ADV-B2a.

ADV-B1.

ADV-A5. *Harriet Hubbard Ayer Make-up Doll*, 14½"
and 16", retailed at $11.39 and $12.98 respectively.
Glued-on Saran wig, vinyl plastic Magic Flesh arms and
face, hard plastic body and legs. Complete with make-up
kit. Shown 1953 and 1954 catalogs. *(Courtesy Sears,
Roebuck & Co.)* A known 14" example is on a hard
plastic "P-90" body by Ideal and the "make-up kit" adds
becoming color to an otherwise unpainted face. Marks:
MK 21/IDEAL DOLL.

ADV-B1. 6½" *Billie-Whipple*. Wire frame covered with
cotton wadding and nylon stockinette, vinyl molded
head, mohair whiskers and hair, burlap hat. Promotion
by Radio Station KMBZ of Kansas City, Missouri, to
benefit Children's Mercy Hospital of that city. Unmarked. 1969. *(Rebekka Anderton collection)*

ADV-B2. *Buster Brown*. Originated by R. F. Outcault as
a comic, Buster Brown and his name have been used to
advertise clothes, shoes and many other items. The
advertisement shown is marked: **"BUSTER
BROWN"/(TRADE MARK REGISTERED)/IVAN
FRANK & CO./MAKERS/NONE GENUINE
WITHOUT THIS LABEL.** Buster Brown is used as
trademark by Buster Brown Hosiery Mills of Chat-
tanooga, Tennessee (formerly United Hosiery Mills).
(Kirtley collection)

At night when I go out to dine,
And want to look all swell and fine,
And want the girls to think I'm cute,
I always wear this stylish suit.
For ti's, you see my very best,
And I am fashionably dressed,
And Tiger as proud as he can be,
And hangs around and looks at me.

$5.00,
5.95,
and
$7.50.

CLOTHE YOUR BOY AT
**THE PALACE CLOTHING CO.'S
BOYS' STORE.**

ADV-B2.

BUSTER

BROWN

VESTEE

SUITS

The author cannot resist the temptation to display an original *Campbell Kid* jingle which occurred to her as this material was being prepared:

*"The Campbell Kids both come on strong,
Such is their constitution
From eating healthful Campbell's soups;
They're now an institution."*

(Campbell Kid information courtesy the Campbell Soup Company)

We blend the best with careful pains
In skillful combination,
And everything we make contains
Our business reputation.

fig. CK

ADV-CK1.

THE CAMPBELL KIDS

The *Campbell Kids* were created in 1900 by artist, Grace Weiderseim, later known as Grace G. Drayton. She continued to draw the *Campbell Kids* until 1933 at which time the task was assigned to a continuing series of artists. Magazine advertisements and car cards were popular vehicles for the *Campbell Kids* in the early days; they currently appear regularly in television announcements. Each spot usually features a jingle such as the one which appears on the Campbell Soup Company stationary written by Charles M. Snyder, along with a typical illustration.

Dolls and spoons, bridge tallies and cut-outs are among the items collectors may be able to add to collections. The advertisements with their illustrations and jingles would comprise an impressive collection. The *Campbell Kids* have been with us a long time and show signs of continuing for many years to come.

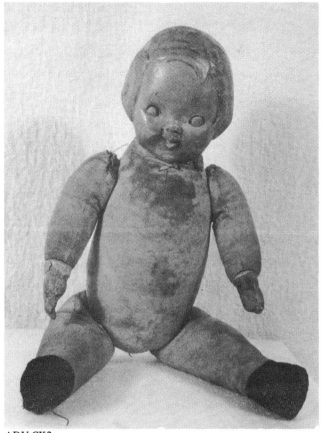

ADV-CK2.

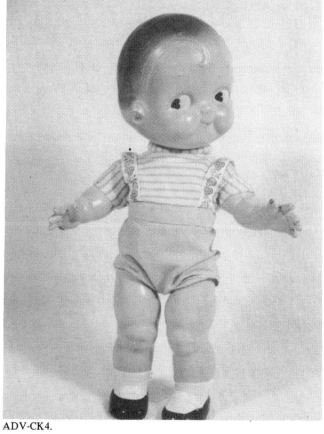

ADV-CK4.

ADV-CK3.

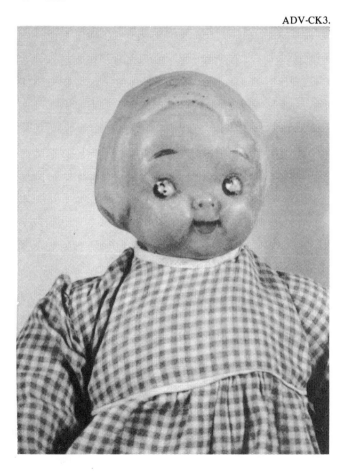

ADV-CK1. 10½ *Campbell Kid.* All cloth construction, including hands, pin and disc joints, sawdust and cork stuffing, side-glancing painted eyes. *(Kirtley collection)*

ADV-CK2. 11" *Campbell Kid.* Cloth construction, sewn-in black cloth feet, composition head and gauntlet hands, pin and disc joints, sawdust and cork stuffing. Note these "Can't Break 'Em" composition heads are in excellent condition even though the paint is worn and chipped. *(Kirtley collection)*

ADV-CK3. 12" *Campbell Kid.* Cloth construction, composition head and gauntlet hands. Doll is similar to ADV-CK2, but larger. *(Zillner collection)*

ADV-CK4. 12½" *Campbell Kid.* All composition, all original. Girl doll in 1949 catalog wore similarly designed dress; boy had cap to match his suit. Girl wore hairbow. — 1948 — Horsman. *(Courtesy Mrs. Theodore W. Glassmire)*

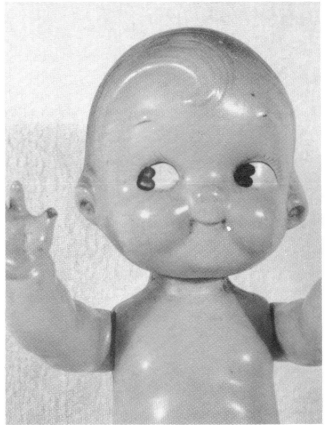

ADV-CK5.

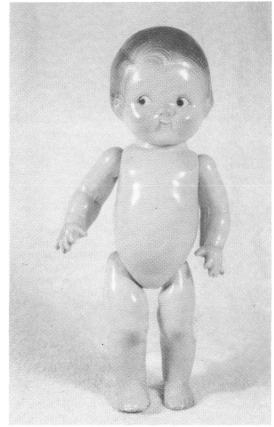

ADV-CK6.

ADV-CK6.

ADV-CK5. 12½" *Campbell Kid.* Close-up of 1948 Horsman doll. *(Kirtley collection)*

ADV-CK6. 11½" *Campbell Kid.* All composition, blue painted eyes. Sometimes called "Dolly Dingle" because of resemblance to the Dolly Dingle paper dolls, both designed by Grace G. Drayton. Marks: **A PETITE / DOLL.** ca. 1925. American Character. *(Wiseman collection)*

ADV-CK7.

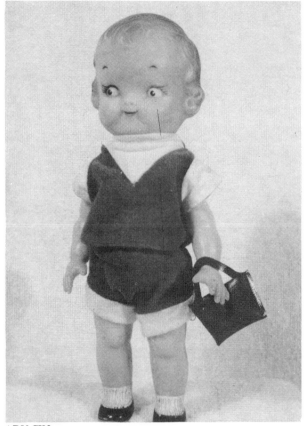

ADV-CK8.

ADV-CK9.

ADV-CK7. 13" *Campbell Kids.* All vinyl plastic, molded hair, jointed heads and arms. 1952 catalog illustration. 1950 catalog offered 12½" composition dolls (ADV-CK5), but no Campbell Kids were shown in 1951, apparently year of change-over from composition to the newer plastics. *(Courtesy Sears, Roebuck & Co.)*

ADV-CK8. 8" *Campbell Kid.* All vinyl, molded hair, shoes and sox, jointed only at shoulder and neck. Original two-piece red and white knit outfit and purse. Marks: **CAMPBELL KID / MADE BY / IDEAL TOY CORP.** *(Author's collection)*

ADV-CK9. 10" *Campbell Kid.* All molded vinyl, painted features, turning head, jointed shoulders and hips. All original: red knit underpants, red flannel blouse, red sox, separate molded vinyl black shoes, white flannel spats with snap on sides, red Campbell tartan kilt and hat. Original mailing carton for this premium doll. *(Author's collection)*

ADV-CL2.

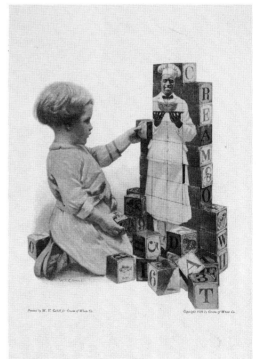

ADV-CL3.

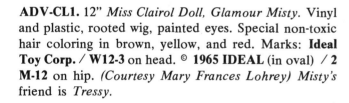

ADV-CL1.

ADV-CR1.

ADV-CR2.

ADV-CL1. 12" *Miss Clairol Doll, Glamour Misty.* Vinyl and plastic, rooted wig, painted eyes. Special non-toxic hair coloring in brown, yellow, and red. Marks: **Ideal Toy Corp.** / **W12-3** on head. © **1965 IDEAL** (in oval) / **2 M-12** on hip. *(Courtesy Mary Frances Lohrey)* Misty's friend is *Tressy.*

ADV-CL2. 1965 Catalog illustration *Glamour Misty,* the Miss Clairol Doll. Also available, *Pos'n Misty,* with bendable limbs. *(Courtesy Sears, Roebuck & Co.)*

ADV-CL3. *Clicquot Club Eskimo.* Composition head, cloth body and limbs, dressed in furry Eskimo suit, this boy doll with painted forelock was display doll for dealers handling Clicquot Club Ginger Ales in the 1920's. Illustration from 1943 magazine advertisement. Effanbee.

ADV-CR1. 18" *Rastus, the Cream of Wheat Chef.* "In brilliant color, ready to sew and stuff," a premium with boxtop and ten cents. 16" size was offered in 1922, 18" in 1930, doll was available during various promotions until 1952. Illustration is from magazine coupon. *(Courtesy John C. Flavin, National Biscuit Company)*

ADV-CR2. Cream of Wheat full-page, inside-cover advertisement from Pictorial Review, August, 1909, painted by W. F. Cahill for the Cream of Wheat Company, one of a series. *(Kirtley collection)*

CR-3.

ADV-CR3. *CrackerJack®* . Sailor boy and his dog. Ideal, about 1917. Doll is dressed to represent the trademark known to children and adults for several generations. *Trademark photograph courtesy CrackerJack® Division of Borden Foods, Borden, Inc.*

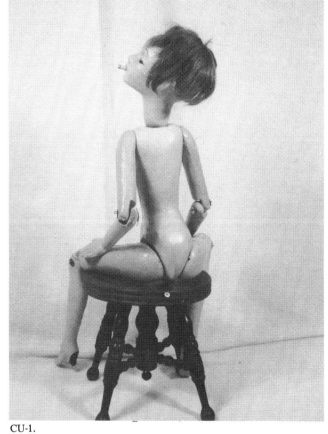

CU-1.

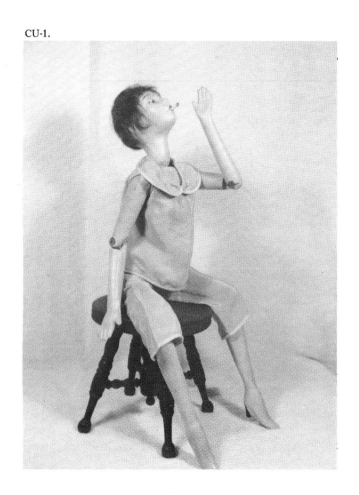

CU-1.

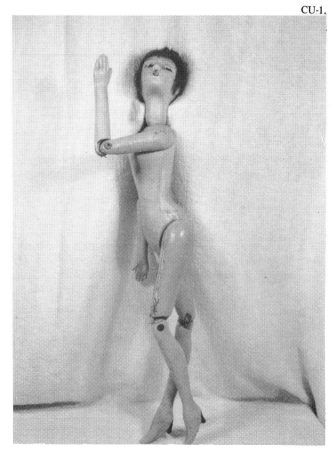

CU-1.

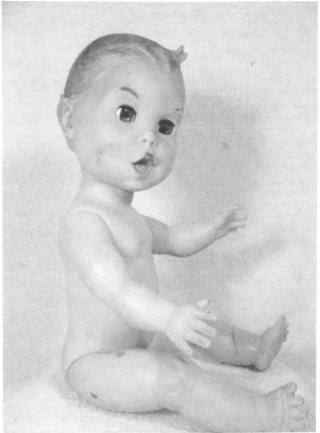

ADV-CU2.

ADV-G2.

ADV-E1.

ADV-CU1. 25" *Cubeb Smoking Doll.* [1] All composition, fully jointed, painted features, mohair bobbed wig, molded shoes, metal pin joints. Used by Cubeb Tobacco Company to promote smoking among women. ca. 1920. Unmarked. *(Kirtley collection)*

ADV-CU2. 14½" *Miss Curity.* Plastic and vinyl doll, saran wig, sleep eyes, complete with first aid book and kit, retailed at $11.39. From a 1953 catalog illustration. Trademark by Kendall Company, 1949. Ideal. Also shown in 1953 was 7½" *Miss Curity,* same type doll as small *Mary Hartline* (which see), Saran hair, white nurse uniform with *Miss Curity* on cap. *(Courtesy Sears, Roebuck & Co.)* Also used the "P-90" series dolls.

ADV-E1. 15" *Eskimo Pie Boy.* Lithographed cloth, flat, sewn and stuffed rag doll may be ordered at this writing from coupon on box of Eskimo Pie ice cream novelties. *(Author's collection)*

The character has been the trademark of *Eskimo Pie Corporation* since the 1930's. It has been updated in attire and the expression refined over the years; present boy appeared in 1961. The rag doll was introduced in 1962; in 1964 during a special promotion over 200,000 were distributed. More than 375,000 have been shipped since 1962. Manufacturer: Chase Bag Company.

[1]Spinning Wheel Magazine, Jan.-Feb., 1969, Hanover, Pa.

ADV-K1.

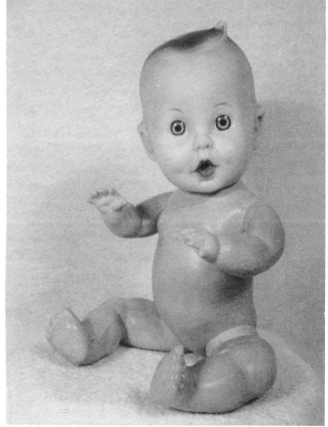

ADV-G1.

ADV-F1.

ADV-F1. 20" *Flossie Flirt.* Illustration is portion of ad in Needlecraft Magazine, December, 1929, in which various toys, including Ideal's Flossie Flirt, are offered as prizes for cash subscriptions. This was a common promotion practice and apparently was quite effective. *(Author's collection)*

ADV-G1. 11" *Gerber Baby.* All rubber, head is different compound than body and has turned yellow-ivory color, set eyes. Marks: **GERBER BABY / © Gerber Products Co.** on head. **Mfg. by / the Sun Rubber Co. / Barberton, O., U.S.A. / Pat. 2118682 / Pat. 2160739.** This doll was obtained as a premium by sending in Gerber baby food labels in 1956. Same doll offered in Sears 1955 catalog: 12" at $5.59, 13" at $8.95, and 18" at $13.89, with layette, travel case, scales, bottles, bubble pipe, everything a baby needs. *(Childhood doll of Joseph Richard Anderton II)*

ADV-G2. 14" *Gerber Baby.* All vinyl, sleep eyes with lashes, molded and painted eyebrows and hair, squeeker and drink and wet feature same as original doll but dimples are missing from this 1967 version. According to information obtained from the Gerber Products Company, this doll "made a brief appearance as a

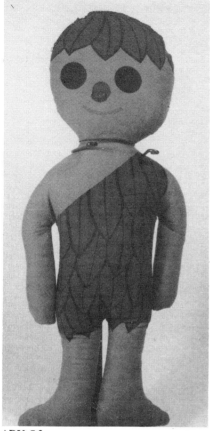

ADV-G3.

ADV-G4.

THE KELLOGG COMPANY

The Kellogg Company of Battlecreek, Michigan, have made use of dolls in their promotions since 1925. The first dolls were *Goldilocks and the Three Bears* printed on cloth for the customer to sew and stuff. Over the years, Kellogg has distributed more than *five million* dolls of various kinds. Following is a partial list of the many offers they have made via cereal boxtops:

1928	Nursery Rhyme dolls (cloth to stuff)
	Bo Peep, Mary & Lamb, Red Riding Hood, Tom Piper's Son
1935	Cloth Animals (Vernon Grant)
1935	Frog, Cat, Dog, Duck.
1954	Sweetheart. This was a standard doll which cost $1.00 and which resulted in requests of over one-half million.
1954	Majorette. Standard Doll.
1955	Magic Mary. This was a paper doll of one dimension mounted on board with several different outfits.
1957 & '58	Toddler walking.
1958	Grown up doll.
1959	Baby Ginger.
1960	Little Miss Kay.
1961	Baby Chris.
1962	Linda Lou.
1964, '65 & '66	Calico Lass.
1966	Stuffed Hillbilly Goat (we stuffed).
1966	Stuffed Woody Woodpecker (we stuffed). (50c)
1969	Mary Kate (regular doll).
1969	Banana Splits stuffed.
1970	Tony Tiger stuffed.

premium offer about 1967, but was discontinued because the doll's expression never quite caught the fresh appeal of the original 'Gerber Baby' sketch." Marks: **GERBER BABY / © GERBER PRODUCTS CO.** on head. *(Author's collection)*

ADV-G3. 16" *Jolly Green Giant.* "From the valley of the Jolly (ho-ho-ho) Green Giant" comes this pre-stuffed lithographed rag doll in varying shades of green. 1960's. *(Rebekka Anderton collection)*

ADV-G4. Green Giant trademark of the Green Giant Company, LeSueur, Minnesota. *(Courtesy Green Giant Company)*

ADV-K1. Kellogg's *Snap, Crackle and Pop.* In this picture they are left to right *Crackle, Snap and Pop.* Molded, painted vinyl heads with cloth hand puppet bodies. 1960's. *(Author's collection)*

ADV-K2. Kodak Display Dolls. 10" Balsa wood dolls painted with casein paint. Designed by New York artist, Stanley Glaubach, and costumed by his wife, for Christmas, 1969, advertising promotions of the Eastman Kodak Company. *(Courtesy J. Walter Thompson Company, New York)*

ADV-K2.

ADV-L2.   ADV-L3.

ADV-L4.

ADV-L1.

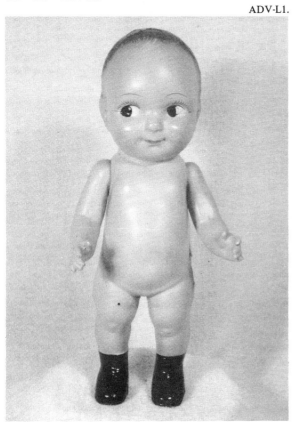

ADV-L1. 13" *Buddy Lee.* Plaster composition, painted features, jointed only at shoulders; head, body and legs one piece. Trademark doll of the H. D. Lee Company, Inc., originated in 1920. Plaster doll was distributed 1920 through 1948. Mold was changed in 1949; legs were thinned and bowed to enhance "cowboy" appearance and facilitate dressing doll. Unbreakable plastic material was used with the new mold. Unmarked. *(Author's collection)*

ADV-L2. 13" *Buddy Lee Cowboy Doll.* Dressed in denim cowboy pants, various shirts, belt, bandanna, cowboy hat, and lariat. Printed on hat band is **"Ride 'Em in Lee Rider Overalls."** Some hat bands read: **"Ride 'Em in Lee Copper-Riveted Riders' Overalls."** Pants and shirt are stitched together at intervals; shirt has two buttons. *(Courtesy The H. D. Lee Company, Inc.)*

ADV-L3. 13" *Buddy Lee Engineer Doll.* Dressed in bib overalls of blue denim or striped white denim, with jacket, shop cap and bandanna. The clothing for *Buddy Lee* dolls was made in Lee plants, but the caps were bought from outside source. *(Courtesy The H. D. Lee Company, Inc.)*

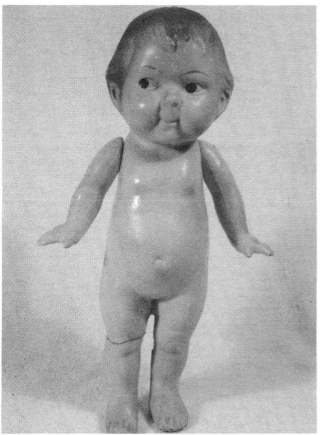

ADV-L5.

ADV-M1.

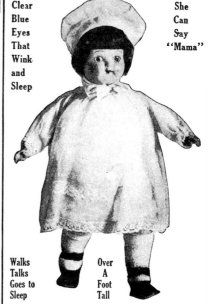

Clear Blue Eyes That Wink and Sleep

She Can Say "Mama"

Walks Talks Goes to Sleep

Over A Foot Tall

GIRLS! THIS DOLL IS YOURS FOR **A FAVOR**

The doll is a real one—20 inches tall, dressed with white lace-trimmed dress, underclothes, and with bonnet to match. Has shoes and stockings that you can put on or take off. Clear, life-like skin that can be washed, mohair wig that can be combed. She can say "Mama" almost perfectly, and by holding the shoulders she can be made to walk almost as if she were alive. The doll is really beautiful, and you'll say so, too, when you receive yours.

How to get the Walking, Talking Doll

Secure three yearly subscriptions to MODERN PRISCILLA at the regular price of $2.00 each, from your relatives and friends. Send the names and addresses to us, together with $6.00, and in return we will send you the doll exactly as described. The subscriptions can be new or renewals. In this way your doll will cost you no money—only the pleasant effort of getting the subscriptions. And when you receive your doll—Oh! how you will jump with joy! It will surely be the loveliest doll you've ever had. Send your orders in as soon as you take them and we'll ship the doll by return parcel post.

The Priscilla Company
85 Broad Street, Boston, Mass.

ADV-M2

ADV-L4. 13" *Buddy Lee Industrial Doll.* Dressed in many colors of shirts, pants, belts, caps, bow ties or overhand ties, and Union-Alls to represent many different types of industrial workers. The Industrial Doll was introduced in 1923. *(Courtesy The H. D. Lee Company, Inc.)*

ADV-L5. 13½" Composition Doll. Dolls of this type are often mistaken for *Buddy Lee,* The H. D. Lee Company advertising doll, especially when dressed in Lee-style clothing. Doll is possibly one of Sears' "Chubby Kids" which were sold over period of many years. Unmarked. *(Wiseman collection)*

These dolls have been found with paper labels on the bottom of one or both feet. The name *"Sweetie"* seems to be associated with the 13½" size while a smaller 11½" size is often marked *"Baby Bud".*

ADV-M1. 16" *Mr. Magoo.* Weak-eyed character from children's television cartoons has been used by The General Electric Corporation in television commercials and as display figures. Doll shown has vinyl head, hat, cloth body stuffed with Dryex©, plastic foam and cotton. Marks: **1962 / UPA Pictures, Inc. / All Rights Reserved.** Sears 1962 catalog lists 12" Mr. Magoo, as above, at $2.89. *(Zillner collection)*

ADV-M2. *Modern Priscilla.* An advertisement in *Modern Priscilla* magazine of October, 1923, offering an unidentified doll as subscription premium.

ADV-Mc1.

ADV-Mc3.

fig. ADV-Mc1

ADV-Mc4

ADV-Mc1. 8" *Betsy McCall.* Fine quality hard plastic with soft vinyl arms, Saran wig rooted in plastic scull cap glued to head, blue sleep eyes, solid plastic lashes. First dolls this size had mohair wigs. 1957. American Character Doll Co. Marks: see fig. ADV-Mc1. *(Author's collection)*

ADV-Mc2. 22" *Betsy McCall.* Rooted saran hair, sleep eyes, jointed waist, wrists, and ankles. 1962 Sears catalog illustration.

ADV-Mc3. 14" and 20" *Betsy McCall.* 1959 Sears catalog illustration. Dolls dressed as bride or in evening gown, 14" with wardrobe and trunk at $11.89 for set, 8" also listed, hard plastic, basic doll $1.97.

ADV-Mc4. 14" *Betsy McCall.* Hard plastic with soft vinyl head, rooted hair, sleep eyes. Marks: **McCALL CORP** on head. **IDEAL DOLL / P-90** on back. Original dress with panties attached. 1952. Sears catalog that year shows this doll with separate patterns available. *(Zillner collection)*

ADV-Mc5. 14" *Betsy McCall.* Same doll as ADV-Mc4, sleep glassene eyes, red Saran hair, included apron pattern. 1953 Sears catalog illustration. 14" *Betsy McCall* in 1958 catalog is a "walker" and 20" has roll and sleep eyes. *(Courtesy Sears, Roebuck & Co.)*

ADV-Mc2.

ADV-Mc4.

ADV-Mc5

ADV-Mc6. 13" *McCall-Peggy the Modern Fashion Model*. Designer kit complete with mannequin, dress form, patterns, sewing book, fabric, thread, tape, and needles. Dolls of this type were very popular 1942-1945. Heirloom Needlework Guild, Inc., A Subsidiary of Dritz-Traum Co., Inc. 1942. *(Wiseman collection)*

ADV-Mc6.

ADV-MU1.

ADV-N1.

ADV-N2.

ADV-MU1. 14" *Arthur Murray Dancing Doll.* Plastic, sleep eyes, Saran wig, velveteen gown, on detachable music platform. 1952 Sears catalog illustration. *(Courtesy Sears, Roebuck & Co.)*

ADV-N1. 13" Nestle Chocolate *Little Hans, The Chocolate Maker.* Pre-stuffed rag doll premium with product labels. Created by ad agency people at Leo Burnett, Hans is a regular on children's television commercials. 1970. Marks: © **The Nestle Company, Inc.** on right foot. *(Courtesy The Nestle Company, Author's collection)*

ADV-N2. 13½" Nestle Chocolate *Little Hans, The Chocolate Maker.* All vinyl with molded vinyl hat attached, red synthetic beard, molded hair and spectacles. Wears brown leatherette trousers, yellow suede shirt, red knit sox, and separate molded vinyl shoes, although there are shoes molded over the feet. Only slightly more than two thousand of this doll were produced. Marks: **1969 THE NESTLE CO.** on head. *(Zillner collection)*

ADV-N3. 13" Nickerson Farms *Honey Bee.* Pre-stuffed, flat lithographed cloth, yellow and black. Unmarked. 1969. *(Author's collection)*

ADV-N4. *Cuddles. Needlecraft* Magazine, December, 1929, offered this doll as a subscription premium. Ideal.

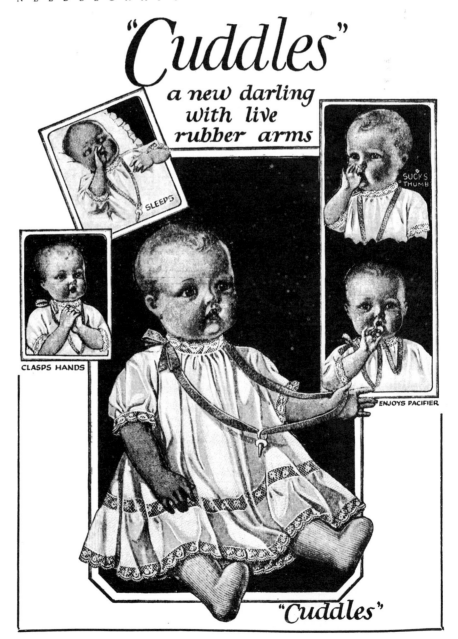

ADV-N3.

ADV-N4.

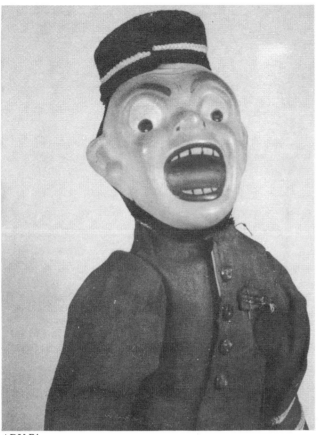

ADV-P1.

ADV-P2.

ADV-P3.

ADV-P1. 15" Phillip Morris *"Johnny"*. Composition head, cloth body, felt hands, all original, separate hat. Mouth wide open in that familiar "Call for Phillip Morris!" slogan. Doll is unmarked; design or lettering of medal on chest is undecipherable. *(Zillner collection)*

ADV-P2. 22" *Mr. Peanut*. Bright yellow and black, prestuffed, lithographed cloth. Trademark of Planters Peanuts Co., Inc. for many years, *Mr. Peanut* may be found in many forms, including salt and pepper shakers. 1960's. *(Zillner collection)*

ADV-P3. 14" Pillsbury *Popin Fresh Dough Boy*. White cloth, blue tie and eyes, flat lithographed cloth. Trademark of Pillsbury Mills has been prominently displayed in television commercials. 1960's. *(Wiseman collection)*

The *Doughboy* rag doll was created in 1967. He has been widely distributed, primarily through order blanks found in stores. Over 300,000 *Doughboy* rag dolls have been distributed in the three years since introduction.

ADV-Q1.

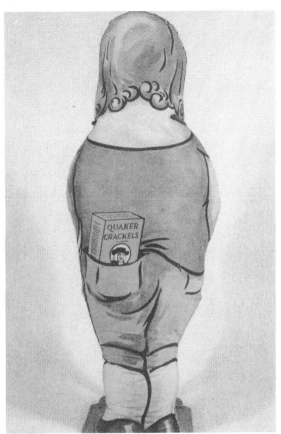

ADV-Q1.

NOTE: ORIGINAL PRICES SHOWN
ARE NOT TODAY'S PRICES.

ADV-Q1. 17" *Quaker Crackels Boy.* Litographed cloth, pale lavendar suit with green vest, gold buttons, and brown shoes. Blonde hair and blue eyes, and a box of Quaker Crackels, short-lived ready-to-eat cereal, in hip pocket. 1924. *(Courtesy Ralph's Antique Dolls)*

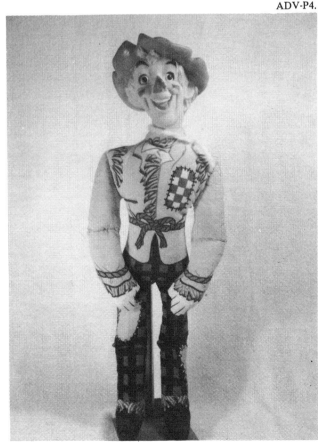

ADV-P4.

ADV-P4. 22" *Purina Scarecrow* (From Checkerboard Square). Molded vinyl head, cloth lithographed body. This friendly fellow is a regular in Purina's television commercials. 1960's. *(Wiseman collection)*

The *"Checkerboard Squarecrow"* was available for $1.50 plus any "CHEX" cereal label from the Ralston Purina Company.

ADV-R2.

ADV-R2.

ADV-R1.

ADV-R1. 10½ *Little Miss Revlon.* Good quality plastic and vinyl, swivel waist, high-heel feet, rooted Saran hair, original dress and shoes, blue sleep eyes, separate fingers, polished nails. Marks: Cloth label in dress reads: **Ideal Toy Corp. / Hollis, N.J.** 1957. *(Author's collection)*

ADV-R2. 18" *Miss Revlon.* Good quality plastic and vinyl, swivel waist, high-heel feet, rooted Saran hair, original dress and shoes, blue sleep eyes, separate fingers, polished nails. 1956 catalog lists three costumes, including *"Cherries A La Mode",* dark blue dress with cherries, $12.95; *"Queen of Diamonds",* shown, $14.95, in red velvet, white fur, and "diamonds". Revlon is a trademark of Revlon, Inc. Dolls came with comb, hair curlers, and Revlon Satin Set hair spray. 1956. Marks: **IDEAL DOLL/VT-18** on head and body. *(Author's collection)*

A 20" version of Miss Revlon is known as *"Kissing Pink".* She was dressed in a pink and white striped cotton dress and wore a pearl necklace.

ADV-S1.

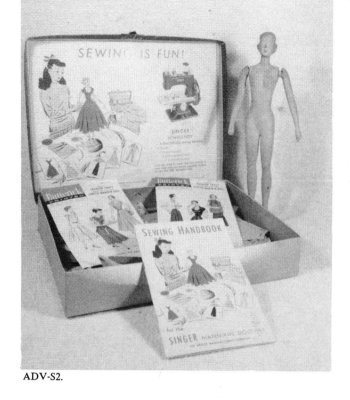

ADV-S2.

ADV-S3.

ADV-S1. 9" Seven-Up's *"Fresh Up Freddie"*. All molded vinyl with squeaker, green pants, red top-knot. Marks: © **1959** on right foot. **The / Seven-Up / Co.** on left foot. *(Author's collection)*

ADV-S2. 13" *Singer Mannikin* Doll Set. Doll is very light weight and somewhat flexible, short flip hair-do differs from other mannequin dolls, teen-ager face, arms attach as others of this type. Cardboard case contains Butterick patterns, thimble, needle threader, sewing handbook, tape measure, doll stand. Additional patterns were available. Patterns made for The Singer Mfg. Co. by The Butterick Pattern Co. Doll set by W. Smith Industries. © 1949 by Singer. *(Baume collection)*

ADV-S3. 16" *Smokey The Bear*. All original, separate yellow ranger hat, faded blue denim pants, Teddy Bear cloth body, head, and feet, felt nose and tongue, plastic eyes, leatherette belt with plastic silver **Smokey** buckle. Badge reads: **SMOKEY RANGER / PREVENT FOREST FIRES**. A representative for the National Park Service, Smokey was introduced in 1953, still in the catalogs at Christmas, 1969, retail $6.99. *(Author's collection)*

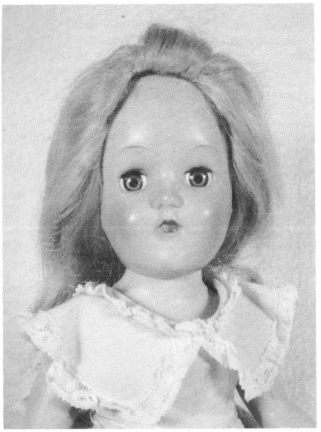

ADV-T1.

ADV-T2.

ADV-S4

ADV-S4 18" *Stuffed Rabbit.* This rabbit, along with a cat and dog, were offered by a large cereal company for ten cents and two boxtops in about 1909. It had been sewn together, along with many others, as Christmas gifts that year. When it became apparent there was an extra, this one was placed, unstuffed, in an old trunk in the attic, where it remained until the trunk was opened in 1969. The rabbit was one of many different figures lithographed on muslin and retailed in dry goods stores, in catalogs, and as premiums. Some of these animals are being reproduced today. ca. 1900. Arnold Print Works. *(Author's collection)*

ADV-T1. 14" *Toni.* All hard plastic, glued-on nylon wig, blue sleep eyes, flat feet, original dress. Marks: **P-90 / IDEAL DOLL / MADE IN U.S.A.** on head. **IDEAL DOLL / P-90** on body. 1948. *(Author's collection)*

ADV-T2. 20" *Toni Walker.* All original, hard plastic, sleep eyes, glued-on nylon wig, flat feet. Marks: **P-92 / IDEAL DOLL / MADE IN U.S.A.** on head. **IDEAL DOLL / 19** on body. 1948. *(Zillner collection)*

ADV-T3.

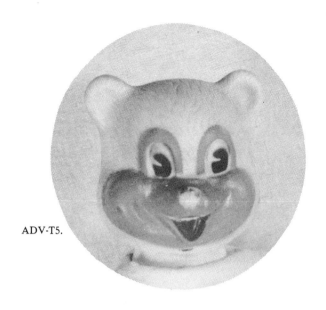

ADV-T5.

fig. ADV-T3

ADV-T4.

ADV-T3. 10½" *Toni.* Fine quality vinyl, rooted hair, blue sleep eyes, all original. This *"Toni"* is a lady with high-heel feet. Marks: see fig. ADV-T3, back of waist. *Toni* dolls, with their curlers, home permanents, and hair setting lotions, were available in catalogs as late as 1958, in 14", 20", and 25" sizes. *(Author's collection)*

ADV-T4. 8" *"Thumbs-Up Victory Doll."* Flexible composition "Lasticoid", head and body one piece, jointed hips and shoulders, all original. Tag reads: **"Your $1.50 purchase / of this doll / helps in sending / ambulance to Britain and Her Allies and Vitamins to / The Undernourished Children of England / An Original / Creation of / Margit Nilsen Studios, Inc. / 71 Fifth Ave., N.Y."** 1941. *(Wingfield collection)*

ADV-T5. *Teddy Snow Crop* Hand Puppet. Molded vinyl head, white flannel "glove". Teddy represents Snow Crop Frozen Foods. 1960's. *(Author's collection)*

Two versions of doll were offered; a plush doll and a hand-puppet as shown. Offer was made in early 1950's as point-of-sale (in-store) premium. At same time, a dwarf dressed in a *Teddy Snow Crop* costume appeared on behalf of *Snow Crop* at supermarkets, fairs, etc., generating good exposure for the Brand. The character is not presently being used. *Snow Crop is a trademark of the Coca Cola Company, Foods Division.*

ADV-T6.

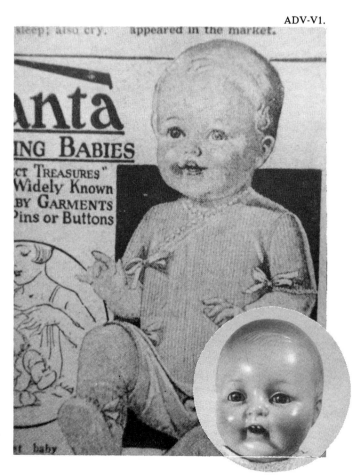

ADV-V1.

ADV-T6. 14" *"Tintair Glamour Girl."* Plastic doll, fully jointed, sleep eyes, rayon dress and panties, had two bottles non-toxic coloring to apply to hair, plastic dish, and hair curlers. © 1951 by Tintex. R & B doll. *(Courtesy Sears, Roebuck & Co.)*

ADV-V1. 14", 19", 21½" *Vanta Baby.* Composition head and limbs, cotton stuffed body. Doll came dressed in doll-size replicas of the Vanta baby garments; "no pins, no buttons", that "thousands of real babies are now wearing". Sleep eyes, cry voice, molded painted hair. 1927 Catalog illustration courtesy Sears, Roebuck & Co. Retail prices: $3.49, $4.89, and $5.98. Marks: **VANTA BABY/AMBERG**.

MADAME ALEXANDER DOLL COMPANY

The Alexander Doll Company, when founded by Madame Alexander in New York in 1923, already had a generation of experience behind it. Madame Alexander's parents were the founders of the first doll hospital in the United States in 1895. First dolls produced by the new company were cloth with dimensional facial features; in contrast, more than 200 different materials go into the production of a single doll today. Several molding processes are used to produce sturdy faces, bodies, and limbs from the finest durable materials.

Madame Alexander believes dolls are important to a child's total educational experience and must contribute to an understanding of other people, other times, and other places. *Alice in Wonderland,* one of the first Alexander doll creations, began a trend that continues with production of dolls representing Louisa May Alcott's *"Little Women",* the Dickens characters, James Whitcomb Riley's *"Little Orphan Annie",* the *"Sound of Music"* characters, and many others. Inspiration for dolls also comes from great paintings and great people. Many types of baby dolls are included in the line; they are invariably cuddly and often large.

Madame Alexander dolls are now, or have been, on display in the Brooklyn Children's Museum, New York; St. Valentine Museum, Richmond, Virginia; Museum of Yesteryear, Florida; The Sandwich Museum, Massachusetts; The Museum of the City of New York; the Congressional Club, Washington, D.C.; the Children's Trust Museum, New Delhi, India; and the Smithsonian Institution, Washington, D.C.

In addition to Madame Alexander, President of the firm, family tradition is carried on by Secretary Richard Birnbaum, her son-in-law, Vice-President William Birnbaum, her grandson, and daughter Mildred Birnbaum, Research Consultant. Philip Behrman, Madame Alexander's late husband, was Vice-President and Treasurer.

ALEX-1.

ALEX-2.

ALEX-3.

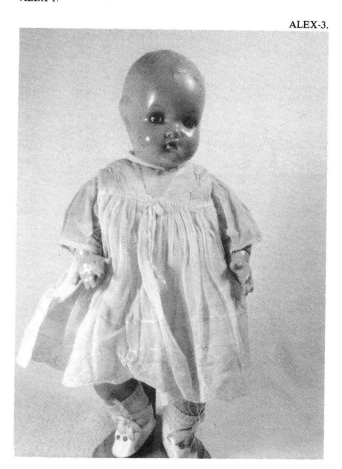

ALEX-3.

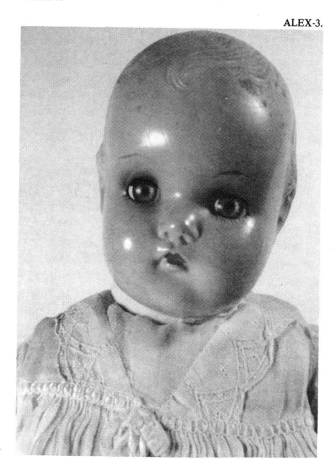

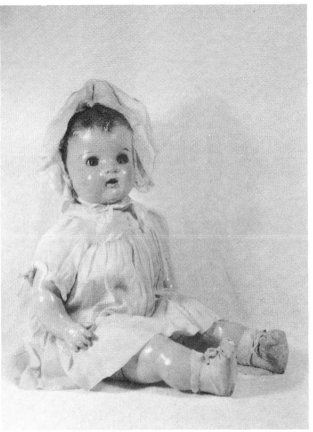

ALEX-5.

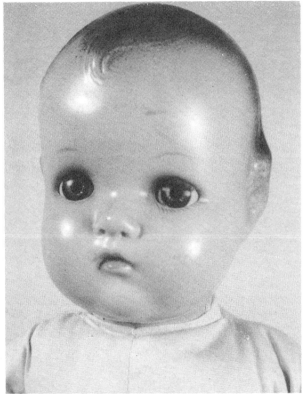

ALEX-4.

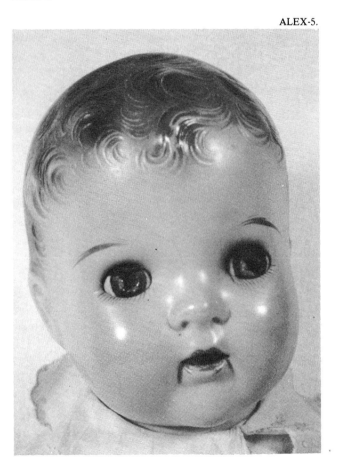

ALEX-5.

ALEX-1. 8½" Girl. Composition, painted eyes, original blonde mohair wig, all original. Marks: **ALEXANDER** on body. **A.D.CO.** on head. **MADAME ALEXANDER** on cloth dress tag. Reminiscent of *Little Bo Peep.* 1930's. Probably one of the early Fairy Tale or Nursery Rhyme series. *(Wingfield collection)*

ALEX-2. 7" *"Alice in Wonderland".* All composition, painted blue eyes, painted shoes and sox, original blonde mohair wig, one-piece head and body, original clothes; never un-dressed. Marks: **ALEXANDER** on back. *(Author's collection)*

ALEX-3. 17" Baby. Composition head, gauntlet hands, and legs, blue sleep eyes, believed to be *"Little Genius."* Original clothes. Marks: **MADAME ALEXANDER** on head. ca. 1936. *(Wiseman collection)*

ALEX-4. 14" Circumference composition head similar to ALEX-3. Marks: **MADAME ALEXANDER** on head. Brown sleep eyes, on replacement body, head was originally mounted on rubber body, ca. 1936. *(Spaulding collection)*

ALEX-5. 24" Baby. Composition head, arms, straight legs, cloth body, brown sleep eyes. Original clothes: Pink dress and bonnet, undies, shoes and socks, very nicely dressed. Probably *"Princess Alexandria",* 1937. *(Wiseman collection)*

ALEX-6

ALEX-6.

ALEX-7.

ALEX-7.

ALEX-8.
                                            ALEX-8.

ALEX-9.

ALEX-6. 18½" *"Scarlett O'Hara."* Composition, green sleep eyes, black mohair wig, original costume. This doll is unmarked but an identical doll in the author's collection is marked **Mme. Alexander** on back of head. 1937. *(Wiseman collection)*

The 1940 Sears Fall and Winter catalog carried a "Southern Belle" doll in 12", 15", and 18" sizes. Since no manufacturer's name is given it is doubtful if this was an Alexander doll, although it was dressed in typical costume of "Scarlett" complete with large floppy hat.

ALEX-7. 21" *"McGuffey Ana".* Composition, brown sleep eyes, new wig, all original clothing: blue print dress, white dotted swiss apron. Marks: Dress tag reads: **McGuffey Ana.** Doll is unmarked. 1936. *(Wiseman collection)*

ALEX-8. 18" *"Flora McFlimsey".* All composition, blue-green sleep eyes, human hair wig of red-brown, freckles, all original costume pale green organza dress. 1938. Marks: **Madame Alex** on head. *(Wingfield collection)*

ALEX-9.

ALEX-10a.

ALEX-10.

ALEX-9. 13" *"Flora McFlimsey"*. Composition, freckles, sleep eyes, red-brown human hair wig, all original costume, blue and white check dress, separate white organdy apron. 1938. Marks: **Madame Alex** on doll. **Flora McFlimsey / Madame Alexander** on original wrist tag. *(Wiseman collction)*

ALEX-10. 24" *"Princess Elizabeth"*. Composition, brown sleep eyes, original blonde human hair wig, open mouth, four teeth. Dress is an original marked McGuffey Ana on cloth tag. Doll and costume are identical to sketch on page 25 of Luella Hart's "Directory of United States Doll Trademarks", which indicates possibility *Princess Elizabeth* doll was dressed and marketed as *McGuffey Ana* at some time. Marks: **PRINCESS ELIZABETH / ALEXANDER DOLL CO** on head. 1937. *(Author's collection)*

ALEX-10a. 15" *"Princess Elizabeth"*. Description and marks same as ALEX-10, except replacement wig. Dress and tiara courtesy Gwen Bower, not original to this doll. Dress tag reads: **"Princess Elizabeth" / Madame Alexander, N.Y.U.S.A. / ALL RIGHTS RESERVED.** Snaps on either side of front neckline to fasten missing royal robe. Dress is magenta pink rayon taffeta. 1937. *(Author's collection)*

ALEX-10a

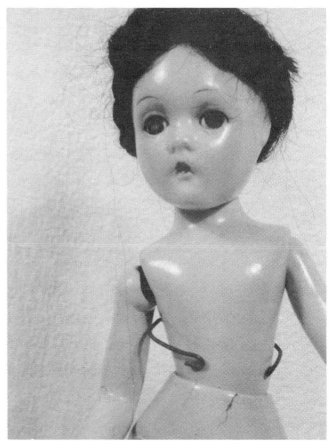

ALEX-11

ALEX-12.

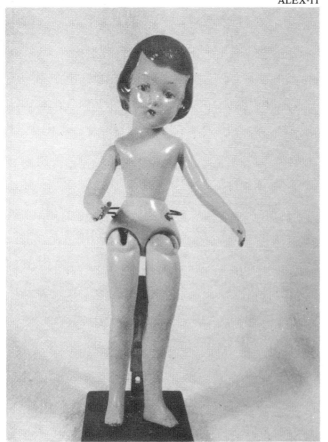

NOTE: ORIGINAL PRICES SHOWN
ARE NOT TODAY'S PRICES.

ALEX-11. 13" *"Wendy-Ann"*. All composition, blue painted eyes, brown molded hair, swivel waist. Marks: **WENDY-ANN / MME. ALEXANDER / NEW YORK.** 1938. *(Wiseman collection)*

ALEX-12. 13" *"Wendy-Ann"*. All composition, green sleep eyes with crazing, replacement wig. Same marks as ALEX-11. *(Wingfield collection)*

ALEX-13.

ALEX-14.

ALEX-15.

ALEX-13. 13" *"Wendy-Ann".* Same as ALEX-12, with brown sleep eyes, human hair wig, original dress, pink organdy with blue ribbon insertion, attached petticoat. Tag on dress reads: **Wendy-Ann / By Madame Alexander / N.Y.** *(Spalding collection)*

ALEX-14. 13" *"Alice in Wonderland".* Green sleep eyes, human hair wig, *Wendy-Ann* doll dressed in "Alice" costume. From 1938. *(Zillner collection)* For full length view this doll see *Sonja Henie.*

ALEX-15. 13" *"Alice in Wonderland".* Same as ALEX-14. Dress tag reads: **Alice in Wonderland.** Note dress styling. *(Wiseman collection)*

ALEX-17.

ALEX-16.

ALEX-16. 21" Composition. Gray sleep eyes, original mohair wig, small waist, all original costume of net and gold ric-rac with tiny flowers entwined in her braids. 1938-1940. Marks: **ALEXANDER** on head and shoulders. *(Wiseman collection)*

ALEX-17. 22" Composition. Blue sleep eyes, original mohair wig, small waist, all original costume of ecru with wine-colored velvet sash, fitted bodice, princess train, pantalettes and long white stockings, ballerina slippers with tiny heels and ribbon ankle ties, gold braid crown set with tiny pearls and jewels. Truly a "royal" personnage. 1938-1940. Marks: Clothes are tagged **MADAME ALEXANDER.** *(Wiseman collection)*

ALEX-16.

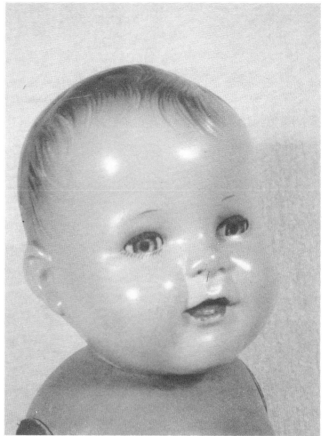

ALEX-18

ALEX-19.

ALEX-18. 21" Baby. Composition head, blue sleep eyes, stuffed rubber body, limbs are missing. Pin and disc joints, head and torso measure 13" tall. Marks: **MADAME ALEXANDER** on head. ca. 1938. *(Author's collection)*

ALEX-19. 14" and 19" *"Jeannie Walker"*. All composition, glass-like eyes, lashes, turning head, brunette mohair wig, blue cotton pique skirt, white dotted blouse, straw hat, shoes, socks, lacy undies. 1942 catalog illustration. Retailed at $3.39 and $5.69 respectively. *(Courtesy Sears, Roebuck & Co.)* Also available 1941 catalog, with human hair wig.

ALEX-20a.

ALEX-20c.

ALEX-20b.

ALEX-20. THE WEDDING PARTY, 1945. Composition, human hair, sleep eyes. *(Courtesy Sears, Roebuck & Co.)*

ALEX-20a. 17" and 22" *"Bride"*, rayon satin dress, rayon marquisette veil, bouquet, $10.39 and $12.79 respectively.

ALEX-20b. 15", 18", and 21½" *"Bridesmaid"*. Pastel rayon marquisette dress and veil, $6.84, $9.98, and $12.45 respectively.

ALEX-20c. 16", 20", 24" *"Flower Girl"*. Sheer rayon net over marquisette dress, flowers in her hair. $8.98, $12.45, and $14.98 respectively.

ALEX-21.

ALEX-22.

ALEX-23.

ALEX-21. 17" and 21½" *"Bride".* Hard plastic, sleep eyes, lashes, mohair wig, retailed at $15.98 and $17.98 respectively. *(1946 catalog illustration courtesy Sears, Roebuck & Co.)*

ALEX-22. 14½" and 17¾" *"Fairy Queen".* High grade polished composition, mohair wig, glass-like sleep eyes, lashes, net and gold braid costume. Retailed $9.98, $14.98. 1947. *(Courtesy Sears, Roebuck & Co.)*

ALEX-23. 15" and 18" *"Babs, The Ice-Skating Girl".* Hard plastic, mohair wig, sleep eyes, lashes, "real" figure skates, gold braid trim on costume, marabou muff. $8.98 and $10.98, 1948 catalog illustration. *(Courtesy Sears, Roebuck & Co.)*

ALEX-24.

ALEX-25.

ALEX-26a.   ALEX-26b.

ALEX-24. 14½" and 17½" *"Fairy Queen"*. Hard plastic, sleep eyes, lashes, rayon satin gown with gold color braid, mohair wig. $9.98 and $14.98. 1948 catalog illustration. *(Courtesy Sears, Roebuck & Co.)*

ALEX-25. 14½" and 17½" *"Nina Ballerina"*. Hard plastic, mohair wig, sleep eyes, lashes, rayon satin and net dress with silver ric-rac, rayon undies, satin shoes. $7.95 and $11.45, 1949 catalog illustration. *(Courtesy Sears, Roebuck & Co.)*

ALEX-26a. 14½" and 17½" *"Polly Pigtails"*. Hard plastic, mohair wig in pigtails with ribbons, sleep eyes, lashes. $6.98 and $8.98, 1949 and 1950 catalogs. *(Courtesy Sears, Roebuck & Co.)*

ALEX-26b. 14" *"Cinderella"*. Hard plastic, "shiny yarn wig", glass-like sleep eyes, lashes, cotton peasant costume, broom, no socks. $6.98, 1950 catalog. *(Courtesy Sears, Roebuck & Co.)*

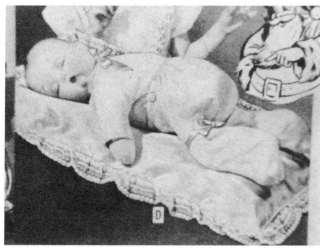

ALEX-26-1.

ALEX-26-2.

ALEX-27.

ALEX-26-1. 14" *Slumbermate*. Vinyl head turned to side, jersey-covered, kapok-stuffed body, two-piece removeable sleeper. Retail, $6.69. *1951 Catalog illustration courtesy Sears, Roebuck & Co.*

ALEX-26-2. 18½" *Bunny-Baby*. Soft vinyl head and limbs, cloth body, sleep glassene eyes, organdy dress and bonnet. *1951 Catalog illustration courtesy Sears, Roebuck & Co.*

ALEX-27. 17" *"Violet"*. Hard plastic, blue sleep eyes, glued-on synthetic wig, jointed wrists and elbows, knees, hips, and shoulders, but not at waist. Marks: **ALEXANDER** on head. ca. 1952. *(Author's collection)*

ALEX-28.

ALEX-29.

ALEX-30.

ALEX-28. 20" *"Cissy"*. Plastic and vinyl, high-heeled feet, all original costume, hose and silver sandals, checked lime taffeta dress, straw hat with yellow rose trim, fur cape. Marks: **Mdm. Alexander.** 1955. *(Kirtley collection)*

ALEX-29. 18" *"Active Miss"*. Apparently *Violet*. Jointed knees, elbows, wrists, all plastic. 1954 Catalog illustration. $12.98 retail. *(Courtesy Sears, Roebuck & Co.)*

ALEX-30. 14" *"Cynthia"*. Hard plastic, brown sleep eyes, rooted hair, original clothes; white with red four-leaf clover print, navy trim, black patent shoes. 1950's. *(Kirtley collection)*

ALEX-31. 15" *"Margot Ballerina"*. Hard plastic, soft vinyl jointed arms, sleep eyes, replacement wig, original costume; pink satin and net. Marks: **ALEXANDER** on head. **MME. ALEXANDER** on shoulders. 1961. *(Author's collection)*

ALEX-31.

ALEX-33.

ALEX-32.

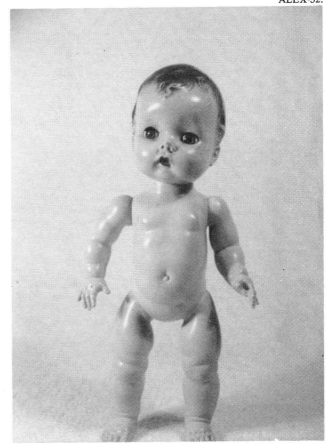

ALEX-32. 12" Boy. Hard plastic, gray sleep eyes, closed mouth, molded painted hair. Marks: **ALEXANDER** on head. ca. 1950. *(Wiseman collection)*

ALEX-33. 17½" *"McGuffey Ana"*. Hard plastic, blue sleep eyes, lashes, closed mouth, original blonde mohair wig in pigtails. Original costume: pink cotton dress, separate lace-trimmed flower-print pinafore, flower-trimmed straw hat, black patent button shoes, long stockings. ca. 1952. *(Charles Vandiver collection)* Reissued 1965.

ALEX-34. 21" *"Kathy"* All vinyl, brown sleep eyes, lashes, drink and wet feature, molded painted hair, body squeeker. Marks: see fig. ALEX-34. 1958. *(Author's collection)* See p. 60 for illustration.

ALEX-35. 15" *"Marybel, The Doll That Gets Well"*. Rigid vinyl with soft vinyl head, rooted blond hair, brown sleep eyes, lashes, original pink satin bloomer suit, carrying case with crutches, leg case, arm cast, bandages, yellow chicken pox spots, and red measles spots. Note jointed waist. Marks: **MME.** © **ALEXANDER** in circle on head appear to be **1958.** *(Author's collection)* See p. 60 for illustration.

ALEX-33.

ALEX-35.

ALEX-34.

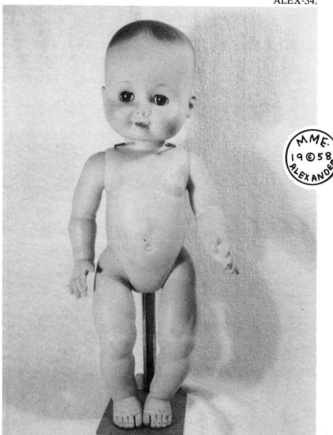

Note: Sears catalogs carried "Perfect Patient" for several years. This was not *Marybel,* but may have been American Character's *"Mendy",* 1967. *Marybel* appeared as shown here in the 1959 Christmas catalog from Sears in same pink suit and case, retail $12.37. *Marybel* was re-issued in different material and case in 1966.

fig. ALEX-34

ALEX-35.

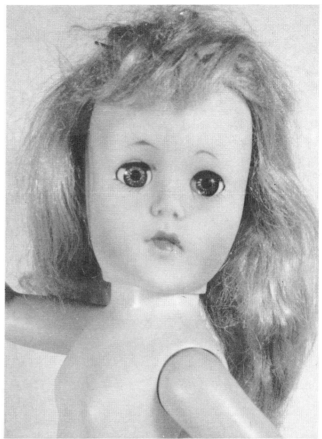

ALEX-37.

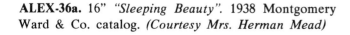

So lovely the Prince had to wake her with a kiss. 16 in. tall, fully jointed, made entirely of hard-to-break composition. Beautiful finish; sleeping eyes, real lashes. Head turns or tilts. Golden, first quality shoulder length human hair wig. Coronet of Gold sequins in her hair. Blue celanese taffeta dress. Gold spangle trim. Blue organdy petticoat. Dress, petticoat have snap fasteners—not pins! Blue rayon panties with lace edging. White rayon stockings. Gold color sandals with real heels. Made by Madam Alexander, one of the foremost designers of dolls. Best quality, best dressed, most attractively finished doll at this price. **$3⁵⁹**

ALEX-36a.

ALEX-36b.

ALEX-36a. 16" *"Sleeping Beauty"*. 1938 Montgomery Ward & Co. catalog. *(Courtesy Mrs. Herman Mead)*

ALEX-36b. 17" and 21" *"Sleeping Beauty"*, 1959 catalog. Hard plastic, soft vinyl arms, jointed elbows and knees, blue rayon satin gown with gold color trim, princess crown of gold-color with rhinestones. *(Courtesy Sears, Roebuck & Co.)*

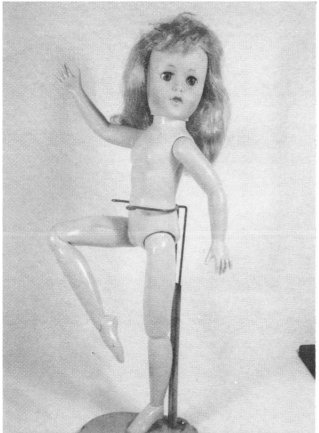

ALEX-37.

ALEX-39a.

ALEX-38.

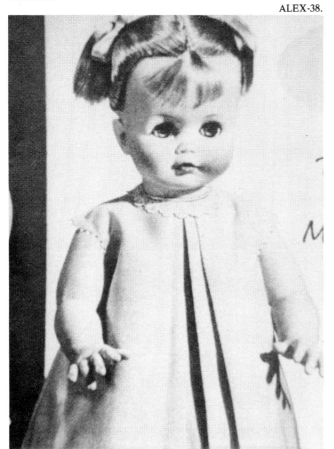

ALEX-37. 17" *"Ballerina Elise"*. Hard plastic, soft vinyl head, rooted synthetic hair, blue sleep eyes. Elise came dressed as bride, in riding outfit, as *Scarlett O'Hara*, ballerina, and other. Marks: **A L E X** on head, ca. 1959. *(Author's collection)*

ALEX-38. 24" *"Chatterbox"*. Hard plastic, soft vinyl head, rooted Saran hair, pique dress. Push button, she talks; lay her down, she stops. Two batteries; she says *"Who is coming to tea?", "I hope we have cookies."* and other phrases. 1961 catalog, $17.88 retail. *(Courtesy Sears, Roebuck & Co.)*

ALEX-39a. 14" *"Caroline"*. Plastic and vinyl, rooted Saran wig, green sleep eyes, dressed in original-wardrobe flannel pajamas. Marks: **ALEXANDER / 19© 61** on head. *(Author's collection)*

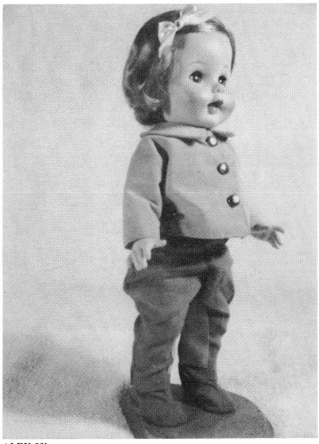

ALEX-39b.

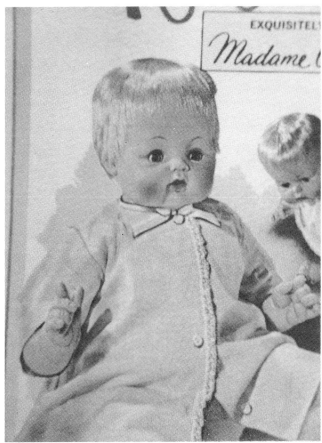

ALEX-40-1.

ALEX-40.

ALEX-39b. 14" *"Caroline"*. Same as ALEX-39a, dressed all original suede cloth riding habit, pink hairbow. *(Zillner collection)*

ALEX-40. 10" *"Jacqueline"*. Plastic, glued-on wig, sleep eyes, lashes, original costume. Marks: **MME. ALEXANDER** on body. *(Zillner collection)* Also available a 21" *Jacqueline* marked **ALEXANDER / 19© 61.**

ALEX-40-1. 14", 18" *Kitten*. Vinyl head and limbs, soft stuffed cotton body, rooted hair, sleep eyes. Retail $6.67 and $8.99. An 18" size with a wind-up knob, moves legs and arms, retails $10.99. *1963 Catalog illustration courtesy Sears, Roebuck & Co.*

ALEX-41.

ALEX-42.

styles. Marks: © **ALEXANDER DOLL CO. INC. / 1965** on head. *(Author's collection)*

ALEX-42. 22" *"So Big "*. Vinyl head and hands, painted eyes, rooted hair, cry voice, soft stuffed body. Since 1954. 1970 Alexander catalog illustration. *"So Big",* Golden Press. *(Courtesy Alexander Doll Co., Inc.)*

Dressed in blue and white checked gingham suit. Marks: **ALEXANDER (c) 1967** on head. Tag reads: **SO BIG/by MADAME ALEXANDER (R)/NEW YORK, U.S.A.** *(Courtesy Alexander Doll Co., Inc.)*

ALEX-41. 17" *"Leslie"*. Plastic and vinyl, rooted hair, sleep eyes, dressed as bride, ballerina, debutante in formal, or as here, in short party dress; various hair

ALEX-44.

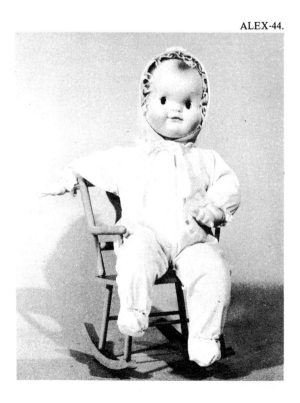

ALEX-43.

ALEX-45.

ALEX-46.

ALEX-43. 12" *Little Huggums"®* , 25" *"Big Huggums"®* . *Little Huggums,* rooted or sprayed hair, sleep eyes, vinyl head, stuffed cloth body and limbs. *Big Huggums,* rooted hair, painted eyes, stuffed cloth, vinyl head and hands. Since 1963. 1970 Alexander catalog illustration. *(Courtesy Alexander Doll Co., Inc.)*

ALEX-44. 22" *"Pumpkin"®* . Stuffed cloth, vinyl head and hands, painted eyes and hair. *(1970 catalog illustration courtesy Alexander Doll Co., Inc.)*

ALEX-45. 21" *"Puddin"®* . Stuffed Cloth, vinyl head and hands, dark sleep eyes, lashes, puckered lips, fine rooted honey blonde hair, cry voice. *1970 catalog illustration courtesy Alexander Doll Co., Inc.)*

ALEX-46. 20" *"Happy"®* . Stuffed cloth, vinyl head and limbs, rooted brown hair, dimples, sleep eyes, lashes. *(1970 catalog Illustration courtesy Alexander Doll Co., Inc.)*

ALEX-47. 14", 20" *"Mary Cassatt Baby"®* . Soft vinyl head and limbs, stuffed cotton body, rooted hair, sleep eyes, cry voice. Inspired by the nineteenth century paintings of Mary Cassatt. *(1970 Illustration courtesy Alexander Doll Co., Inc.)*

ALEX-47.

ALEX-50.

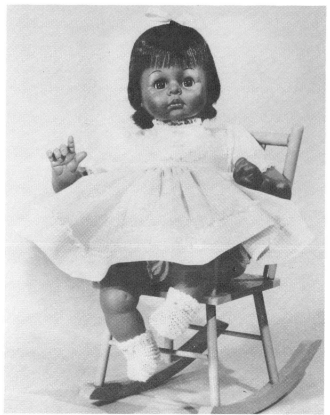

ALEX-48.

ALEX-49.

ALEX-48. 14", 20", 24" *"Pussycat"*® . Same construction as ALEX-47, dark or light hair. *(1970 Illustration courtesy Alexander Doll Co., Inc.)*

ALEX-49. 20" *"Victoria"*® . Soft vinyl head and limbs, sleep eyes, lashes, cry voice, sprayed hair. *(1970 Illustration courtesy Alexander Doll Co., Inc.)*

ALEX-50. 12" *"Lucinda"*® . Plastic, soft vinyl head and arms, rooted hair, sleep eyes, lashes. *(1970 Illustration courtesy Alexander Doll Co., Inc.)*

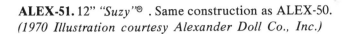

ALEX-51. 12" *"Suzy"*® . Same construction as ALEX-50. *(1970 Illustration courtesy Alexander Doll Co., Inc.)*

ALEX-51.

ALEX-55.   ALEX-52.   ALEX-53.   ALEX-54.

ALEX-52 through **ALEX-59.** These dolls are 14" plastic and vinyl, with sleep eyes, lashes, rooted hair, jointed shoulders and hips. *(1970 Illustrations courtesy Alexander Doll Co., Inc.)*

ALEX-52. *"Madame Doll"*® , in pink silk brocade gown, pink organdy dust cap. "The Secret of Madame Doll" — Frances Cavanah, Vanguard Press.

ALEX-53. *"Heidi"*® , in print cotton dress, white pinafore, straw roller hat.

ALEX-54. *"Rebecca"*® , in pink and white dotted cotton dress, pink poke bonnet.

ALEX-55. *"Alice in Wonderland"*® , in pale blue cotton dress, white pinafore. Alice is based on Lewis G. Carroll's book "Adventures Under Ground". *Facsimile of original manuscript by Xerox U.M.I.*

ALEX-59.

ALEX-56.   ALEX-57.   ALEX-58.

ALEX-61. *Sound of Music.* Dolls representing characters from the movie, *"Sound of Music".* (*Photograph courtesy Madame Alexander Doll Company*)

ALEX-62. *Peter Pan.* Dolls representing characters from the classic which has been produced as a stage play and a movie while also remaining popular as a book. (*Photograph courtesy Madame Alexander Doll Company*)

ALEX-60.

ALEX-56. *"Jenny Lind® and Her Listening Cat".,* blue print cotton dress, white eyelet apron, furry kitten. "Jenny Lind and Her Listening Cat" — Frances Cavanah, Scholastic Book Services, New York. 1969.

ALEX-57. Portrait Children Series, *"Degas Girl"®* wears white eyelet cotton dress, organdy dust cap, after masterpiece paintings by Degas.

ALEX-58. Portrait Children Series, *"Renoir Girl"®* wears pink cotton dress and straw hat, after masterpiece paintings by Renoir.

ALEX-59. *"Grandma Jane"®* , wears blue line shift dress and coat, has rimmed spectacles, pearl necklace, gray hair.

ALEX-60. *"Cinderella® ".* Matte finish vinyl and plastic, blue sleep eyes, solid plastic lashes, rooted hair, closed mouth. Doll is unmarked; dress tag reads: *"Cinderella"* / by **MADAME ALEXANDER, NEW YORK U.S.A.** The Alexander card is attached to wrist. 14" doll. (*Rebekka Anderton collection*)

ALEX-61.

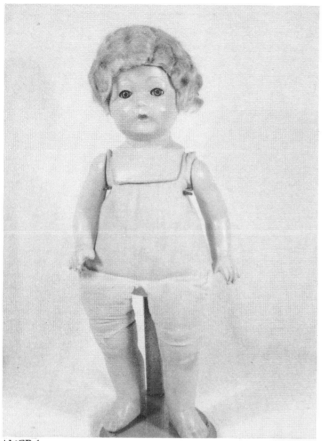

AMER-1.

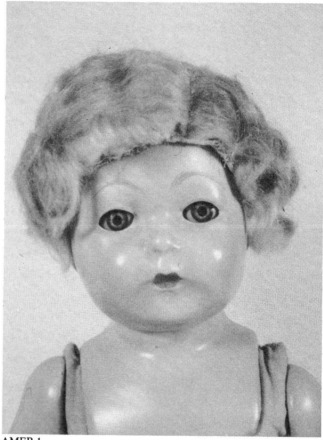

AMER-1.

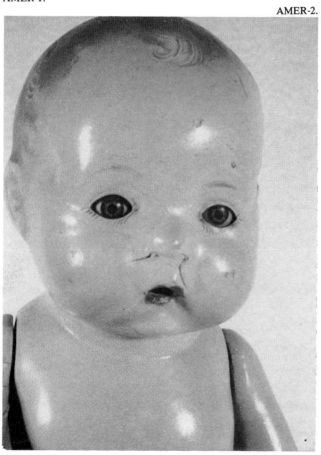

AMER-2.

AMERICAN CHARACTER DOLL COMPANY

The company dates from about 1918 or 1919, when American industry was supplying the market vacated by the German doll manufacturers because of World War I. Dolls were marked in several ways as the illustrations in this book will indicate. The company is now out of business; molds, patents, copyrights, and equipment have been liquidated. Some of the molds were purchased by the Ideal Toy Corporation.

AMER-1. 17" Mama Doll. Composition shoulder head, arms and legs, cloth body, gray tin eyes, original blonde mohair wig. Marks: **PETITE / Amer. / Character Doll Co.** 1920's. *(Spalding collection)*

AMER-2. 23" Bent-leg Baby. Composition, dark blue tin sleep eyes, holds bottle in hand. Marks: **PETITE / AMERICA'S WONDER BABY DOLLS** (curved). 1920's. *(Wiseman collection)*

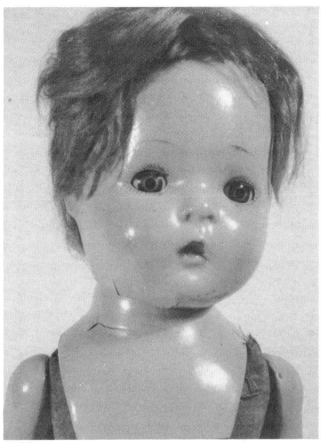

AMER-3.

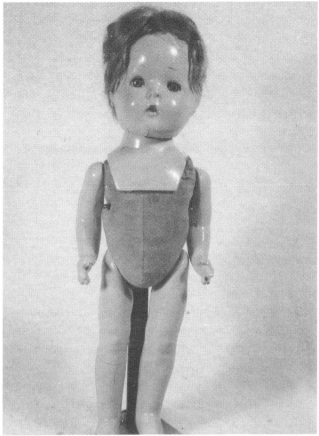

AMER-3.

AMER-3-1.

NOTE: ORIGINAL PRICES SHOWN
ARE NOT TODAY'S PRICES.

AMER-3. 16" *Sally.* Composition swivel shoulder head, arms and legs, gray tin sleep eyes, original blonde mohair wig. Marks: **PETITE / SALLY.** 1920's, 1930's. *(Wiseman collection)*

AMER-3-1. *Bottletot.* Composition head and arms, cloth body and legs, sleep eyes, painted hair. Listing reads: "Bottletot, a Petite Baby, 'Baby B' Holds Her Own Bottle". *1926 Catalog illustration courtesy Sears, Roebuck & Co.*

AMER-4.

AMER-5.

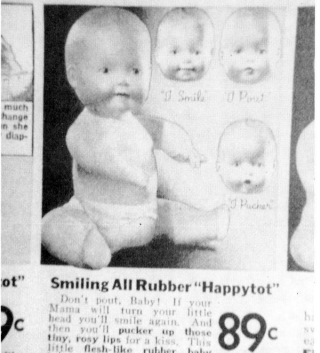

AMER-51.

AMER-4. 18", 21", 24" *Toddle-Tot.* Composition head and limbs, soft body, mama voice, sleep eyes, lashes, "natural" face with dimples and narrowed eyes. *1930 catalog illustration courtesy Sears, Roebuck & Co.* Retailed at $3.48, $4.69, and $5.95.

AMER-5. 24" *Perfect Beauty.* Composition head and limbs, stuffed body, mama voice. Retailed at $6.95. *1930 catalog illustration courtesy Sears, Roebuck & Co.*

AMER-5-1. 10½" *Happytot.* All rubber, changeable-faced baby. This may be the "Marvel Tot" patented by American Character in 1936, as listed in Luella Hart's Directory of United States Doll Trademarks. *1936 Catalog illustration courtesy Sears, Roebuck & Co.*

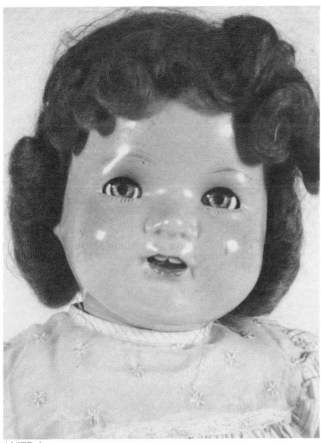

AMER-6.

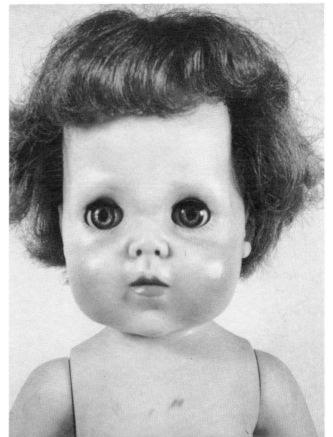

AMER-6-1.

AMER-7.

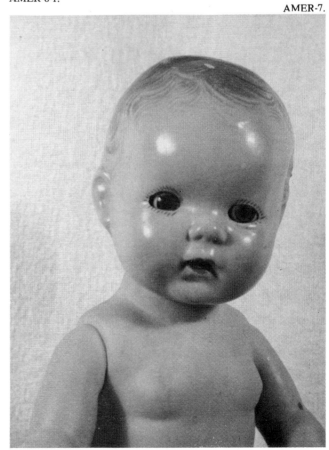

AMER-6. 19" Mama Doll. Composition head and limbs, stuffed body, blue sleep eyes, big smile with two teeth. Marks: **AM. CHAR. DOLL.** ca. 1938. *(Wiseman collection)*

AMER-6-1. 16" Child. Stuffed vinyl body, sleep eyes, rooted hair, closed mouth. Legs and body are one-piece construction. Marks: **Amer. Char. Doll** on head. 1950's. *(Spalding collection)*

AMER-7. *Toodles.* Open mouth, composition head, on replacement vinyl body. Marks: **"TOODLES"** on head. 1955. *(Kirtley collection)*

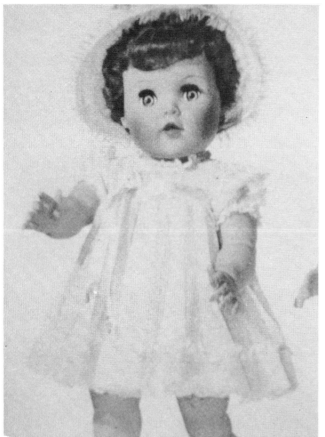

AMER-8.

AMER-9.

AMER-9.

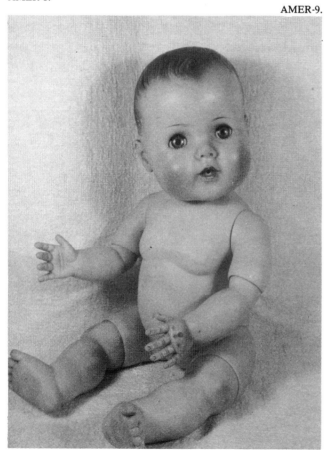

AMER-8. 23" *Toodles Toddler.* Vinyl, rooted saran hair, sleep glassene eyes, lashes. Also with molded hair. *1959 catalog illustration courtesy Sears, Roebuck & Co.*

AMER-9. 21" *Toodles.* All vinyl, blue sleep eyes, open mouth, drink and wet feature, jointed elbows and knees, molded hair. 1955. *(Kirtley collection)*

AMER-10.

how to have more fun with your
AMERICAN CHARACTER DOLL

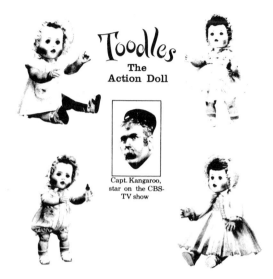

Capt. Kangaroo,
star on the CBS-
TV show

You will actually believe TOODLES is a real live baby. She can kneel, sit, play with her toes and fingers, and assume a 1000 different positions. She is soft and cuddly and feels as lifelike as a real infant.

She drinks and wets too, her head moves in any direction. She is washable, unbreakable. Make believe becomes almost real for the little girl who has a TOODLES to love.

AMER-10a.

AMER-11.

AMER-12.

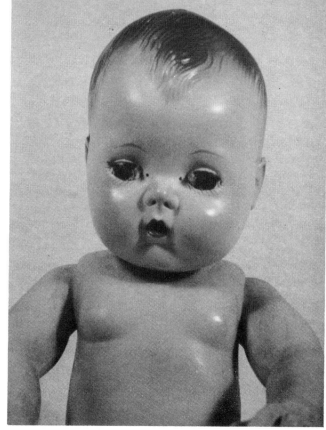

AMER-10. 25", 30" *Toodles Toddlers.* All vinyl, rooted saran hair, glassene sleep eyes, lashes. Retailed at $14.99 and $16.99. *1960 catalog illustration courtesy Sears, Roebuck & Co.*

AMER-10a. *Toodles.* Illustration from a 1953 brochure.

AMER-11. 21" *Toodles, The Action Baby.* "First all jointed vinyl doll": jointed elbow and knees, detailed fingers, molded hair. Wore sandals, nylon playsuit, rayon taffeta bonnet. Retailed $15.95. See AMER-9. *1955 catalog illustration courtesy Sears, Roebuck & Co.*

AMER-12. 13" *Tiny Tears.* Rubber, hard plastic head, molded hair, hands in early, palm-down position. Marks: **Pat. No. 2675644 / Ame-Character.** 1950. *(Spalding collection)*

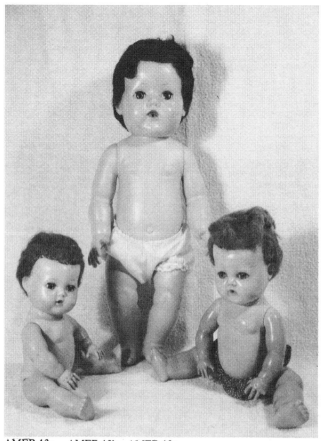

AMER-13a. AMER-13b AMER-13c.

AMER-13b.

AMER-14.

AMER-13a. 11" *Tiny Tears.* Rubber, hard plastic head, washable synthetic hair rooted in skull cap, sleep eyes, hands in early, palm-down position. Marks: Same as AMER-12. *(Author's collection)*

AMER-13b. 19" *Tiny Tears.* All vinyl, hard plastic head, rooted saran hair in skull cap, sleep eyes, hands turned palm to body. Marks: Same. *(Author's collection)*

AMER-13c. 13" *Tiny Tears.* Rubber, hard plastic head, saran hair rooted in skull cap. Marks: Same. Note "tear" openings at inner corner of eye on these three dolls. *(Author's collection)*

AMER-13d. From a *Tiny Tears* brochure. ca. 1955.

AMER-14. 8½" and 12" **New** *Tiny Tears.* All vinyl, rooted hair, blue sleep eyes, drink and wet feature, no "tear" openings, solid molded plastic lashes. 8½" size is marked: **19© 64 / AMER.CHAR.DOLL** on head. 12" is marked only **AM. CHAR.®** on head. Smaller doll's wig is just as it came from a thrift shop, will comb down nicely with care. *(Author's collection)*

You can even play in the tub with

  Tiny Tears THE DOLL THAT CRIES REAL TEARS

- **AMERICA'S BEST LOVED BABY DOLL** — Tiny Tears, the star pupil on Miss Frances' Ding Dong TV show, likes to play in water. Her head is plastic with sleeping eyes.
  She drinks her bottle, wets her diaper, and cries.
  You can have Tiny Tears with rooted Saran hair that can be washed, brushed and curled just like your own! She comes with a suitcase packed full of extra clothes and accessories.
- **FEEDING TINY TEARS** — Like all babies, Tiny Tears gets hungry. Feed her only plain water. Lay her on her back and gently place the nipple in her mouth. Sometimes your baby will be very hungry and drink rapidly, other times she will take her bottle more slowly.
- **TO MAKE TINY TEARS CRY** — After she has had her bottle, *place the pacifier in her mouth securely* and hold her in an upright position. Squeeze her body slowly and gently with both hands and she will cry REAL TEARS. If you do not want Tiny Tears to wet too much, watch oz. marks on nursing bottle and feed her only one oz.
- **CHANGING TINY TEARS** — When Tiny Tears needs a change of diaper, it is advisable to dry and powder her arm and leg joints.
- **PLAYING WITH TINY TEARS** — Tiny Tears is a playful infant too. In her layette you will find a bubble pipe. A good soapy solution will help Tiny Tears to blow big bubbles in her playtime hour. Place the bowl of the pipe in the soapy mixture and then put the stem in your baby's mouth. Hold her in an upright position, press her tummy several times and you will get nice big bubbles.

JUST LIKE A REAL LIVE BABY

You can wash her ears, play with her fingers and toes, powder her . . . and dress Tiny Tears in the prettiest outfits.

Tiny Tears can do almost anything a real baby can do including play in her own play pen. You'll have more fun with Tiny Tears than any other baby doll in the whole world. You'll love her because she is so wonderful.

Drinks, Wets, Changes   Blows Bubbles   Bathes

AMER-13d.

AMER-14a.

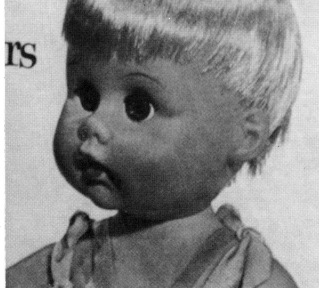

AMER-14a. 12" *Teeny Tiny Tears*. All vinyl, sleep eyes, rooted hair. 8½" size was called Teeny Weeny Tiny Tears. *1963 Catalog illustration courtesy Sears, Roebuck & Co.*

AMER-15. 20" *"Sweet Sue Sophisticate"*. Good quality plastic, rooted hair, sleep eyes, jointed waist, high-heel feet, adult hands. 1953. Marks: **AMERICAN © CHARACTER** in circle on Back. *(Author's collection) Sweet Sue Coed* is offered 1955 catalog in 18", 22", 25" sizes at $10.98, $12.98, and $18.98. Has rooted Saran wig, flat feet. In 1954, *Sweet Sue* is dressed as *"Annie Oakley"* of television series.

AMER-15-1. Illustration from a mid-1950's brochure enclosed with a Sweet Sue Sophisticate *"Queen of Diamonds"*. *(Author's collection)*

AMER-15-2. Illustration from a mid-1950's brochure enclosed with a Sweet Sue Sophisticate *"Queen of Diamonds"*. *(Author's collection)*

AMER-15.

AMER-15

AMER-15-1

Sweet Sue SOPHISTICATE
the most glamorous doll in the world...
SHE WALKS

How to walk and play with SWEET SUE SOPHISTICATE, America's glamorous girl doll, that does practically everything!

She walks, she sits, she turns her head. She has high heeled shoes and nylon stockings. SWEET SUE SOPHISTICATE can do almost anything.

HERE'S HOW TO MAKE HER WALK:

1. straighten her legs in standing position.
2. take her arms, balance her on one foot and lead her forward.
3. shift her weight free from one foot to the other.
4. alternately repeat this action on each leg and SWEET SUE SOPHISTICATE will walk

Here's how to wash, comb and set SWEET SUE SOPHISTICATE'S rooted hair—that cannot pull out:

SWEET SUE SOPHISTICATE is a wonderful doll with beautiful hair. By washing it and changing her hairdo, you can give your SWEET SUE SOPHISTICATE doll a brand new personality—she becomes practically a new doll. Use your own curlers and bobby pins, you need no special wavelotion or kits because SWEET SUE SOPHISTICATE'S hair curls easily and keeps the soft lustre.

Another Brand New
Sweet Sue
with FLEXIBLE FOOT

Sub-teen SWEET SUE is the newest of the family, whose ankles are jointed so that she can stand on her toes like a ballerina or wear flat shoes or high heels. She bends at the waist, walks, and comes complete with a model's carrying case which includes an extra pair of shoes, ballet slippers and dancer's leotard. She is beautifully constructed in Bisque finished vinyl with rooted Saran hair that can be washed and combed and she's as much fun to play with as a real live little girl.

A
Jointed ankle permits ballet positions.

B
Jointed ankle permits walking in flat heeled loafers.

C
Jointed ankle permits walking in high heeled shoes.

Right out of the pages of McCall's Fashion Magazine

BETSY McCALL

a real true-to-life personality
with a
wonderful wardrobe.

BETSY McCALL can do 'most everything. She has jointed knees, can walk, sit and kneel. She is active every moment of the day, providing loads of exciting playtime fun. By changing her inexpensive costumes she can be any type of playmate you like from a bathing beauty to a bride. BETSY McCALL is just 8" high.

You'll see her wonderful wardrobe of 18 different costumes at your favorite toy or department store.

AMER-15-2.

AMER-16.

AMER-17.

se, hair that
Cricket has
key, just like
and you can
hair any way
. . . she always
cute. She wears
ballet dress,
nd and shoes.
-inch costumes
Wt. 7 oz.
843. . . . $2.94

AMER-16. 12" *Tressy,* "The dress-up doll with dress-up hair." Doll has mechanism to allow hair to "grow" and then to retract. Glamour paks of pins, brushes, combs, rollers, hats, and other accessories were available. Plastic and vinyl, rooted hair, painted eyes, doll unmarked. *1963 catalog illustration courtesy Sears, Roebuck & Co.*

AMER-17. 9" *Cricket,* Tressy's Little Sister. She has magic key, hair grows, legs pose, rooted hair, painted eyes. Also shown in 1966 catalog. *1965 catalog illustration courtesy Sears, Roebuck & Co.*

The cutest little baby you have ever loved

TEENIE WEENIE

TEENIE WEENIE is the new 11" all vinyl baby doll that drinks and wets. She has sleeping eyes and a movable head that is jointed so that she can assume hundreds of life-like positions. She has rooted Saran hair that can be washed and combed . . . and what's even more important, TEENIE WEENIE gives you a choice of seven complete changes of costume. She's ready for anything from a bath to a party.

EVERYBODY LOVES A **Pretty Baby**

YOU'LL LOVE HER TOO!

Every little girl wants a Pretty Baby to care for. Just like a real baby, she cries when you squeeze her. Closes her eyes to sleep, moves her arms and legs. Made of unbreakable washable vinyl, she is dressed in a long embroidered nylon dress and pastel petticoat. Her cap is shirred and trimmed in lace and she wears a diaper and booties.

For additional clothes for SWÉET SUE and TINY TEARS, write to American Character Doll Corp., Dept. C-I, 1107 Broadway, New York.

AMER-19.

AMER-18.

AMDOLL-1.

AMER-18. *Teenie Weenie.* Illustration from a 1955 sales brochure.

AMER-19. *Pretty Baby.* Illustration from a 1955 sales brochure.

AMER-20. 21" *Whimsies.* All vinyl, stuffed, rooted hair, painted eyes. It is difficult to know which character of the many *Whimsies* was represented by this much-played-with example. See *Multi-Faced Dolls* for *Hedda Get Bedda.* 1960 American Doll & Toy (American Character). *(Kirtley collection)*

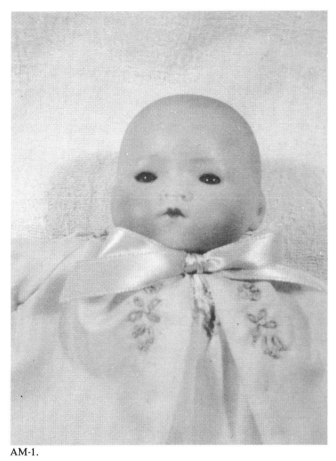

AM-1.

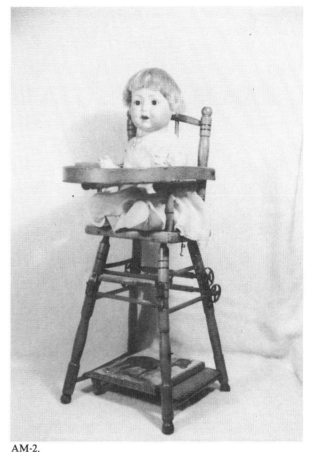

AM-2.

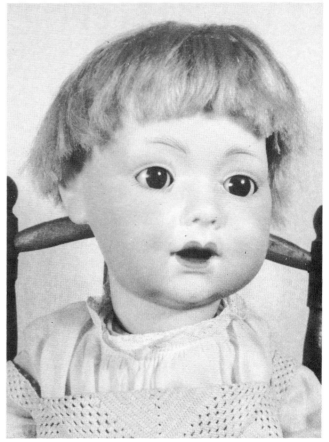

AM-2.

ARMAND MARSEILLE

These German bisque head dolls are among the most plentiful and are therefore most available to the average collector. The No. 370 and No. 390 mold numbers are commonly found in a variety of sizes and treatments and could constitute a collection in themselves. The firm produced a wide range of babies, toddlers, children, and some lady types.

AM-1. 10" *Kiddie Joy.* Tiny glass sleep eyes, closed mouth, tinted hair, bisque head, composition arms, cloth body, straight legs. AM made some of these heads; this doll has the AM head (note resemblance to *Dream Baby*). Marks: **GERMANY / KIDDIE JOY / 1 / 0,** on head. *(Battagler collection)*

AM-2. 17" Baby. Brown stationary eyes, open mouth, two upper teeth, original blonde mohair wig, bisque socket head, bent-leg baby body of papier mache. Marks: **GERMANY / 327 / A. 9 M.** *(Battagler collection)*

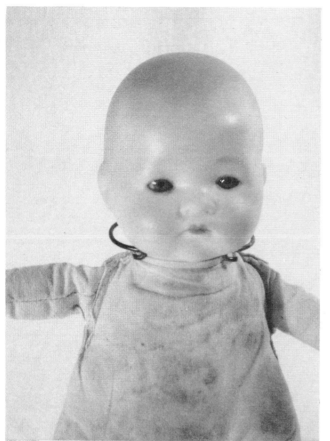

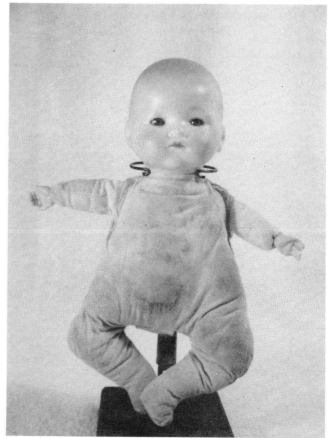

AM-3.

AM-4.

AM-3.

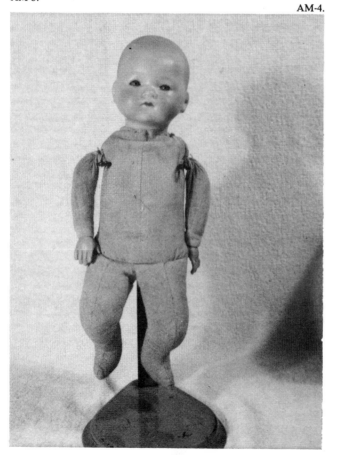

AM-3. 10" *Dream Baby.* 9" circ. bisque head, *Bye-lo* type cloth body with celluloid hands is original, has never been off the head. Same marks as A&M-4. *(Bower collection)*

AM-4. 12" *Dream Baby,* 9" circ. bisque head, original cloth body with Turtle-mark celluloid hands, blue sleep eyes, closed mouth, cry voice. Marks: **AM / Germany / 341 / 2.** *(Author's collection)*

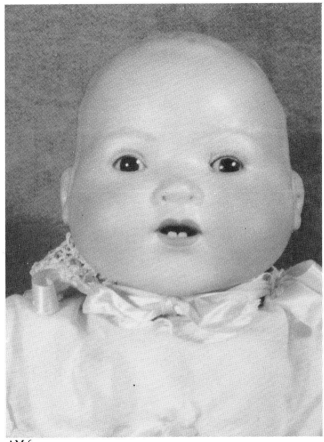

AM-6.

AM-5

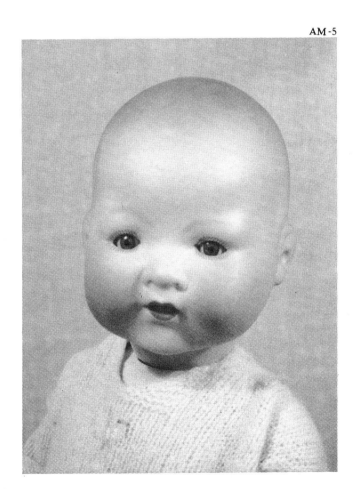

AM-5

AM-5. 17" Baby. Bisque socket head, blue sleep eyes, open mouth, two teeth, papier mache bent-leg baby body, red painted lines between fingers, toes and around nails, red dots in nostrils and inner eye corners. Marks: **A.M. / GERMANY / 351.14.K.** *(Author's collection)*

AM-6. 17" Baby. Bisque flange-neck head, sleep eyes, open mouth, two teeth, cloth body, composition hands. Marks: **A.M. / GERMANY / 351.** *(Battagler collection)*

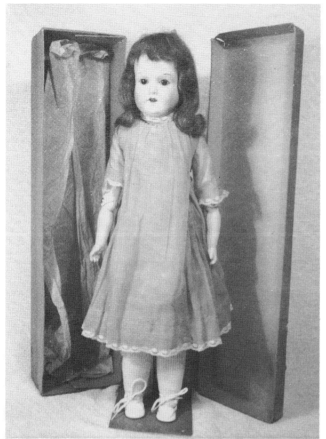

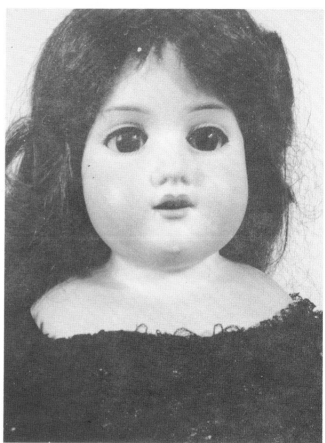

AM-9.

AM-8.

AM-9.

AM-7.

AM-7. 12" Baby. Bisque flange-neck head, blue sleep eyes, open mouth, two teeth, new cloth body, composition hands and lower limbs. Marks: **A.M. / GERMANY / 352.** *(Author's collection)*

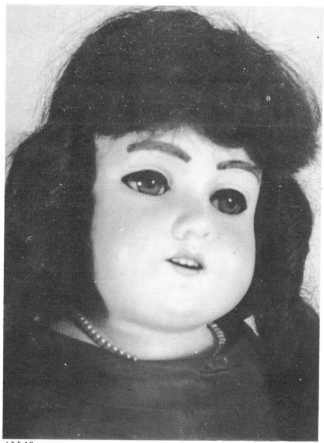

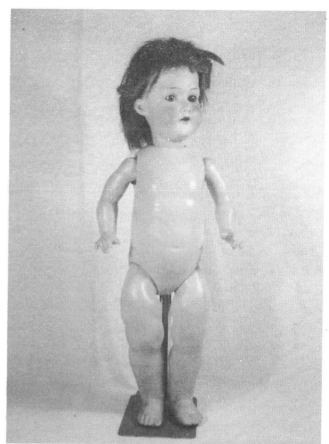

AM-10.

AM-11.

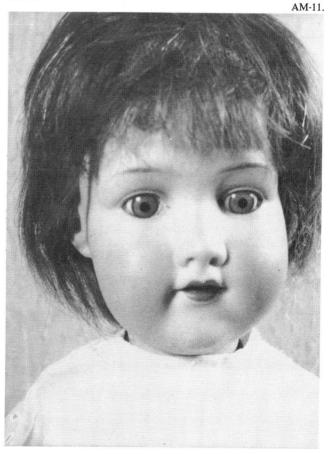

AM-11.

AM-8. 22" Bisque Shoulder Head, brown glass eyes, open mouth, four teeth, red-brown human hair wig, kid body with universal joints, bisque hands, cloth lower legs and feet. Marks: **A. & M. / 370 / GERMANY / 5.** (Battagler collection)

AM-9. 20" Bisque shoulder head, brown glass eyes, open mouth, four teeth, original wig was red-brown mohair, kid body, universal joints, composition lower arms with red lines between fingers and around nails, cloth lower legs and feet. Original clothes, never removed from doll. Doll never played with, found in original box with Montgomery Ward label. Marks: **ARMAND MAR-SEILLE / GERMANY / 370 / 0.** (Author's collection)

AM-10. 24" Bisque shoulder head, blue sleep eyes, fur brows inserted in slit in bisque, real hair lashes, replacement wig, open mouth, four teeth, kid body with gusseted knees, replacement bisque hands. Marks: **3 7 0 / A . M . - 3 - D . E . P . / A R M A N D   M A R-SEILLE / MADE IN GERMANY.** (Courtesy Phyllis Odell)

AM-11. 21" Bisque socket head, glass eyes, open mouth, four teeth, original human hair wig, chubby-legged toddler papier mache body, composition arms. Marks: **ARMAND / MARSEILLE / GERMANY / 390 / A. 6½ M.** (Author's collection)

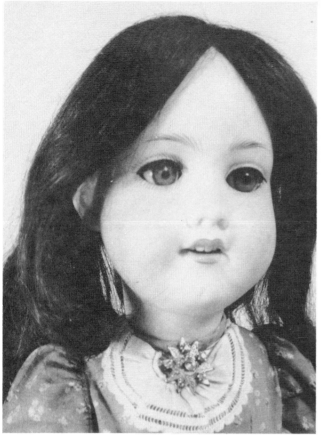

AM-12.

AM-13.

AM-14L.   AM-14R.

AM-12. 17" Bisque socket head, glass sleep eyes, hair lashes, open mouth, four teeth, ball-jointed body, unusually pale bisque. Marks: **ARMAND MARSEILLE / GERMANY / 390 / A. 4 M.** *(Bower collection)*

AM-13. 15½" Bisque socket head, stationary glass eyes, replacement wig, ball-jointed papier mache, wood and composition body with "stick" legs. Marks: **390 / A. O M.** *(Courtesy Phyllis Odell)*

AM-14L. 13½" Boy. Bisque socket head, stationary brown glass eyes, original mohair wig, open mouth, four teeth, red dots nostrils and inner eye. Marks: **ARMAND MARSEILLES / GERMANY / 390 / A.3 / OX   M.** *(Battagler collection)*

AM-14R. 10" Boy. Bisque socket head, brown sleep eyes, replacement wig, open mouth, two teeth, papier mache baby body. Marks: **GERMANY / 971 / A. 4 / 0 M.** *(Battagler collection)*

Both 14L and 14R were found in an attic dressed as illustrated in what appear to be original clothes. 14L wears dark blue velvet belt and tie, blue cotton knickers, white shirt. 14R dressed in very old cotton romper suit. The "attic babies" play with old marbles and other toys from Mrs. Battagler's collection.

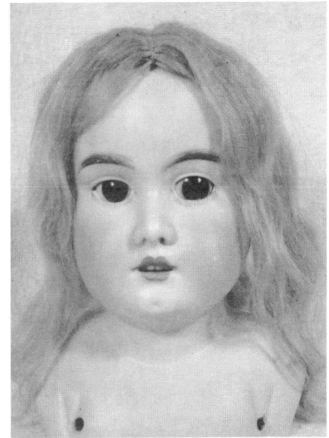

AM-15L.   AM-15R.   AM-16.   AM-16.

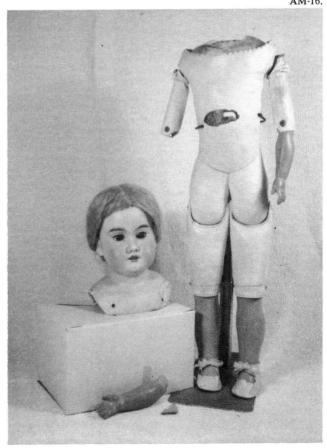

AM-15L. 13" Young Lady. Blue sleep eyes, painted lashes, bisque shoulder head, red mohair wig, kid body, very old, probably original costume of silk, tan with tiny white stripes, Gibson Girl sleeves, lace petticoat and chemise, straw hat with silk, lace, veiling, ostrich and other feathers. Marks: **390 / GERMANY / A 4 / 0 M. / D.R.G.M.** *(Battagler collection)*

AM-15R. 9" Boy. Bisque socket head, blue painted intaglio eyes, closed mouth, dimples, ball-jointed body but originally on papier mache baby body. Marks: **A.M. 8 / 0 / Germany** on head. *(Battagler collection)*

AM-16. 23" *Rosebud.* Bisque shoulder head, original blonde mohair wig, brown glass sleep eyes, open mouth, four teeth, kid body, metal pins hold celluloid forearms and hands, lower legs and feet, wooden ball joint at shoulder, upper arms kid-covered wood. Marks: **ROSE-BUD / A. 5½ M. / MADE IN GERMANY,** on head. Stamped in blue under shoulder head on body: **48.** Red label on abdomen reads: **SUPER ---- / HAIR STUFFED.** *(Author's collection)*

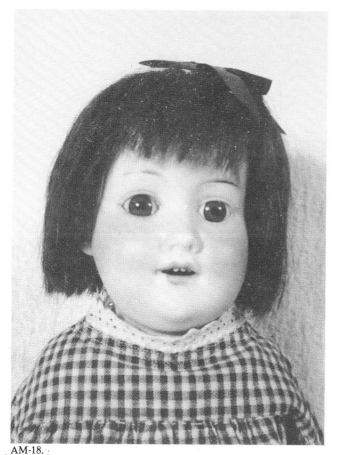

AM-18.

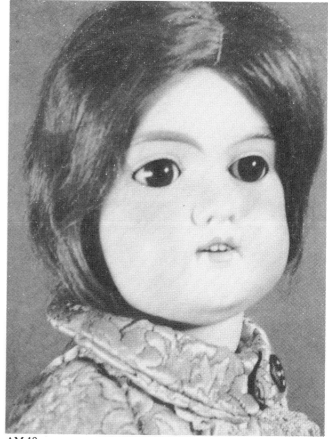

AM-19.

AM-17.

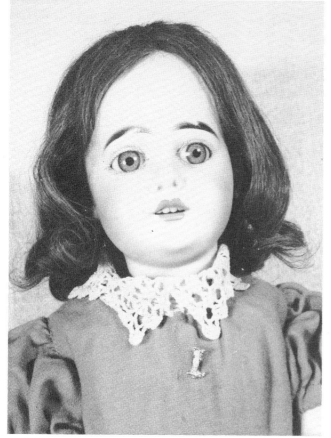

fig. AM-18

AM-17. 22" *Miss Columbia.* Bisque socket head, blue threaded stationary glass eyes, French human hair wig exactly matches her painted brows, open mouth, four teeth, ball-jointed wood and composition body. Marks: **1894 / AM 9 DEP / MADE IN GERMANY.** *(Author's collection)*

AM-18. 20" *Baby Betty.* Bisque shoulder head, blue stationary glass eyes, old human hair wig, dimpled chin, kid body with universal hip joints and gusset knee joints, cloth lower legs and feet, well modeled bisque hands and lower arms, old dress. Marks: See fig. A&M-18. *(Battagler collection)*

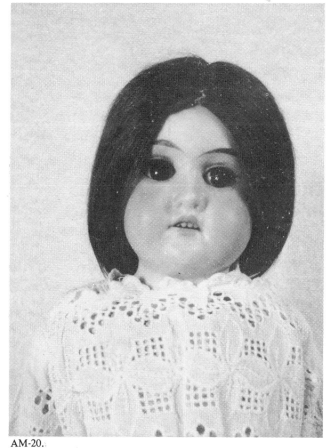

AM-19.

AM-20.   AM-20.

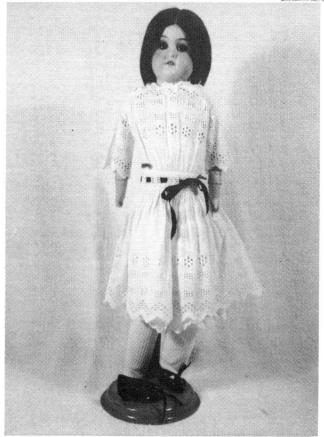

NOTE: ORIGINAL PRICES SHOWN
ARE NOT TODAY'S PRICES.

AM-19. 22" *Florodora*. Bisque socket head, brown glass eyes, molded painted brows, open mouth, four teeth, composition and papier mache ball-jointed body, original dark blonde mohair wig. Marks: **Florodora / A 7 M** on head. *(Battagler collection)*

AM-20. 19" *Florodora*. Bisque shoulder head, brown sleep glass eyes, hair lashes, open mouth, four teeth, kid body, gusset knees, bisque hands, cloth feet. Old, but not original dress. Childhood doll of Ada Aurora Vannucci Dillard, this doll was purchased in Spokane, Washington, in 1910. Mrs. Dillard remembers the original dress was of light tan satin trimmed with a light blue braid and her stockings were of black knit. Even the women wore black hose in those days. When the doll came to the author she brought along another old white cotton lawn dress and a finely crocheted collar made by little Ada's aunt. Marks: **FLORODORA / A 210 XM / MADE IN GERMANY.** *(Author's collection)*

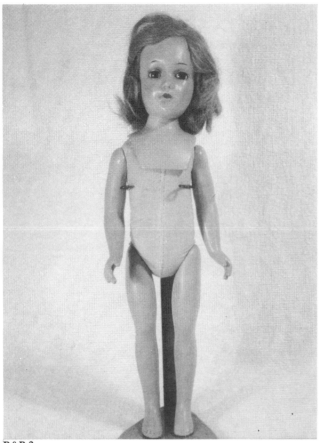

R&B-2.

R&B-2.

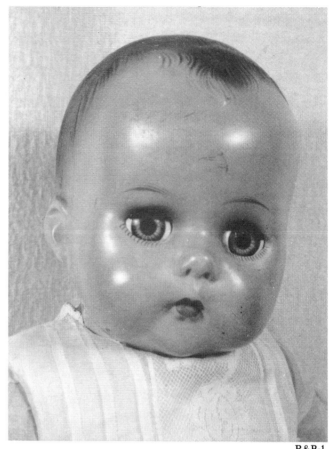

R&B-1.

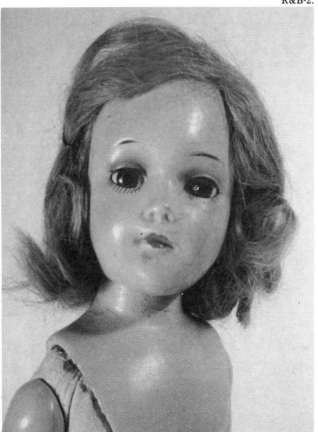

ARRANBEE DOLL COMPANY

Arranbee (R&B) Doll Company made dolls from 1922 until it was purchased by Vogue Dolls, Inc. in 1958. Use of the name and manufacture of the company's products was discontinued in 1960. Dolls may be found marked either with the spelled-out name **ARRANBEE,** or simply with the initials, **R & B,** or **R & B** in an oval. *(Courtesy Vogue Dolls, Inc.)*

R&B-1. 22" Baby. Composition head, arms and bent legs, brown sleep eyes, stuffed cloth body. Marks: **R & B** on head. ca. 1940. *(Kirtley collection)*

R&B-2. 17" *Debu Teen.* Composition swivel shoulder head and limbs, brown sleep eyes, hair lashes, original blonde human hair wig, stuffed cloth body. Originally dressed as a debutante in long pink taffeta dress with pink net overskirt, white rabbit fur jacket, pink slippers, according to original owner. Marks: **R & B** on head. 1938. *(Courtesy Gwen Bower)*

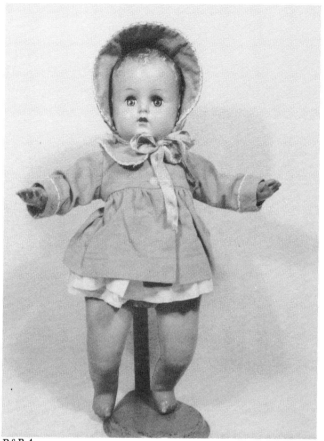

R&B-4.

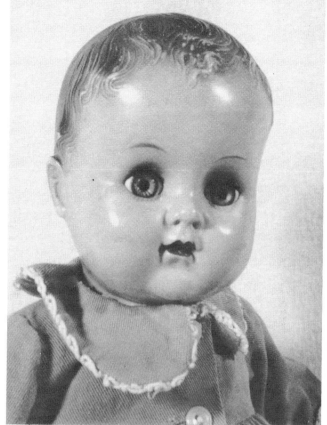

R&B-4.

R&B-3L.   R&B-3R.

R&B-3R. 17" Girl. Hard plastic, blue sleep eyes, head turns as she walks. Unmarked, but similar to R&B-3L. *(Charles Vandiver collection)*

R&B-3L. 17" Girl. Hard plastic, bright blue sleep eyes, long lashes, red mohair wig looks original, original clothes. Marks: **R & B** on head. ca. 1950. *(Charles Vandiver collection)*

R&B-4. 17" Baby. Composition head, stuffed rubber limbs, separate fingers, cotton stuffed body, sleep eyes, hair lashes, original clothes. Doll purchased 1944 for Mrs. Battagler's daughter, also shown in 1947 catalogs. Marks: **R & B** on head. *(Battagler collection)*

R&B-5c.

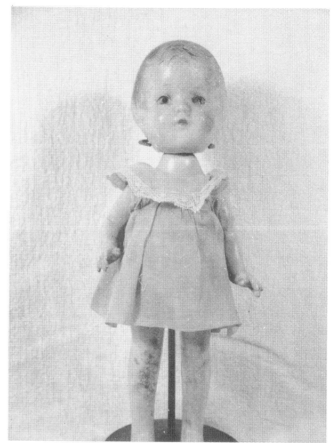

R&B-6.

R&B-5L, R&B-5C, R&B-5R

R&B-5L. 16" Girl. All composition, sleep eyes, original mohair wig, unmarked.

R&B-5C. 17" Girl. All composition, original mohair wig, sleep eyes. Marks: **R & B** on head. ca. 1940. *(Author's collection)*

R&B-5R. 14" Girl. All composition, blue sleep eyes, found wearing buckskin-color flannel panties, may have been dressed as American Indian since her skin color is darker than that of other two dolls in picture. Marks: **R & B** on head. ca. 1940. *(Author's collection)*

R&B-6. 12" *Nancy,* All composition, painted blue eyes, molded painted hair, original green organza dress. Marks: **NANCY / AN ARRANBEE DOLL** on dress tag. **ARRANBEE / DOLL CO.** on back. ca. 1930. *(Kirtley collection)*

R&B-7.

R&B-8.

R&B-9.

R&B-9.

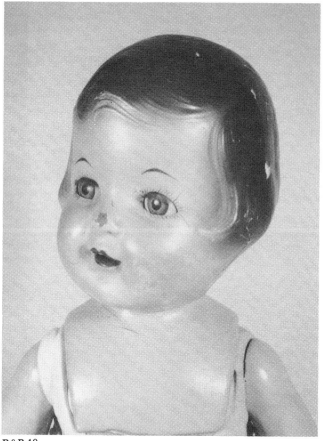

R&B-10.

R&B-10.

R&B-10.

R&B-7. 21" Girl. All composition, golden brown sleep eyes, original blonde mohair wig. Marks: **R & B** on head. ca. 1938. *(Wiseman collection)*

R&B-8. 10" Girl. Soft vinyl head, hard plastic jointed body, green sleep eyes, bright orange rooted hair. Marks: **R & B,** head and body. 1960's. *(Rebekka Anderton collection)*

R&B-9. 11½" Girl. All composition, painted blue eyes, molded hairbow loop, molded painted hair. Marks: **ARRANBEE / DOLL CO.** ca. 1925. *(Wiseman collection)*

R&B-10. 20" Child. Composition swivel shoulder head and limbs, cotton stuffed body, molded painted hair, blue tin sleep eyes, hair lashes plus painted upper and lower lashes, cry voice, open mouth, two teeth, original clothes, shoes, and socks; dress is pink organdy. Marks: **ARRANBEE** on head. ca. 1930. *(Baume collection)*

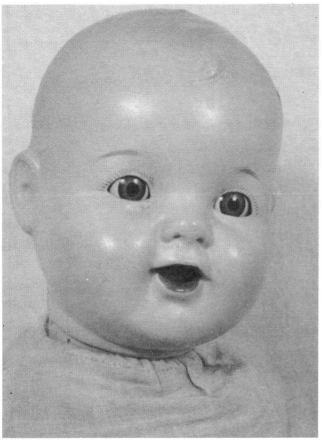

R&B-11.

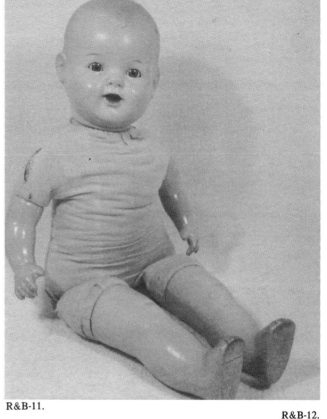

R&B-11.

R&B-12.

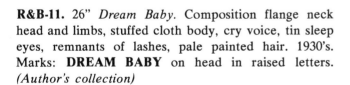

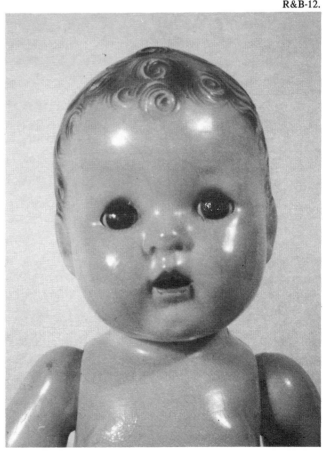

R&B-11. 26" *Dream Baby.* Composition flange neck head and limbs, stuffed cloth body, cry voice, tin sleep eyes, remnants of lashes, pale painted hair. 1930's. Marks: **DREAM BABY** on head in raised letters. *(Author's collection)*

R&B-12. 16" *Dream Baby.* All composition, brown sleep eyes, molded, painted brown hair, open mouth, two teeth. Marks: **DREAM BABY** in raised letters on back of head. The eyes on this doll date it a few years after R&B-11; ca. 1940. *(Wiseman collection)*

A 21" *Dream Baby* is shown in 1944 Sears Christmas Catalog. Dressed in assorted baby dress and bonnet outfits, it had composition arms, legs, and head with stuffed cotton body, molded ringlet hair. Retail $3.19. Head is similar to that of R&B-12.

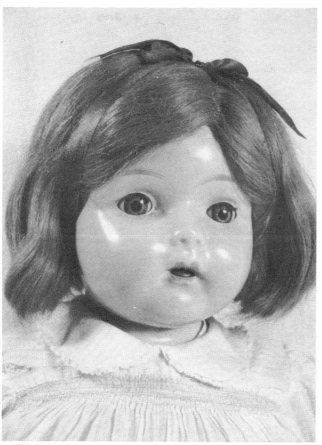

AVRL-1ª.

AVRL-1b.

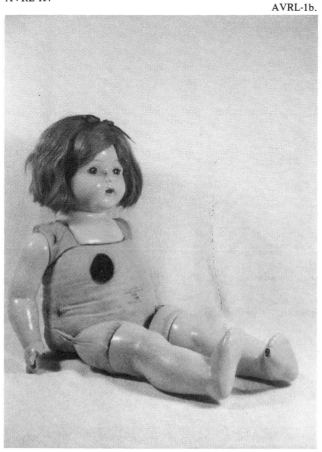

AVRL-1c.

AVERILL MANUFACTURING COMPANY

Dolls from this company are known variously as *Madame Hendren* dolls, *Madame Georgene* dolls, or *Georgene Novelties*. Dolls from Averill date from about 1913; the company ceased operation in 1965 and the assets were liquidated at that time. A full line of baby dolls, walking dolls, girl dolls, etc. was produced over the years.

———————

AVRL-1a. 26" *Dolly Record.* Composition shoulder head, arms and legs, gray tin sleep eyes, cloth body, human hair wig, changeable records and record player in body.

AVRL-1b. Round opening in chest for speaker. Stamped on lower left front of cloth body: **GENUINE / MADAM HENDREN / DOLL / 26.**

AVRL-1c. Opening in back of cloth body for record player. On the table left to right: record player mechanism, cylinder record, and face plate. On record: **Averill Manufacturing Co. / New York City, U.S.A.** On mechanism: **Pat. 1355525 / 1357936.** Stamped on body: **Genuine / Madame Hendren / Doll / "26".** Recording is *"London Bridge"*, one of several nursery rhymes recorded for these dolls. Record mechanism appears identical to that found in *Mae Starr* dolls, (which see) and made by Universal Talking Toys Co. *(Wiseman collection)*

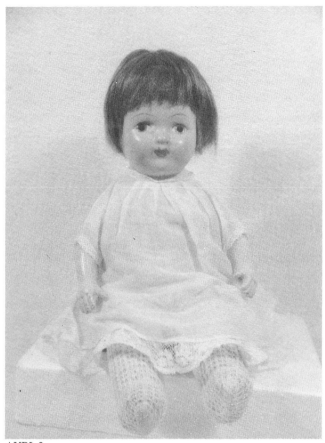

AVRL-2.

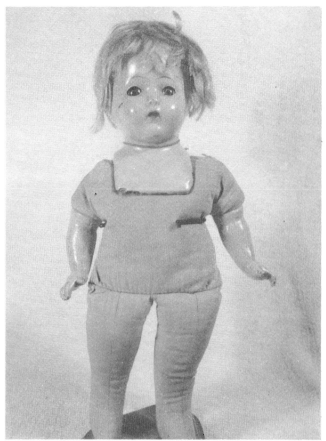

AVRL-3.

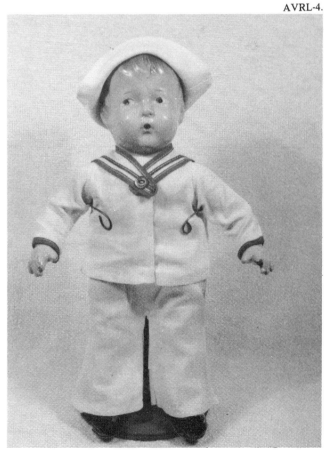

AVRL-4.

AVRL-2. 12" Baby. Composition shoulder head, arms, cloth body and legs (pink muslin), original mohair wig, cry voice, painted blue eyes, original clothes. Marks: Stamped on body front in blue-green ink: **GENUINE / MADAM HENDREN / DOLL / 12 / MADE IN U.S.A.** 1910's-1920's. *(Wingfield collection)*

AVRL-3. 14" Baby. Composition shoulder head, arms, cloth body and legs, open crown, mohair wig, gray tin sleep eyes. Marks: **GENUINE / MADAM HENDREN / 818M / MADE IN U.S.A.** on shoulder plate. Similar doll appears in 1924 Sears catalog in 19½" size in voille dress and hat at $3.98, identified as Mme. Hendren doll. *(Wiseman collection)*

AVRL-4. 13½" *Whistling Sailor.* Composition head, flange neck, composition arms, cloth body, blue-green painted eyes. Whistle operated by standing doll on table and pressing downward, thus compressing coil spring bellows which constitutes the entire structure of the legs. 1929. *(Wingfield collection)*

Shown in the Sears 1925 catalog is an identical doll described as being 15" tall. Two possibilities suggest themselves: either the doll was made in two sizes or this example has lost some of its height with age, that is, the springs in the legs have compressed enough to account for the height difference.

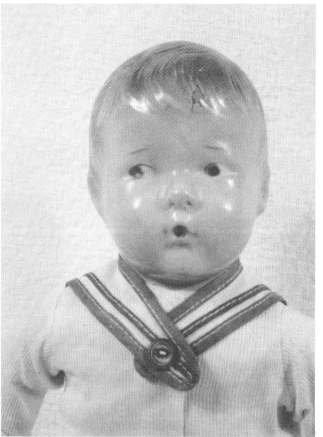

AVRL-4.

AVRL-5.

AVRL-6.

AVRL-5. 13½" *Cowboy Whistler.* 1927 Sears catalog illustration. 1928 catalog offered a Whistling Cop, 1929 listed a Whistling Sailor. *(Courtesy Sears, Roebuck & Co.)*

AVRL-6. 18" *Rock-a-Bye Baby.* Composition head and limbs, stuffed cotton body, cries with three voices, sleep eyes, mohair wig, walks in toddling fashion like baby's first steps. Dressed in white organdy and lace, came in heavy cardboard cradle packing box. Retailed in 1921 at $11.50; by 1924 price was down to $6.95. *1921 Catalog illustration courtesy Sears. Roebuck & Co.*

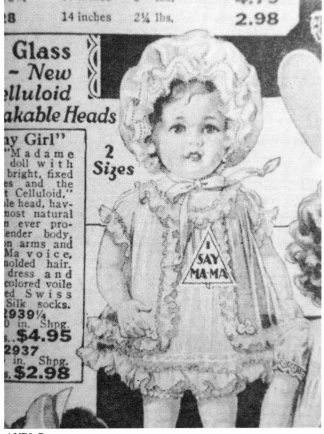

AVRL-7.

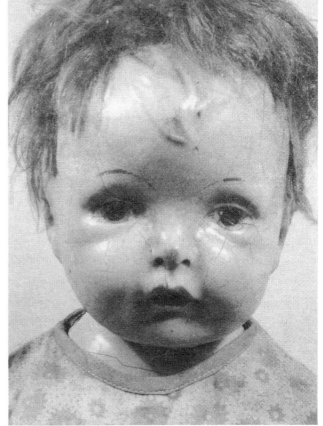

B-1.

B-1.

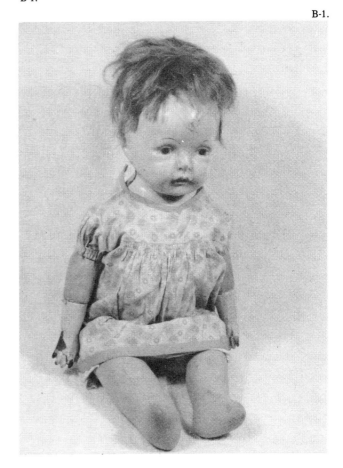

AVRL-7. *Sunny Girl.* Celluloid head, composition limbs, slender stuffed cloth body, painted, molded hair, mama voice, fixed glass eyes. 14" size was $2.98; 20" size was $4.95. *1927 Catalog illustration.* In 1928 another of the smiling babies typical of the period is shown in this line, called Sunny Babe. Had "art" celluloid head, open mouth with teeth and tongue, fixed glass eyes, cry voice, dressed in colored organdy, 19", coat $4.85. *Catalog information courtesy Sears, Roebuck & Co.*

 B

B-1. 22" Baby. Composition head, painted blue eyes, closed painted mouth, original mohair wig, deep shoulder plate, composition arms to elbows, cloth body and legs. Doll was Christmas gift to Pearl Fairchild Dunlap in 1918, purchased at Sears. *"Baby Ruth"* character face doll in Sears 1918 catalog listed with molded papier mache body, undressed, has similar face.

B-2.

fig. B-3

B-3.

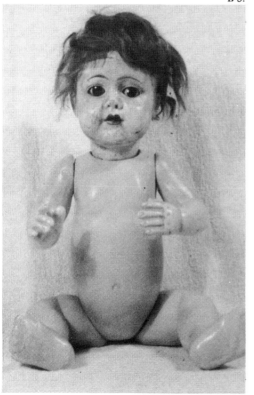

B-4.

B-2. 18" *Bannister Baby* ® All vinyl, jointed arms, legs, glassene sleep eyes, drink'n'wet feature, cries, blows bubbles with plastic pipe, dressed in terry robe, booties and undies. 1954. *Catalog illustration from 1954 courtesy Sears, Roebuck & Co.* Inspired by the famous baby photographs of Constance Bannister. Marks: **32/Constance Bannister/New York, New York/Mfd. by/The Sunn Rubber Co.,/Barberton, Ohio, U.S.A./under one or more U.S. Pats. 2118682/2160732, 2552218, 2629131, 2629134, and other Pats. Pending.**

B-3. 18" Baby. Composition, body is in excellent condition while head is peeling badly; may be different materials or exposure since doll was well dressed and thus protected. Closed mouth, sleep eyes, original mohair wig of soft light brown color. Marks: Fig. B-3 on head. *(Author's collection)*

B-4. 32" Bed Doll. French Dandy, cloth mask face, silk floss hair with pigtail, cloth body, sawdust stuffed, teal blue velvet coat, silver lame pants. From France. Unmarked. *(Courtesy Kimport Dolls)*

B-5. 24" Bed Doll. French Girls, cloth mask faces, embroidery floss hair, woven metallic cloth dresses, painted features, hats decorated with holly and flowers, dolls are all cloth construction. 1920's. *(Courtesy Kimport Dolls)*

B-5L.

B-5.

B-4.

B-5R.

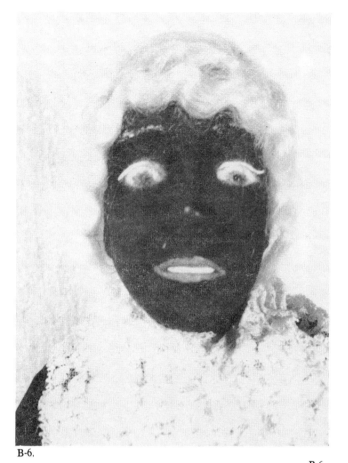

B-6.

B-6.

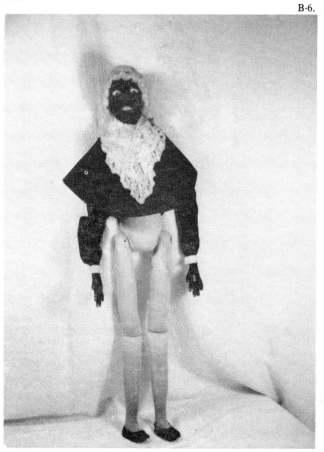

B-6.

B-6. 28" Bed Doll. *"Melissa"* is cloth with leather hands, white wavey mohair wig, face covered with some type of flocking material, head is composition or a reinforced felt. Black silk hat and shoes, black taffeta dress, lace jabot. Clothes are sewn on. Doll came from the Deep South of the United States and is believed to be what is called a *household doll,* representing a nanny who cared for the children of a family. Buttons on the joints are hand carved. Doll may date in the nineteenth century. *(Kirtley collection)*

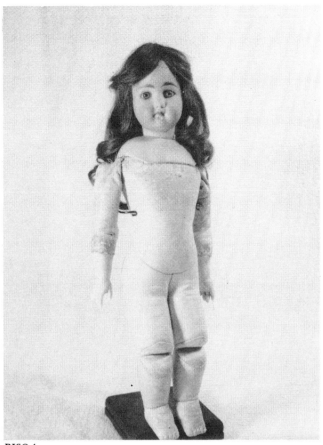

BISO-1.

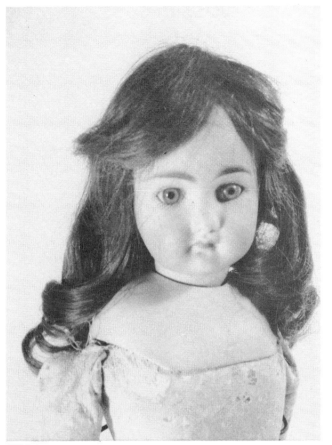

BISQ-1.   BISQ-2.

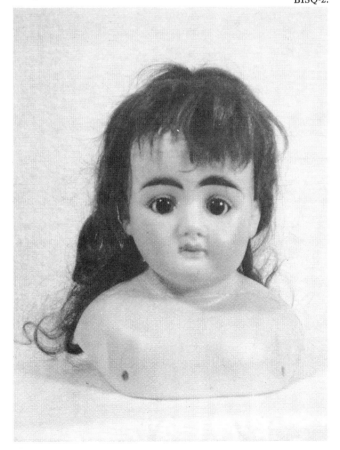

BISQUE DOLLS
Doll collectors use the term *bisque* to define the ceramic dolls or dolls parts which are tinted and unglazed, giving a soft, life-like finish to the material. (See also China).

BISQ-1. 15" Child. Not of this century, she is shown as an example of the beauty of the old German bisques. Stationary blue bulging glass eyes, swivel head, deep shoulder plate, pink kid body, gusset joints, original bisque hands, human hair wig, closed mouth. Marks: **6** on head. *(Bower collection)*

BISQ-2. 15" Child. Another closed mouth German, bisque shoulder head is 4½" tall, 7½" circ. Brown blown glass eyes, original mohair wig, gusseted kid body, bisque hands. Marks: **1235 Germany AS (or NS) DEP.** *(Author's collection)*

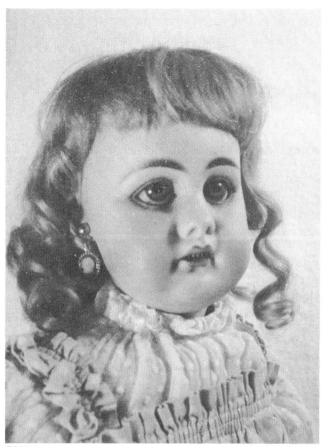

BISQ-3.

BISQ-3.

BISQ-3.

BISQ-3. 20" Treasure. Swivel-head bisque, original blonde mohair wig, blue sleep eyes, open mouth, six teeth, pierced front-to-back ears, original bisque hands and arms, cloth feet, kid body with very narrow waist, wood upper arms covered with kid. Marks: **S & H 461 or SH 11 461.** *(Courtesy Phyllis Odell)*

This doll was brought from Paris about 1880 to Olive Garrison, by an aunt who traveled extensively in Europe. The doll and her trunk of clothes have been in the same family beginning the fifth generation. Dresses, coats, capes, raincoat, aprons, umbrella, sheets, pillowcases, hats, handkerchiefs, nightgowns, robes, and jewelry are among the large trousseau packed in the round-top trunk. Olive Garrison, whose name is painted on one end of the trunk, was an aunt of the present owner. The clothes have a great deal of hand finishing on them in addition to fine machine stitching. The doll is known as "Olive Lavice"; she is named after the two aunts.

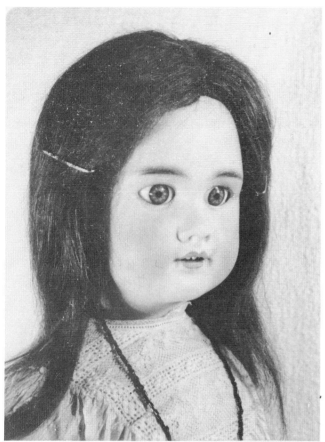

BISQ-5.

BISQ-5.

BISQ-4.

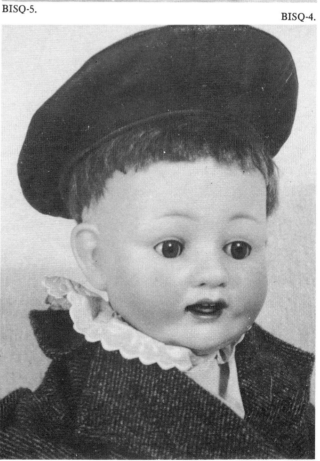

BISQ-4. 17" Boy. Blue sleep eyes, mohair wig, bisque socket head, typical bent-leg baby body. Tongue disappears when eyes close. Marks: **F. S. & Co. / 1272 / 40 / Deponiert** on head. Coleman Collectors Encyclopedia of Dolls identifies these initials as Franz Schmidt & Co., Germany. *(Battagler collection)*

BISQ-5. 25" Child. Bisque socket head, ball-jointed composition and wood body, new human hair wig, stationary blue blown glass eyes, open mouth, four teeth, molded, painted brows, painted lashes. Original dress of silk and lace in a faded pink, original underwear of cotton and lace. Marks: **DEP / 11** on head. *(Author's collection)*

BISQ-6.

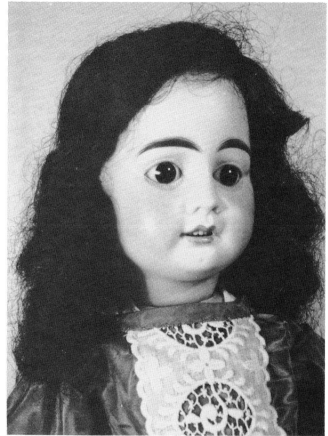

BISQ-6.

BISQ-7

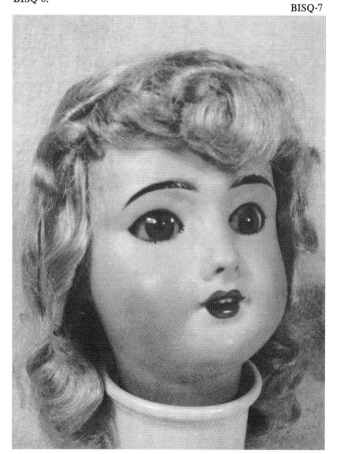

BISQ-6. 19" SFBJ Child. Bisque socket head, ball-jointed, composition and wood body, stationary dark brown eyes, painted lower lashes only, open mouth, five teeth, pierced-in ears, replacement wig. Marks: **4** on head. Red and blue **SFBJ** label on back of body. Her small owner, who mowed lawns all one summer to pay for her, has christened her "Antonia". *(Rebekka Anderton collection)*

BISQ-7. SFBJ Head. Bisque socket head, cornflower blue eyes, open mouth. Marks: **SFBJ / 30 / Paris / 10.** *(Kirtley collection)*

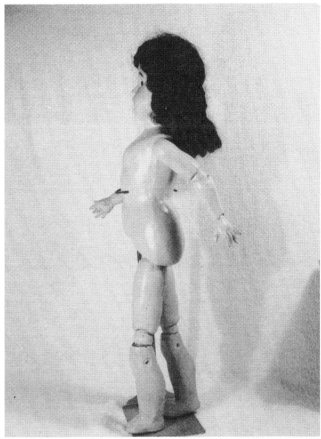

BISQ-8.

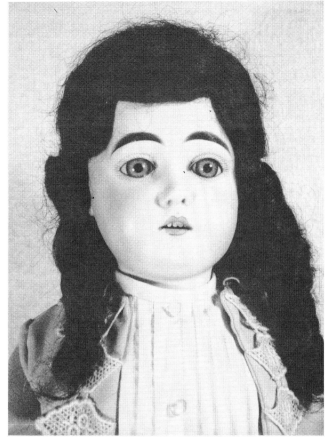

BISQ-8.

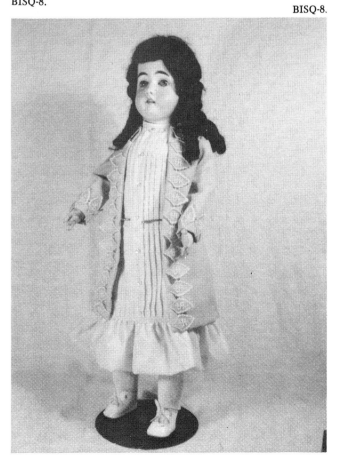

BISQ-8.

BISQ-8. 24" Bisque. Blue blown glass threaded eyes, open mouth, five teeth, bisque socket head, composition and wood ball-jointed body. Marks: **A.S.** / **11** on head. Much washing of dishes and dusting of furniture is paying for this doll. *(Rebekka Anderton collection)*

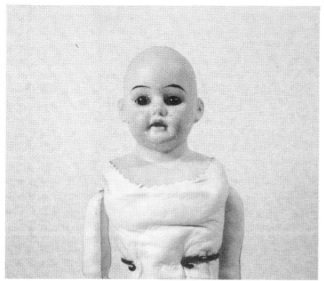

BISQ-9.

BISO-10.

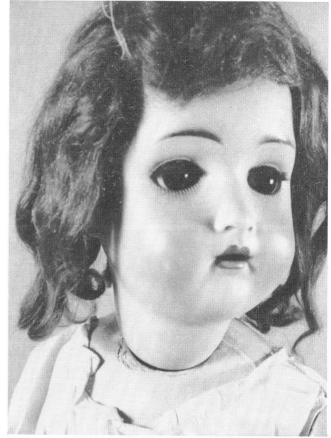

BISQ;10.

BISQ-9. 14" Bisque. Stationary brown glass eyes, open mouth, teeth, bisque shoulder head, gusseted kid body, bisque hands. Marks: **Germany / P.Sch. 1899-5 / 0.** An identical head has initials **A.M.** (for)**Armand Marseille**) over the **Germany.** Coleman Collectors Encyclopedia of Dolls identifies these initials as Paul Schmidt, Germany. Early 1920's. *(Author's collection)*

BISQ-10. 23" Bisque. Brown sleep eyes, hair lashes, painted lower lashes, molded, painted brows, open mouth, four teeth, ball-jointed body, bisque socket head, has the distinctive Kestner coloring. Marks: **Made / in / Germany / 136 / 9 (or 0).** 1920's. *(Childhood doll of Mrs. W. R. (Pearl) Anderton)*

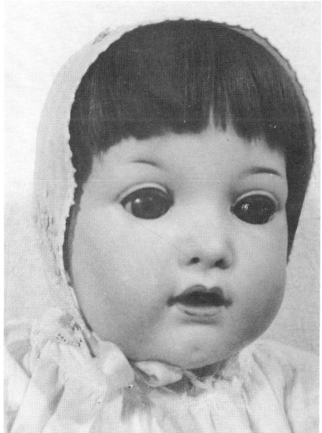

BISQ-11.

BISO-12.

BISO-13.

fig. BISQ-13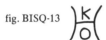

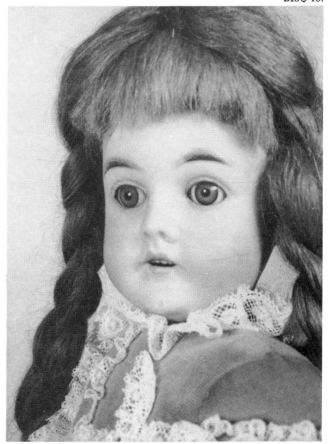

BISQ-11. 20" *Melitta.* Bisque socket head, composition and papier mache baby body, open pierced nostrils, blown glass eyes, hair lashes, human hair wig, beautiful peaches and cream complexion. Marks: **Melitta / 11.** *(Battagler collection)*

BISQ-12. 23" Bisque. Shoulder head, original mohair wig, kid body, open mouth, four teeth, painted, molded brows. Marks: **Germany / 3.** *(Battagler collection)*

BISQ-13. 23" Bisque. Socket head, ball-jointed body with red lines around nails, at knuckles, open mouth, four teeth, blue sleep eyes, painted, molded brows, two wigs, one atop the other create this effective hairdo. Marks: See fig. BISQ-13. This may be a *Heinrich Handwerck* mark. *(Battagler collection)*

BISQ-14.

BISQ-15.

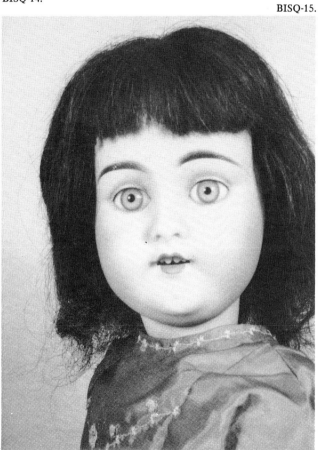

BISQ-14.

BISQ-14. 25" *Dollar Princess.* Bisque socket head, ball-jointed body, brown sleep eyes, painted lashes, molded, painted brows, open mouth, four teeth, original mohair wig. All original from top of her lacy bonnet to tip of high-button kid shoes, except the little beaded purse. Marks: **THE DOLLAR PRINCESS / 62 / SPECIAL / Made in Germany** on head. *(Battagler collection)*

BISQ-15. 22" Bisque. Socket head, very pale bisque, ball-jointed body, open mouth, four teeth, deep dimple, definite double chin, molded, painted brows, blue stationary eyes, human hair auburn wig with bangs. Marks: **S & Q / 101 / Dep. / 11.** 1920's. *(Battagler collection)*

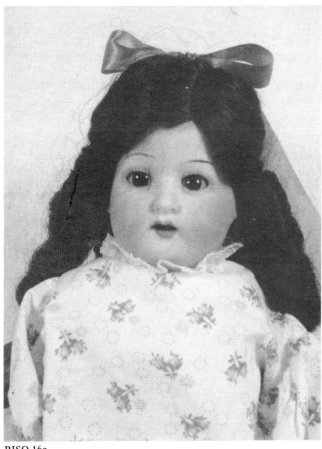

BISQ-16a.

BISQ-16a. BISQ-16b. BISQ-16c.

BISQ-16c.

BISQ-16a. 15" Bisque. Shoulder head, kid body, stationary brown eyes, new wig, open mouth, four teeth, painted brows, bisque hands. Marks: **Germany / M 275 10 / 0 / Heubach-Koppelsdorf,** on head. *(Author's collection)*

BISQ-16b. 15" *Florodora.* Bisque shoulder head, sleep eyes, kid body, bisque hands. Marks: **Florodora / A 5 / OX M / Made in Germany.** *(Rebekka Anderton collection)*

BISQ-16c. 15" Child. Bisque shoulder head, white bisque hands, kid body, legs and feet, molded, painted brows, sleep eyes, open mouth, four teeth. Marks: **Gbr. 170 K / 5 / 0.** Coleman's Collectors Encyclopedia of Dolls gives three choices for this mark: Gebruder Krauss, Gebruder Knoch, or Gebruder Kuhnlenz. Since this doll is very similar to a Knoch doll pictured on page 364 of that work, this writer is inclined to believe BISQ-16c is a Gebruder Knoch. Note the shiny eyebrows which nearly meet above the nose. *(Author's collection)*

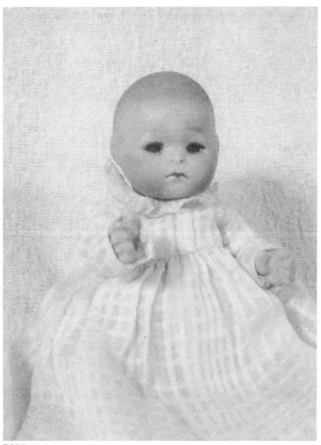

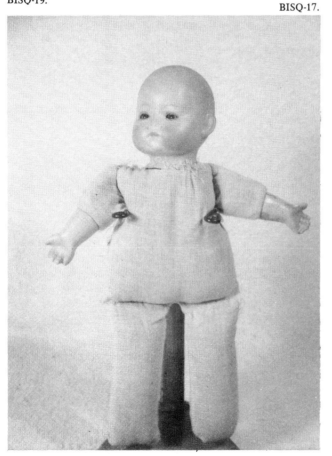

BISQ-19.

BISQ-17.

BISQ-18.

BISQ-17. 10" Baby, 7" circ. bisque head. Composition hands, cloth body of crude proportion and design. Marks: **73. / HS** (Superimposed) **/ Germany / 240.** According to Coleman's Collectors Encyclopedia of Dolls, *New Born Babe* was apparently first doll representing a very young infant; 240 appears on the Hermann Steiner version. Doll was re-issued as competition to the Bye-lo about 1924-1925. *(Author's collection)*

BISQ-18. 6½" Baby. Bisque socket head, papier mache body, closed mouth, painted eyes. Marks: **Germany / 1924 17 / 0.** Apparently another Bye-lo competition. *(Author's collection)*

BISQ-19. 6½" Baby. All bisque, with enamel-over-bisque body and limbs, blue sleep eyes, closed mouth. Marks: **Germany 2 / 0 R127A.** Probably Recknagel of Alexandrinenthal, which made *New Born Babe* for Louis Amberg. This head is of that type and probably of that date. Doll identified by Coleman's Collectors Encyclopedia of Dolls. *(Battagler collection)*

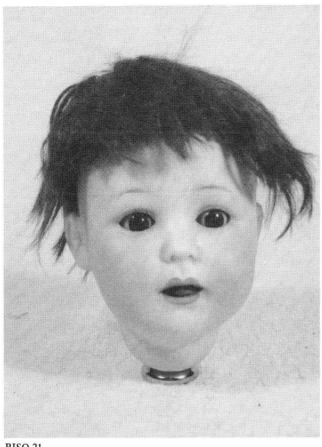

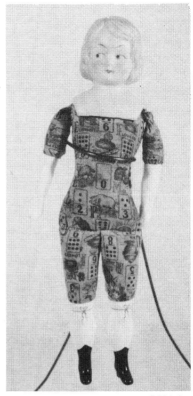

BISQ-23.

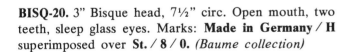

BISQ-21.

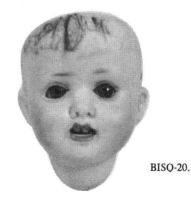

BISQ-20.

BISQ-22.

BISQ-20. 3" Bisque head, 7½" circ. Open mouth, two teeth, sleep glass eyes. Marks: **Made in Germany / H** superimposed over **St. / 8 / 0.** *(Baume collection)*

BISQ-21. 5" Bisque head, 11" circ. Open mouth, original mohair wig, brown sleep eyes, hair lashes, composition baby body. Marks: **Jutta / 1914 / 8½.** *(Baume collection)*

BISQ-22. 5½" and 5 3 / 8" *Nancy Ann Story Book Dolls.* Left, **Seasons Series, Autumn, 92.** Right, **A Dillar, a Dollar, A Ten O'Clock Scholar, 112.** Paint over bisque, painted features and shoes, glued-on mohair wigs. *(Author's collection)*

BISQ-23. 9¼" *ABC Doll.* Pink tinted bisque head, blue painted side-glancing eyes, closed mouth, molded, painted blonde hair, alphabet and toy print body. Arms and legs are reproductions chosen to match the old ones. *(Courtesy Mary Lou Highlander)*

BISQ-25

BISQ-24.

BISO-26a. BISQ-26b. BISQ-26c.

BISQ-24. Miniature bisque baby marked **Germany.** Shown in metal buggy 5" tall and 5" long, painted pastel pink, stamped **Made in Germany.** *(Kirtley collection)*

BISQ-25. 4" Baby. All bisque, painted hair and features, blue eyes, closed mouth, shiny brows, new clothes. *(Courtesy Phyllis Odell)*

BISQ-26a. 6" Pink Bisque. Stationary blue glass eyes, closed mouth, painted shoes with small heels, blue-banded stockings, new wig.

BISQ-26b. 3½" Pale Pink Bisque. Painted features, painted blue shoes and sock tops.

BISQ-26c. 4¼" All Bisque. Light blue sleep eyes, closed mouth, black painted Mary Jane slippers with tiny heels. Marks: **Germany.** *(Courtesy Phyllis Odell)*

BISQ-29

BISO-28.

BISQ-27.

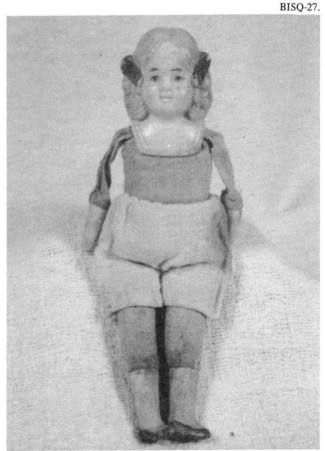

BISQ-27. 6½" Girl. White bisque shoulder head, hands and feet, cobalt blue painted eyes, blonde painted hair, blue hair-bows, original body excelsior stuffed, medium brown painted shoes. Doll was purchased in 1919. Unmarked. *(Courtesy Mrs. Charles (Wilma) Knox)*

Another example with this same head has an alphabet-printed body and is marked **PATENT/NO 30441** across the back of the shoulders.

BISQ-28. Doll House Dolls. All bisque, jointed shoulders and hips, some with painted hair, others have glued-on wigs. Sizes 1-3 / 8" to 3½" tall. All marked: **GERMANY**. First quarter of Century. *(Courtesy Gwen Bower)*

BISQ-29. 3" Girl. All bisque, painted and molded clothes and features, elastic-strung turning head. Marks: **758 / BB / GERMANY** on back of dress. ca. 1920. *(Author's collection)*

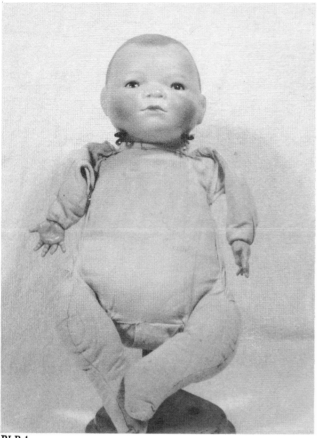

BLB-1.

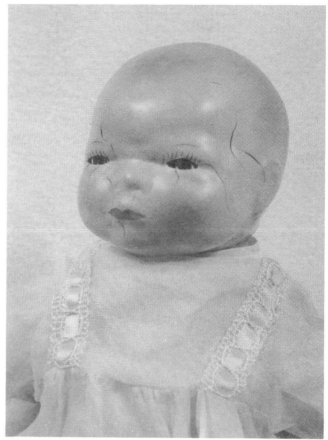

BLB-2.

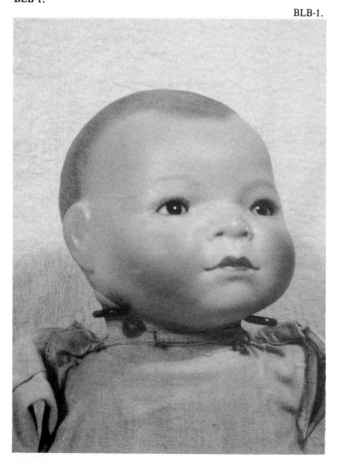

BLB-1.

BYE-LO BABY

This famous baby doll was created by Grace Storey Putnam in 1922. The *Bye-lo* is generally accepted as the first doll modeled from a new-born infant; however, some authorities believe it was preceded in 1914 by the Amberg *New Born Babe*. The *Bye-lo* was manufactured in a variety of materials.

BLB-1. 14" *Bye-lo Baby*, 13" circumference bisque head, brown sleep eyes, dark blond painted hair, hollow celluloid hands, cry voice. Marks: **Copr. by / Grace S. Putnam / MADE IN GERMANY** on head. **GRACE S. PUTNAM**, red mark, on body. *(Battagler collection)*

BLB-2. 13" *Bye-lo Baby*, 11¾" circumference composition head and hands, bent leg cloth body. All original, never played with. Marks: **Grace Storey Putnam** on head. **Bye-lo Baby / Reg. U.S. Pat. Off / © GRACE STOREY PUTNAM / GEO. BORGFELDT CORPORATION / New York, N.Y.** on dress tag. *(Wingfield collection)*

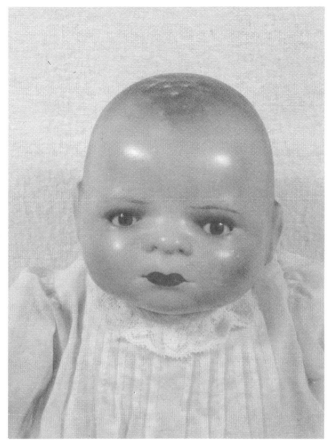

BLB-3.

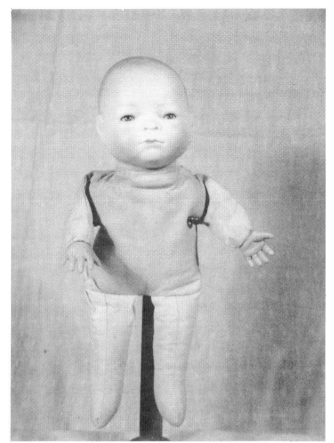

BLB-4.

BLB-4.

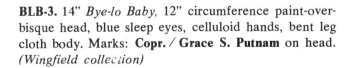

fig. BLB-4

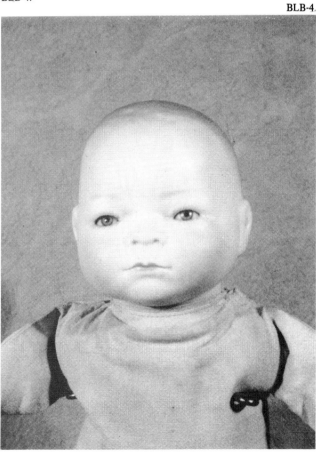

BLB-3. 14" *Bye-lo Baby,* 12" circumference paint-over-bisque head, blue sleep eyes, celluloid hands, bent leg cloth body. Marks: **Copr. / Grace S. Putnam** on head. *(Wingfield collection)*

BLB-4. 11" *Bye-lo Baby,* 10¼" circumference bisque head, all original, blue sleep eyes, straight leg cloth body. Marks: Same as BLB-1, plus dress tag as shown in fig. BLB-4. *(Childhood doll of Mrs. Charles M. Kennedy)*

118

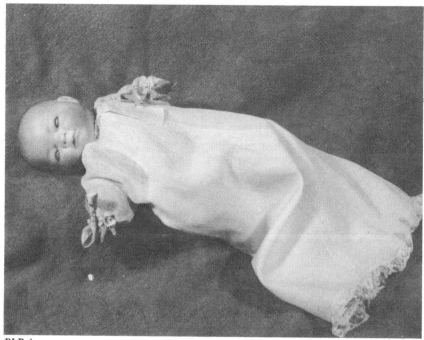

BLB-4.

BLB-5. 12" *Fly-lo Baby*, 10¾" circumference composition head and celluloid hands, green tin sleep eyes, cloth body, re-dressed. ca. 1928. Marks: **Copr. by / G. S. Putnam / MADE IN U.S.A.** on head. Hands unmarked. *(Wingfield collection)*

BLB-5.

BLB-5.

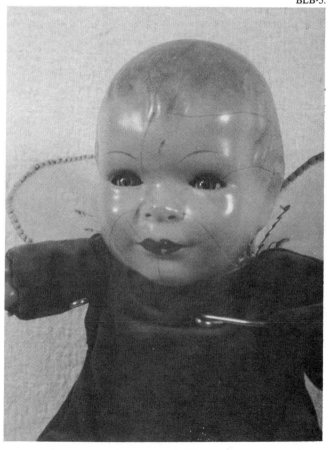

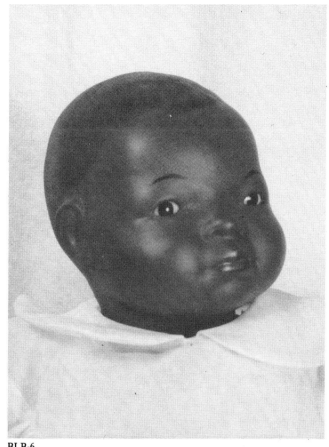

BLB-6.

BLB-8.

BLB-7.

BLB-6. 12" Reproduction Colored *Bye-lo Baby,* 12" circumference colored-in-bisque head, bisque hands, bent leg brown cotton body. 1970. Unmarked. *(Kirtley collection)*

BLB-7. 2½" *Bye-lo Baby Salt,* 1 5 / 8" tall, glazed pink porcelain, unmarked, beautifully painted face. ca. 1925. *(Arthur's collection)*

BLB-8. *Bye-lo Baby* box showing end label. Note price. *(Kirtley collection)*

CAMEO DOLL PRODUCTS COMPANY

Cameo, Kewpies, and *Kallus* — the researcher finds the three nearly inseparable. Mr. Joseph L. Kallus, founder and owner of Cameo Doll Products Company, worked with Rose O'Neill in the development of her *Kewpies* as dolls. As a student at Pratt Institute, Mr. Kallus answered a school bulletin-board advertisement for artists who could draw and sculpt children and was chosen to assist Rose O'Neill with her *Kewpie* dolls. Working from her sketches, he modeled an "in-the-rough" *Kewpie* doll, after which she put her finishing touches to the model, giving it her own individual style. During this time, Rose O'Neill was kept busy with magazine illustrations of *Kewpies,* illustrations for fiction, and with magazine covers, all of which are treasured by today's collectors.

Mr. Kallus continued to work in the doll field while furthering his studies both at Pratt Institute and at the Art League with Robert Henri, George Bridgman, Frank V. DuMond, and William D. L. Dodge. *"Portrait of an Old Man"* was painted during this period.

Wood pulp composition carnival *Kewpies* were produced by Mr. Kallus' Rex Doll Company about 1916 and in 1918 he obtained his first doll copyright for *Baby Bundie.* After military service during World War I, he became president of Mutual Doll Company, then founded the Cameo Doll Company in 1922. Cameo has been in continuous production since that date, both in the *Kewpie* line and with other doll creations. A large sampling of these dolls are shown on the following pages. Cameo operated a plant at Port Allegany, Pennsylvania, from 1932 until January, 1970, when the entire doll production, including equipment, was acquired by the Strombecker Corporation of Chicago, Illinois.

In 1933, Mr. Kallus was called to the White House to confer with President Franklin Delano Roosevelt regarding the Small Business Administration for Pennsylvania. The aim of the commission was to suggest ways of improving the general economy of the nation which had been at a disastrous low since October of 1929. His own company, Cameo, continued to struggle for survival and by 1935 was beginning to stabilize, when the plant was completely destroyed by fire. The factory was on the site of an old tannery which is the present site of the Pittsburgh Corning plant. At the time of the fire the building was filled with completed and nearly-completed merchandise. Many irreplaceable Rose O'Neill artifacts were also destroyed. Following the fire, a modern doll plant was developed at another location.

Mr. Kallus has a definite philosophy about his dolls. He feels the real profit (in making dolls) comes from the service and the sense of satisfaction in providing an artistic doll the child can appreciate and play with in safety. It is his belief that his life's work is in good hands with the Strombecker Corporation which continues the standards of quality he has worked to maintain. Mr. Kallus enjoys an active retirement with his new company, Cameo Exclusive Products, which deals with the licensing of products based on his copyrights and patents.

CAM-1. © J.L.K.

© J.L.K. CAM-2.

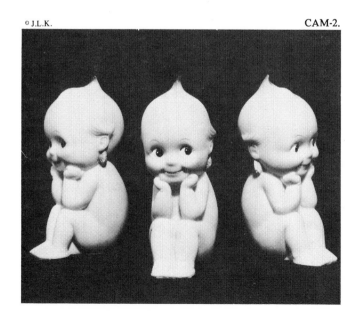

CAM-3.   © J.L.K.

CAM-5.   © J.L.K.

CAM-4.

© J.L.K.

   fig. CAM-5

© J.L.K.   CAM-5.

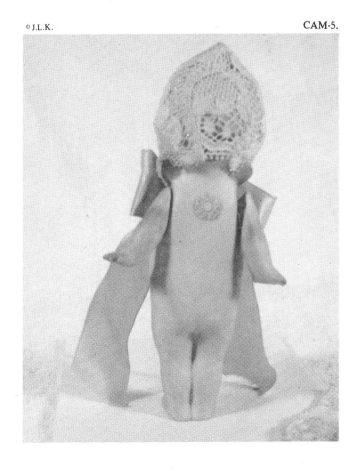

© J.L.K.

CAM-1. Joseph L. Kallus in his studio, surrounded by *Kewpies®* . Photograph made about 1944. *(Courtesy Joseph L. Kallus)*

CAM-2. Sitting *Kewpies®* . One of the best-known of all the *Kewpie®* poses, sometimes called "The Thinker Kewpie® ". *(Photograph courtesy Joseph L. Kallus)*

CAM-3. Two 1947 *Kewpies®* . Fully jointed, latex bodies. *(Photograph courtesy Joseph L. Kallus)*

CAM-4. Floppy *Kewpies®* . Soft bodies. *(Photograph courtesy Joseph L. Kallus)*

CAM-5. 5" Bisque *Kewpie®* . Fine bisque with the Kestner coloring. Marks: See fig. CAM-5. Adornment old but not original. *(Courtesy Lois and Sallye Antiques)*

CAM-8L.   © J.L.K.   CAM-8R.

CAM-6.   © J.L.K.   CAM-7L. CAM-7R.

fig. CAM-6

CAM-6. 14" Composition *Kewpie®* . Much loved, paint peeling, but still most personable. Wears an original *Kewpie®* dress not original to this doll. Marks: Cloth dress label, see fig. CAM-6. *(Zillner collection)*

CAM-7L. 5¼" Bisque *Kewpie®* . Painted hair, blue wings. Marks: **O'neill** across both feet. *(Battagler Collection)*

CAM-7R. 9" Vinyl *Kewpie®* . Painted eyes, turning head. Marks © **Rose O'Ņeill** on left foot; **Kewpie** on right foot. **Cameo** © on head and shoulder. *(Battagler collection)*

CAM-8L. 3¾" Vinyl *Kewpie®* . This one rides the dashboard of author's automobile as a reminder to "keep smiling".

CAM-8R. 2¼" Celluloid *Kewpie®* . Tiny blue wings, all one piece. Marks: **Japan** across shoulders. 1920's. *(Author's collection)*

CAM-10.   © J.L.K.

CAM-9.

© J.L.K.   CAM-11.

CAM-9. 11" Composition *Kewpie®* . Painted features, jointed shoulders, stationary head. Original red *Kewpie®* heart label and red ribbon costume. *(Author's collection)*

CAM-10. Modern Vinyl *Kewpie®* . Dressed in red and white striped dress and red apron trimmed with holly, especially for the Christmas season. *(Photograph courtesy Joseph L. Kallus)*

CAM-11. *Kewpie® Gal©* . Sculptured by Joseph L. Kallus. Vinyl, molded, painted hair and features, body and limbs identical to CAM-10. She is quite a "gal" with her two-strand pearl choker and molded hair-band. *(Photograph courtesy Joseph L. Kallus)*

CAM-12. Vinyl *Kewpie®* . Modeling by Joseph L. Kallus. Unjointed body and limbs, turning head. Sunsuit is a favorite *Kewpie®* costume. *(Photograph courtesy Joseph L. Kallus)*

CAM-13. *Ragsy© Kewpie®* Three sizes, all vinyl, molded-in color, soft and "bathable", coos and cries. 1964. *(Photograph courtesy Joseph L. Kallus)*

CAM-14. Composition *Scootles® ., The Baby Tourist.* Created by Rose O'Neill in 1925; sculptured by Joseph L. Kallus. These are wood pulp composition dolls of the 1930's. *(Photograph courtesy Joseph L. Kallus)*

CAM-12.

© J.L.K.

CAM-14.

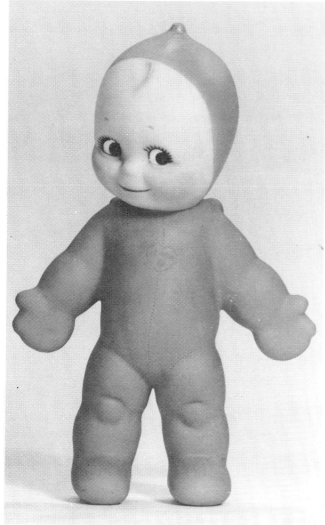

© J.L.K.

© J.L.K.   CAM-15.

CAM-13.

© J.L.K.

The Kewps gave a hugsome Kewpie doll
To Ragsy, the peach of the town;
And they did not part, but heart to heart
Were Ritzy and Ragsy Brown.

FROM "THE KEWPIES AND RAGSY AND RITZIE"®
PAPER DOLL BOOK BY ROSE O'NEILL

© J.L.K.   CAM-16.

CAM-15. 19" *Scootles®* . All vinyl, sleep eyes, assorted outfits, retailed in 1965 at $10.00 *(Photograph courtesy Joseph L. Kallus)*

CAM-16. *Scootles®* . Wood pulp composition, about 1929. Dresses by B. R. Cromien; shoes by Braitling of Bridgeport, Connecticut. *Scootles®* was re-issued in 1964. *(Photograph courtesy Joseph L. Kallus)*

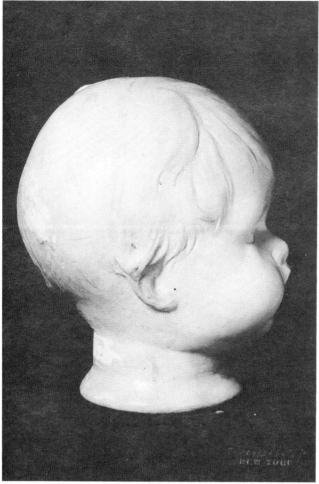

CAM-17.   © J.L.K.

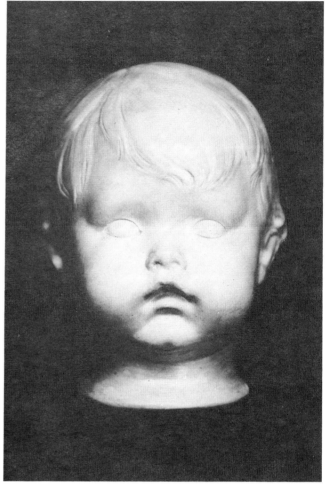

CAM-17.   © J.L.K.

CAM-18-1

CAM-17. *Baby "Bo-Kaye"*© . Sculptured by Joseph L. Kallus, licensed to Geo. Borgfeldt & Co. Made in bisque in 1925, later in celluloid and other mediums. Copyright GXXC-77991 July 10, 1926. Photograph shows *Baby "Bo-Kaye"* head in plaster which has received finishing touches in preparation for producing molds. *(Photographs courtesy Joseph L. Kallus)*

Mr. Kallus tells the story of the origin of the name, *"Bo-Kaye"*: He and Mr. Fred Kolb, president of Geo. Borgfeldt & Co., were seated at a desk on which had been placed a bouquet of flowers. The problem that day was the naming of a new doll; the solution came with the inspiration from the flower bouquet. The name could also represent Borgfeldt (Bo) and Kallus (Kaye).

CAM-18. *Little Annie Rooney*© . Character from a newspaper cartoon strip by Jack Collins. Doll designed and sculptured by Joseph L. Kallus after the Mary Pickford characterization in a motion picture, *"Little Annie Rooney"*. Dolls were manufactured by Cameo exclusively for Geo. Borgfeldt & Co. Illustration is January, 1926, advertisement from Playthings. *(Courtesy Joseph L. Kallus)*

The Latest Novelty Doll

Representing the irresistible romping child spirit so ably played by Mary Pickford in her recent most successful motion picture "Little Annie Rooney."

This doll should appeal to every child because of the happy, humorous expression of the face; the most realistic, brightly colored get-up, and the wig with two long braids of hair.

For at once delivery.

Write for Samples—Dept. 25.

Sole Licensee and Distributor

GEO. BORGFELDT & CO.
111-119 East 16th Street   ::   New York

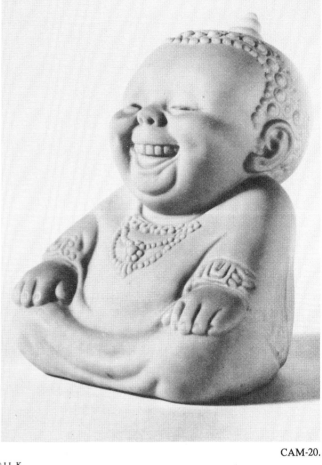

CAM-20.

© J.L.K.

CAM-19.

I am your little friend HO-HO
The wisdom of ages I know-ho,
So I bring you JOY
And hope and pluck,
I bring you a LAUGH
And LOVE ❤
and LUCK ♣

A **CAMEO DOLL** PRODUCT
Port Allegany, Pa. U.S.A.

© J.L.K.

CAM-18-1. 11" *Giggles.* Composition, molded and painted features, molded hairbow loop. Unmarked. *(Photograph courtesy Warner Studio, doll from Mrs. Warner's collection)* Ca. 1946. (See p. 126 for illustration)

CAM-19. *Betty Boop*© . Character from an animated cartoon by Paramount Pictures, Max Flesche Studios. Segmented wood and composition doll designed, modeled, and copyrighted by Joseph L. Kallus. Copyright on doll is G9089 dated July 21, 1932. Illustration is from photograph of large department store window entirely filled with *Betty Boop*© dolls for a special promotion. Dolls sold for $1.49 and $1.00. *(Photograph courtesy Joseph L. Kallus)*

CAM-20. *Ho-Ho*© . Rose O'Neill's last doll creation. ". . . *he is a little clown Buddha, the wisdom of the ages finding its last words in the supreme wisdom of laughter.*" Created in 1940, *Ho-Ho*© was listed in 1965 Playthings in four sizes in soft vinyl, produced by Cameo. *(Photograph courtesy Joseph L. Kallus)*

A plaster of Paris HO-HO candle holder marketed in 1941 is marked on the back **Rose O'Neill 1940.**

MARCH, 1942—PLAYTHI♦

CAMEO TO MAKE DISNEY DOLLS

An interesting news story of the past week, is the appointment of Joseph A. Kallus, well-known doll manufacturer and proprietor of Cameo Doll Products Company, Port Allegany, Pa., to manufacture Walt Disney's Dumbo and Timothy Q. Mouse from the recent Walt Disney motion picture success. Dumbo dolls will be manufactured and shipped immediately— Timothy Q. Mouse will follow. As soon as production is under way on the above two items, Mr. Kallus will start production on Baby Weems—the child phenomenon— from the Walt Disney feature picture, "The Reluctant Dragon."

Dumbo

Baby Weems

There are few manufacturers in the doll industry as well known or with as much experience as Mr. Kallus. He has been producing dolls depicting well-known characters and personalities for over 25 years, and has been credited with items whose sales have reached great volume. The Walt Disney items which Mr. Kallus will produce will be designed in his own inimitable way—of segmented wood and composition, to retail at from $1.00 up. It has always been Mr. Kallus' aim to give full value to the consumer—and in his new Walt Disney Line the values are very apparent—with full markup for the retailer. First models will be shown at the Toy Fair.

Timothy Mouse

CAM-21.

CAM-22.   © J.L.K.

NOTE: ORIGINAL PRICES SHOWN ARE NOT TODAY'S PRICES.

CAM-21. *Disney* Dolls. Three characters from the Disney Studios, modeled by Joseph L. Kallus and produced by Cameo. Illustration is article from March, 1942, Playthings. *(Courtesy Joseph L. Kallus)*

CAM-22. *Pinkie*© . Sculptured by Joseph L. Kallus. Wood pulp composition, April, 1930. Vinyl and plastic, 1950. Sleep eyes, rooted hair. Doll was handled by Sears during early 1950's. *(Photograph courtesy Joseph L. Kallus)*

YOUNG AMERICAN BOYS GET A B

Meet **CHAM**

CHAMP

THE ALL AMERICAN BOY DOLL — FOR THE ALL AMERICAN BOY OR GIRL

Here's a swell little guy any active little boy and girl will want for a playmate. No curls or frills on him. He's just the right kind of regular, mischievous fellow, so typical of every real American boy. Freckled faced, pug nosed, with a wisp of hair falling carelessly over his forehead. Wears a cotton striped jersey with the name "Champ" on it—and is ready for a friendly scrap, anytime—anywhere. Handsomely proportioned, made of wood pulp composition with a head that tilts and turns. Adjustable arms and legs enable "Champ" to assume many different positions.

©J.L.K.

PUT 'EM UP
CHAMP

CAMEO DOLL PRODUCTS CO,   PORT ALLEGANY, PA.

CAM-23.

©J.L.K.

CAM-24.

CAM-23. 16" *Champ®* . Sculptured by Joseph L. Kallus. Wood pulp composition, freckled face, pug nose, wisp of painted hair falling across forehead, painted features. Wears striped cotton jersey bearing his name. Jointed hip, shoulder and neck. October, 1942. Retailed at $2.98 in 1956. *(Courtesy Joseph L. Kallus)*

CAM-24. *Dyp-a-Babe®* . Sculptured by Joseph L. Kallus, produced by Cameo of "Pink Magic" vinyl by Dublon. Sleep eyes, drink and wet feature, cry voice, came with complete layette, or in romper suit. U.S. Patents 2728947, 2728948, and 2728980. 1956. *(Photograph courtesy Joseph L. Kallus)*

CAM-25. © J.L.K.

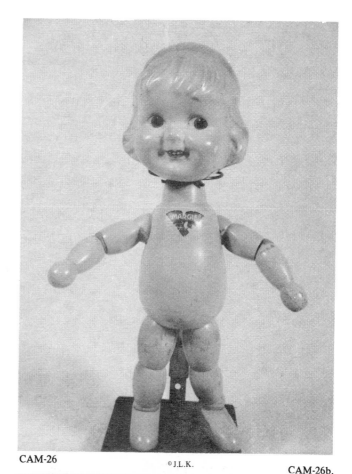

CAM-26. © J.L.K.

CAM-26b.

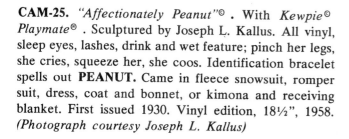

CAM-25. *"Affectionately Peanut"*© . With *Kewpie*© *Playmate*© . Sculptured by Joseph L. Kallus. All vinyl, sleep eyes, lashes, drink and wet feature; pinch her legs, she cries, squeeze her, she coos. Identification bracelet spells out **PEANUT.** Came in fleece snowsuit, romper suit, dress, coat and bonnet, or kimona and receiving blanket. First issued 1930. Vinyl edition, 18½", 1958. *(Photograph courtesy Joseph L. Kallus)*

CAM-26. 9½" *Margie*© . Segmented wood and composition, molded, painted features. Marks: Red label on chest with black and white lettering reads: **"MARGIE"** / Des. & Copyright / by Jos. Kallus. 1929. *(Spalding collection)*

CAM-26b. 17" *Margie*© . Soft vinyl, glassene eyes, rooted Saran hair, jointed at elbows, patent leather shoes, rayon sox. 1958 Catalog illustration. *(Courtesy Sears, Roebuck & Co.)*

Margie © *Doll*

Truly a Work of Art Modeled from Life

all VINYL
★ NEW

★ Fully jointed

★ Ball and socket universal joint type. Can assume 1000 and one poses.

★ In segments. Split at waistline of body, arms at shoulder and legs at body. Head, universal joint at neckline: head will tilt and swivel in socket.

No. 9093/60

©J.L.K.

No. 9013/60

©J.L.K.

CAM-26a.

CAM-27.

CAM-26a. 17" *Margie©* . Sculptured from life by Joseph L. Kallus. All vinyl, fully jointed, ball and socket universal joints, swivel waist, rooted hair, sleep eyes. *(Illustration courtesy Joseph L. Kallus)*

CAM-27. 18½" *Miss Peep©* . Sculptured by Joseph L. Kallus. All vinyl, stationary inset eyes, dressed in snowsuit, in pink blanket, or as illustrated. Also 16" size. Marks: ® **Cameo** © on head; **Cameo**© on back. 1960's. *(Photograph courtesy Joseph L. Kallus)*

CAM-28. 20" *Baby Mine* © **TM.** Sculptured by Joseph L. Kallus. All vinyl, painted features, several different versions. 1961. *(Courtesy Joseph L. Kallus)*

CAM-28

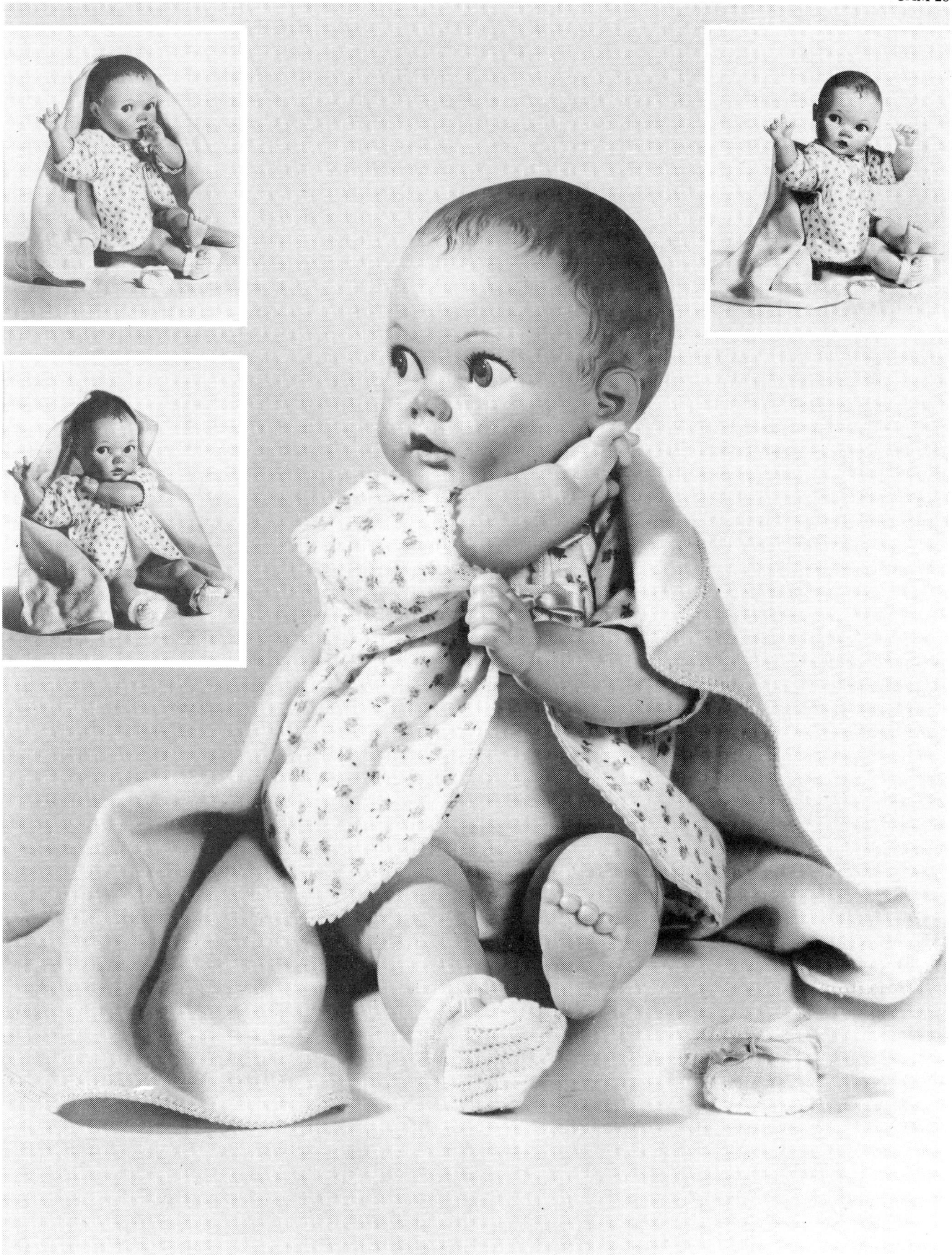

CAM-29.   ©J.L.K.

CAM-29. *"Landscape".* From the original by Joseph L. Kallus.

CAM-30. *"Portrait of a Child".* From the original by Joseph L. Kallus, 1927.

CAM-31. *"Portrait of an Old Man".* From the original oil painting by Joseph L. Kallus.

Examples of the *serious* art of Joseph L. Kallus.

CAM-30.   ©J.L.K.   CAM-31.   ©J.L.K.

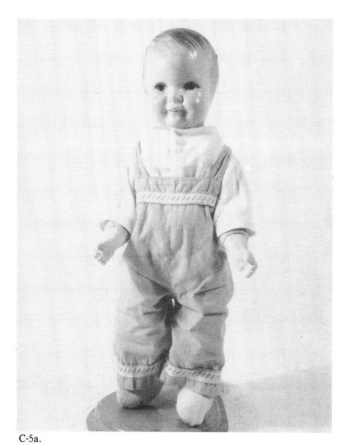

C-5a.

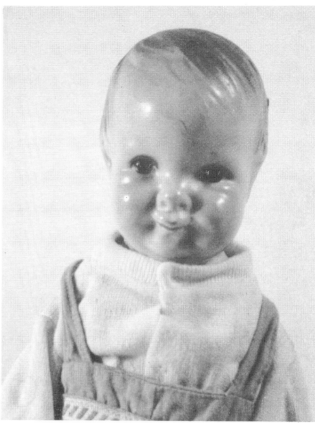

C-5a.

CELLULOID DOLLS

Celluloid has been used to produce dolls almost since its discovery in 1870. This compound of cellulose nitrate and camphor is known by several trade names: celluloid and biskoline are two. This first synthetic plastic used in manufacturing is the forerunner of many plastics we have in use today which explains why it is sometimes difficult to determine whether a late doll is plastic or celluloid.

Celluloid is highly flammable but its other features seem to outweigh this one undesirable characteristic, except in the case of play toys for children. Celluloid can be sawed, molded, turned, drilled, planed, polished, buffed, and painted. Resistance to oil, acid and water, plus a wide range of color variations and low cost are other desirable properties. Sunlight will discolor it, as will storage above 120 degrees F and it will begin to decompose when stored above that temperature.

The first dolls manufactured from celluloid in the United States were made about 1880 by the Celluloid Manufacturing Company as an economy move to salvage scrap material from their regular production line. Germany had gone into production shortly after the material came on the market; therefore some of their dolls pre-date the American-made ones. Many bisque head dolls from companies such as Kammer & Reinhardt have twins in the celluloid heads made by the Rheinische Gummi & Celluloid Fabrik Co. These dolls are marked with the **"K (STAR) R"** as well as the *turtle mark* of Rheinische.

The *turtle mark* is found on dolls, doll parts and tiny dollhouse figures. American firms imported turtle-marked parts for dolls assembled in this country (see *Bye-lo Baby*). Celluloid heads may be found on kid, cloth or ball-jointed bodies. The metal *"Minerva"* heads were also produced in celluloid, with the mark picturing the *Goddess Minerva helmet.*

In the United States, the Parsons-Jackson Celluloid Collar Company began using scrap materials about 1914 to make dolls with painted eyes, closed mouths, and metal-spring stringing which were practically water-proof. Although the company went out of business before 1920, dolls were marketed for several years thereafter, probably from stocks on hand. Early 1920's catalogs show a *"heavy celluloid doll - these are the better quality, not the light weight dolls."* Although no manufacturer or trade name is given, the illustration strongly resembles the *Parsons-Jackson Baby.*

Many less prominent companies have manufactured celluloid dolls, a few of which are illustrated in CEL-12. The low cost of celluloid dolls has made them attractive for use in promotions. Good quality celluloid is sometimes a beautiful ivory color, and CEL-4 is a fine example. Her cameo-like beauty gives her a fragile, youthful appearance which belies her fifty years.

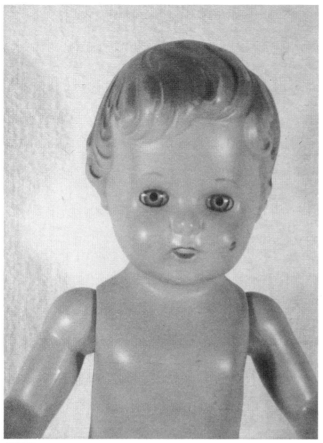

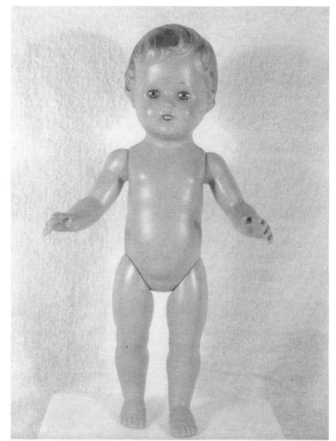

CEL-2.   CEL-1.   CEL-2.

fig. CEL-1

CEL-1. 8" Girl, 8½" Boy, all original, painted features, felt and cotton clothes, marked Diamond Turtle Mark. Brought to the United States prior to World War II; original wooden box covered with lithographed paper showing view of mountains. *(Author's collection)*

CEL-2. 13½" Child, set glass eyes, painted features, marked Turtle Mark on head and Diamond Turtle Mark with numbers **34** on back. *(Kirtley collection)*

CEL-3. 22" Boy, blue glass eyes, open mouth, two molded teeth, marked Diamond Turtle Mark on head and back. Note exquisite modeling. *(Spalding collection)*

CEL-4. 17" Girl, celluloid shoulder head, lower arms and hands, cloth body and legs, blue glass sleep eyes, original underwear, shoes, stockings, old dress not original. Marks: Turtle Mark. ca. 1920 *(Zillner collection)*

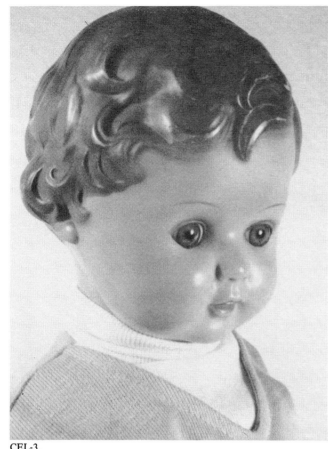

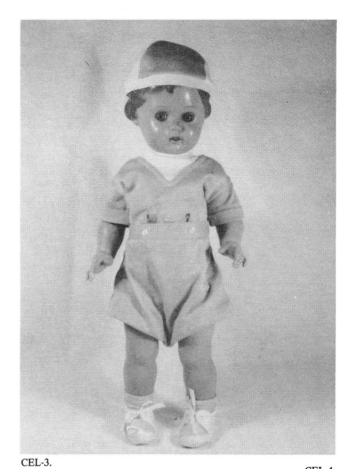

CEL-3.   CEL-4.   CEL-3.   CEL-4.

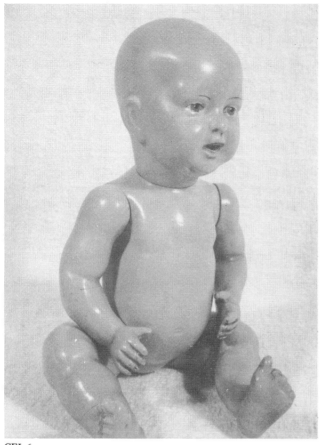

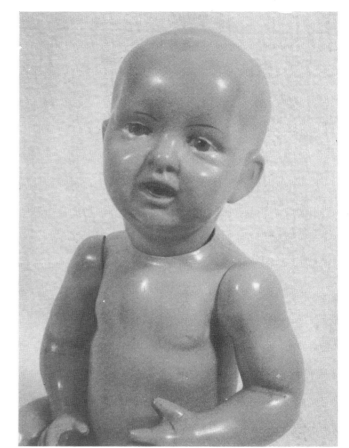

CEL-6.   CEL-5.   CEL-6.

fig. CEL-6

fig. CEL-10

PARSONS-JACKSON CO.
CLEVELAND, OHIO.

CEL-5. 10½" Babies, *Parsons-Jackson,* blue painted eyes (note differences in work of finishing artists), found dressed as twins (from original owner), marks, see fig. CEL-6. 1914-1920. *(Wingfield collection)*

CEL-6. 12" Baby, *Parsons-Jackson,* painted eyes, jointed with metal springs, marks, see fig. CEL-6. Ca. 1920. *(Author's collection)*

CEL-7. 2½" Heads for hand puppets, thin celluloid, painted accents, marked with **Turtle Mark.** *(Courtesy Kimport Dolls)*

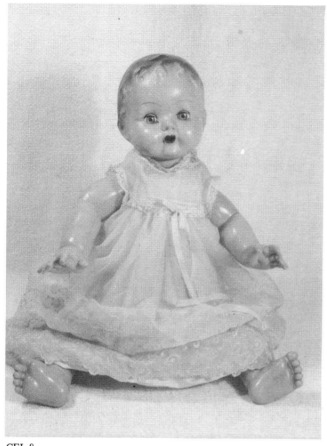

CEL-8.

CEL-9.

CEL-7.

CEL-10.

CEL-8. 19½" Baby, celluloid head and limbs, excelsior-stuffed cloth body, cry box, light blue sleep eyes, unmarked. Note modeling of limbs. *(Kirtley collection)*

CEL-9. 5" Soldier, jointed, painted shoes, suede cloth uniform, unmarked. With him is 4¾" papier mache maiden, painted features and clothes, marked **GERMANY.** Ca. 1920. *(Vandiver collection)*

CEL-10. 13" Clown, stuffed body and legs, unmarked. 6" Fiddler girl, wisp of mohair wig, painted eyes, marks, see fig. CEL-10. *(Vandiver collection)*

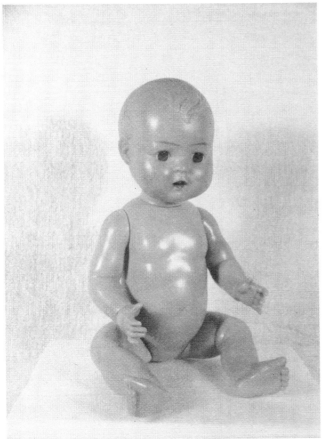

CEL-12.

fig. CEL-12d

CEL-11.

CEL-13.

CEL-11. 12¼" Baby, jointed wrists, blue sleep eyes, marked on head **3512¼**, on shoulder **B3512¼** and **OK** on a world globe. Made in Hong Kong. *(Vandiver collection)*

CEL-12. Front row L to R:
a) 11" Carnival type, heavy celluloid, painted features, jointed shoulders, marked **FETHALITE**.
b) 5" Girl, swivel head, jointed shoulders, hips, painted features, shoes, marked, see fig. CEL-12b.
c) 2¼" *Kewpie,* unjointed, painted features, marked **JAPAN** just below his little blue wings, plus another illegible mark.
d) 6" Carnival type, thin celluloid, gold painted hair, painted features, pink feathers, gold bead earrings and necklace, elastic strung arms, marks, fig. CEL-12d and **OCCUPIED JAPAN.**
e) 3½" molded, painted hair, hairbow, dress and shoes, rubber hat, marks, fig. CEL-12d plus **PAT. / JAPAN.**
f) 6" Girl, molded, painted hair with hairbow loop, painted features and shoes, jointed shoulders only, marked: **KNICKERBOCKER / PLASTIC CO. / GLEN-DALE, CALIIF. / DES. PAT. / PEND.**
Back row: 6½" painted features and hair, jointed shoulders only, marked, see fig. CEL-12.

CEL-13. 6" Boy, thin celluloid, painted features and clothes, red helmet and shirt, dark blue knickers, green stockings, marked, see fig. CEL-10. Ca. 1920. *(Author's collection)*

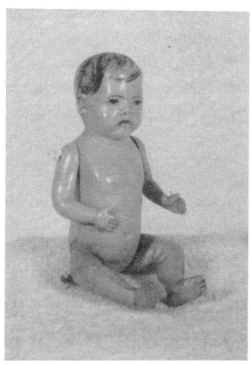

CEL-14.

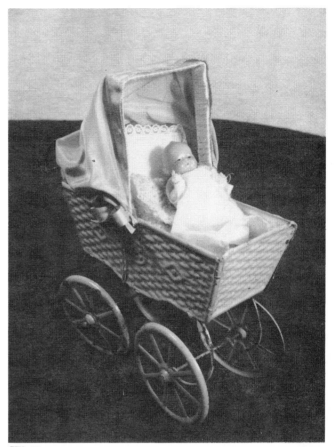

CEL-15.

CEL-16.

fig. CEL-12b

fig. CEL-12

CEL-14. 5" Baby, dark blue painted eyes, painted brush stroke hair. ca. 1917. Marks: **MADE / IN / U.S.A.** *(Courtesy Mrs. Charles Knox)* Celluloid babies to dress were featured in the Sears, Roebuck & Co. catalog of 1919. There were 5" at 33 cents, 6½" at 43 cents, 9" at 95 cents, and 12" at $1.35.

CEL-15. 2½" Baby, resplendent in pink all-metal buggy 6¾" long. *(Kirtley collection)*

CEL-16. 8" Baby, all celluloid, blue painted eyes, blonde painted hair with blue painted bow, bent legs. Marked: **YANOCO / U.S.A.** *(Courtesy Kimport Dolls)*

CHI-1.

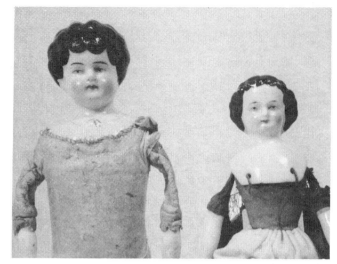

CHI-2a.   CHI-2b.

CHINA DOLLS

China dolls offer such a wide choice of hair, face and shoulder types that a comprehensive collection would require considerable display area. *China,* in terms of doll collecting, is meant to define the porcelain heads with glazed surface, having two or three holes for sewing to a body, and painted, molded features, usually *under glaze.*

Bisque, on the other hand, is porcelain left *unglazed,* resulting in a soft, matte finish with a natural appearance. Many novice collectors and non-collectors refer to all porcelain head dolls as *china.* Technically, this term is appropriate although it tends to confuse when applied to dolls. An easy method of distinguishing the two terms as pertaining to dolls is to remember that *china* dinner services, as well as *china* dolls, are glazed and shiny. It then follows that *bisque* must be the correct term for the *unglazed* porcelain heads.

CHI-2b.

CHI-1. 19" *Ruth.* Homemade cloth body with very small waist, composition lower arms and hands, blue and white china high-button boots. Blonde hair and blue eyes, molded collar and blouse, name **RUTH**, touched with gold. Shoulder seams and collar also molded in back. Head measures 4¾" tall, 9" circ. Marks: **PATENT APP'D FOR / GERMANY.** *(Author's collection)*

CHI-2a. 12" *Bertha.* Kid body, china hands and lower arms, cloth feet which have been replaced for the fourth time, molded blouse collar and name **BERTHA.** Collar molded in back. Marks: **PATENT APP'D FOR / GERMANY.** Doll was given to Lucile May Yahns Cullings in 1913; she shared it with her two sisters for many years, which explains the need for four sets of replacement cloth feet. *(Author's collection)*

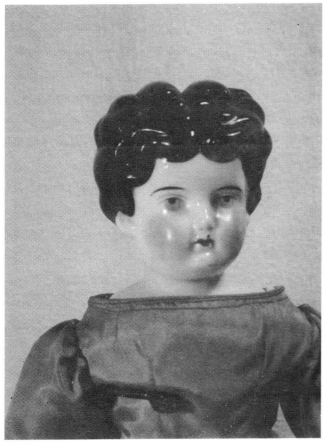

CHI-4a.   CHI-4b.   CHI-4c.

CHI-3.

CHI-3

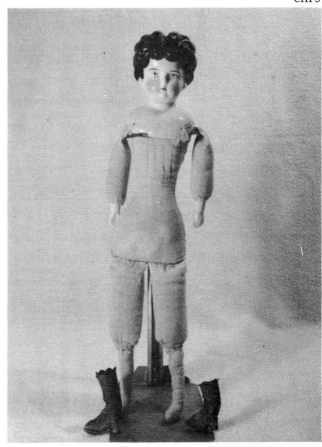

CHI-2b. 8½" China. Very old cloth body, china limbs, blue garters, flat shoes. Small-waisted body has been slip-covered and repaired at least twice. Stuffed with saw-dust, this doll has older-style hair-do which has been called Civil War type; however, it is more probable the date is nearer 1880. *(Author's collection)*

CHI-3. 17" China. Cloth body and feet, china hands and arms, tiny waist, red line above eyes, blue painted eyes. Marks: **4** on back of shoulder plate. *(Courtesy Phyllis Odell)*

CHI-4a. 6" Dresser Doll. All china powder box, marked: **Madame Pompadour / Dresser Dolls / -E & R / Germany.**

CHI-4b. 7½" Dresser Doll. Powder puff doll, china head and torso, 2¾" tall, silk skirt over wire frame, pockets hold cotton puffs each with silk ribbon bow. Marks: **6099 / Germany.**

CHI-4c. 6½" Dresser Doll. China head and torso 1½" tall, red **GERMANY** stamp. Original silk and lace dress. Manufacturer's name is gone from powder box, but price of 50 cents remains. *(Author's collection)*

CHI-6.

CHI-5.

CHI-7.

CHI-5. 23" Blonde China. Blue eyes, original china hands, cloth body with two red seams down the front. White china shoulder head has two attaching holes. China legs and feet have molded-on boots and thick, curvy calves. Doll belonged to the mother of Fairy Electra Cunningham Ryerson, dancer in movies and on television. *(Battagler collection)*

CHI-6. 4¾" Miniature China. White china, black hair, original body, old dress, slip and pantaloons. One collector remembers the Christmasses of her childhood. The tree at Church was always decorated with numbers of these tiny chinas, all dressed with loving care by the mothers of the church. After the program, each little girl received at least one of the tiny dolls for her own. *(Battagler collection)*

CHI-7. 19" Blonde. White china shoulder head 4¼" deep, two sewing holes, gold painted necklace with applied gems of red and green glass. *(Battagler collection)*

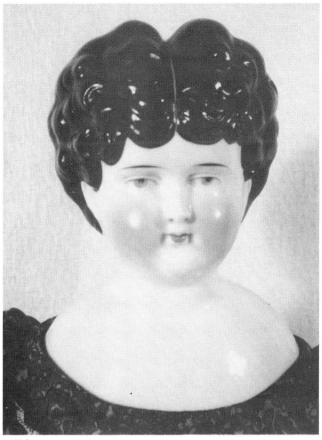

CHI-8.

CHI-10.

CHI-9.

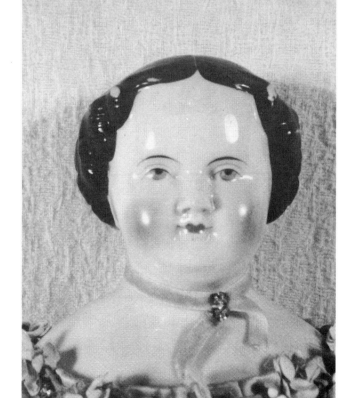

CHI-8. 25" Deep Shoulder China. Shoulder head measures 6½", blue eyes, white center part, rosy apple cheeks. White china head has large numeral **9** center back. *(Battagler collection)*

CHI-9. 23" Old China. This doll predates the twentieth century by perhaps fifty years, but the author could not resist showing her. She has no marks, a very old hair style, blue eyes, white china shoulder head, three sewing holes. Body is cloth with original leather hands. *(Battagler collection)*

CHI-10. 4" Half-Doll. Dressed in lavendar silk skirt, lavendar china cloche and blouse, mounted on a pin cushion also covered with lavendar silk. Only mark: Incised numerals **9493**, probably German. *(Rebekka Anderton collection)*

COM-B1.

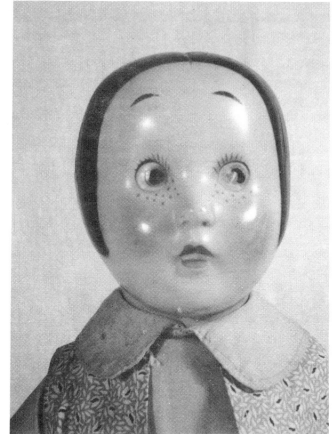

COM-C1.

COM-B2.

DOLLS FROM THE COMICS

Cartoons, funny papers, or comic strips — whatever you may call them — have been a popular source of doll designs for many years. Comic characters have been translated into rag, composition, bisque, celluloid, and plastic dolls. Many have gone on to fame in movies and television; all are imminently collectible.

COM-B1. 15" *Buttercup.* Baby from Jimmy Murphy cartoon strip, "Toots and Casper" (King Syndicate), soft cotton construction, painted features, squawker voice. Also 18". ca. 1925. Modern Toy Co. *(Courtesy Sears, Roebuck & Co.)*

COM-B2. 7½" *Charlie Brown.* All vinyl, original clothes, white skin, black eyes, molded shoes. Marks: **United Features Syndicate, Inc. 66.** *(Zillner collection)*

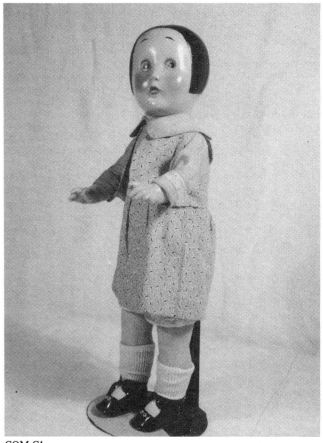

COM-C1

COM-D2.

COM-D1.

COM-C1. 18" *Ella Cinders,* the Rags to Riches Heroine of a comic strip by Bill Conselman and Charlie Plumb, (Metropolitan Newspaper Service). Composition head and limbs, soft body, painted features and hair, original clothes. Horsman, 1925. Marks: © **1925 MNS** on head. Tag on dress reads: **Ella Cinders Trademark / Reg. U.S. Pat. Ofc. 1925/Metropolitan Newspaper Service.**

Actress Colleen Moore played the part of *Ella Cinders* in a 1920 movie. *(Zillner collection)*

COM-D1. 18" *Dagwood.* All cloth, from "Blondie" strip, one of a series which included Alexander (from "Blondie"), Popeye, Little Iodine, Olive Oyl, Wimpey, Snuffy Smith, Sweetpea, and Annie Rooney. Date uncertain. Research revealed manufacturer, Columbia Toy Products, had been out of business "several years". © **King Features Syndicate, Inc.** *(Zillner collection)*

COM-D2. 15" *Dennis the Menace.* Vinyl head and limbs, cloth body and removeable clothes, all original. From the comic by Hank Ketcham (Hall Syndicate). *(Zillner collection)*

COM-D3.

COM-F2.

COM-F1.

COM-D3. 13" *Dennis the Menace.* Two versions from different molds, both all vinyl, jointed neck only. 1955 Catalog shows 16" Dennis with vinyl head, latex body, stationary glassene eyes, cotton T-shirt, denim overalls with name on bib. Head is from different mold than either shown here. Also available 22" vinyl Dennis dressed as above and a 5¾" string puppet Dennis. Hand puppets of Dennis, his family, father Henry, and mother Alice, and his friends, Margaret, Joey, Mr. Wilson are also shown in several catalogs. Marks: **DENNIS THE MENACE/(c) H.K.K./1958** on back. Initials stand for Hank Ketcham, creator of *Dennis.*

COM-F1. 8" *Elmer Fudd.* All vinyl, all original. Tag reads: **R. Dakin & Co. / SAN FRANCISCO / "ELMER FUDD" / No. 2202 / PROD. OF HONG KONG.** Reverse of tag includes picture of pig and: **LOONEY TUNE / © WARNER BROS-SEVEN ARTS INC.** Marked on head: **© WARNER BROS-SEVEN ARTS INC 1968.** Marked on back: **MADE IN HONG KONG.** *(Wiseman collection)*

COM-F2. 12" *Flintstones Characters.* All vinyl, from "The Flintstones" of television, movie cartoons and comics. Left, *Bam-Bam* with jointed right arm to hold "club". Right, *Pebbles,* original clothes. Also: 8" size, *Tiny Bam-Bam* and *Tiny Pebbles,* a cave house, log cradle, dinosaur stroller, other accessories. 1960's. Ideal. *(Author's collection)*

COM-F3.

COM-G1.

COM;G2.

COM-F3. 8½" *Felix.* All wood, cartoon cat. Marks: "FELIX" / COPYRIGHT-1922, 1924 BY / PAT SULLI-VAN / PAT. APPLIED FOR. By Schoenhut. *(Wiseman collection)*

COM-G1. *Gasoline Alley,* by Frank King. Included array of characters, many of which have been re-created as dolls. *Uncle Walt, Skeezix,* and *Skeezix'* dog are shown here. Bisque dolls are L to R: 2½" *Skeezie,* 3½" *Uncle Walt,* and 3½" *Skippy* from comic of that name. Other of Frank King's characters made up in bisque dolls were *Rachel, Mrs. Blossom,* and *Jean, Skeezix's* playmate. Dolls date from 1922, and are marked with name of character. *(Author's collection.*

COM-G2. *Gasoline Alley Characters. Skeezix* and his dog in oilcloth type material, flat printed and stuffed, sewn on outside. Material is called "imitation leather". *1927 Catalog illustration courtesy Sears, Roebuck & Co.*

COM-L1.

COM-L2.

COM-L2.

NOTE: ORIGINAL PRICES SHOWN
ARE NOT TODAY'S PRICES.

COM-L1. 8¼" *Linus.* Character from Charles Schultz cartoon *"Peanuts".* All vinyl, painted clothes and features, his security blanket is missing. Marks: **UNITED FEATURES SYNDICATE** © . 1960's. *(Author's collection)*

COM-L2. 15" *Little Lulu.* All cloth, molded painted features, string hair, red cotton dress. Unmarked. From comic strip by Marjorie Henderson Buell. *(Zillner collection)* 1958 Sears catalog shows 14½" fabric doll as above. 1959 catalog shoes 16½" doll in western outfit, same type doll as above, retails at $5.87.

COM-L3.

COM-L4.

COM-L5.

COM-L3. 13½" *Little Orphan Annie* and 9" *Sandy*. "Imitation leather", looks like oil cloth, sewn on outside, stuffed, flat. *1927 Catalog illustraation courtesy Sears, Roebuck & Co.*

COM-L4. 5½" *Little Orphan Annie*. All wood, red and white painted outfit. Marks: **Made in U.S.A.** on right foot. **LITTLE ORPHAN ANNIE / HAROLD / GRAY** on back of skirt. *(Author's collection)*

COM-L5. 18" *Little Orphan Annie*. Rag, stiffened mask face, separate dress and panties of same material, original red-brown mohair wig. Cloth tag on doll reads: **Saturday Evening Post.** One of a series offered as premiums. *(Courtesy Ralph's Antique Dolls)*

COM-L6.

COM-L7.

COM-L8.

COM-L6. 12" *Little Orphan Annie*. All composition, unmarked, body has characteristics of Effanbee dolls. Painted features, yellow hair, blue eyes. There is also a 10" size in this model. ca. 1930. *(Zillner collection)*

COM-L7. *Little Orphan Annie* Dishes. All done in "comic book colors". Platter, center front, is 4¼", teapot is 3" without cover. Marks: **LICENSED BY / FAMOUS ARTISTS / SYNDICATE / MADE IN JAPAN** on platter and teapot. **MADE IN / JAPAN** on saucers, plates, creamer and sugar. All marks in red. *(Childhood toy of Mrs. Dennis (Nora Lee) Hulen)*

COM-L8. 10" *Little Orphan Annie*. All composition, painted hair and features. Note difference in hair molding from COM-L6. Unmarked. ca, 1930. *(Doll and Electric Range, Zillner collection; Book and Jacks Game, Author's collection)*

COM-M1.

COM-N1.

COM-01.

COM-M1. 9½" *Mighty Mouse.* One-piece, all vinyl, originally had a red felt flying cape. Marks: © **TERRY-TON.** *(Author's collection)*

COM-N1. 15½" *Nize Baby.* From cartoon by Milt Gross; cloth with pressed features, baggy costume. Madame Hendren doll. *1927 Catalog illustration courtesy Sears, Roebuck & Co.*

COM-O1. 10" *Olive Oyl.* Vinyl head, cloth body, bright colors. Marks: On tag: **SEMCO LTD / MADE / IN ENGLAND; OLIVE OYL / © KFS INC.** on reverse. King Features Syndicate, Inc. *(Zillner collection)*

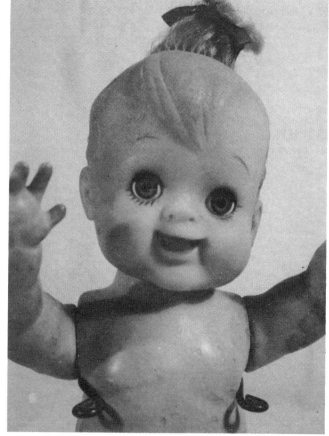

COM-P2.   COM-P1.   COM-P1.

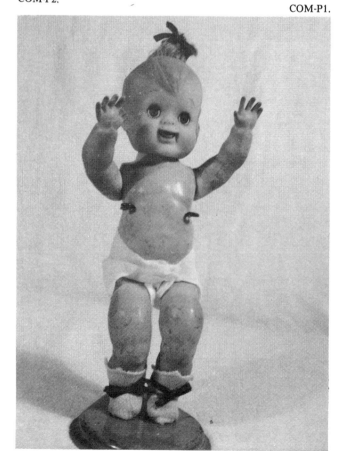

COM-P1. 14" *Joan Palooka.* Stuffed vinyl with rooted topknot. Doll represents daughter of title character in *"Joe Palooka"* comic strip. Marks: © **1952 / HAM FISHER / IDEAL DOLL.** *(Zillner collection)*

COM-P2. *Pogo and Friends.* Vinyl, turning heads, some with jointed arms. Premiums in shrink-paks of Proctor & Gamble laundry products. All are marked © **1969 / Walt Kelly / Made in Japan.** Back row left to right: *Beauregard Hound, Howland Owl,* and *Albert Alligator.* Front row left to right: *Churchy La Femme, Pogo Possum,* and *Porky Pine. (Rebekka Anderton collection)*

COM-P3.

COM-P4.

COM-P5.

fig. COM-P3

COM-P3. 10½" *Popeye.* Wood and composition, steel springs, natural colors. Marks: © / **King Features / Syn. Inc. / 1932** on left foot. Fig. COM-P3 on right foot. *(Author's collection)*

COM-P4. 5" *Popeye.* All wood, enameled colors. Marks: **POPEYE** © **BY K.F.S.** on back of blouse. **MADE IN U.S.A.** on right foot. Made by same company as doll in COM-L4. *(Author's collection)*

COM-P5. 13" *Popeye.* All soft vinyl, jointed shoulders, hips, swivel head. Marks: **Cameo K.F.S.** © . Available in catalogs 1957 through 1959. Should be a pipe in his mouth. *(Zillner collection)* 21" *Popeye,* cotton stuffed body, vinyl face and arms, handle turns at back, doll laughs. *Shown in 1959 Sears, Roebuck & Co. catalog.*

COM-P6.

COM-P6. 7" *Porky Pig,* 8" *Elmer Fudd.* All vinyl, separate clothing. Dolls are marked back of head: © **Warner Bros.-Seven Arts Inc. 1968, Looney Tunes.** *(Zillner collection)*

COM-S1.

COM-S1. 16" *Sad Sack.* From the World War II cartoon by Sgt. George Baker, made famous in "Stars and Stripes", a GI newspaper. All vinyl, jointed only at neck, molded-on shoes, painted eyes. Doll is shown in 1959 Sears catalog dressed in Buck Private uniform. *(Kirtley collection)*

COM-S2. 11½" *Brenda Starr.* From cartoon strip by Dale Messick (Chicago Tribune, World Rights Reserved). All vinyl, rooted hair, wears most teen fashion doll clothes. Poor likeness of that gorgeous redhead, but usual Madame Alexander quality. Shown 1964 Sears catalog at $3.87. *(Zillner collection)*

COM-S2.

COM-S1.

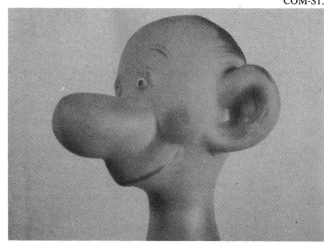

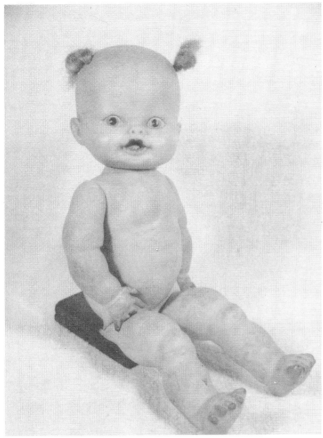

COM-T1.

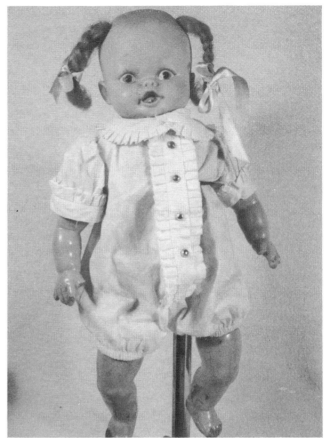

COM-T2.

COM-T3.

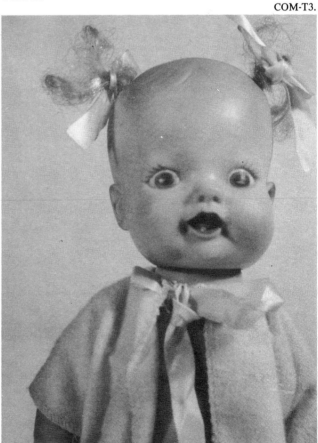

COM-T1. *Dick Tracy* Character, 14" *Bonnie Braids.* All rubber, open molded mouth, two lower teeth, body and legs one piece. There is a hole in each ear, has blue painted eyes. Marks: **CHICAGO TRIBUNE** (Curved) **IDEAL DOLL.** 1951. *(Author's collection)*

COM-T2. *Dick Tracy* Character, 15" *Bonnie Braids.* Soft vinyl head, composition arms and legs, cloth body, painted features, open closed mouth, one lower tooth, wears an Eloise combination suit. Dick Tracy comic strip by Chester Gould. Marks: **Copr. 1951/Chi. Tribune/Ideal Doll/U.S.A.** 1953 catalog shows "Bonnie Braids walks this year, head turns side to side, soft vinyl head. $7.59 retail." *(Spalding collection)*

COM-T3. *Dick Tracy* Character, 12" *Bonnie Braids.* Stuffed vinyl, rooted braids, painted eyes. 1952 Sears catalog shows 12" key wind, molded plastic, crawling Bonnie Braids at $2.94 retail. *(Zillner collection)*

COM-T4.

COM-T6.

COM-T5.

COM-T4. *Dick Tracy* Character, 14" *Sparkle Plenty.* Stuffed vinyl body, hard plastic head, yellow string hair, bright blue sleep eyes, pierced nostrils. 1950's. *(Zillner collection)*

COM-T5. *Dick Tracy* Character, 15" *Honey Moon.* Soft vinyl head and limbs, stuffed cotton body, white string hair, painted eyes, blue and silver original costume. Marks: © **1965-C.T.-N.Y.N.S. / IDEAL TOY COR-P. / HM / 4-2-2H.** *(Zillner collection)*

This doll also found in a blue and gold striped dress, booties and bib with name, moon, and stars printed on it. Sold for $7.99 in 1965.

COM-T6. *Dick Tracy* Character, 13" *Moon Maid.* Plastic with soft vinyl head, painted eyes, rooted pale platinum blonde synthetic wig, silver lame costume, blue net tu-tu. Marks: © / **UNEEDA / DOLL CO. / IN / 1966** on head. *(Author's collection)*

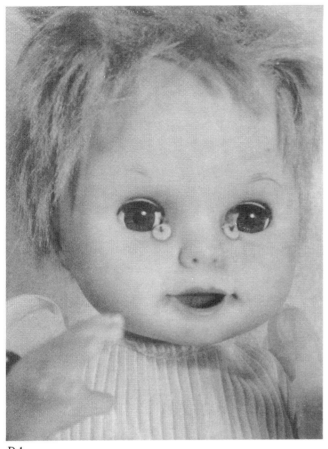

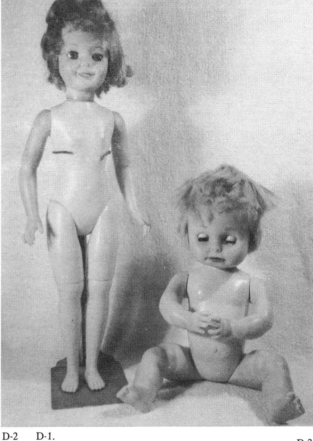

D-1

D-2 D-1.

D-2.

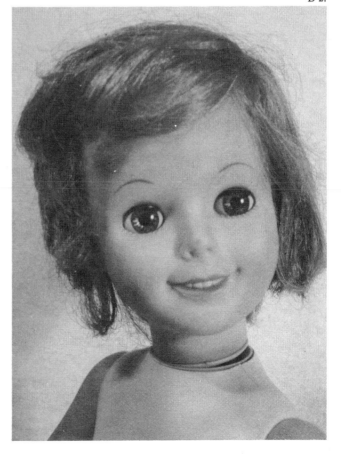

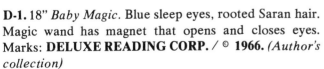

D-1. 18" *Baby Magic.* Blue sleep eyes, rooted Saran hair. Magic wand has magnet that opens and closes eyes. Marks: **DELUXE READING CORP.** / © **1966.** *(Author's collection)*

D-2. 21" *Suzy Homemaker.* Rooted hair, sleep eyes, swivel neck, vinyl doll, jointed at knees. Marks: **K21 / Deluxe Reading Corp.** / © **1966.** *(Author's collection)*

D-5.

ou met

nny

rite

head

tilts . .

oses

29

g 8-incher
some little
, flexible
l legs. In
red dress,
nties. She
the other
on this
stic ward-
e. Shpg.

6. $1.29

PCBKM

D-3.

D-4.

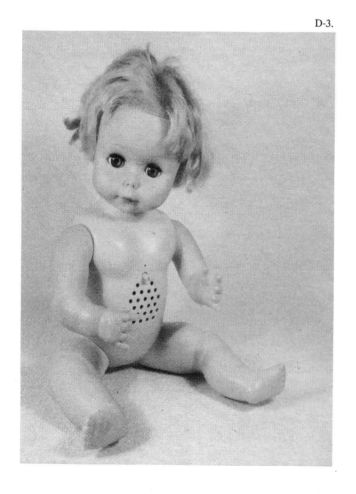

D-3. 21" *Nancy Nurse.* All vinyl, rooted hair, sleep eyes, operates on batteries to declare "I feel sick," and "I'm all better now". Marks: **6 / 19© 63 / Deluxe Reading** on head. *(Courtesy Mary Frances Lohrey)*

D-4. 8" *Penny Brite.* Rooted hair, painted blue eyes. Bendable leg model marked: **A-9 / B150 / DELUXE READING CORP. / © 1963.** Straight leg model marked: **A-9 / B65 (or 3) / DELUXE READING CORP. / © 1963.** Back of shoulders: **DELUXE READING CORP. / ELIZABETH NJ / PAT PENDING.** *1964 Catalog illustration courtesy Sears, Roebuck & Co.*

D-5. 7" *Suzy Cute.* Vinyl, rooted hair, blue stationary eyes, drink and wet feature, push her arms down then press her chest and her arms come up "reaching for mommy". This doll went to the hospital with Rebekka for her tonsilectomy and caused many comments because she was the picture of Rebekka. Marks: **Deluxe Reading Corp. / © 1964 / 229 / 4** on body. **Deluxe Reading Corp. / © 1964 67 / X** on head. *(Rebekka Anderton collection)*

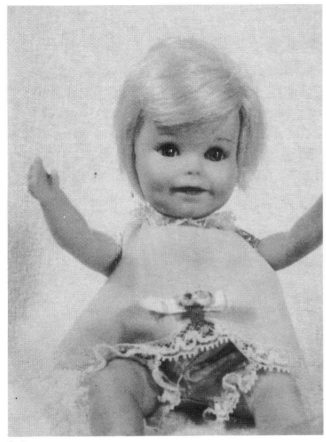

D-5.

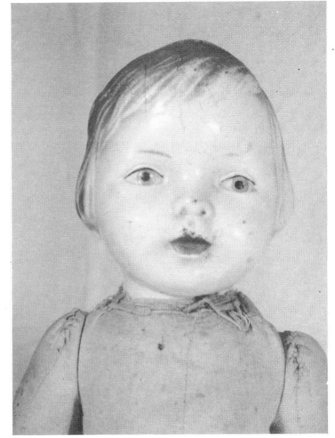

D-6.

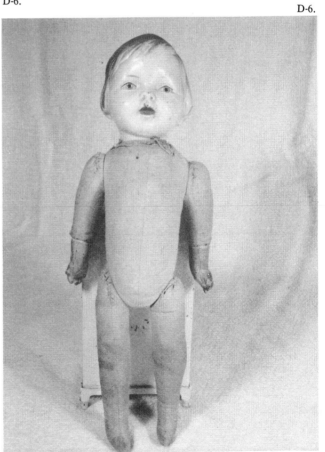

D-6.

NOTE: ORIGINAL PRICES SHOWN
ARE NOT TODAY'S PRICES.

D-6. 16;' Child. Composition head and gauntlet hands, cloth body, blue painted eyes, open closed mouth, molded, painted hair. Marks: © **D. 1910's.** *(Zillner collection)*

DIS-1.

DISNEY DOLLS

No one can truly say how many dolls have evolved from the characters created by Walt Disney. Since the 1930's, one after another of his little creatures have attained doll status and the parade continues to grow. Here is a sampling.

DIS-2.

DIS-3.

DIS-1. *Donald Duck.* Here is Donald, that most famous duck of all.

DIS-1a. 11" tall, all hard plastic, unmarked, roly-poly pop-up toy.

DIS-1b. 3" tall, old Japanese bisque, marked across tail: © **WALT DISNEY.** Stamped right foot: **JAPAN** in black.

DIS-1c. 2 3 / 8" late soft vinyl flexible one piece doll. Marks: © **WALT DISNEY PROD. HONG KONG.**

DIS-1d. 7" All vinyl squeeze toy with squeeker. Marks: © **W.D.P. H.H.** on right foot.

DIS-1e. (Front) 4¼" Candy dispenser, one of series now available including *Captain Hook, Peter Pan* and others. Marks: **U.S. PATENT 2 620 061 MADE IN AUSTRIA.**

DIS-2. 12½" *Sleepy.* One of *The Seven Dwarfs* from movie, "Snow White". Painted buckram face, plush beard, blue eyelids, clothes are part of body; green shirt, orange pants, brown shoes. ca. 1938. *(Wiseman collection)*

DIS-3. 12½" *Grumpy.* One of *Seven Dwarfs* from movie, "Snow White". Painted buchram face, plush beard, gold jacket, brown pants, black belt, black and white eyes. ca. 1938. *(Wiseman collection)*

DIS-6.

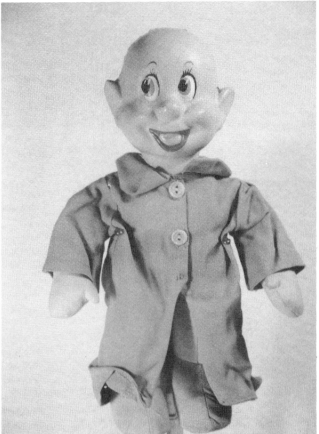

DIS-4.

DIS-5.

DIS-4. 11" *Dopey.* A member of the *Seven Dwarfs,* from a different series than DIS-2 and -3. Composition shoulder head, cloth body and limbs, original clothes, blue painted eyes. ca. 1938. *(Wiseman collection)*

DIS-5. 12" *Christopher Robin,* 8" *Winnie the Pooh.* Flexible plastic, molded clothes, natural colors, Made in England. From "Winnie the Pooh" by A. A. Milne. *Christopher Robin* was the writer's son, *Pooh, Piglet* and *Eeeyore* were his toys which became characters in the books. *1966 catalog illustration courtesy Sears, Roebuck & Co.*

DIS-6. 11" *Christopher Robin,* 3½" *Winnie the Pooh.* All vinyl, painted eyes, rooted Saran hair, all original. Marks: **HORSMAN DOLL INC. / 66111.** *(Zillner collection)*

DIS-8.

DIS-7.

DIS-9.

DIS-7. 19" *Christopher Robin.* Molded vinyl head, cloth body, blue painted eyes, original clothes. Tag reads: **Walt Disney / Character / COPYRIGHT WALT DISNEY PROD. / J. SWEDLIN INC. LICENSEE.** *(Wiseman collection)*

DIS-8. 9" *Jiminy Cricket.* Lithographed cloth in green, black and red. Unmarked. *(Courtesy Ralph's Antique Dolls)* see Rag-18, p. 375.

DIS-9. 12" *Tinker Belle.* Vinyl, molded hair, set-in eyes, green costume, hook to hang doll from ceiling in flying attitude. This doll also found with moulded-on shoes. *(Kirtley collection)*

DIS-10. 3" *Minnie Mouse,* 3½" *Orphan Annie. Minnie* is plaster, orange dress, green hat and trim. Marks: © **WALT DISNEY.** *Annie is bisque, orange hair, red dress.* Marks: **MADE IN JAPAN,** incised.

DIS-10.

DIS-11.

DIS-14.

DIS-12.

DIS-11. 4" Character Hand Puppets. Left, *GUS,* marked cloth tag: **GUND / SWEDLIN.** Center, *Minnie Mouse,* Marks: © **W.D.P. / 631 / MINNIE.** Cloth tag: **"The Wonderful World of Gundikins" / T.M. Reg. Applied for / J. Swedlin Inc. Licensee / Gund Mfg. Co.** Right, *Dumbo.* Marks: Cloth label, **"Dumbo, the Flying Elephant / Copyright Walt Disney Prod. / Gund Mfg. Co. / J. Swedlin Inc. Licensee.** *Dumbo* has a squeeker and is plush fabric, other two are cotton bodies. *Minnie* has red molded hairbow.

DIS-12. 10" *Mickey Mouse,* 12" *Mouseketeer Girl.* Vinyl, molded clothes, turning heads, girl has jointed hips. Marks: **WALT DISNEY PROD. / SUN RUBBER CO.** 1950's. *(Kirtley collection)*

DIS-13.

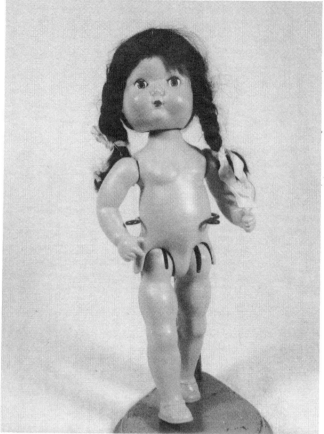

E-2.

E-1.

DIS-13. *"Famous Movie Stars". 9½" Big Bad Wolf, 6" Three Little Pigs, 6" Mickey Mouse.* All rubber, painted in brilliant, life-like colors, turning heads. 1934 Catalog illustration. *(Courtesy Sears, Roebuck & Co.)*

DIS-14. 8" *Pinocchio* and *Jiminy Cricket.* Wooden dolls, turning heads, jointed arms and legs, non-poisonous painted colors, 45 cents each. These are segmented figures similar to *Felix* and *Margie* in construction. Ideal. 1940 Catalog illustration, Sears, Roebuck & Co., was model for sketch.

E

E-1. 7" *Eugenia.* Composition, one piece body and legs, molded-on sailor sunsuit. Marks: **EUGENIA DOLL.** 1920's. *(Kirtley collection)*

E-2. 12" English plastic. Highly colored hard plastic, sleep eyes, solid plastic lashes, nodding head turns as legs "walk", blued-on dynel wig, molded-on shoes. 1950's. Marks: **RODDY / Made in / England.** *(Spalding collection)*

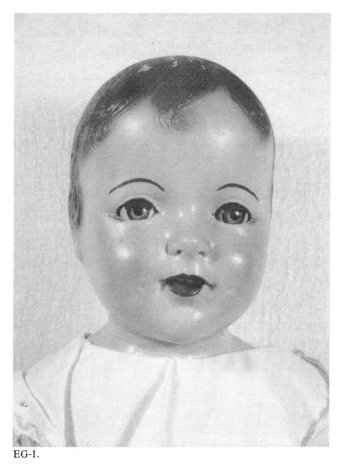

EG-1.

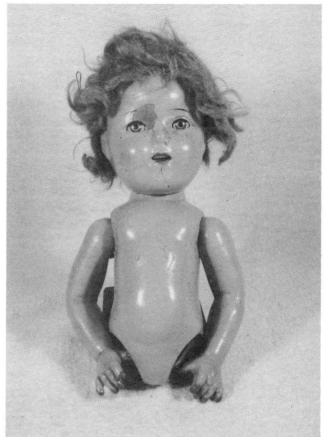

EG-2.

EG-2.

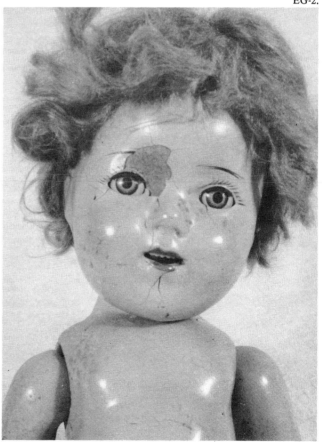

EEGEE

GOLDBERGER DOLL MFG., CO., INC.

This company founded by Eugene Goldberger, has been manufacturing dolls since 1917. E. G. was the original mark used on dolls; E. Goldberger and EEGEE are also found on this firm's products. In 1968 the logo was changed to that shown on packaging in the illustrations on these pages. *(Information courtesy Goldberger Doll Mfg., Co., Inc.)*

EG-1. 29" Composition. Tin sleep eyes, straight composition legs, arms, and shoulder head, molded hair, may have had wig at one time, open mouth, four teeth, felt tongue, dimples, cry voice, cloth body, head has been repainted. Marks: **E.G.** on head and each limb. *(Courtesy Kimport Dolls)*

EG-2. 18" Composition. Blue tin or decal eyes, original blonde mohair wig, open mouth, six tiny teeth, hair and painted lashes. Note resemblance to Shirley Temple dolls. Legs, though not available for this photograph, are of proper modeling and proportion and also resemble Shirley Temple. Marks: **E.G.** on head. ca. 1935. *(Baume collection)*

EG-3a.

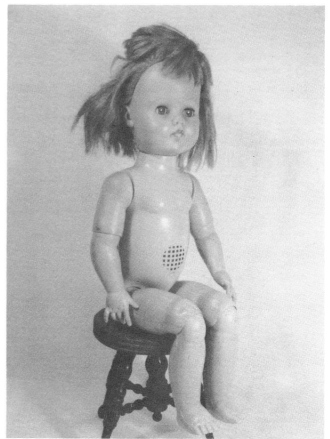

EG-3a.

EG-3b.

NOTE: ORIGINAL PRICES SHOWN
ARE NOT TODAY'S PRICES.

EG-3a. 23" *Susan Stroller.* Hard plastic body and legs, soft vinyl head and arms, rooted Saran hair. Also available in 29" size. Marks: **EEGEE** on head. 1955. *(Author's collection)*

EG-3b. 19½", 23", 26" *Susan Stroller.* Vinyl and hard plastic, rooted hair, closed mouth. Retailed at $7.49 and $11.98. *1955 Catalog illustration courtesy Goldberger Doll Mfg. Co. Inc.*

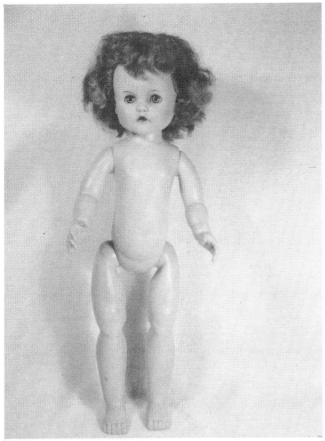

EG-4a.

EG-4a. EG-4b.

EG-4a. 27" Walker. Rigid plastic, soft vinyl head, rooted Saran hair, "walking" hip action, sleep eyes. 1955. *(Author's collection)*

EG-4b. 19½", 23", 26 Walker. *1955 Catalog illustration courtesy Goldberger Doll Mfg. Co. Inc.*

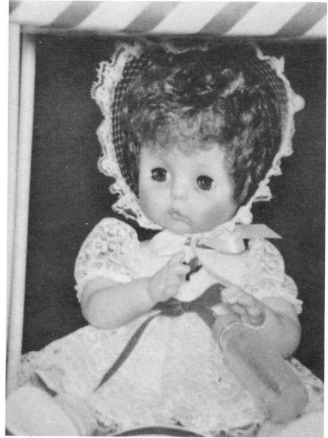

EG-7.

EG-5.

EG-6.

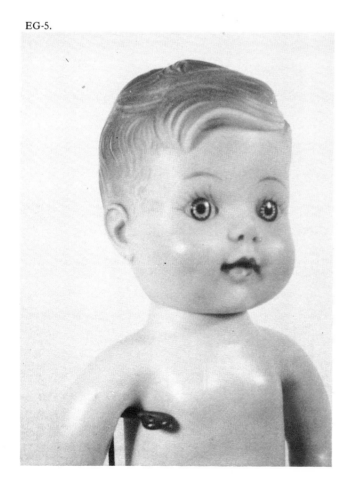

EG-5. 13" Boy. Deeply molded hair, vinyl head, stuffed vinyl one-piece body and limbs, stationary set-in glassene eyes. Purchased in 1956. Marks: **EEGEE.** *(Childhood toy of Joseph Richard Anderton II)*

EG-6. *Sugar Kandi.* Vinyl, sleep eyes, lashes, rooted hair, drink and wet feature. *1967 Catalog illustration courtesy Goldberger Doll Mfg. Co. Inc. Kandi is shown in 1970 catalog.*

EG-7. 18" *Baby Care.* Vinyl, molded or rooted hair, sleep or set glassine eyes, drink and wet feature, with complete nursery set. *1969 Catalog illustration courtesy Goldberger Doll Mfg. Co. Inc.*

EG-9.

EG-8.

EG-10.

EG-8. 14", 18", 24" *Baby Carrie.* Rooted or molded hair, sleep or set glassine eyes. 14" size comes in plastic carriage, 1970. 18" and 24" come in carry seat. *1970 Catalog illustration courtesy Goldberger Doll Mfg. Co. Inc.*

EG-9. 16" *Camilla.* Foam, in body stocking and lace trimmed striped dress, rooted hair. A "Posi Playmate" doll. *1970 Catalog illustration courtesy Goldberger Doll Mfg. Co. Inc.*

EG-10. 22" *Carol.* All vinyl, rooted wig in dutch, long twin-tailed or bob wigs, sleep eyes, walk feature. *1970 Catalog illustration courtesy Goldberger Doll Mfg. Co. Inc.* Available several prior years.

EG-12.

EG-11.

EG-13.

EG-11. 16", 32", 36" *Annette.* Vinyl, sleep eyes, rooted wig both long and short bob, walk feature. Since 1961. *1970 Catalog illustration courtesy Goldberger Doll Mfg. Co. Inc.* Also colored Annette.

EG-12. 12" *Posi Playmate.* Foam body, bendable arms and legs, rooted curly or straight hair, sleep eyes. Also molded hair and hat, or painted eyes and molded hair. *1969 Illustration courtesy Goldberger Doll Mfg. Co. Inc.*

EG-13. 16", 19", 25" *Bundle of Joy.* Foam stuffed cloth body, vinyl head and limbs, with or without mama voice. Colored *Bundle of Joy:* "Black ethnic features, assorted hairstyles, vinyl head and arms." Since 1963. *1970 Illustration courtesy Goldberger Doll Mfg. Co. Inc.*

EG-14. 18" *Softina.* Patented vinyl foam floppy washable baby, drink and wet feature, glassine eyes, molded or rooted pixie hair. Since 1967. *1970 Illustration courtesy Goldberger Doll Mfg. Co. Inc.* Also 21" size.

EG-15. *Flowerkins.* 1963 Illustration courtesy *Goldberger Doll Mfg. Co. Inc.*

EG-16. 15", 25" *Babette.* Soft chubby baby cloth body, soft stuffed vinyl arms and legs, painted eyes, pixie rooted hair in angel twin tail style. 25" also available with sleep eyes. *1970 Illustration courtesy Goldberger Doll Mfg. Co. Inc.*

EG-17. *Puppetrina.* Vinyl doll, rooted hair, glassine eyes, has pocket in back for insertion of child's hand for manipulation of doll's head and arms. *1970 Illustration courtesy Goldberger Doll Mfg. Co. Inc.* Since 1963.

EG-14.

EG-16.

EG-17.

EG-15.

F&B-2.

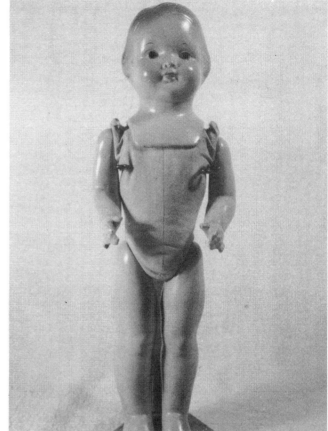

F&B-1.

F&B-1.

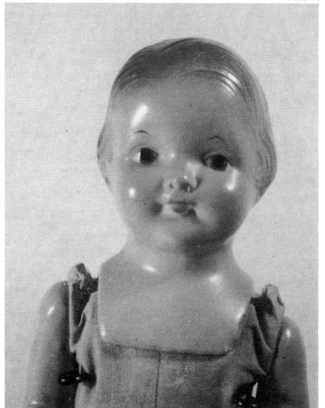

EFFANBEE DOLLS

EFFanBEE dolls are truly Twentieth Century dolls; the firm of Fleischaker & Baum began manufacturing dolls in 1910. The "F & B" dolls are numerous, varied and usually well-marked. Many are even dated; some have their given names embossed on the shoulder plates — to the delight of today's collectors.

F&B-1. 14" *Baby Dainty.* Composition shoulder head and limbs, blue painted eyes, orange-brown painted hair, cry voice. Marks: **EFFANBEE / BABY DAINTY** on shoulder. 1912. *(Wiseman collection)*

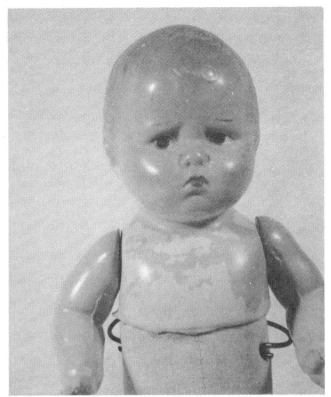

F&B-3.

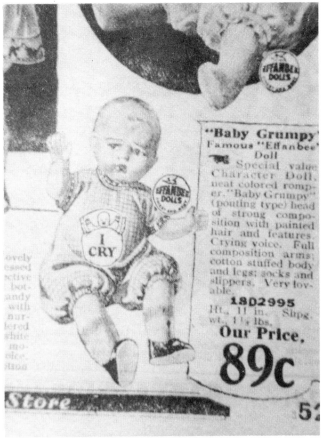

F&B-3a.

F&B-3.

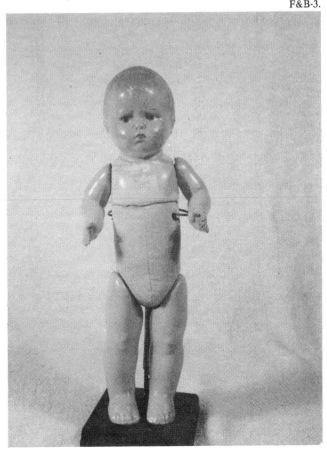

F&B-2. *Mary Jane.* Advertisement in the Ladies' Home Journal, December, 1919. American manufacturers had raced to fill the needs of a market cut off from the large German suppliers by World War I. Much of what was produced in this country was of composition. Few of this type remain intact today because in recent years these bodies have been used as replacements for bisque heads and the original composition heads have been discarded. These dolls featured human hair, long curl wigs, sleep eyes, and were available in 16", 18", 20", and 24" at prices ranging from $6.95 to $11.75. *"Mary Jane"* was available from Sears in 1917, 1920, and 1923, in the same style shown in the Journal advertisement. *Dolly Dumpling,* a composition shoulder head doll was also advertised in 1918 and 1919 Ladies' Home Journal, but without illustration.

F&B-3. 12" *Baby Grumpy.* Deep composition shoulder head and limbs, stuffed cloth body, painted eyes. Marks: Fig. F&B-3 on back of shoulder. ca. 1924. These dolls are so similar to the *Baby Grumpy* marked dolls that collectors tend to group them together. *(Wiseman collection)*

F&B-3a. 11" *Baby Grumpy.* 1925 Catalog illustration courtesy *Sears, Roebuck & Co.*

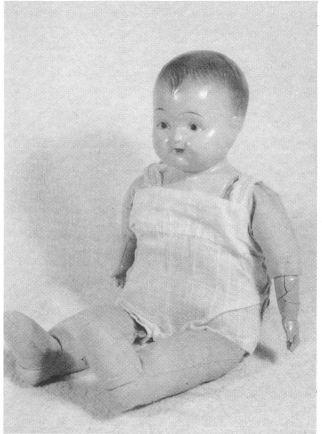

F&B-4.

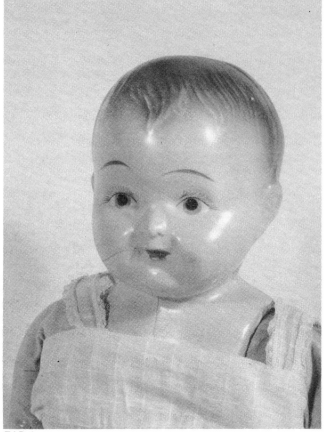

F&B-4.

F&B-4-1.

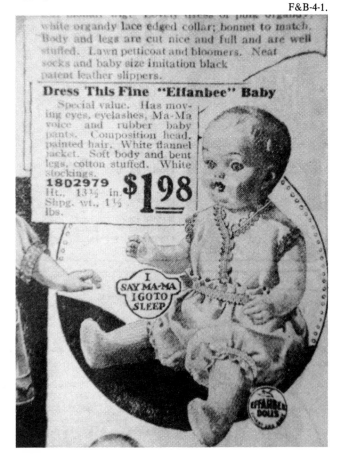

white organdy lace edged collar; bonnet to match.
Body and legs are cut nice and full and are well
stuffed. Lawn petticoat and bloomers. Neat
socks and baby size imitation black
patent leather slippers.

Dress This Fine "Effanbee" Baby

Special value. Has moving eyes, eyelashes, Ma-Ma
voice and rubber baby
pants. Composition head,
painted hair. White flannel
jacket. Soft body and bent
legs, cotton stuffed. White
stockings.

18D2979 **$1⁹⁸**
Ht., 13½ in.
Shpg. wt., 1½
lbs.

I SAY MA-MA I GO TO SLEEP

Effanbee   fig. F&B-4

fig. F&B-3

F&B-4. 16" Baby. Composition shoulder head and gauntlet hands, molded, painted hair, painted blue eyes. Pink cloth cutton-stuffed body and limbs, original garment. This may be one of the Dolly Dumpling dolls which included a full line. Marks: Fig. F&B-4 on back of shoulder. *(Baume collection)*

F&B-4-1. 13½" Baby. Possibly *"Baby Effanbee"*. 1925 Catalog illustration courtesy *Sears, Roebuck & Co.*

F&B-5.

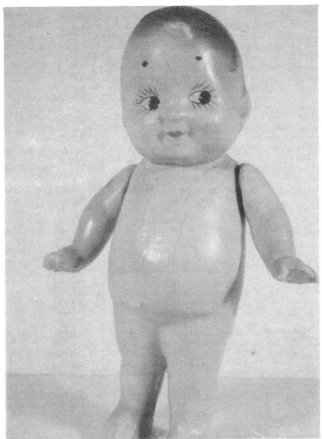

F&B-6.

F&B-7.

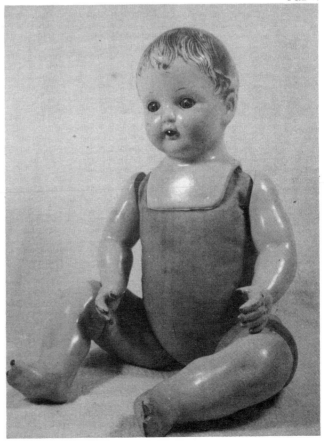

F&B-5. 12" Colored Baby. All composition, one-piece body and head, painted eyes and hair. Marks: Fig. F&B-4. *(Kirtley collection)*

F&B-6. 7" Chubby Boy. All composition, black painted eyes, faintly molded sunsuit. Marks: Fig. F&B-4 on back. Refer to Sears' stated policy; Effanbee may have supplied these dolls in off season at special prices to fill Sears' need for "Chubby Kids". 1910's. *(Wiseman collection)*

F&B-7. 19" Baby. Composition shoulder head and limbs, stuffed cloth body and upper legs, gray tin sleep eyes, pin and disc joints. Marks: Fig. F&B-4 on shoulder. ca. 1920. *(Wiseman collection)*

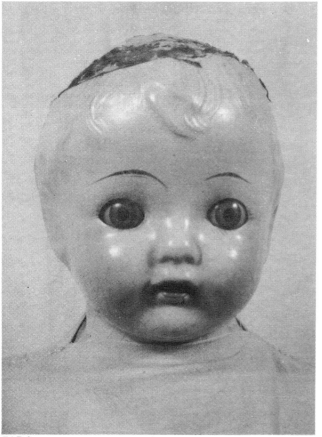

F&B-9.

F&B-8.

F&B-10.

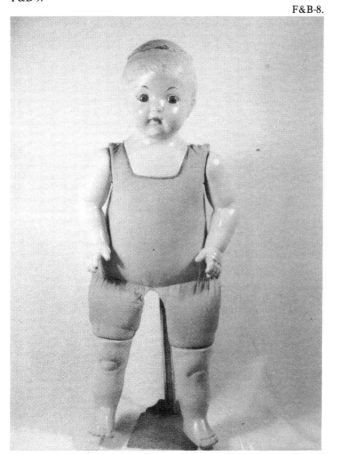

F&B-8. 24" Baby. Composition shoulder head and limbs, stuffed cloth body, gray tin sleep eyes. Marks: Fig. F&B-4 on back of shoulder and on both arms. ca. 1920. *(Wiseman collection)*

F&B-9. 20" Baby. Identical head to that of F&B-8, but this body has been replaced and original proportions were not maintained. Marks: Fig. F&B-4 on back of shoulder. *(Author's collection)*

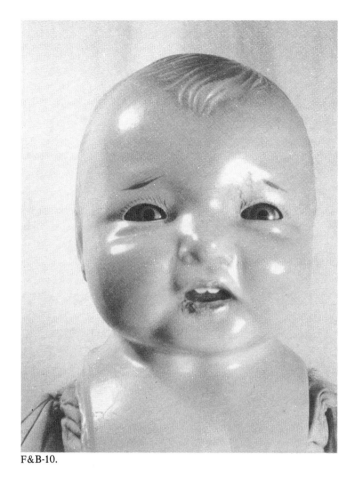

F&B-10.

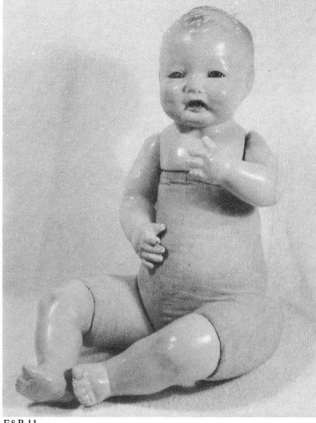

F&B-11.

F&B-11

EFFANBEE
BUBBLES
COPR. 1924   fig. F&B-11
MADE IN U.S.A.

F&B-10. 20" Baby. Composition shoulder head, green-blue tin eyes, open mouth, two teeth, molded hair, dimples. Unmarked. Shoulder heads such as this were sold in quantities to be completed at home; this may well be a home-made cloth body. Note resemblance to *Bubbles* and *Grumpy.* ca. 1924. *(Kirtley collection)*

F&B-11. 22" *Bubbles Twins.* Composition shoulder heads and limbs, stuffed cloth bodies, gray-blue tin sleep eyes, all original. One twin has been undressed to show body construction. Marks: Fig. F&B-11 on shoulder plate of both. *(Wiseman collection)*

F&B-12.

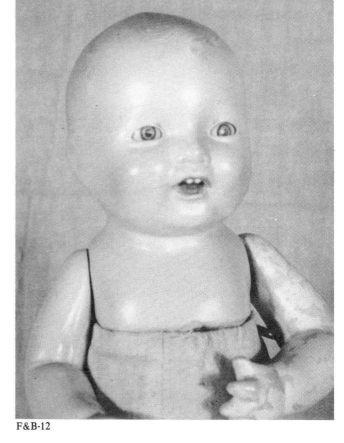

F&B-12

F&B-12

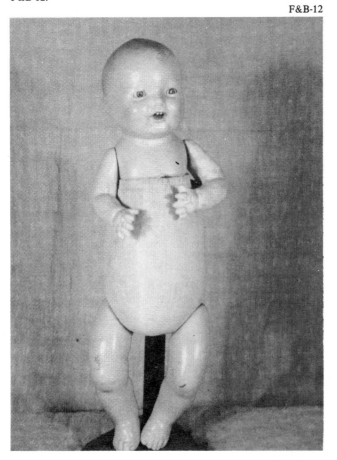

fig. F&B-12

F&B-12. 14" *Bubbles.* Same construction as F&B-11, except legs are all composition. All three *Bubbles* have cry voice, open mouth, two teeth, elongated bodies, deep dimples. Marks: Fig. F&B-11 on shoulder plate. Fig. F&B-12 on cloth tag sewn to dress. *(Author's collection)*

F&B-13.

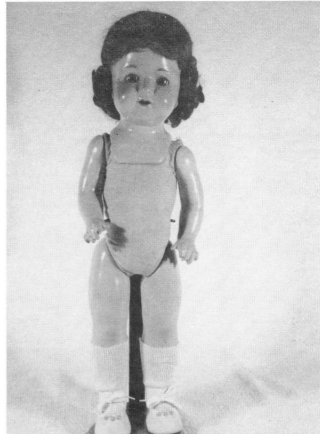

F&B-14.

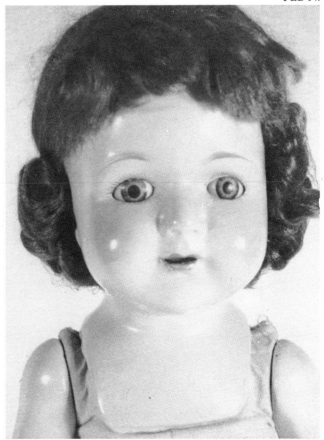

F&B-14.

fig. F&B-14

F&B-13. 29" Mama Doll. 1923 Catalog listing reads: "Genuine Effanbee mama doll, stuffed body, large child head, chubby full length composition arms and legs, sleep eyes, real hair. Pink organdy and lace dress and bonnet with gold heart necklace." Price in 1923, $8.95, in 1924 $8.75. This is one of the earliest dolls shown in Sears catalogs to carry the name of the manufacturer. *Catalog illustration courtesy Sears, Roebuck & Co.*

F&B-14. 18" *Rosemary.* Composition shoulder head and limbs, stuffed cloth body, blue tin eyes. ca. 1925. Marks: Fig. F&B-14 on shoulder. *(Wiseman collection)*

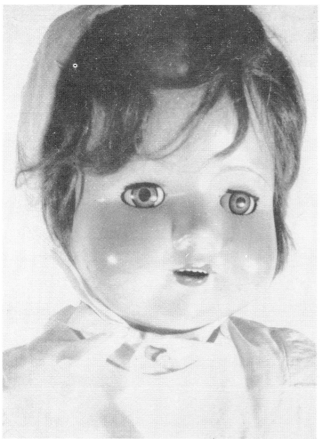

F&B-16.

F&B-15.

F&B-17.

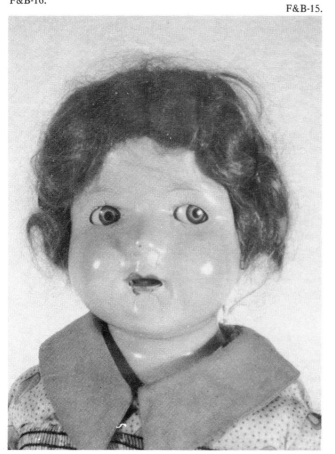

F&B-15. 18" *Rosemary.* Same as F&B-14, with flirty tin sleep eyes and original mohair wig and dress. Compare these dolls with some of the unmarked dolls of the period. ca. 1925. *(Wiseman collection)*

F&B-16. 22" *Rosemary.* Same as F&B-14, with original light brown mohair wig. Note different sizes of same doll often are slightly different in appearance. ca. 1925. *(Wiseman collection)*

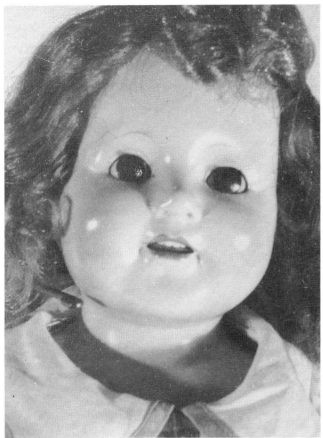

F&B-17.

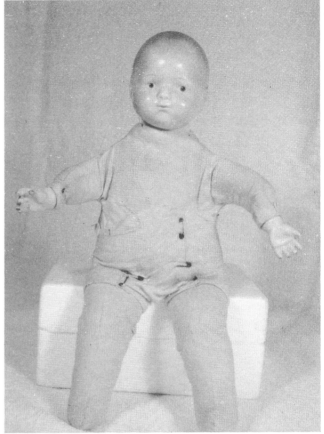

F&B-19.

F&B-18.

 fig. F&B-17

F&B-17. 22" *Marilee.* Composition shoulder head and limbs, brown sleep eyes, cry voice, all original except new wig. Original wig was in long, long curls. White romper suit with blue flower print, original shoes and socks. Also 29" Marilee. ca. 1925. Marks: Fig. F&B-17. *(Wiseman collection)*

F&B-18. 22" *Marilee.* Same as F&B-17, with original long blonde mohair wig. *Marilee* was also dressed in ruffled pastel dress and matching undies. *(Wiseman collection)*

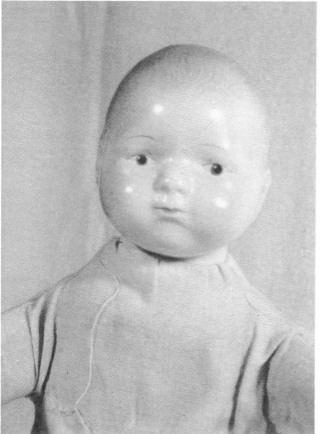

F&B-19.

F&B-20.

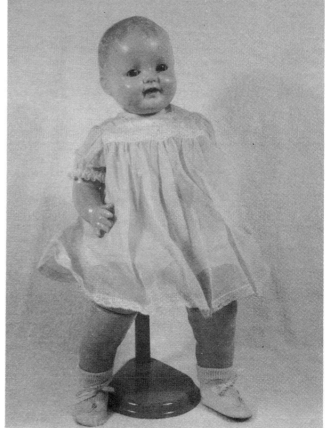

F&B-20.

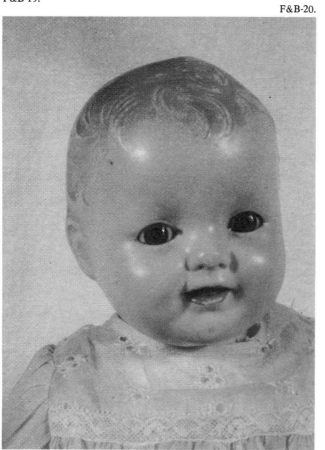

F&B-19. 14" *Pat-o-Pat.* Composition swivel head and gauntlet hands, stuffed cloth body and limbs, painted features. Press mechanism in body and hands clap together. Marks: **EFFANBEE / MADE IN U.S.A.** on head. ca. 1925. *(Zillner collection)* See also p. 185.

F&B-20. 20" *Lovums.* Composition swivel shoulder head, arms and legs, stuffed cloth body, blue-green sleep eyes, all original yellow organdy dress and bonnet (not shown). ca. 1928. Marks: **EFFANBEE / LOVUMS / © / Pat. 1283,558.** *(Wiseman collection)*

F&B-21. 17½" *Lovums.* Same as F&B-20, with lamb's wool wig and bent legs. Note seam and dart shaping of body. Marks: **LOVUMS / EFFANBEE / © / Pat. 1283,558.** *(Courtesy Camelot of Springfield, Missouri)*

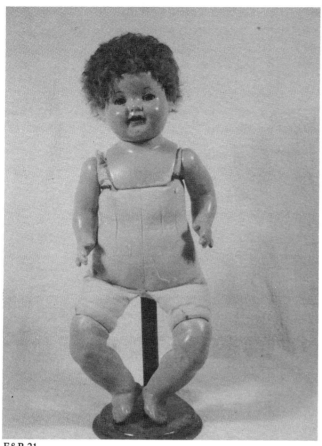

F&B-21.

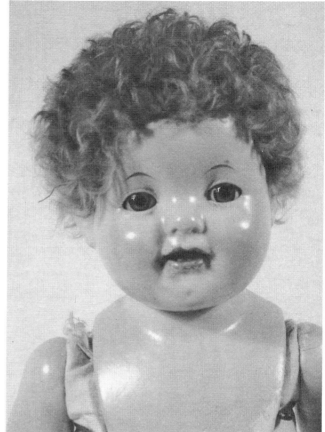

F&B-21.

F&B-22.

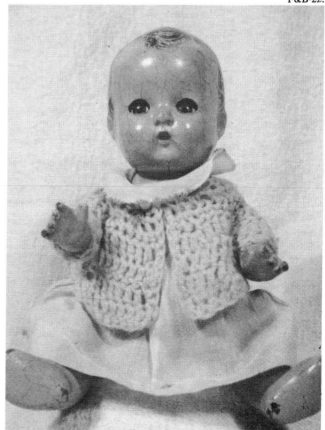

F&B-22. 8½" *Patsy Baby-ette.* All composition, blue sleep eyes, molded, painted hair. Marks: **EFFAN-BEE / PATSY BABY-ETTE** on back. ca. 1927. *(Author's collection)*

This doll is also found with glued-on skin and fur wig.

F&B-23. 19" *Patsy Ann.* All composition, blue sleep eyes, closed mouth, original clothes, shoes and socks. Marks: **EFFANBEE / "PATSY-ANN" / © / Pat. No. 1283558** on shoulders. ca. 1927. *(Author's collection)*

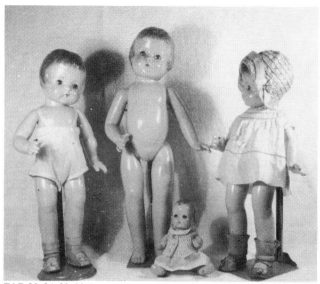

F&B-23, 24, 22, 23.

F&B-23.

F&B-24.

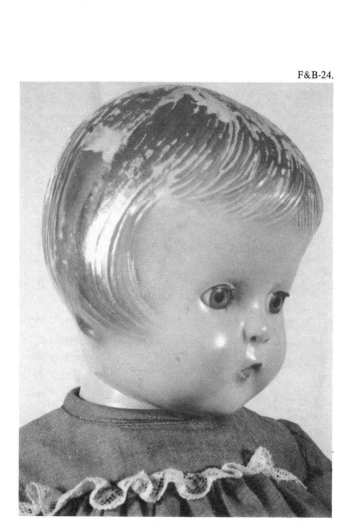

F&B-24. 22" *Patsy Lou.* All composition, blue-green sleep eyes, closed mouth. Marks: **EFFAN-BEE** / **"PATSY LOU"** on back. ca. 1927. *(Author's collection)*

F&B-24a. *Patsy Lou* poses with Effanbee doll trunk of pink leather-textured paper over card, metal hinges, handles and latch. Heart-shaped emblem in upper left hand corner inside cover reads: **"An EFFANBEE Play Product."** Baby doll pictured on inside cover wears an Effanbee heart bracelet. The little "mother" wears a typical 1920's bob hair-do. Size: 7½ x 12 x 5¼ inches tall. *(Author's collection)*

F&B-25. 9" *Patsyette.* All composition, painted eyes, all original, mohair wig, blue hairbow and blue print clothes with sewn-in cloth tag, bracelet. Marks: **EFFAN-BEE** / **PATSYETTE** / **DOLL** on back. **EFFAN-BEE** / **PATSY** / **ETTE** on heart bracelet. *(Author's collection)*

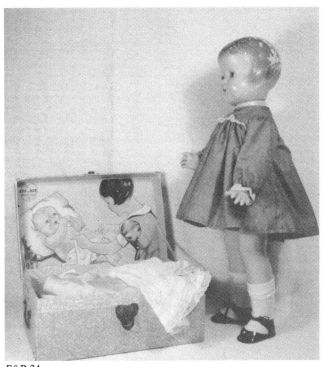

F&B-24a.

F&B-25, 26, 27.

F&B-28.

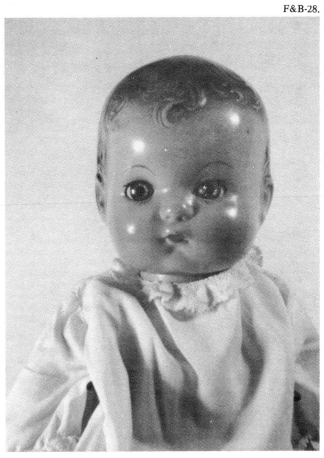

fig. F&B-25

F&B-26. 11" *Patsy Jr.* All composition, painted side glancing eyes, molded hair band painted same as hair, new dress. Marks: **EFFANBEE / PATSY JR. / DOLL** on back. *(Author's collection)*

F&B-27. 9" *Patsyette.* Same as F&B-25, with molded, painted hair, all original. Electric range is unmarked; plug it in and it still works. *(Author's collection)*

F&B-28. 13" *Patsy-Baby.* Composition head, cloth body similar to that of AM-4, blue sleep eyes. Marks: **EFFAN-BEE / PATSY-BABY** on back of head. *(Wiseman collection)*

F&B-29.

F&B-29.

F&B-30.

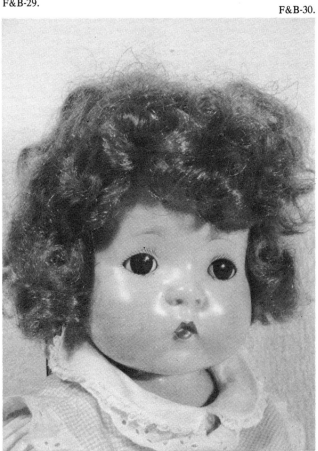

F&B-30.

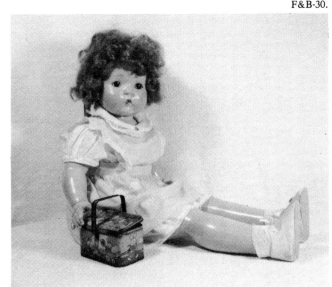

F&B-31.

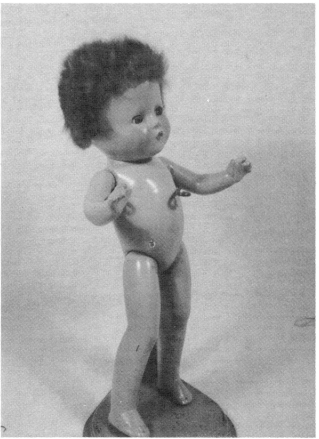

F&B-32.

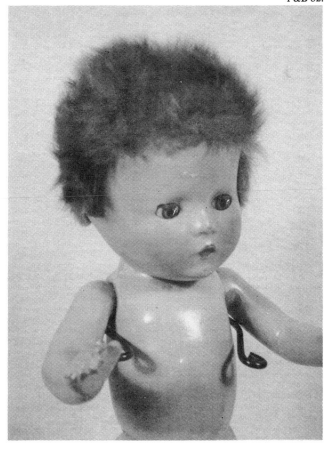

F&B-32.

F&B-29. 27" *Patsy Ruth.* All composition, brown sleep eyes, smooth head under original human hair wig, original heart tag bracelet, new dress. Marks: **EFFAN-BEE / PATSY RUTH.** *(Wiseman collection)*

F&B-30. 30" *Patsy-Mae.* Composition swivel shoulder head and limbs, stuffed cloth body, brown sleep eyes, new wig. Marks: **EFFANBEE / PATSY-MAE** on head. **EFFANBEE / LOVUMS / © / Pat. No. 1283558** on shoulder plate. *(Wiseman collection)*

F&B-31. 16" *Patsy-Joan.* All composition, brown sleep eyes, color worn off molded hair. Marks: **EFFAN-BEE / PATSY-JOAN.** *(Wiseman collection)*

F&B-32. 12" *Patsy Type.* All composition, green tin sleep eyes, fur wig, molded Patsy bob under wig. Body is unmarked, but is definitely a *Patsy* type. Horsman made some *Patsy* type dolls which are shown in Sears 1931 catalog. Another catalog listing reads: "Made especially for us by a leading maker under our own name "Dainty Dorothy" and "Sally". These two dolls are exactly like *Patsy.* This fur-wigged, tin-eyed doll ca. 1928. *(Author's collection)*

F&B-33.

F&B-34.

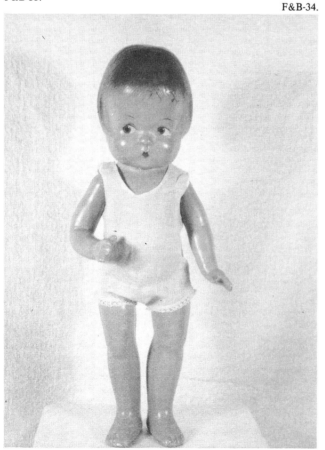

F&B-35.

**NOTE: ORIGINAL PRICES SHOWN
ARE NOT TODAY'S PRICES.**

F&B-33. 13½" *Patsy.* Late composition in perfect condition, blue sleep eyes, all original in red and white checked dress. Doll is unmarked, was purchased in doll shop in 1950. Sears 1947 Christmas Book lists 13½" *Patsy* and 17" *Patsy Joan,* the last such listing until the vinyl *Patsy Ann* issue. *(Wiseman collection)*

F&B-34. 14" *Patsy Type.* All composition, painted eyes, original clothing, unmarked. Feature by feature comparison of these unmarked dolls with a marked doll of same size is often necessary to establish authenticity. *(Kirtley collection)*

F&B-35. 15" *Patsy Ann.* Vinyl, rooted Saran hair, gray-blue sleep eyes, hair lashes, closed mouth, rigid body and limbs, soft head. Marks: **EFFANBEE / PATSY AN-N /** © **1959** on head. *(Author's collection)*

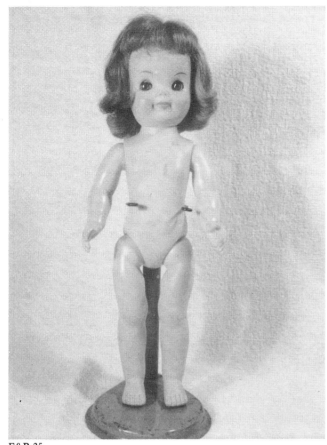

F&B-35.

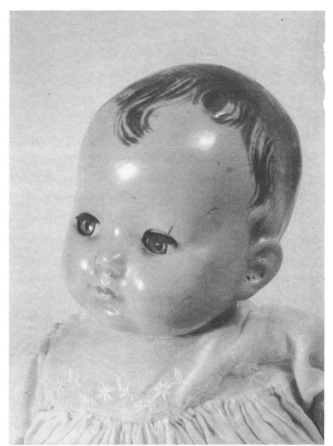

F&B-36.

F&B-35a.

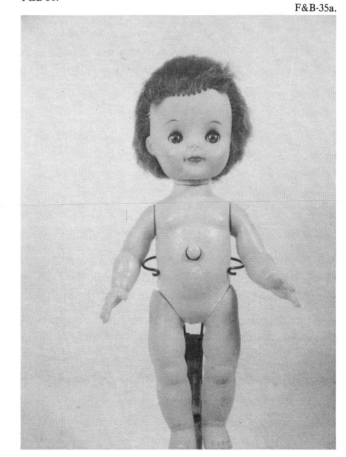

F&B-35a. 10½" *Yes-No Patsy Ann.* Head of soft vinyl is identical to that of F&B-35, although unmarked. Blue sleep eyes, solid plastic lashes, rooted saran hair. Refer to Horsman for other yes-no dolls. *(Kirtley collection)*

An 11" doll with same head is offered in Sears catalogs 1960 through 1962 and is listed as *"Fluffy".* Apparently did not have the yes-no feature.

F&B-36. 17" Baby. Composition head and limbs, cloth body, blue flirty sleep eyes, brown molded, painted hair. Note elongated, new-born baby shape of head. ca. 1928. Marks: **EFFANBEE / MADE IN U.S.A.** on head. *(Wiseman collection)*

F&B-37.

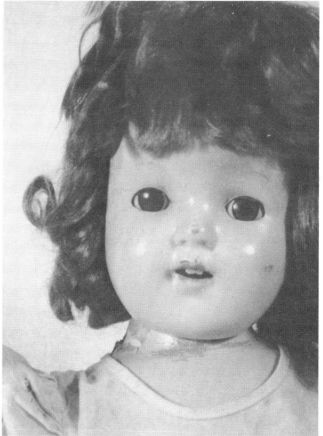

F&B-37.

F&B-38.

F&B-37. 20" *Mary Ann.* All composition, original blonde mohair wig, green sleep eyes, original clothes. Early 1930's. Earlier *Mary Ann* had cloth body. Marks: **MARY ANN** on head. *(Wiseman collection)*

F&B-38. 20" *Mary Ann.* All composition, fat toddler body very similar to PORT-D5, brown sleep eyes, original brown mohair wig. Early 1930's. *(Wiseman collection)*

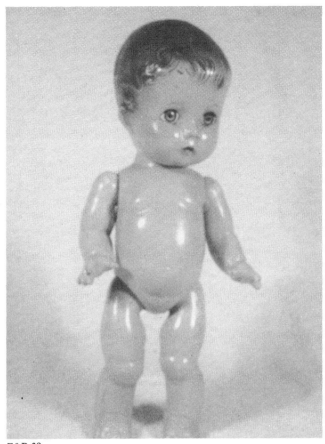

F&B-39.

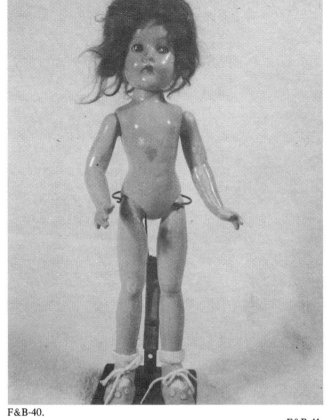

F&B-40.

F&B-41.

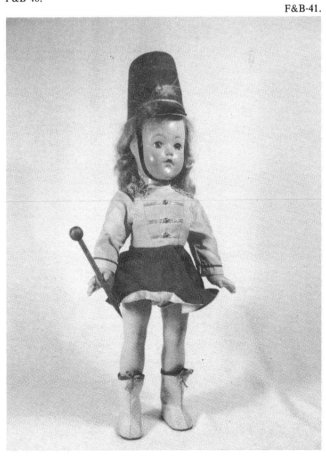

F&B-39. 13" *Candy Kid.* All composition, blue sleep eyes, brown moulded, painted hair. These dolls were dressed in all manner of outfits and were also sold as twins. 1946. *(Wiseman collection)*

F&B-40. 14" *Suzanne.* All composition, light blue sleep eyes, original mohair wig. Marks: **SUZANNE / EFFAN-BEE / MADE IN / U.S.A.** ca. 1942. *(Wiseman collection)*

F&B-41. 18" Majorette. All composition, dark blue sleep eyes, mohair wig, all original costume. Marks: **EFFAN-BEE / U.S.A.** on head and shoulders. 1936-1942. *(Wiseman collection)* Probably one of Effanbee's *"Little Lady"* line.

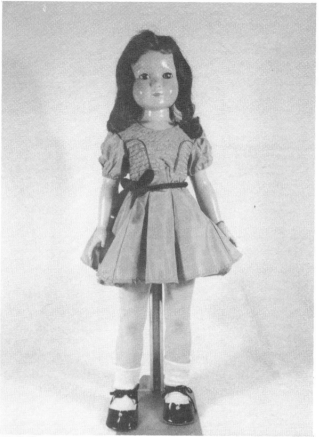

F&B-42.

F&B-42.

F&B-43.

F&B-42. 20" *Dewees Cochran.* All composition, brown sleep eyes, new wig, original dress. One of a series of four designed by doll artist, Dewees Cochran, while under contract to Effanbee in 1936.[1] Marks: **EFFAN-BEE / AMERICAN / CHILDREN** on head. **EFFAN-BEE / ANNE SHIRLEY** on body, an example of inter-mixing of parts at the factory. Effanbee issued these heads on Anne Shirley bodies, much as Ideal used the Shirley Temple bodies with various heads. *(Wiseman collection)*

F&B-43. 16" Baby. Composition head and limbs, cloth body, bright blue sleep eyes, with whitest whites, synthetic wig glued on over molded hair, original blue slip with lace edge, white organdy dress with blue trim. Marks: **EFFANBEE** on head and shoulder. *(Purchased in 1945 for Mrs. Battagler's daughter.)* Probably *"Baby Bright Eyes".*

F&B-44. 20" *Mickey.* Composition head and hands, cloth body and feet, blue sleep flirty eyes. Remembered by the owner as being called *"Sweetie Pie";* however, the doll may easily have been the same model as was marketed under the names *"Tommy Tucker"* and *"Mickey."* Often a company will market the same doll in different costumes under several different names. Hair was originally in

[1] Young, Helen, "The Complete Book of Doll Collecting", G. P. Putnam's Sons, New York, 1967.

F&B-43.

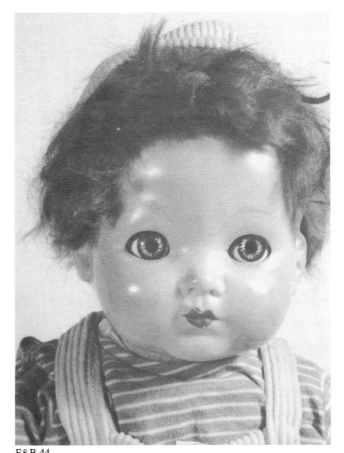

F&B-44.

F&B-44.

ringlets and the skin-fur wig was used on all three of these dolls. All three dolls also had flirty eyes and came in a variety of sizes. Doll shown was purchased in 1944, the first year EFFANBEE abandoned use of the metal wrist tags. *(Childhood doll of Mrs. Lawrence Zillner)*

F&B-45. 12", 16", *Sister and Brother.* Composition heads and hands, cloth bodies and limbs, painted features, embroidery floss hair, all original costumes. Girl is dressed in pink, boy is in blue. Purchased as a pair for $7.50 in 1943; boxed in a seated position. They represent dollmakers' attempts to provide attractive play dolls despite war shortages. Marks: **EFFANBEE** on head. Sometimes the marks are barely discernible. *(Childhood dolls of Mrs. Lawrence Zillner)* See p. 198 for illustration.

F&B-46. 14¼", 18" *Honey Walker.* Plastic, glassene eyes, saran hair. Shown in 1952 through 1954 catalogs, retailed at $7.39 and $9.49. *Catalog illustration courtesy Sears, Roebuck & Co.* See p. 198 for illustration.

F&B-47. 16" *Dy-Dee Baby.* Rubber with hard plastic head, lamb's wool wig, applied rubber ears, sleep eyes, drink-wet-tears feature. 1956. *(Wingfield collection) Dy-Dee Baby* was one of a large family which included *Dy-Dee Lou, Dy-Dee-Ette, Dy-Dee-Wee* and *Dy-Dee-Kin.* Found in soft rubber, hard rubber, vinyl and hard plastic. See p. 198 for illustration.

F&B-45.

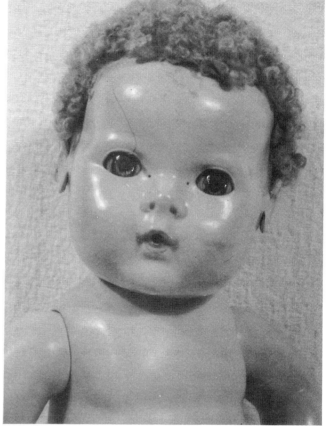

F&B-47.

F&B-46.

F&B-48. 18" *Dy-Dee Darlin'.* Vinyl body, soft vinyl head, arms and legs, rooted hair, sleep eyes, dressed all in pink and white. *1968 Catalog illustration courtesy Sears, Roebuck & Co.*

F&B-49. 11" *Mickey, the All-American Boy.* All original, vinyl, painted eyes, molded hat. Marks: **Mickey / EFFANBEE.** *(Wiseman collection)*

F&B-50. 11" *Mickey, the All-American Boy.* Sailor and Football Star, (lost his uniform in one of those skirmishes).

F&B-51. 11" *Mickey, the All-American Boy.* Another sailor. First catalog listing was 1957: Baseball Player, Football Star, Sailor. In 1959, Boy Scout was added and in 1960, *Mickey* Boxing Champion with black eye, terry robe, gym shoes and boxing gloves was new. Still available in 1970, Aviator, Soldier, Fireman, and Policeman have been added to the list, each with appropriate molded-on hat and removeable uniform. *(Kirtley collection, Catalog information courtesy Sears, Roebuck & Co.)*

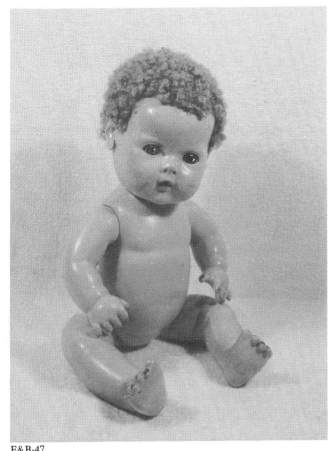

F&B-47.

F&B-51.   F&B-48.   F&B-50.   F&B-49.

F&B-51-1.

F&B-52.

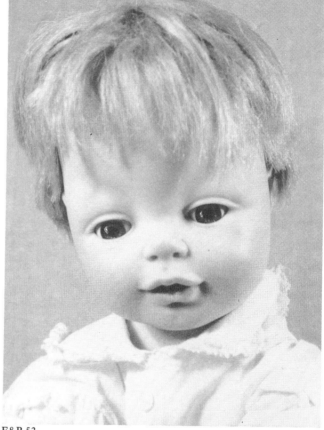

F&B-53.

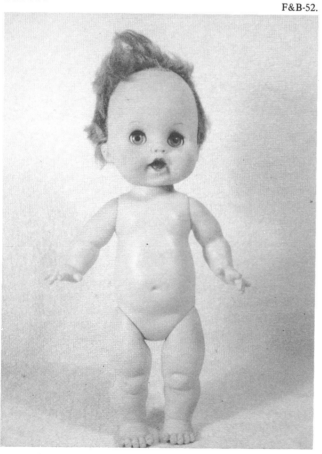

F&B-51-1. 15" *Girl Scout.* Vinyl and plastic, rooted hair, sleep eyes, authentic uniforms. Also available: *Blue Bird, Brownie,* or *Camp Fire Girl.* Listed 1960, 1961. 1962 Catalog illustration courtesy *Sears, Roebuck & Co.*

F&B-52. 12½" *Half Pint"*, also known as *"1/2 Pint".* All vinyl, blue sleep eyes, rooted Saran hair, nursing mouth. Marks: **EFFANBEE/19(c)62** on head and body. Also a black version. *(Author's collection)*

F&B-53. 16" *Lil Sweetie.* All vinyl, blue sleep eyes, no lashes, no brows, rooted dynel hair, drink and wet feature. Came in long christening gown with lace and embroidered rosettes, sweater, cap and booties, on a pillow trimmed with embroidery and organdy ruffle, with her own baby bottle. Marks: **5667 / EFFAN-BEE / 19© 67** on head and **EFFANBEE / 19© 67** on shoulder. *(Courtesy Sharon Denise Brink)*

For at least one year this doll was marketed as *Dy-Dee Darlin'* although it is definitely not the same doll as that shown in illustration F&B-48. Note the unique moulded eye-lids.

F&B-54. 16" *Dy-Dee Baby.* All vinyl, molded hair, sleep eyes, "coo" voice, drink and wet, completely equipped at $12.99. 1970 Catalog illustration. 14" shown in 1968, both singly and as Dy-Dee Bunting Twins, bundled together in flannel wrapper. *Catalog information courtesy Sears, Roebuck & Co.*

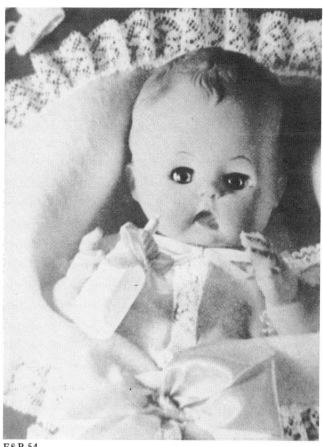

F&B-54.

ETH-1.

ETH-2.

ETHNIC DOLLS

ETH-1. 16" Man, Woman with Babies. Cloth over wire, mask faces well molded, inset eyes of glass bead with painted pupils, stitched fingers and toes. Mexico, 1941. *(Kirtley collection)*

ETH-2. 6½" *Skookum*. Molded, painted features, dress in bit of authentic Indian blanket, handmade. Early ones had dried-apple heads; this is a later composition one. Body built up over sticks. Designed by Mary McAboy, executed by Tammen Mfg. Co. and Arrow Novelty Co. *(Author's collection)*

ETH-3. 10" Baby. Bixque-like composition, open cry-voice box in abdomen, well-loved, some of front hair is missing, colorful woven silk kimona. Marks: **JAPAN** blue stamped on left leg. 1953. *(Courtesy Cheryl Jean Lynn)* See p. 202 for illustration.

ETH-4. 9½" Seated, Chief. Paint-over-celluloid head, cloth body, seated on silk-covered pillow. Elaborate and authentic clothes are sewn on; red and yellow shirt, navy pants, real leather belt with silver buckle ornament, yellow feather headdress, back of head covered with black plush, braids of embroidery floss, jointed hip and shoulder. Unmarked. *(Charles Vandiver collection)* See p. 202 for illustration.

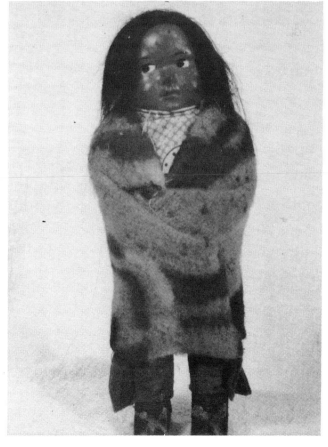

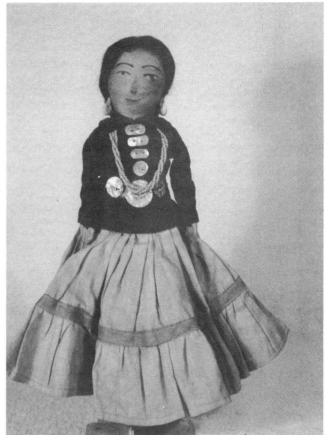

ETH-4.

ETH-3.

ETH-5.

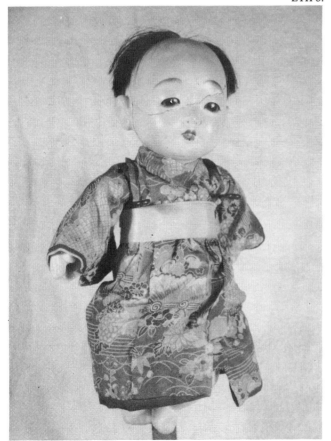

ETH-5. 12" Navajo. All cloth, hand painted features, mohair wig, stitched fingers, yellow skirt, red velvet shirt, silver belt and buttons, turquoise beads. Purchased 1940 on wedding trip, between Alburquerque and Santa Fe, New Mexico. *(Battagler collection)*

ETH-6. 9" Chinese Girl with Lotus. Wire construction, cloth padded, composition head and hands, silk kimona, hand painted features, parasol for right hand is missing. Marks: **MADE IN CHINA** on base. *(Battagler collection)*

ETH-7. 10", 10¾" Seminole Indians. Handmade of cypress fibre by Seminole Indians, dressed in colorful authentic costumes. 1938. *(Battagler collection)*

ETH-8. 13½" Hula Girl. All cloth, grass skirt, padded nose, painted features, yarn hair, stitched fingers. Brought from Honolulu in 1945. *(Battagler collection)*

ETH-9. 8½" Sioux Indians. Doeskin, bead features, authentic dress. Handmade by Lillian Shaw, Sioux Indian Reservation, Devil's Lake, North Dakota. Purchased in 1938 by Miss Lida J. Curtin. *(Battagler collection)*

ETH-6.

ETH-7.

ETH-9.

ETH-8.

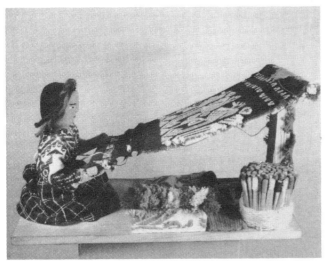

ETH-11.

ETH-11.

ETH-10.

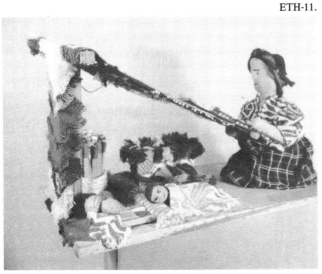

ETH-10. 3" Guatamalean Dolls. Completely handmade, sticks, cloth, yarn. These dolls are sold in Kansas City, Missouri, by Dr. J. E. Kendrick to help finance a medical mission in Guatamala. *(Rebekka Anderton collection)*

ETH-11. 5" Seated, Guatamalean Woman Weaving. Dolls are dressed in bits of hand woven cloth, baby sleeps in shade of loom work, sticks wound with dyed yarns and swatches of cloth make up an authentic display of the primitive methods employed by these weavers. *(Courtesy Dr. J. E. Kendrick)*

ETH-12. 14" Korean Girl. Composition head, arms and straight legs, card body, nose, eyelids, and mouth delineated by incisions, black hair may be seaweed, painted on red slippers, note darker lip and lip pucker lines. Original silk clothes in traditional style. *(Childhood doll of Denise Spalding)*

ETH-13. 13" Swedish Girl. Good quality hard plastic, blue flirty sleep eyes, blond mohair wig, authentic Swedish costume. ca. 1952. *(Childhood doll of Denise Spalding)*

ETH-14. 8" Alaskan. All plastic, dressed in native animal skins and furs. Purchased in Anchorage, Alaska, in 1970. Unmarked. *(Courtesy Kristie Lynn Gast)*

ETH-15. 8" Chinese Baby. All composition, beautifully finished, Oriental features, dressed in silk. Purchased in Hong Kong in 1970. Unmarked. *(Courtesy Kristie Lynn Gast)*

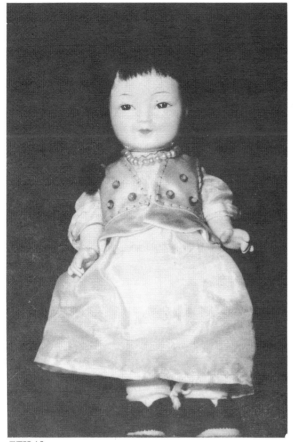

ETH-15.

ETH-13.

ETH-12.

ETH-14.

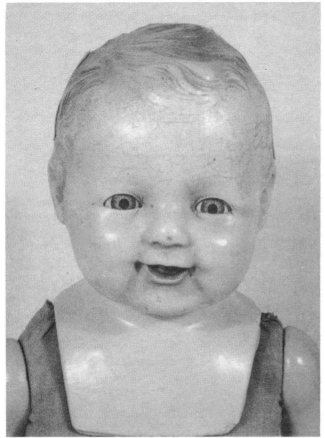

F-1.

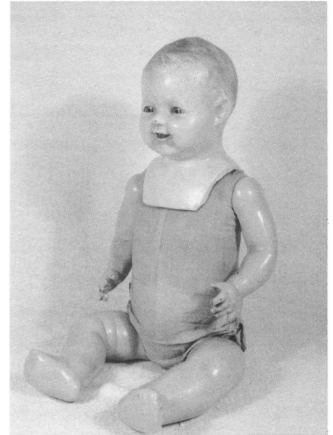

F-1.

F-2.

F-5.

F

F-1. 21" Baby. Open mouth, two teeth, molded tongue, blue tin sleep eyes, composition shoulder head and limbs, cloth stuffed body, cry box, molded, painted hair. Marks: **F.D.P. Co.**, probably Federal Doll Products Company. 1920's. *(Baume collection)*

F-2. 4½" Flapper Head. Papier mache; paste saturated card pressed into a mold, in this case; mohair wig, painted features, separate lavendar organdy cloche. Marks: **Germany** in a circle, stamped inside shoulder.

F-3.

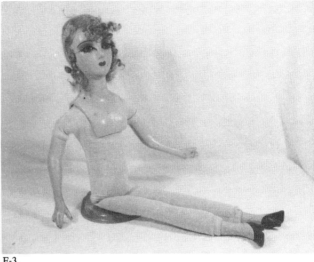

F-3.

F-4.

F-3. 28" Flapper Bed Doll. Composition shoulder head, arms and feet with molded shoes, excelsior-stuffed cloth body, applied and painted lashes, painted eyes, original mohair curls. Marks: **W-K/IN** on back of shoulder plate. 1920's. *(Courtesy Mrs. Theodore Warren Glassmire)*

F-4. 21" Flapper Cigarette Smoker. Composition head, different composition hands, lower arms, and feet, original white mohair wig. Original silk pants suit of pale beige was probably white originally, trim is black, original felt hat. Marks: **Germany** impressed on head. *(Zillner collection)*

F-5. 24", 30" Flapper Vamp. "Rayon brocade body, cotton stuffing, fluffy white mohair wig, arms and legs tie into innumerable poses." This type doll shown in catalogs throughout the 1920's, retailed at 97c and $1.79 in 1926. *(Sketched from catalog, courtesy Sears, Roebuck & Co.)* Soft dolls such as this were made by many companies in a variety of fabrics.

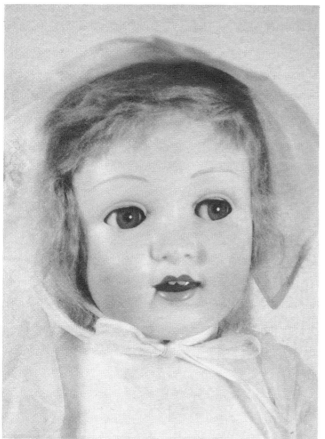

FR-2.   FR-1   FR-2.

FRENCH MODERNS

FR-1. 18" *Clodrey Toddler.* Vinyl head and limbs, polyurethane-foam filled body, blue sleep eyes. By Clodrey of France. *1970 catalog illustration courtesy Sears, Roebuck & Co.*

FR-2. 20" *Raynal Child.* Lightweight hard plastic, blond mohair wig, glass flirty eyes, open mouth, two molded teeth and tongue, spring strung, well modeled hands. All original costume; organdy slip, dress, apron and bonnet. Late 1940's, early 1950's. Marks: Back of head and pin on dress read **RAYNAL**. From France. *(Courtesy Kimport Dolls)*

FR-3. 19½" *French Composition.* Original mohair wig, composition shoulder head, gauntlet hands. Body and legs are one piece, shaped in cutting, cotton stuffed. Marks: **Protected through / Patent Office, U.S.A.** Brought from France. *(Kirtley collection)*

FR-4. 24" *French Child.* Composition shoulder head, legs, and arms. Blue painted eyes, open closed mouth, human hair wig. Bought in Paris in the 1920's by an American family in government service who were living in Switzerland at the time. *(Wingfield collection)*

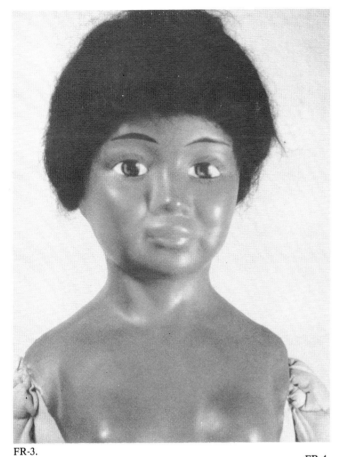

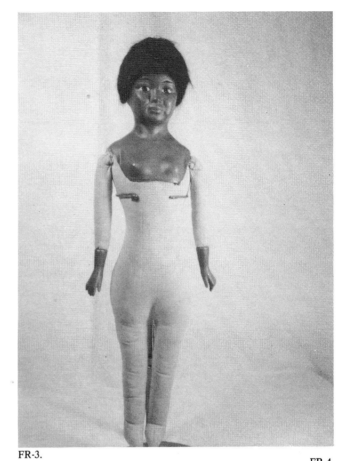

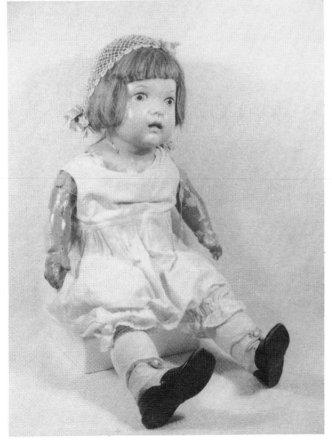

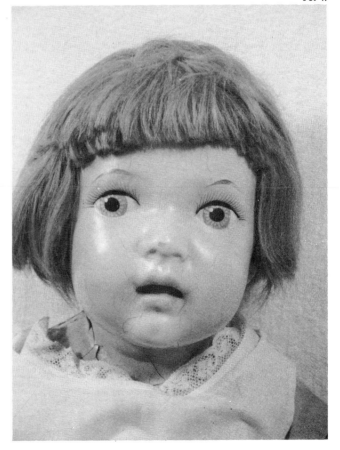

FR-5.

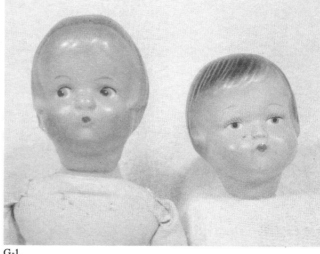

G-1.

FR-5. 20" *Pettitcollin*. All vinyl, fully jointed, rooted hair with upswept hair-do and Paris-designed clothes. Basic doll was $7.98 and outfits $4.98 to $5.98. *1963 Catalog illustration courtesy Sears, Roebuck & Co.*

fig. G-1

G-2.

G

G-1. 15" Composition Doll, 3½" Head. Painted features and hair, body with leather buttons and heavy wire at hip. Marks: Doll on left marked as in fig. G-1. Head on right marked **Germany.** *(Author's collection)*

G-2. 16" *Hansel and Gretel*. Hard plastic bodies, clear blue eyes, lashes, rooted blonde hair, fully jointed; place on face, they cry mama. Made in Germany. *1963 Catalog illustration courtesy Sears, Roebuck & Co.*

G-3. 9½" Girl. Composition head, papier mache body, jointed hip and shoulder, blue painted eyes, closed mouth. Head material has color all through, is a very smooth compact type of composition. Original gauze and felt costume, cheesecloth underwear. Marks: **Germany / 150.** 1920's. *(Author's collection)*

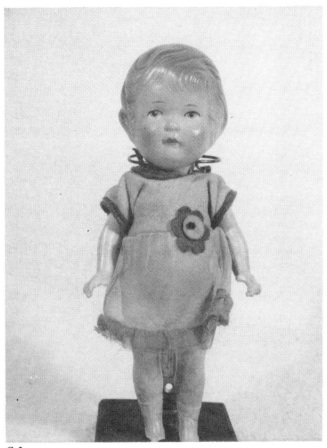

G-3.

G-4.

G-5.

G-4. 17", 12" *Poor Pitiful Pearl.* Stuffed vinyl, one piece body and limbs on 17" size; jointed vinyl on 12". Rooted hair, sleep eyes. Large one marked **GLAD TOY** on head and large **A** in relief on body. Small doll marked: © / **A** / **BROOKGLAD** / **CREATION**. 1950's. *(Author's collection)*

G-5. 17" *Poor Pitiful Pearl.* Original dress, navy blue print, no hem and red patch. 1958 Sears catalog lists doll with "rejuvenation outfit", $4.98 retail. *(Spalding collection)*

Another example of this character doll has a body very like the doll on the right in G-4 above and is marked **(c)** **1963/WM. STEIG/HORSMAN DOLLS, INC.**

G-6. 11" *Billy Boy.* All composition, painted eyes and hair, all original outfit. Tag on clothes as in fig. G-6. Listed in Sears 1928 and 1929 catalogs at $1.29, black velveteen beret, trousers and jacket, white shirt, all composition. *(Wiseman collection)* See p. 212 for illustration.

H-1.

H-1.

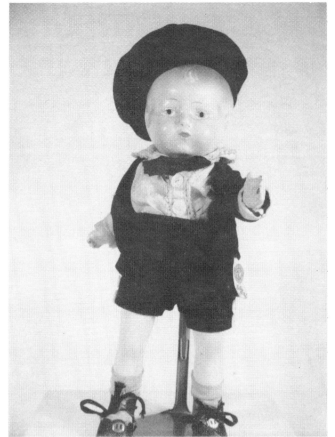

G-6.

fig. G-6

G-7. 16" *GEM 5-In-One-Doll*. "A doll for every occasion". Composition shoulder head and limbs, molded hair and features, cloth stuffed body. Came with separate wig and costumes for girl, sailor, clown, maid, and Indian Princess, with extra shoes and stockings. Boxed outfit, $3.98. Several other GEM dolls shown in mama and baby line. *1925 Catalog illustration courtesy Sears, Roebuck & Co.*

H

H-1. 10" Girl. Composition swivel head and arms, all original, molded, painted features, molded loop for hair ribbon, cloth body and legs. Marks: **Hansi** / **M E,** on head. From Germany. *(Courtesy Kimport Dolls)*

H-2. 5¼" *Bonnie Blue Bell*. Composition, painted features and shoes, mohair wig, jointed shoulder and hip. Blue dress, pink ribbons. Hollywood Doll Mfg. Co. 1947. *(Author's collection)*

G-7.

H-3. 14" *Mary Hoyer.* Good quality hard plastic, saran glued-on wig, golden brown eyes. Also an 18" size. Dolls were sold through needlework magazines to dress in knit or crochet. Booklets patterns, yarns, kits and accessories were available. Advertised as "Most Beautiful Doll in America." 1940's, 1950's. Marks: **ORIGINAL / Mary Hoyer / DOLL** (in a circle). By The Mary Hoyer Doll Mfg. Co. *(Wiseman collection)*

H-2.

H-3.   H-3.

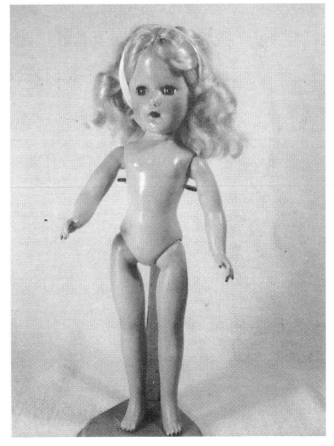

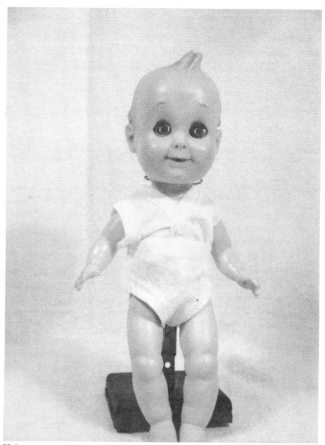

HMD-1.

H-5.

H-4.

H-4. Hummels, *Peterle and Rose.* Vinyl, all original, represent the famous Hummel figurines. Marks: **ORIGINAL / M. T. HUMMEL / Made In Germany / W. Goebel, Oeslau,** on tag. **M. J. Hummel** / © **W. Goebel** on head. *(Zillner collection)*

These dolls were made earlier in rubber from different moulds than those used for the vinyls. The rubber examples are marked with the bee-in-a-V mark of the Goebel factory as well as with the *Hummel* signature. Vinyl models are presently on the market. Peterle is 11½" tall and Rose is 11".

H-5. 12" *Baby Hungerford.* Vinyl, jointed hip and shoulder, drink and wet feature, brown sleep eyes. Resembles, but is not, the *Gerber Baby.* 1960's. Marks: **HUNGERFORD.** *(Kirtley collection)*

This doll was distributed as the "Heinz Baby" on a 1957 premium offer and came complete with diaper and bib.

HANDMADE DOLLS

Some of the most cherished dolls of yesteryear are those made with loving, careful hands in sewing room or home studio. A fascinating array of handmade dolls is available to the collector. In fact, the most famous rag dolls of all time, Raggedy Ann and Raggedy Andy, began as the inspired gifts of two mothers for their little girls (See Rag Dolls). Only a tiny sampling of handmade dolls is shown in this limited space; many more, equally as interesting and collectible, await discovery.

HMD-2.

HMD-3.

HMD-1. *Uncle Pink* and *Aunt Jenny.* Hand-carved, wooden dolls representing an early pioneer couple who settled in Tennessee near what is now Pleasant Hill, sometime in the 1800's. These dolls have been carved by several artists over the years; Polly Page now carries on the tradition. The dolls, carved from red cedar, are dressed in blue denim overalls and calico dress. *(Photograph courtesy Polly Page)*

HMD-2. Polly Page at her work table. *Uncle Pink, Aunt Jenny* and several of her farm animals are shown; she also carves animals for a Christmas Creche. *(Photograph courtesy Polly Page)*

Polly Page tells how she feels about carving her dolls: "I put myself in my work when I am carving. If I am sad I can't make *Aunt Jenny* smile; I must be humble to carve *Baby Jesus* in his manger. The value of the money is not all, because you never get the full value of your time. Its good for your mind and soul. It relaxes me and I forget all my little troubles and cares and try to make *Uncle Pink* and *Aunt Jenny* smile." Words from the heart of a true artist.

HMD-4.

HMD-3. *Huck Finn.* Only 4" tall, bendable to some extent, fashioned of artist's composition, hand painted. Designed and executed by Mrs. Clarence McOwan of Hannibal, Missouri. Mrs. McOwan also makes a 4" *Tom Sawyer* and *Becky Thatcher,* and a 6" *Mark Twain* and *Aunt Polly.* Dolls are beautifully costumed, meticulously finished. *(Rebekka Anderton collection)*

HMD-4. 11" Ozark Woman. All cloth, painted and stitched features, stitched fingers and toes, wisp of gray mohair wig, removeable clothes. Purchased in the Missouri Ozarks about 1947. *(Rebekka Anderton collection, courtesy Gwen Bower)*

HMD-6.

HMD-7.

HMD-6, -5, -7.

HMD-5. *"Irvin Wallace".* Hand-carved, wooden doll, cloth stuffed body. Portrait of a family friend by Mulvane, Kansas, artist, Carolyn Battagler Sims, 1968. *(Battagler collection)*

HMD-6. 12" Bride. Beautifully carved, detailed hair-do with hairnet, stuffed cloth body. Carolyn Battagler Sims, 1967. *(Battagler collection)*

HMD-7. *"Virginia Mae".* Pioneer Woman with well-done hands and carved boots to the knees for "marching through Kansas". Blue painted eyes, carved lids. An original by Carolyn Battagler Sims; this is Mrs. Sims' first doll, done in 1965. *(Battagler collection)*

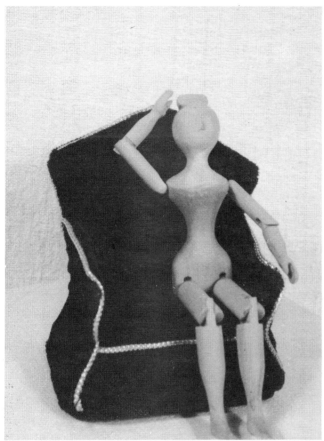

HMD-8.

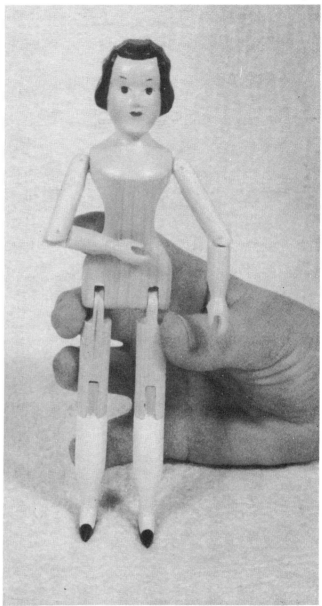

HMD-9.

HMD-9a.

HMD-8. 6" Spanish Lady. Hand carved, beautifully jointed and finished, sample doll without features. Note "comb" in hair. Marks: **S. Smith, Date: 9 / 16 / 65** on back. Hand carved by Mr. Sherman E. Smith of Utah. *(Courtesy Kimport Dolls)*

HMD-9. 6" *Hitty*. Hand carved and finished by Mr. Sherman E. Smith. Dolls are of Black Willow wood, dowels, and round toothpicks (used for joint pins). Although he has made larger and smaller sizes on occasion, Mr. Smith believes Hitty should be just this size to represent the character in Rachel Field's book [1]. The dolls receive five coats of lacquer, then features are painted, after which two coats of varnish are added. The artist mixes his own colors to achieve the desired flesh color for face and hands; body is left natural wood color. All dolls are signed and dated. *(Author's collection)*

HMD-9a. *Hitty*. Waiting for a new costume, *Hitty* examines the contents of an old doll trunk. Doll by Sherman E. Smith. *(Author's collection)*

[1] Field, Rachel, "Hitty, Her First Hundred Years", The MacMillan Company, New York, 1957.

HMD-10a.

HMD-12.

HMD-10.

HMD-11.

HMD-10. *Ped-a-Dolls.* Handmade of artists' composition, mounted on ceramic pedestals. Beautifully costumed dolls represent (top) *Marie Antoinette* and *Queen Elizabeth I;* (front) *Mary, Queen of Scots, Swan Lake,* and *Colonial Lady.* Barbara Brooks originals. *(Courtesy Kimport Dolls)*

HMD-10a. *Queen Elizabeth I.* Barbara Brooks original Ped-a-Doll. *(Courtesy Kimport Dolls)*

HMD-11. Helen Young Dolls. China heads and limbs, stuffed cloth bodies, handmade by author Helen Young[1]. Doll on left has black hair, pink ribbon; one on right has red hair, freckles and green hair ribbon. Redhead is marked **HY;** other doll is unmarked. *(Kirtley collection)*

HMD-12. Mammy. Hand made of black cloth, stuffed firmly, cotton wad for white hair, painted features. Purchased in New Orleans about 1946. *(Battagler collection)*

[1] Young, Helen, "The Complete Book of Doll Collecting", G. P. Putnam's Sons, New York, 1967.

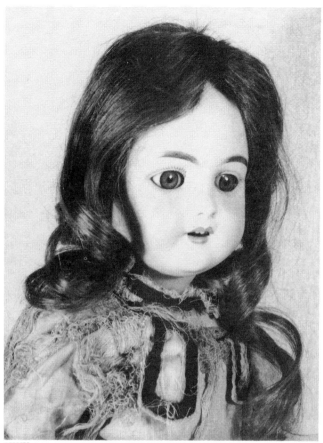

HWK-1.

HWK-1.

HMD-13.

HMD-13. Peddlar. Only 2¾" tall, with jointed hips and shoulders. On her tray are a doll, string of beads, bit of lace, plate, fan, bit of gold braid, flowers, purse, shell, book, and three tiny bottles. This amazing bit of miniatura was created by Irma Park. *(Courtesy Gwen Bower)*

HANDWERCK DOLLS

HWK-1. 21" Child. Bisque socket head, ball-jointed body, blue paper weight eyes, open mouth, four teeth, pierced front-to-back ears, replacement human hair wig. All original, though her clothes are in shreds and tatters: Pink trimmed with black velvet ribbon, undergarments are cotton trimmed with hand crocheted lace, original pink stockings and white leather shoes with flat heels, eyelets and pink shoe laces. There is a numeral **6** on sole of shoes. Marks: **HANDWERCK / 109 11 / Germany / 2½** on head. *(Author's collection)*

HWK-2. 32" Child. Bisque socket head, ball-jointed body, brown glass sleep eyes, molded-painted brows, open mouth, four teeth, original blonde mohair wig, pierced front-to-back ears. Doll wears size 3 baby shoes and an old baby dress cut down slightly to fit. Marks: **GERMANY / Heinrich Handwerck / Simon Halbig / 6½** on head. Although doll is now in Battagler collection, it belonged to Mrs. Battagler's aunt. See p. 220 for illustration.

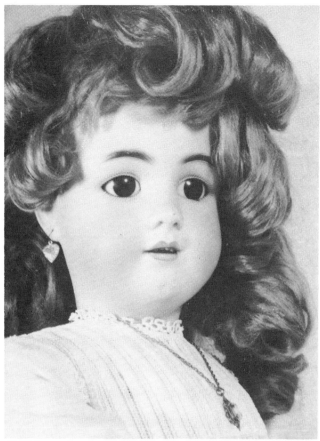

HWK-2.

HWK-2.

HWK-3.   HWK-4.

HWK-2 Contd.

This doll was the grand prize in a contest sponsored by the Zest Coffee Company about 1911. Packed in each pound of coffee was one letter of the word ZEST and the letter Z was the key to the prize. The father of year-old Gertrude Mobley was the lucky winner and brought the large doll home to his little daughter. The doll was hung on the parlor wall and was played with only during Spring and Fall cleaning sessions when it was removed to Gertrude's tiny rocking chair. The doll's hair was brushed and combed and her clothes refurbished before she was returned to the hook in the corner. *(Childhood doll of Gertrude Mobley Hessenflow)*

HWK-3. 21" Nurse. Bisque socket head, ball-jointed body, brown glass sleep eyes, hair lashes, open mouth, four teeth, ears pierced front-to-back. Nurse uniform is old and handmade. Marks: **Germany / HEINRICH HANDWERCK / SIMON HALBIG / 2¼** on head. *(Battagler collection)*

HWK-4. 23" Walker. Bisque socket head, ball-jointed body, gray-blue glass sleep eyes, ears pierced front-to-back. Note unusual arm construction. Marks: Letter **W** on head just below crown opening. **Made in Germany** stamped in red on left hip. *(Battagler collection)*

HAS-1.　　　　　　　　HAS-2.　　　　　　　　　　　　　　　　HAS-4.

HAS-3.

HASBRO

(HASSENFELD BROS.)

HAS-1. 15" *Little Miss No Name.* Vinyl, rooted hair, inset stationary brown eyes, originally a large tear from left eye. Marks: © **1965 HASBRO** ® . Original red and white checked overall. Created by doll designer, Deet D'Andrade. *(Author's Collection)*

HAS-2. 8" *Sad Eyes.* Vinyl, molded painted features, rooted synthetic hair, jointed hip and shoulder. Unmarked doll. **Chadwick-Miller / Made in Hong Kong** on original box. 1960's. Shown to compare with HAS-1. *(Spalding collection)*

HAS-3. 11½" *GI JOE®* . Vinyl and plastic, painted features, fully jointed. Doll's hands are curved to allow him to hold hand grenades, guns, and other implements of warfare. No army in the world is better equipped than *GI JOE.* On left in photograph is *GI JOE* Astronaut; pull talking tag and he says "Ten seconds to lift-off . . . and . . . counting". At right is black *GI JOE* dressed for a night Commando mission. Marks: **GI JOE®** / **COPYRIGHT 1964 / BY HASBRO® / PAT. NO. 3277602/MADE IN U.S.A.** on right hip. Later models, copyrighted 1970, have "life-like hair" of flocked material, sprayed on. *(Courtesy Joseph Richard Anderton II)*

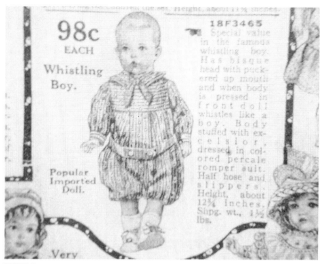

HEU-1.

HEU-2a.   HEU-2b.   HEU-2c.

HAS-4. 12" *G.I. JOE Action Nurse.* Regulation nurse's uniform, cap and shoes, medical bag, stethoscope, plasma bottle, crutches, bandages, and splints. Doll fully jointed, rooted hair. *1967 Catalog illustration courtesy Montgomery Ward & Co.* © **HASBRO / MADE IN U.S.A.** See p. 221 for illustration.

HEU-3.

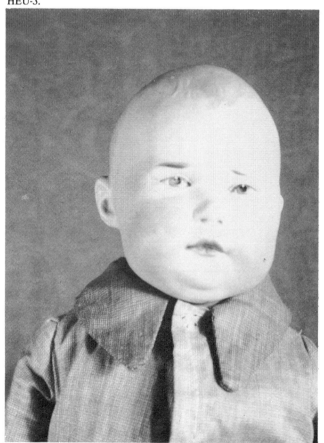

HEUBACH DOLLS

Heubach bisques were produced well into the Twentieth Century, following roughly the same pattern as other German firms and gradually losing the market to American firms. Several Heubach families engaged in dollmaking; most often found are the Gebruder (Bros.) Heubach and the Heubach-Koppelsdorf marks.

HEU-1. 12¾" *Whistling Boy.* Bixque head, puckered mouth, body stuffed with excelsior. Press body to make doll "whistle" like a boy. Identified only as "popular imported doll"; most likely Heubach. *1921 Catalog illustration courtesy Sears, Roebuck & Co.*

HEU-2a. 9" Child. Open mouth, tiny teeth, shoulder and hip joints, molded, painted shoes and stockings, brown sleep eyes, replacement wig and new costume. Marks: **128 / HERM STEINER / H S** (superimposed) / **Germany / 11 (or 14) / 2** on bisque head.

HEU-2b. 9" Child. Open mouth, two teeth, shoulder and hip joints, chubby papier mache body is very rough. New clothes. Marks: **HEUBACH KOPPELSDORF / 320 / 14 / 0 / Germany** on bisque head.

HEU-2c. 7" Child. Open mouth, row of six tiny teeth, bit of mohair for wig, black pupil-less eyes. rough papier mache body, hands and feet, painted shoes and stockings. Marks: **185 / 18 / O / X** on bisque head. *(Battagler collection)*

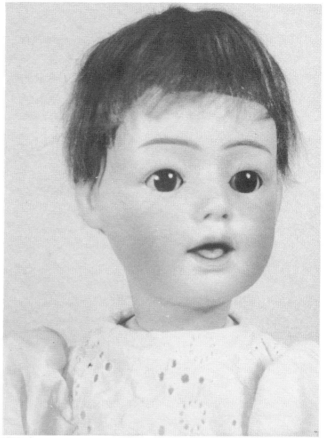

HEU-4. HEU-5.

HEU-6.

HEU-7. HEU-7a.

HEU-3. 20" Boy. Bisque shoulder head and hands, kid body. Marks: **B/HEUBACH** (in a square)/**Germany 7845,** on head. On green paper sticker: **7 DAYS.** *(Zillner collection)*

HEU-4. 9" Boy. Bisque head, intaglio blue eyes, open closed mouth, molded painted hair, bent limb papier mache body, original clothes and sox. Marks: **2 over 0 / 60 / HEUBACH** (in square), **11 / Germany.** *(Battagler collection)*

HEU-5. 8" Boy. Bisque head, blue sleep eyes, painted lashes, open closed mouth, two lower teeth, bent leg papier mache body, original light brown mohair wig. Marks: **87, HEUBACH**(in square) / **Germany.** *(Battagler collection)*

HEU-6. 15" Baby. Bisque head, open closed mouth with molded tongue, brown sleep eyes, painted lashes, bent limb papier mache baby body. Marks: **Daisy** over **G H** (superimposed), **7 / Germany.***(Battagler collection)*

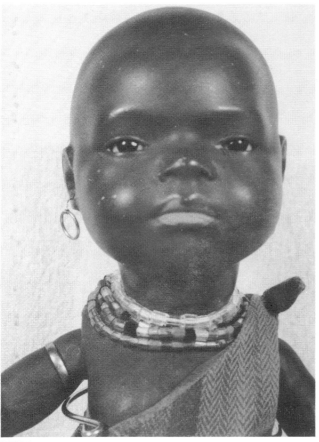

HEU-8.

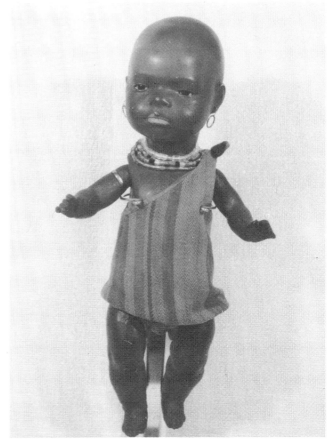

HEU-8.

HEU-9.

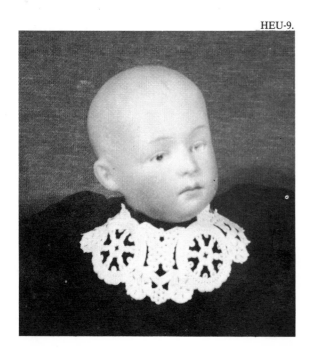

HEU-7. 7½" Girl. Bisque head, painted eyes, straight leg papier mache body, molded painted stockings and blue shoes, blue hairbow, painted blonde hair. Marks: **A crown / P,W G** (superimposed), **12 / 0 / Germany.** She just happened to wander into the picture with that cute Heubach boy). *(Battagler collection)* See p. 223 for illustration.

HEU-7a. 8½" Boy. Bisque head, brown painted eyes, closed mouth, papier mache straight leg body. Marks: **15 HEUBACH** (in square) **189 / Germany** under a **D.** Stamped **49** in green. *(Battagler collection)* See p. 223 for illustration.

HEU-8. 16" African Baby. Painted bisque head, pierced-in ears, composition body, stationary black glass eyes, redressed. Armband is a real gold wedding ring. This head is found on both straight-leg and bent-leg bodies. Marks: **Heubach-Koppelsdorf / 399 2 / 0 D R G M / Germany.** *(Wingfield collection)*

HEU-9. Bisque Boy. Socket head, painted intaglio eyes, closed mouth. Marks: **2 / 0 76 HEUBACH (insquare) 02 / Germany.** *(Author's collection)*

HORS-1.

HORSMAN DOLLS, iNC.

This company dates back to 1865 when E. I. Horsman first distributed, then began assembling, dolls. The history of the company traces a pattern through the years of the early *Campbell Kids,* the *Rosebud* girl dolls, the *HEbee-SHEbees* based on the drawings of illustrator, Charles Twelvetrees, *Tynie Baby* and many other of the very collectible dolls of today. The early Horsman compositions are among the most time-defying of materials (see *Campbell Kids*). Horsman maintains a large plant in Columbia, South Carolina.

HORS-2.

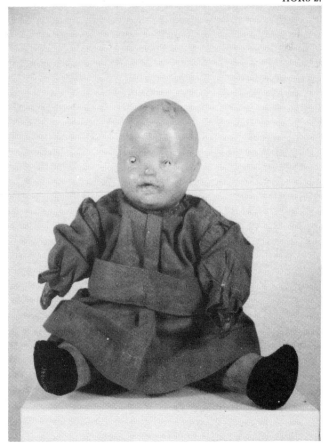

HORS-1. 11" *Billiken.* Ivory velvet body, may have been white originally. Pink and white cloth label sewn on body reads: **"Licensed Stamp / Copyright 1909 by / The Billiken / Company".** In upper left corner is letter **N;** in upper right corner is numeral **6.** Heavy layers of paint completely gone on back of head revealing excellent quality composition, smooth as ivory. On right foot is **Billiken** and other illegible lettering. *(Baume collection)*

HORS-2. 11" Boy. Composition head with very short neck has two sew holes to aid in attachment to body. Composition hands and body construction are identical to earliest *Campbell Kids.* Blue painted eyes, sawdust stuffing. Very old romper suit, carefully sewn to body at several points. Unmarked, but has appearance of very early Horsman. *(Baume collection)*

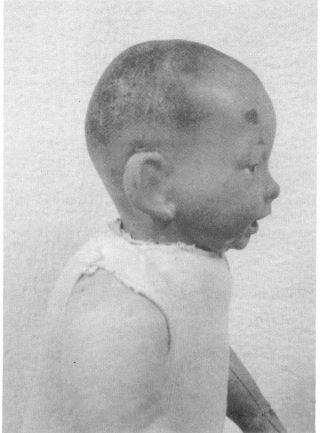

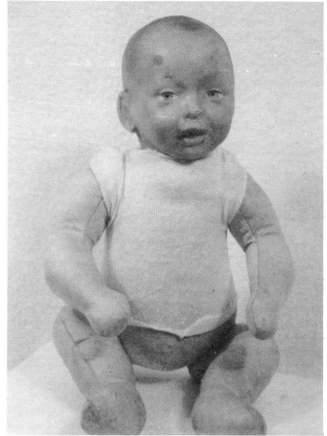

HORS-3.

HORS-3-1.

HORS-3.

HORS-3. 12" *Baby Bumps.* Can't Break 'Em composition head, cloth body and limbs, painted blue eyes, sprayed hair, flange neck, muslin body, pink sateen arms and legs. Also found in colored baby doll, identical to this one. Unmarked. About 1912. Compare with Kammer and Reinhardt No. 100 *Baby. (Wingfield collection)*

HORS-3-1. *Nurse Doll.* Composition head and gauntlet hands, stuffed cloth body and limbs, painted features, mohair wig, authentic uniform. Horsman also made *"Rookie",* a soldier boy, and *"Middie",* a sailor boy. *1917 Catalog illustration courtesy Sears, Roebuck & Co.* Four sizes: 12½" at $1.48, 15" at $1.69, 18½" at $2.63, and 25½" at $3.98.

HORS-4.

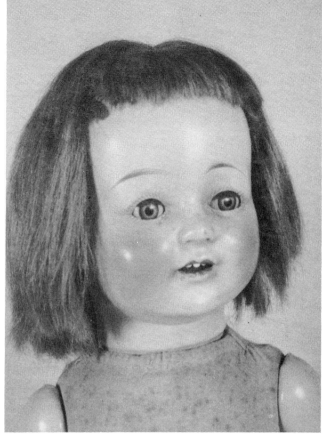

HORS-4.

HORS-4.

NOTE: ORIGINAL PRICES SHOWN
ARE NOT TODAY'S PRICES.

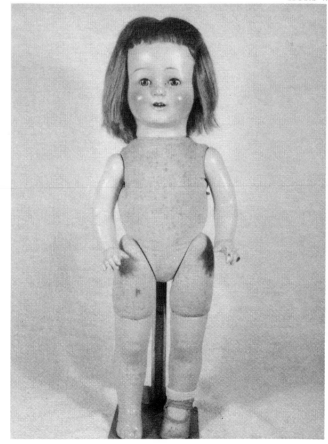

HORS-4. 20" Child. Composition swivel head, arms and legs, blue tin eyes, hair and painted lashes, open mouth, three teeth, original human hair wig, open crown, kapok stuffing, dimples. Marks: © / **E.I.H.CO. INC.** on head. ca. 1920. *(Baume collection)*

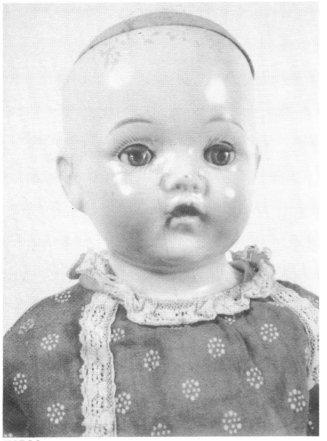

HORS-5.   HORS-5.   HORS-6.

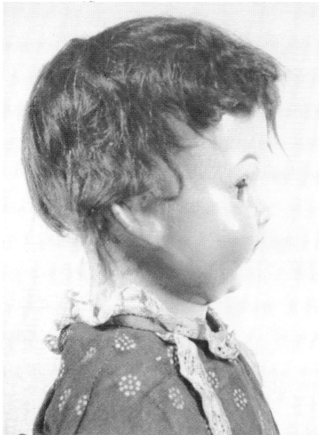

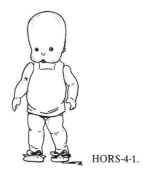

HORS-4-1.

HORS-4-1. HEbee - SHEbee. Doll in bisque or composition in several sizes, based on illustrations by Charles Twelvetrees. *Sketch by the author.*

HORS-5. 17" Child. Composition shoulder head, open crown, gray tin sleep eyes original mohair wig and clothes. Excellent quality composition, good painting. Note profile. Marks: **E.I. H. Co. / E.I. HORSMAN CO. / INC.** on shoulder plate. ca. 1925. *(Courtesy Dot & Joe's Browse Shop)* This model also was available with painted eyes.

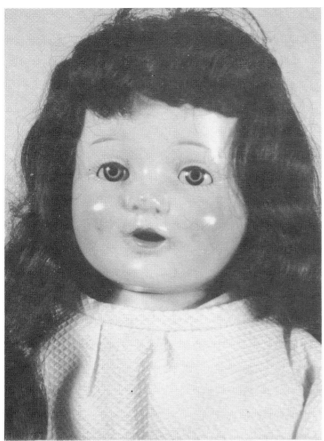

HORS-6.

HORS-6a.

HORS-6-1.

HORS-6. 18½" *Rosebud.* Composition swivel shoulder head, arms and legs, cloth body, gray tin eyes, dimples, open mouth, three teeth, tongue. Marks: **ROSEBUD** in relief on shoulder plate. ca. 1928. *(Spalding collection)*

HORS-6a. 17", 20" *Dolly Rosebud.* Composition head and limbs, stuffed cloth body, legs have hard stuffed thighs so doll can stand alone, mama voice, sleep eyes, hair lashes, mohair wig, open mouth, teeth. *1928 Catalog illustration courtesy Sears, Roebuck & Co.*

HORS-6-1. *Tynie Baby.* Composition head and hands, soft stuffed cloth body and limbs, spread-out baby hands, painted hair, sleep eyes, cry voice, sloping forehead and puffed-out cheeks. An 11" with layette sold for $2.98, an 18" in long white baby dress was $1.95, 18" twins were $4.98 a set in bunting, and a 20" was $4.45 with blanket. Also came with bisque head in 1924. Sometimes called *"The Horsman Bye-lo",* it was definitely offered in competition to the Bye-lo. *1925 Catalog illustration courtesy Sears, Roebuck & Co.*

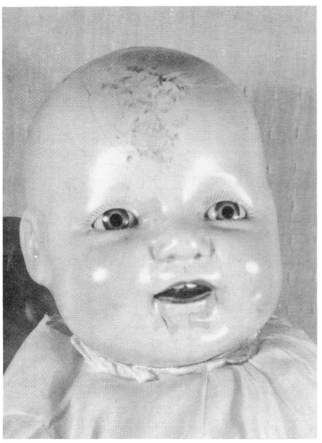

HORS-9.   HORS-7.   HORS-8.

HORS-7. *Baby Dimples* in 14½", 17½", 20" and 22". Natural looking sleep eyes; opening is cut so part of pupil is covered (see close-up photograph of HORS-9). Composition turning head, baby-shaped arms and legs. 1928 *Catalog illustration courtesy Sears, Roebuck & Co.* Also shown in 1930, 1931 and 1932.

HORS-8. 15" *Baby Dimples.* All original, gray tin eyes, open mouth, two teeth. Clothes are marked with tag: **HORSMAN / DOLL / M'FD IN U.S.A.** © / **E.I.H. CO. INC.** on head. *(Wiseman collection).* In December, 1929, issue of Successful Farming Magazine, the J. C. Penney Company advertised *"Baby Dimples"* by E. I. Horsman Doll Company, $1.98 to $5.90. 22" size was illustrated.

HORS-9. 22" *Baby Dimples.* Very soft, fat stuffed cloth body, cry voice, tag on dress reads **HORSMAN DOLLS / MADE IN U.S.A.** Doll marked same as HORS-8. Note resemblance to Effanbee's *"Bubbles"*. *(Courtesy Lois & Sallye's Antiques)*

Also in the 1928 Sears catalog are two dolls called *"Tee Wee"* and *Baby Aire".* *Tee Wee* is a hand doll; a puppet-type doll with sleeve for child's hand instead of body, with a composition head and celluloid hands, 19"

HORS-10-2.

HORS-10-1.

HORS-11.

long. *Baby Aire* was 18½" long, with composition head and the remainder of rubberized cloth which was "easily inflated or deflated." Both these dolls had smiling, dimpled faces similar to *Baby Dimples* and *Bubbles*, although no manufacturer is listed for either doll.

HORS-10-1. *Gold Medal Baby.* Composition head and limbs, stuffed cloth body, tilting, turning head, cries and toddles like a baby, sits alone. Each doll with medal which reads: *"Modeled by a famous sculptor, is most beautiful baby ever produced."* Dressed in organdy dress and bonnet with lace and embroidery, separate slip, flannel vest, rubber pants. First time author has noticed a choice of color offered: white, pink, or blue dresses. 18", 20", and 22" at $2.95, $3.95, and $4.79. *1931 Catalog illustration courtesy Sears, Roebuck & Co.*

HORS-10-2. 12", 16" Buttercup. Composition head, rubber body and limbs, outstretched arms, curved baby legs, sleep eyes, came on a satin pillow, retailed $5.39 for 16" size. 1932 Catalog illustration courtesy Sears, Roebuck & Co.
   An 18" Buttercup was produced by Modern Toy Company ca. 1925; however, this is apparently not the same doll.

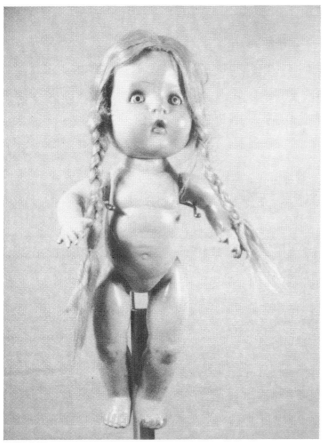

HORS-11.

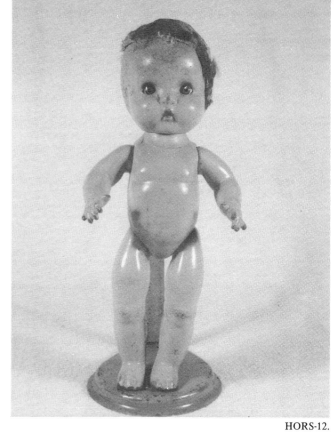

HORS-12.

HORS-13.

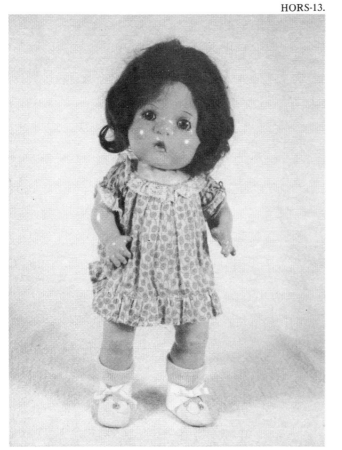

HORS-11. 13" Toddler. All composition, blue sleep eyes, original blonde mohair pigtail wig, closed mouth. Marks: **HORSMAN** on head. 1935. *(Childhood doll of Mrs. Marion S. Lynn)*

HORS-12. 13" *JO-JO.* All composition, blue sleep eyes, remains of wig over molded hair. Marks: **HORSMAN JO JO** / © **1937.** *(Wiseman collection)*

HORS-13. 13" Toddler. Composition, brown sleep eyes, original dress, wig. Marks: **HORSMAN.** 1937. *(Wiseman collection)*

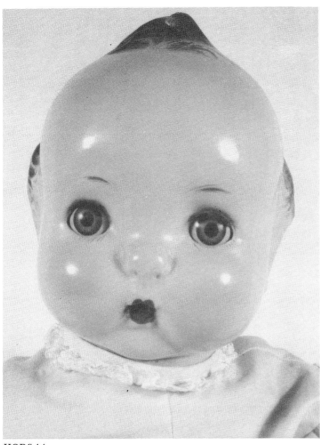

HORS-14

HORS-15.

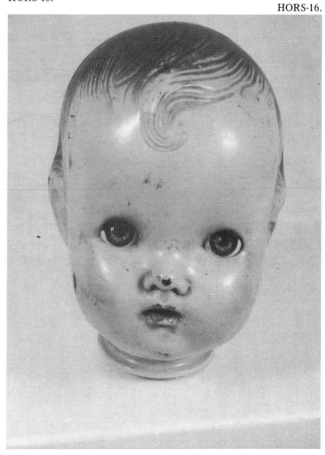

HORS-16.

HORS-14. 22" *Sister.* Composition head, arms and legs, cloth body, brown eyes, painted tufts of hair, closed mouth. Marks: © **1937 HORSMAN** on head. For picture of *Brother* see chapter, *"The Dolls in My Attic".* (*Wiseman collection*)

HORS-15. 17" Girl. All composition, red-brown mohair wig, brown sleep eyes. All original costume. Doll is unmarked, but original box is marked **HORSMAN.** 1930's. (*Wiseman collection*)

HORS-16. 6" Composition Head. Large dark gray eyes, open mouth, two teeth, molded painted hair. Marks: **HORSMAN.** 1938-1942. (*Spalding collection*)

**21-inch Horsman Doll
Blue Rayon Coat, Hat**

Easily worth $3. 21 in. tall. **$198** Bright Blue glass-like go-to-sleep eyes, real lashes. Cry voice. Blonde Mohair curls securely sewed to a cloth foundation ... prettier than poor quality, coarse human hair generally offered at this price. Head, arms, legs of hard-to-break composition. Swivel head turns, tilts. Mouth shows teeth, tongue. Full length composition arms, legs. (Arms inside jointed with double washers so they move freely.) Body filled with soft, clean cotton.

Beautifully tailored Blue Rayon coat and smart jockey hat. Box-pleated silky rayon Peach color dress. White undy, White rayon socks, Blue imitation leather slippers. "Jitter-bug" pin on collar of dress is a tiny bead doll.

HORS-16-1.

**Our Finest Baby—21 in. Tall
With Lovely Pure Silk Coat, Hat**

Not the biggest Doll, but **$295** prettiest, best dressed, finest we've ever seen at this price! Glass-like sleeping eyes, real lashes. Open mouth shows tongue, teeth. Cry voice. Beautifully shaped turning head, painted Brown hair. Arms, legs, head of hard-to-break composition. Cotton stuffed body.

White Organdy dress pleated very full, has deep hem, lace panels and puffed sleeves. Lace trimmed White Organdy slip. Pink rubber panties, White rayon socks, White slippers. Coat and hat Pink **Pure Silk** Crepe de Chine. Full cut coat. Pleated edges on flaring collar, cuffs. Bonnet has ribbon ties, lace net trim.

**17-Inch Baby Doll
With Go-To-Sleep Eyes**

The BEST QUAL- **95c** ITY Baby Doll we've ever offered at this price. She's as dainty and sweet as most dolls selling for $1.49. 17 in. tall. Go-to-sleep eyes. Cry voice. Painted hair. Arms, legs, head hard-to-break composition. Arms inside jointed—better construction used only on quality dolls. Cotton stuffed body. Head turns. Rosy cheeks. White organdy dress cut full, lace trimming, neck gathered with Pink smocking. Pink slip, rubber panties. Rayon socks, imitation leather booties, White. Ship. wt. 2 lbs. 4 oz.

**16-Inch Girl Doll
With Rain Cape, Beret**

16 in. tall. Her big **95c** eyes are framed with real lashes and she goes to sleep. Human hair Brown ringlets securely sewed to a cloth foundation. Fastened with hairpins and bound with a ribbon. (Of course, her wig is not first quality but is exceptionally good for a Doll at this low price.) Made of hard-to-break composition; very nicely proportioned. Arms, legs jointed; head turns, tilts. Red rubber raincape and beret for rainy days. White cotton dress, Red dots, Red ruffles. 1-pc. White undy, rayon socks, imitation leather slippers. Ship. wt. 2 lbs.

NOTE: ORIGINAL PRICES SHOWN
ARE NOT TODAY'S PRICES.

HORS-16-1. Illustration from 1938 Montgomery Ward catalog. *(Courtesy Mrs. Herman W. Mead)*

HORS-17. 25" Baby. Composition swivel flange head, open mouth, two teeth, bright blue and white white eyes, molded hair, cloth stuffed body. Eyes are typical of period. Note resemblance to Ideal's *"Poppa-Momma"* doll; as noted before dolls of a period bear resemblances even across company lines. Marks: **A / HORSMAN / DOLL** on head. ca. 1940. *(Author's collection)*

HORS-18. 17" *"Chubby Baby"*. All composition, glass-like eyes, lashes, open mouth, teeth, tongue, separate fingers, straight legs, mohair wig with bangs. Dressed in flocked dot organdy dress, pink spun rayon coat, matching bonnet. *1942 Catalog illustration courtesy Sears, Roebuck & Co.*

HORS-19. 12" *Bi-bye Baby*. Vinyl head and hands, painted eyes, body is an open mitt for child's hand to use doll as a puppet. Dressed in soft flannel baby garments, wrapped in pink and white baby blanket marked over and over with **"Bi-bye Baby"** print. Marks: **HORSMAN** on head. *(Author's collection)*

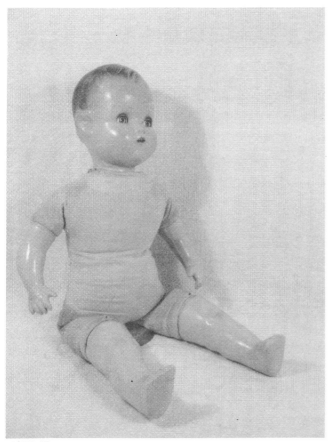

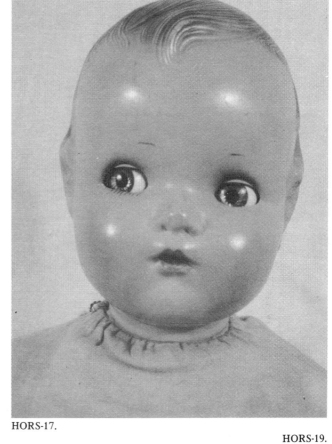

HORS-17.

HORS-17.

HORS-18.

HORS-19.

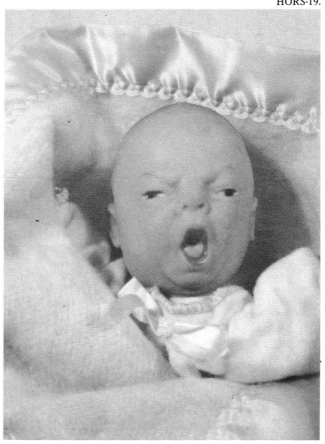

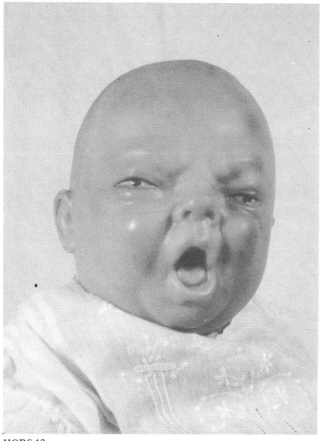

HORS-19a.

HORS-19.

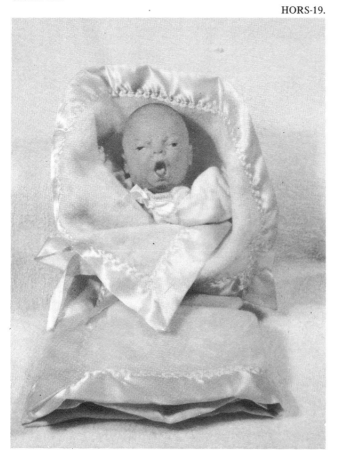

HORS-19b.

HORS-19a. 20" Squalling Baby. Stuffed soft vinyl head and limbs, cloth body, painted blue eyes. Marks: **COPR. LASTIC PLASTIC 49** on flange of head. This plastic is type that has become sticky with age. *(Author's collection)*

HORS-19b. 18" Squalling Baby. Stuffed early vinyl head, hands and legs, stuffed body and upper legs, loud cry voice, wide open-closed mouth, deeply modeled ears, molded, painted features. Unmarked. ca. 1946. *(Author's collection)*

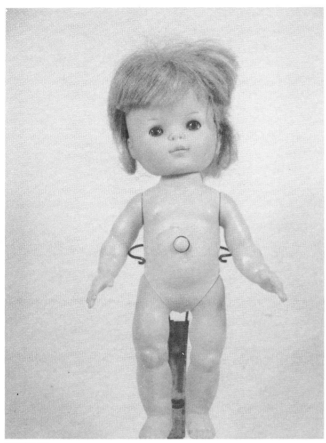

HORS-20.

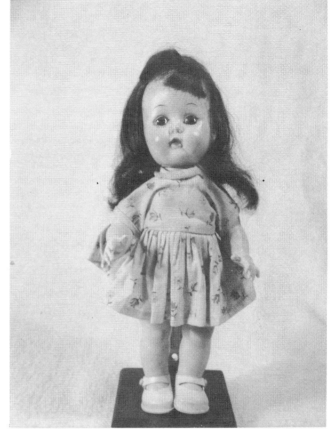

HORS-20b.

HORS-20a.

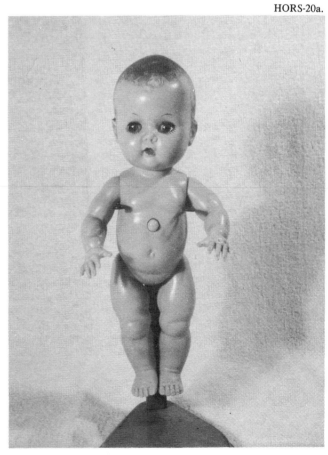

HORS-20. 10½" Yes-No Toddler. Rooted synthetic wig, soft vinyl head, rigid vinyl body and limbs, bright blue sleep eyes, solid plastic lashes, closed mouth. Marks: **66 100 / 7 / © Horsman Dolls Inc. / 1966.** Button in body goes through front to back; press front, doll nods "yes", press back, doll nods "no". *(Spalding collection)*

HORS-20a. 11" Yes-No Toddler. Early celluloid-like hard plastic, blue sleep eyes, same feature as HORS-20. Marks: **PAT. PEND.** on body. *(Author's collection)*

HORS-20b. 11" Yes-No Toddler. Same as HORS-20a, with glued-on synthetic wig, has molded hair under wig, original clothes and shoes. *(Wiseman collection)* Believed to be much earlier than HORS-20 because of older type hard plastic used in construction; compare with *"Brother Coos"*.

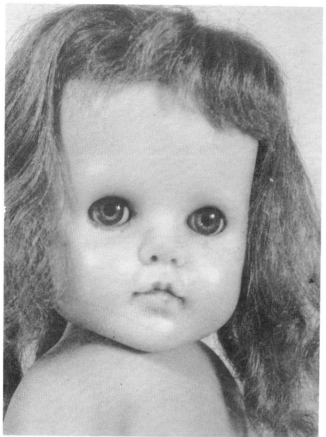

HORS-23.

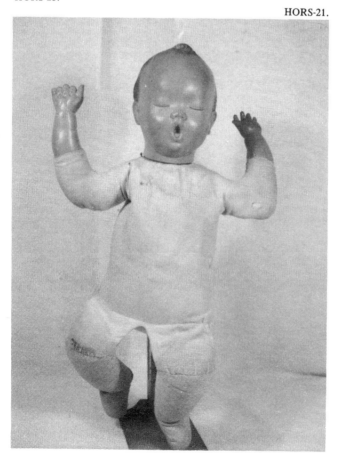

HORS-21.

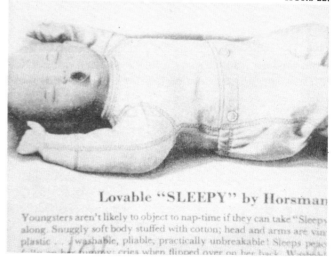

HORS-23.

Sleepy was used as an advertising doll by at least two manufacturers of children's sleepwear. The doll has been found wearing both the Hanes and the Merrichild brands of "sleepers", a suit of knit material with sewn-in feet.

HORS-22.

Lovable "SLEEPY" by Horsman

Youngsters aren't likely to object to nap-time if they can take "Sleepy" along. Snuggly soft body stuffed with cotton; head and arms are vinyl plastic . . . washable, pliable, practically unbreakable! Sleeps peacefully . . . cries when flipped over on her back. Washable.

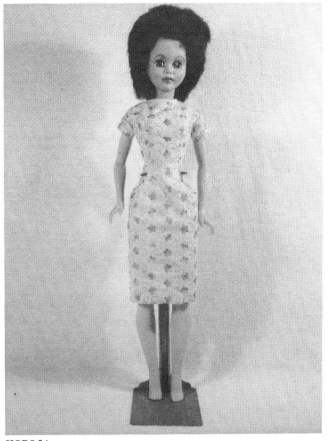

HORS-24.

HORS-24.

HORS-25.

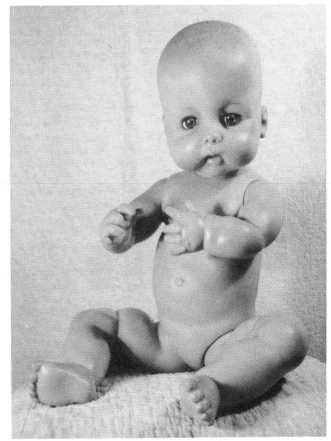

HORS-21. 21" *Sleepy.* Stuffed soft plastic head, lower arms and legs, cloth body, closed eyes, open, yawning mouth. Unmarked. 1951. *(Kirtley collection)*

HORS-22. 21" *Sleepy.* Same doll as HORS-21. *1951 Catalog illustration courtesy Sears, Roebuck & Co.*

HORS-23. 22" Child. Stuffed vinyl one piece body with squeekers in head and body, stuffed vinyl head, rooted hair, blue sleep eyes, closed mouth. Marks: **96 / HORSMAN.** ca. 1952. *(Author's collection)*

HORS-24. 25" Lady Doll. Rigid vinyl, soft vinyl head, rooted hair, blue sleep eyes, long lashes, closed mouth, high-heel feet, very small waist, beautifully modeled adult hands. Original Schiffli embroidered dress. Marks: **HORSMAN / 19© 61 / JK 25 / 4.** *(Charles Vandiver collection)* Mr. Vandiver calls this his "Jacqueline Kennedy doll".

HORS-25. 18" Baby. All vinyl, molded or rooted hair, drink and wet feature, blue sleep eyes. Also 12" size. Marks: **HORSMAN / 19© 61 / BC18.** *(Childhood doll of Rebekka Suzanne Anderton)*
    This doll was used in several baby products promotions. In 1961 Spiegel Christmas book it is billed as the "Even-Flo Baby", advertising baby nursing bottles.

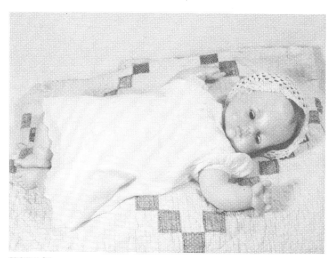

HORS-26.

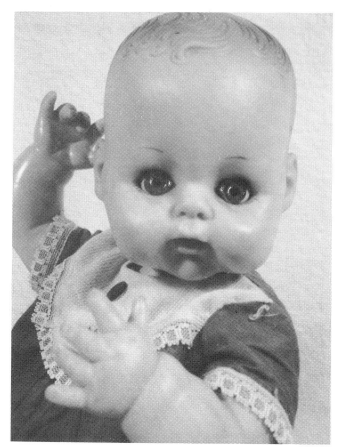

HORS-27.

HORS-28.

HORS-26. 22" Floppy Baby. Vinyl head, arms and legs, cloth body, rooted hair, closed mouth, blue sleep eyes, wears baby clothes, including antique hand crocheted baby cap. Marks: **HORSMAN DOLLS INC. / 1961 / 8 22.** *(Author's collection)*

HORS-27. 16" Baby. All vinyl, molded hair, sleep eyes, flattened back as does HORS-25. Right hand fingers fit into right ear; left hand fingers fit into mouth, separate toes and fingers with well defined nails and dimples, deeply modeled ears. Marks: © **HORSMAN DOLLS INC. / 1963 / No. BC11B.** *(Courtesy Mrs. Joseph R. Gast)*

HORS-28. 4¾" *Kewpie Kin.* All vinyl, painted features, original clothes and box. Marks: **KEWPIE KIN / A HORSMAN DOLL / MADE IN USA / Originally designed by Rose O'Neill / licensed by Cameo Doll Prod. Co. Inc. / to Horsman** on box. © / **Cameo** on body of doll. *(Kirtley collection)*

HORS-30.   HORS-31.

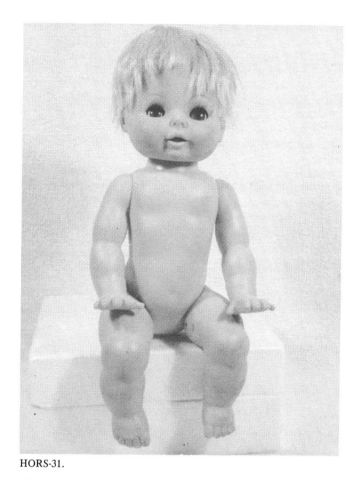

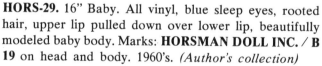
HORS-31.

HORS-29.

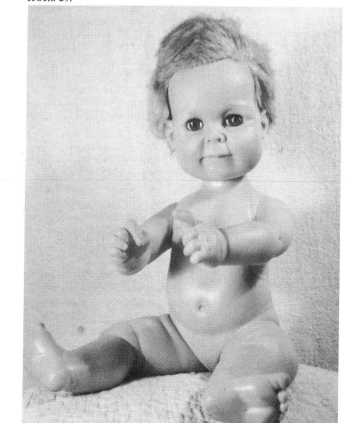

HORS-29. 16" Baby. All vinyl, blue sleep eyes, rooted hair, upper lip pulled down over lower lip, beautifully modeled baby body. Marks: **HORSMAN DOLL INC. / B 19** on head and body. 1960's. *(Author's collection)*

HORS-30. 12" *Lullabye Baby.* Rigid vinyl, soft vinyl head, rooted hair, inset stationary blue eyes, drink and wet feature, plays Brahms' Lullabye as head turns sleepily. Wooden knob key wind on back. Marks: **2580 / B144 8 / HORSMAN DOLLS INC. / 19© 67** on head. Shown in Sears 1968 Christmas book, came on suedette pillow with lace edge, wore terrycloth pajamas, price $5.99. *(Author's collection)*

HORS-31. 14" Crawling Baby. Rigid vinyl, soft vinyl head, rooted hair, head adjusts to two positions as shown by means of slot at neck, no mechanism involved. Marks: **2700 / 14EYE / 3 / HORSMAN DOLL INC. / 19© 67,** on head. **23 (or 25) / HORSMAN DOLLS INC. / PAT. PEND.** on body. *(Author's collection)*

INC./PAT. PEND. on body. *(Author's collection)*
  This doll was sold by Portland Bon Marche with gold tag reading **Mademoiselle Dolls/Mincenter** with **HORSMAN** on head and body. See MTCD for a girl doll marked **HORSMAN** and sold under the *Mademoiselle* label.

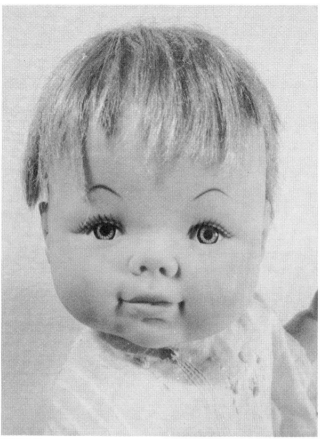

HORS-32.

HORS-32. 20" *Baby Tweaks*. Moulded vinyl head and limbs, firmly stuffed cloth body, inset stationary eyes, rooted Saran hair, wears baby dress and slip worn by author's daughter as an infant. Marks: **54/HORSMAN DOLLS INC./Copyright 1967/67191** on head. *(Author's collection)*

I

IDEAL TOY CORPORATION

The company was founded in 1902 by Morris Michtom, proprietor of a Brooklyn candy store, who created the *Teddy Bear* (which see). The Ideal Novelty & Toy Company was established to handle the production and marketing of *Teddy Bears* and other stuffed toys. In 1915 the company introduced the mechanism which closes doll eyes to simulate sleep. Ideal's *Shirley Temple* doll (which see), introduced in 1934 and modeled after the nation's most popular child actress, was marketed so successfully with movie star flavor and excitement that the doll registered more than *six million dollars* in sales.

In 1937, *Betsy Wetsy* was introduced as part of Ideal's "true life" play toy program. In 1940, Ideal developed a synthetic material that looked and felt like human skin,

with a flexibility which permitted dolls to bend to life-like poses. Much of the company's production was in defense work during World War II, when non-essential materials were used to produce toy jeeps, telephones and dolls.

Sparkle Plenty (which see), based on the *Dick Tracy* comic strip character, introduced in 1947 sold more than *seven million dollars*. "Purpose dolls", such as the *Toni* dolls with nylon hair that could be washed and set were popular in the 1950's. Ideal was the first toy company to use plastics in the manufacture of dolls (see *Plassie*). Mr. Benjamin F. Michtom, son of the founder, has been active in the company since 1924. *(Information courtesy Ideal Toy Corporation and John De Nigris Associates, Inc.)*

IDL-1.

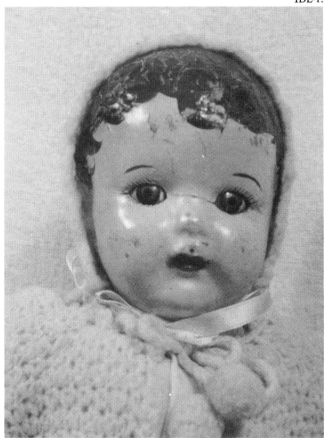

IDL-1. 18" Baby. Composition head and hands to elbow, cloth body and legs, tin sleep eyes, repainted by owner during her daughter's childhood. Purchased at Sears in 1922; box was marked AMERICAN BEAUTY. Doll is marked as in fig. IDL-1. *(Childhood doll of Mrs. Wingfield)*

fig. IDL-2

IDL-2.

IDL-3. *Tickle Toes.* A *Flossie Flirt* baby doll, came with painted hair or fur wig in five graduated sizes from 14½" to 23½". Composition head, rubber limbs, separate toes, open mouth, painted teeth, cried when leg was squeezed. Introduced in 1929, available through 1934. Little sister, 13" *Ticklette,* joined the family in 1931. 1929 Catalog illustration. *(Courtesy Sears, Roebuck & Co.)*

IDL-3.

IDL-2. *Flossie Flirt.* One of a large line of dolls beginning in 1925 which included babies and girl dolls of many sizes and combinations of construction. In 1931 the girl dolls were named *Grace, Joan, Louise* and *Clara Ann.* 1929 Catalog illustration. *(Courtesy Sears, Roebuck & Co.)*

In 1926 "marcelled" short bobs and Nile green organdy dresses were featured. *Vanity Flossie,* with comb and other accessories, joined the group in 1927 along with *Happy Flossie,* a "pacified" baby. *Happy* had rubber arms and legs, flirty sleep eyes and an open mouth. *Baby Smiles* arrived in 1928, the same year *Flossie's* dress was designed especially for her by Helen Oakes Grant (see fig. IDL-2). By 1934 *Flossie's* body was cloth and her head, arms and long, slim legs were composition. She came in three sizes: 18", 22½", and 26". Real lashes and hair in long curls, a girl doll figure, and a mama voice were all 1934 features.

IDL-5.

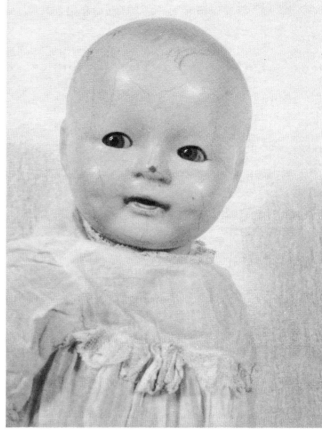

IDL-4.

IDL-4.

fig. IDL-1

IDL-4. 14" Baby. Composition head, rubber arms and legs, separate toes and fingers, cloth body, voice, green-celluloid-over tin sleep, flirty eyes, all original. Probably one of the *Flossie Flirt* line, *"Tickletoes".* 1929. Marks: Fig. IDL-1 on head. *(Childhood doll of Roberta Wells Seehorn and her sister, Mary; Author's collection)*

IDL-5. *Honeysuckle "Ducky". Honeysuckle* line began in 1932. *Ducky* had composition head, "Truflesh" rubber body and limbs, flirty eyes, two voices, legs squeeked when pressed, came in 10", 12", 14", and 16" sizes. Price: $2.49 to $4.98. 1932 Catalog illustration. *(Courtesy Sears, Roebuck & Co.)*

IDL-7.

IDL-6.

IDL-8.

IDL-6. *Honeysuckle "Snoozie".* Composition head, rubber arms, rubberized cloth body and legs, kapok filling. *Winnie, Cuddles,* and *Suck-A-Thumb* are members of the *Honeysuckle* family. 1934 Catalog illustration. *(Courtesy Sears, Roebuck & Co.)*

IDL-7. 11" *Pinocchio.* Wood, molded composition head, painted features and clothes, yellow felt hat, red suit with yellow buttons, brown shoes. Marks: **PINOCCHIO / Des.© by Walt Disney / Made by Ideal Novelty & Toy Co.** on front. **Cop. W.D.P. / Ideal Doll / Made in U.S.A.** on back. 1940. *(Courtesy Kimport Dolls)*

IDL-8. 13" *Girl.* All composition, brown sleep eyes, replacement wig and new dress. This is one of the dolls made up from *Shirley Temple* bodies on which the *13* still shows and the *Shirley Temple* is partially visible. 1930's. *(Spalding collection)*

IDL-9.

IDL-10.

IDL-11.

IDL-9. 13" *Nancy Lee*. All composition, sleep eyes, original mohair wig, original red and white checked sunsuit and dark red shoes. Marked same as IDL-8. 1930's. *(Wiseman collection)*

IDL-10. 13" *Nancy Lee*. Same as IDL-8, original pink crepe pantie-slip combination, original blonde mohair wig. 1930's. *(Author's collection)*

IDL-11.

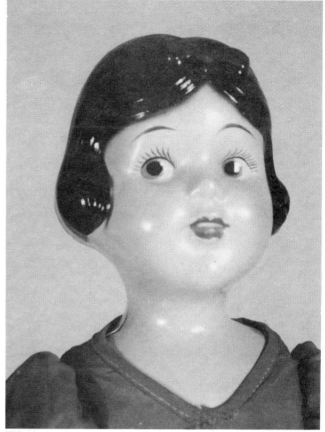

IDL-13.

IDL-12.

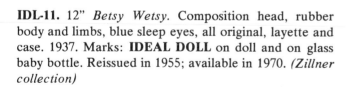

IDL-11. 12" *Betsy Wetsy.* Composition head, rubber body and limbs, blue sleep eyes, all original, layette and case. 1937. Marks: **IDEAL DOLL** on doll and on glass baby bottle. Reissued in 1955; available in 1970. *(Zillner collection)*

IDL-12. 15" *Snow White.* All cloth, had glued-on wig, original red dress with white organdy apron and **"Snow White and the Seven Dwarfs"** with illustrations printed in red. Mask face with painted features. ca. 1937. *(Author's collection)*

IDL-13. 19" *Snow White.* Composition shoulder head, arms and legs, cloth body, painted features. Original dress with red bodice and white skirt, printed with Disney design same as IDL-12. **IDEAL DOLL** on head. Note molded hair-bow. ca. 1937. *(Zillner collection)*

IDL-14.

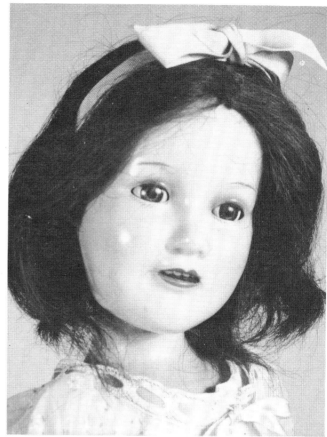

IDL-16.

IDL-15.

IDL-14. 14" Girl. All composition, blue painted eyes, remains of mohair wig over molded hair and hair-bow. Unmarked. Compare with *Snow White* above. *(Wiseman collection)*

IDL-15. 16", 19" *Poppa-Momma.* Composition head and limbs, cotton-filled body, glass-like sleep eyes, lashes, molded-painted hair. Popular two-voice feature: tilt doll forward to hear "Momma", tilt back for "Poppa". Retailed at $2.19 and $3.19. From 1940. 1941 Catalog illustration. *(Courtesy Sears, Roebuck & Co.)*

IDL-16. 21" Teen Star. All composition, brown sleep eyes, open mouth with teeth, human hair original wig. Shown with marked *Deanna Durbin* doll (see PORT-D12). IDL-16 is one of three dolls seen by the author which are marked **IDEAL DOLL / Made in U.S.A.** on head and **IDEAL DOLL / 21** (imprinted backwards) on body. These *"backwards 21"* dolls have been represented to collectors both as *Deanna Durbin* and *Judy Garland;* however, they are not like the 21" *Deanna Durbin* and in no way resemble the 18" *Judy Garland* (see PORT-G1). Pending further research we must not assign either name

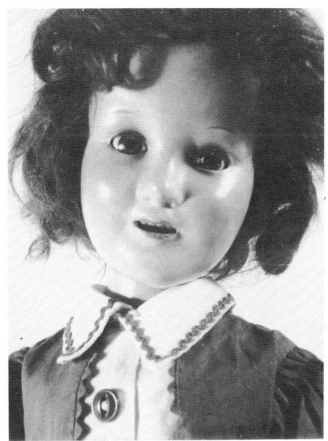

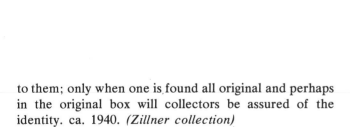

PORT-D12. IDL-16.

IDL-17.

IDL-18.

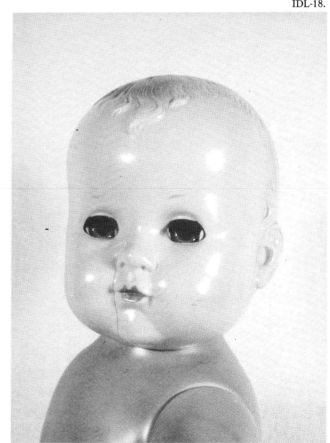

to them; only when one is found all original and perhaps in the original box will collectors be assured of the identity. ca. 1940. *(Zillner collection)*

IDL-17. Another *"backwards 21"* doll, this one with original red brown mohair wig. Old dress but not original. *(Wiseman collection)*

IDL-18. 20" *Magic Skin Baby.* Composition head, stuffed rubber body, sleep eyes, molded-painted hair, jointed shoulders and hips. Note anatomical detail of molded body. ca. 1940. *(Author's collection)*

IDL-19. 13" *Magic Skin Baby.* Same construction details as IDL-18 except hands are turned with palms toward body while those of larger doll have palms turned down, indicating it is oldest of two dolls. *(Author's collection)*

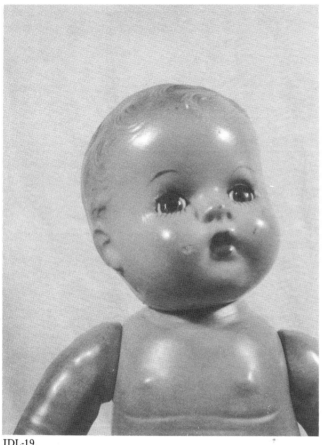

IDL-19.

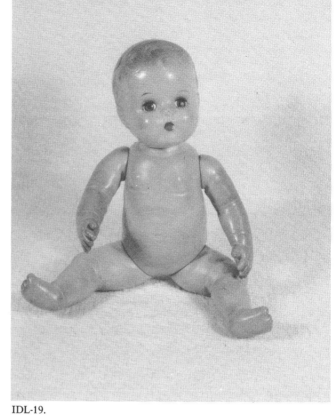

IDL-19.

IDL-18.

IDL-20.

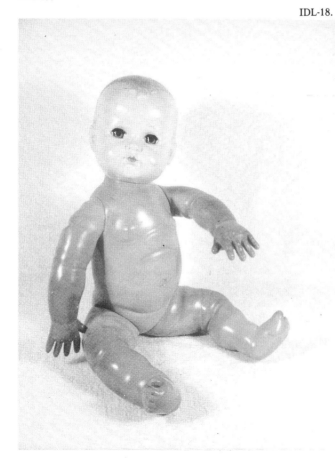

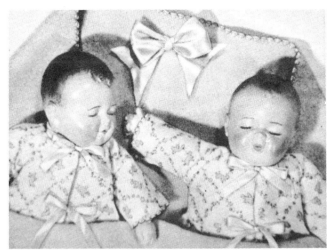

IDL-21.

IDL-23.

IDL-20. 12½" *Flexy Soldier.* Composition head, hands and feet, painted features, flexible spring construction, original World War II army uniform. Same series as *Fanny Brice* and *Mortimer Snerd,* which see. Marks: **IDEAL** on head. ca. 1942. Also available as a sailor. *(Wiseman collection)*

IDL-21. 15" *Sleepy-Time Twins.* Composition head, hands and legs, remainder stuffed cloth, painted features. One is sleeping peacefully; the other is yawning. Set sold for $9.98 in flannel wrappers and bunting. 1945 Catalog illustration. *(Courtesy Sears, Roebuck & Co.)*

IDL-22. *Magic Skin Babies.* Hard plastic heads, synthetic rubber bodies and limbs, stuffed with cotton. Arms jointed at shoulder with pin and disc; legs are flat-seam jointed at hips. Note position of hands: palm down; on later ones palm is turned toward body. 1941 Magic Skin babies were of latex rubber; 1942 began use of synthetic rubber because of World War II restrictions on use of genuine rubber. Dolls came with complete layettes right down to powder and pins. 1947 Catalog illustration. *(Courtesy Sears, Roebuck & Co.)*

IDL-22.

IDL-23. 16", 18" *Plassie.* Hard plastic head, Magic Skin (synthetic) rubber bodies and limbs, stuffed with cotton, choice of mohair wigs or molded hair. Prices $5.69 to $9.47. See also *Plassie.* 1949 Catalog illustration. *(Courtesy Sears, Roebuck & Co.)*

14-in. size $5.79   16-in. size $7.79   18-in. size $9.69   20-in. size $11.59

Every little girl dreams of owning a doll as sweet and lifelike as this one, with go-to-sleep eyes and skin that feels almost human to the touch . . . a doll that she can sponge off and powder, dress and undress. Quality workmanship throughout . . . will outlast

IDL-25.

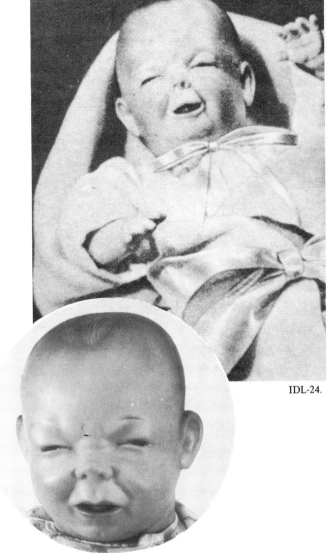

IDL-24.

IDL-26.

IDL-24. 21" *Kiss Me*. Soft vinyl head and limbs, stuffed cotton body push plunger in back to make her cry, pout or pucker up for a "kiss". Shown in 1950 and 1951 catalogs. *Illustration courtesy Sears, Roebuck & Co.*

This doll is also known as *"Blessed Event"*. Catalogs of 1950 list that name whereas the 1951 catalogs refer to the same doll as *"Kiss Me"*. Marks: **Ideal Doll/PAT. PENDING** on head. *(Author's collection)*

IDL-25. 16" *Snoozie*. Vinyl head, hands and legs, cotton stuffed body, Swiss music box played lullaby. 1949 Catalog illustration. *(Courtesy Sears, Roebuck & Co.)*

IDL-26. *Tickletoes*, 15", 19", 23". Hard plastic head, latex arms and legs stuffed with cotton, mohair wig, open mouth with teeth and tongue except 15" size, glassene sleep eyes, lashes. 1950 Catalog illustration. *(Courtesy Sears, Roebuck & Co.)*

IDL-27.

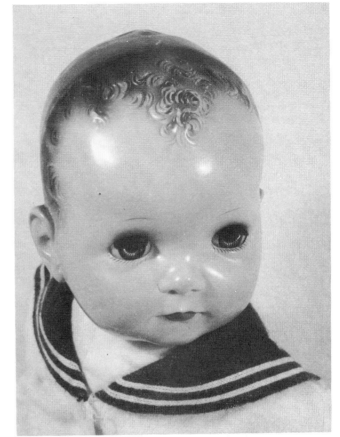

IDL-28.

IDL-28.

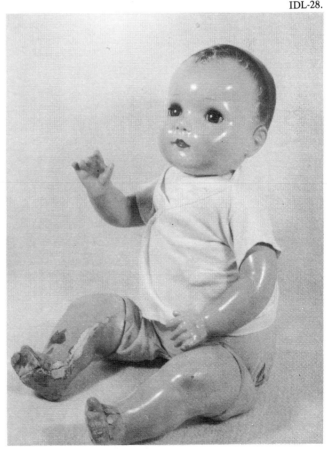

IDL-27. 17" *Sara Lee.* Vinyl head and limbs, stuffed cotton body, real-life features, sleep eyes, cries when tilted, organdy dress and bonnet. Doll designed by Sarah Lee Creech and modeled by Sheila Burlingame, sculptress. 1950. 1951 Catalog illustration. *(Courtesy Sears, Roebuck & Co.)*

IDL-28. 30" *Brother Coos.* Beautifully finished hard plastic head, stuffed cotton body, composition arms and bent legs, blue sleep eyes. Marks: **IDEAL DOLL / MADE IN U.S.A.** on head. 1948. *(Author's collection)*

One of the *Coos* babies was modeled by Bernard Lipfert, the renowned doll designer, after his small granddaughter.

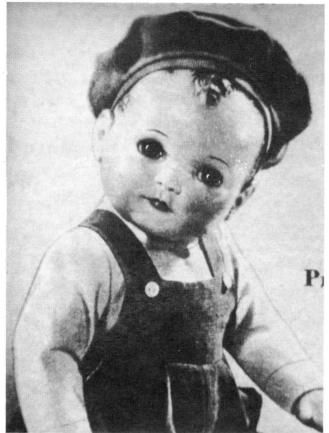

IDL-29.

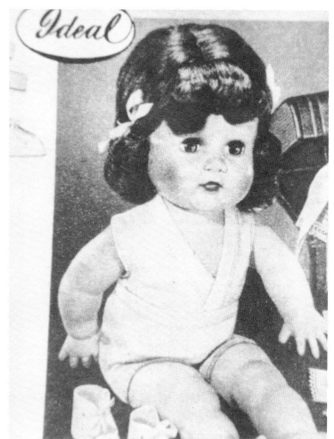

IDL-31.

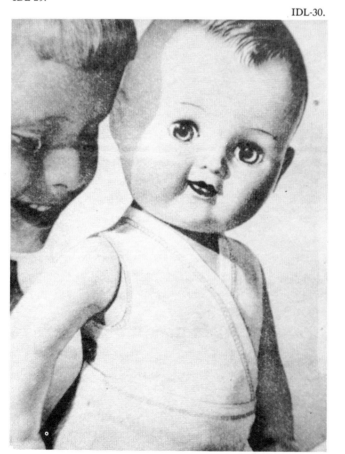

IDL-30.

IDL-29. 30" *Brother Coos.* Same as IDL-28, catalog listing reads: "makes sounds like a baby when you squeeze him". 1951 Version wore cotton gabardine trousers and matching tam, sporty jacket, open-collared knit shirt, rayon socks and real leather baby shoes. 1950 Edition shown was dressed in corduroy bib crawlers and matching tam, knit shirt, socks and baby shoes. *Catalog information courtesy Sears, Roebuck & Co.*

IDL-30. *Baby Coos,* 14", 18", 22", 27". Hard plastic head, Magic Skin body and limbs stuffed with cotton and foam rubber, lucite sleep eyes, lashes. The *"Coos"* family is shown in catalogs 1948 through 1952; babies of several sizes as listed plus a 30" baby sold without layette, which wore its owner's outgrown baby clothes. *Catalog information courtesy Sears, Roebuck & Co.*

IDL-31 *Baby Coos.* Magic rubber skin stuffed with foam rubber, hard plastic head, glued-on mohair wig, sleep eyes. 1950 Catalog illustration. *(Courtesy Sears, Roebuck & Co.)*

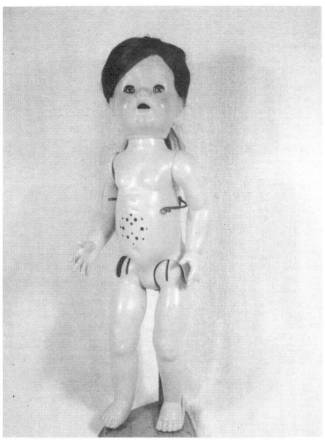

IDL-34.

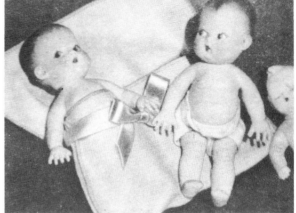

IDL-32.

IDL-33.

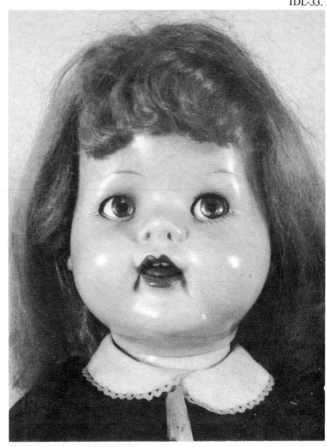

IDL-32. 9¼" *Pete and Repete.* Twin magic skin rubber baby dolls; cry when squeezed. From 1950. 1951 Catalog illustration. *(Courtesy Sears, Roebuck & Co.)*

IDL-33. 23" *Saucy Walker.* All hard plastic, flirty sleep eyes, original synthetic wig. Marks: **IDEAL DOLL** on head. Saucy Walker shown in 1952 Sears catalog is endorsed by movie actress, Dorothy Lamour. 22" size was $14.89, 16" size was $9.29. *(Spalding collection)*

IDL-34. 19" *Saucy Walker.* Hard plastic, sleep eyes, new wig. This doll went through 1951 flood which inundated large areas of Kansas City. She lost only her wig, teeth and tongue and gained a somewhat rusty outlook plus a permanent rattle of dried mud. Unmarked. *(Author's collection)*

IDL-36.

IDL-37.

IDL-35.

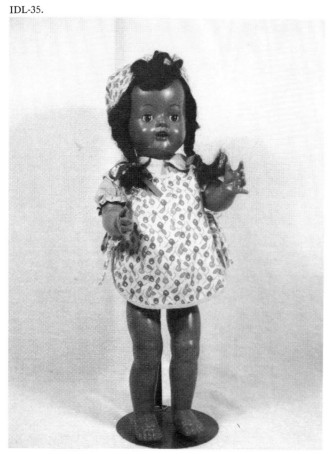

IDL-35. 19" Colored *Saucy Walker*. Hard plastic, brown sleep eyes, original black wig. *(Kirtley collection)*

IDL-36. *Baby Big Eyes.* 23", vinyl head and limbs, vinyl-coated, cotton-stuffed body, cry voice, rooted Saran hair, retail $9.79. From 1954. 1955 Catalog illustration. *(Courtesy Sears, Roebuck & Co.)*

IDL-37. 24" *Posie.* Hard plastic, rolling sleep eyes, long Saran curls, glued-on wig, jointed knees. 1954 Catalog illustration. *(Courtesy Sears, Roebuck & Co.)*

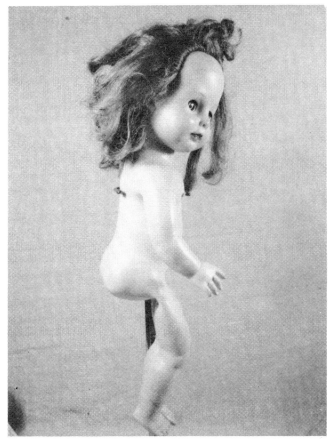

IDL-39.

IDL-39

IDL-38.

IDL-38. 24" *Magic Lips.* Vinyl head and limbs, stuffed vinyl-coated body, rooted Saran hair. Press her back, she closes her lips, release, mouth opens with cooing sound. Flocked organdy dress, rayon slip, panties, socks, vinyl shoes, toothbrush for her three teeth. 1955 Catalog illustration. *(Courtesy Sears, Roebuck & Co.)*

IDL-39. 17" Girl. Stuffed vinyl head and one-piece body and limbs, rooted Saran hair, blue sleep, flirty eyes, original dress. Marks: **IDEAL DOLL / VP-17-Z** on head and **IDEAL DOLL / P17 / 0** on shoulder. 1957. *(Childhood doll of Linda Louise Brink)*

IDL-40.

IDL-41.

IDL-42.

Upswept hairdo

IDL-40. *Betsy Wetsy.* All vinyl, rooted Saran hair or molded hair. Three sizes: 12", 13½", and 16". 1959 Catalog illustration. *(Courtesy Sears, Roebuck & Co.)*

IDL-41. 19", 21", 24" *Cream Puff.* All vinyl, closed mouth, sleep eyes, lashes, coo voice, rooted Saran hair. Sold for $7.99 to $10.97. 1959 Catalog illustration. *(Courtesy Sears, Roebuck & Co.)*

IDL-42. *Miss Ideal,* 25", 30". Molded plastic, shaped like grammar school girl, rooted hair, sleep eyes, thick lashes, jointed waist, wrists, ankles. Came with beauty kit: comb, curlers, wave lotion. 1961 Catalog illustration. *(Courtesy Sears, Roebuck & Co.)* 1962 listing, Miss Ideal "Terry Twist". Retail, $15.99 to $19.99.

Here's Tammy

teenag
vot
mo
like

succee

Meet my fam
on next pag

IDL-43.

IDL-44.

IDL-45.

IDL-43. 12" *Tammy*. All vinyl, rooted hair, painted features. 1963 Catalog illustration. *(Courtesy Sears, Roebuck & Co.)*

IDL-44. *Tammy's* Family: 13" *Dad*, 12" *Mom*. All vinyl, painted features, *Dad* has molded hair, *Mom* has rooted hair. 1963 Catalog illustration. *(Courtesy Sears, Roebuck & Co.)*

IDL-45. *Tammy's* Brother, 13" *Ted*. All vinyl, painted features, molded hair. 1963 Catalog illustration. *(Courtesy Sears, Roebuck & Co.)*

IDL-47.

IDL-46.

IDL-48.

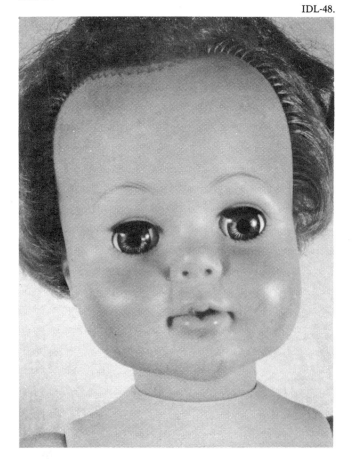

IDL-46. *Tammy's* Sister, 9" *Pepper.* All vinyl, painted features, molded hair. Extensive wardrobe available for entire family. 1963 Catalog illustration. *(Courtesy Sears, Roebuck & Co.)*

IDL-47. *Tammy's* Little Brother, 8" *Pete* and His Pony. All vinyl, painted features, molded hair. Pony measures 9" tall, 10" long. 1964 addition to the family. *Catalog illustration courtesy Sears, Roebuck & Co.*

IDL-48. 22" *Kissy.* Soft vinyl head, hard vinyl body, rooted Saran hair, sleep eyes, lashes, jointed wrists, soft vinyl hands. "Go get Kissy if you want a little kiss, do her arms like this, she'll give a little kiss," was the ditty heard in television commercials advertising this doll. Marks: ©️ **IDEAL CORP. / K-21-L** on head. **IDEAL TOY COR-P. / K-22 / Pat. Pend.** on body. 1962. *(Author's collection)*

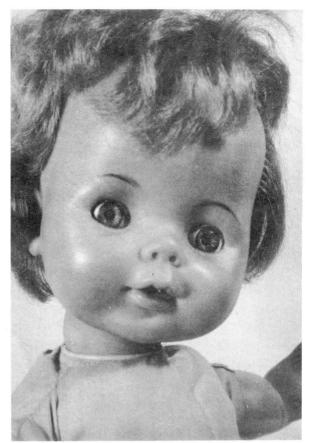

IDL-49.

IDL-48.

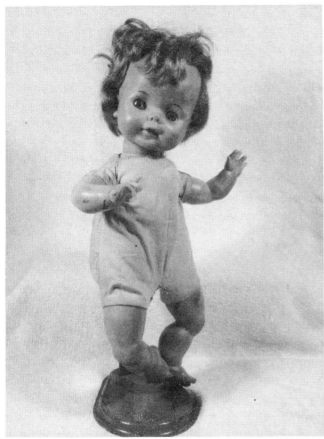

IDL-49.

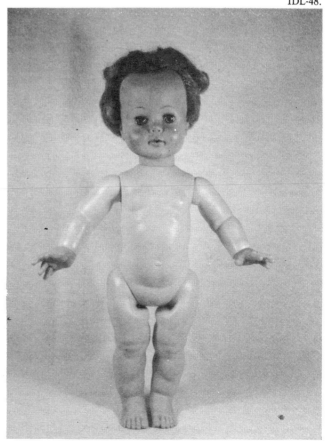

IDL-49. 16" *Kissy Baby.* Vinyl head and limbs, stuffed cloth body, rooted hair, sleep eyes. Also available: 16" *Tiny Kissy,* 17" *Cuddly Kissy,* 11½" *Kissin' Cousins,* a boy and girl, and 22" *Deluxe Kissy.* Doll's mouth "puckers" and mechanism makes "kissing" sound when arms are brought together in front of body. 1962. *(Author's collection)*

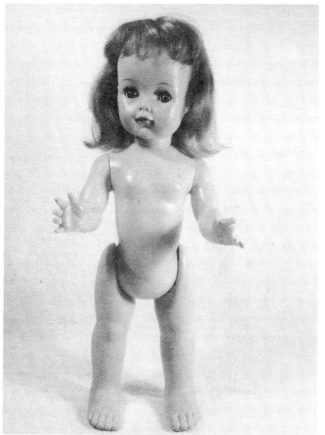

IDL-50-1.

IDL-50-1.

IDL-50.

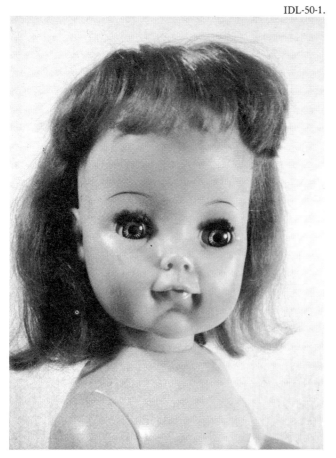

IDL-50. *Thumbelina,* 14", 17", 20". Vinyl head and limbs, foam-filled cloth bodies, rooted Saran hair. 20" Cries and wiggles. 1963 Catalog illustration. *(Courtesy Sears, Roebuck & Co.)*

IDL-50-1. 18" *Goody Two-Shoes.* Plastic and vinyl, rooted hair, sleep eyes, long feathery lashes, closed mouth. Off-on switch on back, vibrator mechanism in feet for walk action, plate with three screws allows access to mechanism, operates on two "D" batteries. Marks: © **1965 / IDEAL TOY CORP / TW 18-4-L-H4** on head. *(Author's collection)*

IDL-51.

IDL-52.

IDL-52a

IDL-53.

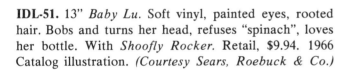

IDL-51. 13" *Baby Lu.* Soft vinyl, painted eyes, rooted hair. Bobs and turns her head, refuses "spinach", loves her bottle. With *Shoofly Rocker.* Retail, $9.94. 1966 Catalog illustration. *(Courtesy Sears, Roebuck & Co.)*

IDL-52. 18" *Giggles.* Vinyl head, rooted hair, sleep eyes, speaker mechanism "giggles" with movement of arms. Marks: © **1966 / IDEAL TOY CORP. / GG-18-H-77** on head. © **1967 / IDEAL TOY CORP. / GG-18** on right hip. *(Author's collection)*

IDL-52a. 16" *Baby Giggles.* Soft vinyl head and limbs, rooted hair, sleep eyes, open-closed mouth, rigid plastic body. Doll "giggles" when arm is moved. Marks: **(c) 1968/IDEALTOYCORP/BG-16** on right hip; **(c) 1968/IDEAL TOY CORP./BG-16-H-11** on head. Original clothes are of soft knitted fabric in two shades of pink. *(Rebekka Anderton collection)*

IDL-53. 22" *Little Lost Baby.* Vinyl three-face head rotates by means of knob at back from happy to sad to sleep, with cry voice for sad face and cooing, gurgling voice for happy face. Stuffed cloth body, non-removeable snow suit of bright pink with "fur" trim, vinyl hands. 1968 Catalog illustration. *(Courtesy Sears, Roebuck & Co.)*

IDL-54.

IDL-56.

IDL-55.

IDL-54. 9" *Betsy Wetsy*. Vinyl and polyethylene, rooted hair, sleep eyes, with folding car bed. Retail, $4.99. 1970 Catalog illustration. *(Courtesy Sears, Roebuck & Co.)*

IDL-55. 18" *Beautiful Crissy*. All vinyl, dark brown, almost pupil-less eyes, open closed mouth, long rooted synthetic auburn wig with "grow" feature: hair winds into head by turning knob on doll's back. Wears orange lace "mod" dress and orange vinyl strap shoes. 1970 Edition wears aqua outfit; many wardrobe items available. 1969. Marks: © **1969 / IDEAL TOY CORP. / 4-17-4129** on head. **1969 / IDEAL TOY CORP. / GH-18 / U.S.PAT. 3-162-976** on right hip. Also Black *Beautiful Crissy*. *(Rebekka Anderton collection)*

IDL-56. 18" *Tressy*. All vinyl, large blue sleep eyes, long, dark "grow" hair, body is same as Crissy, closed mouth, skin tone slightly darker than Crissy. Tressy is 1970 Sears' exclusive. Catalog illustration. *(Courtesy Sears, Roebuck & Co.)*

IDL-57. 15" *Velvet*. *Crissy's* younger cousin with blonde "grow" hair and violet sleep eyes, dressed in violet dress, shoes and hairbow. *(Photograph courtesy Ideal Toy Corp.)*

IDL-57.

© Ideal Toy Corp.

IT-1.

IT-2.

ITALIAN MODERNS

IT-1. 16" *Bettina by Sebino*. Good quality vinyl, rooted high quality synthetic wig, closed mouth, blue sleep eyes, all original blue crepe-black satin costume. 1960's. *(Kirtley collection)*

IT-2. 16" *Ratti*. Vinyl and plastic, mohair wig, blue sleep eyes, original costume. Marks: © / **Made in Italy.** *(Wiseman collection)*

IT-3.   IT-5.

IT-4.

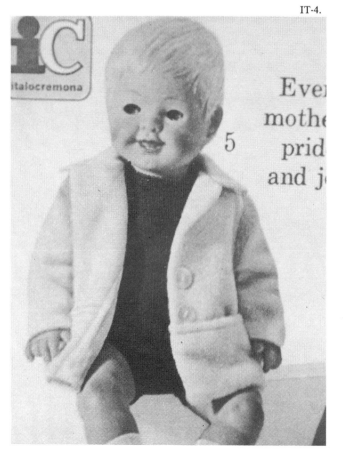

IT-3. 22" *Furga Baby.* Vinyl head, arms, legs, polyurethane-foam filled body, rooted platinum or dark brown hair. Wears knit leggings, sweater and bonnet. *1970 catalog illustration courtesy Sears, Roebuck & Co.*

IT-4. 17" *Bonomi Boy.* Vinyl, fully jointed, rooted pale blonde hair. By italiocremona (Bonomi). *1964 Catalog illustration courtesy Sears, Roebuck & Co.* Shown in 1970 Sears Christmas catalog.

IT-5. 15" *Bonomi Girl.* Vinyl with rooted platinum or chestnut bouffant hair-do. Many chic outfits made in Italy for Bonomi dolls. *1963 Catalog illustration courtesy Sears, Roebuck & Co.*

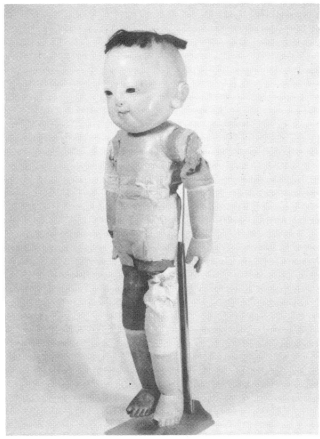

JAPA-1.

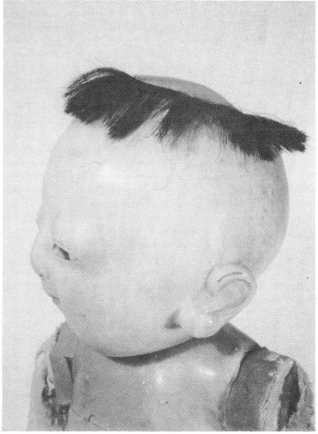

JAPA-1.

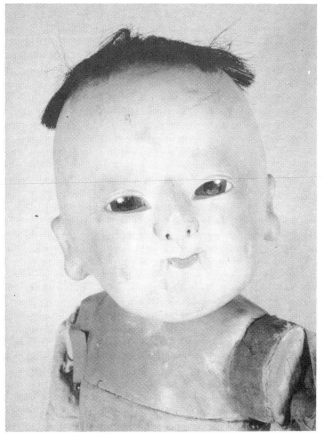

JAPA-1.

J

JAPANESE DOLLS

Several categories of Japanese dolls are shown. First, the traditional dolls; handmade and fascinating, they exhibit the Japanese skill with simple materials. The Japanese bisques were often copied from German models and bisque quality varied widely. Many souvenier dolls produced by Japanese factories represent native figures from many lands.

Although the traditional dolls pre-date the twentieth century, they are shown as examples of an early type directly related to some modern Japanese dolls. The Thomas Nast cartoon (JAPA-3-1), first published ca. 1863, has been in almost continuous publication since and provides an interesting inventory of the toys of that period.

———————

JAPA-1. 23" Baby. Traditional construction; papier mache heads, shoulder plates, hips, lower legs and feet, jointed wrists and ankles. Pasted cloth middle body, cloth upper arms and legs. These dolls flop beautifully, like real baby. Heads are on unique arrangement that causes head to assume natural poses. *(Baume collection)*

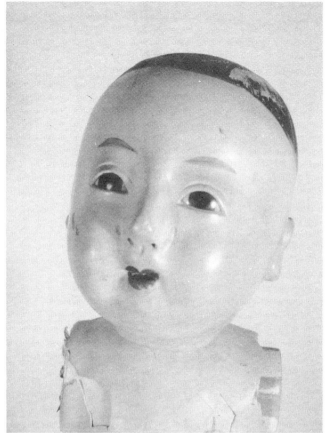

JAPA-2.

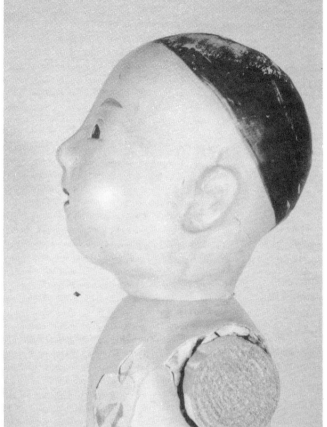

JAPA-2.

JAPA-3.

fig. JAPA-5

fig. JAPA-4

JAPA-2. 23" Baby. Same description as JAPA-1. *(Baume collection)*

JAPA-3. 9" Baby. Similar in construction to JAPA-1 and -2. *(Courtesy Kimport Dolls)*

JAPA-3-1. Reproduction of a Thomas Nast cartoon of 1860's showing Saint Nicholas with one of the traditional Japanese baby dolls tucked under his arm.

JAPA-4. 12" Circumference Bisque Head. Bisque socket head 5" tall, eyes and teeth are paper placed for the photo, open crown. Marks: See fig. JAPA-4. *(Baume collection)*

JAPA-5. 12" Baby. Bisque socket head, blue stationary eyes, open mouth, four teeth, new wig, bent-leg composition body, jointed shoulders and hips. Marks: See fig. JAPA-5. Marks stand for Morimura Brothers. 1910's, 1920's. *(Courtesy Phyllis Odell)*

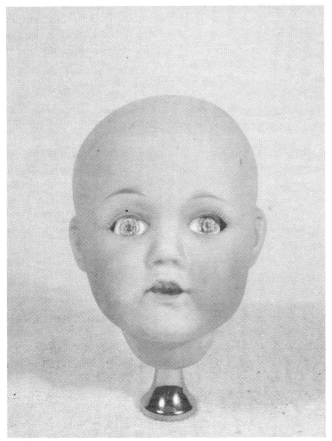

JAPA-4.

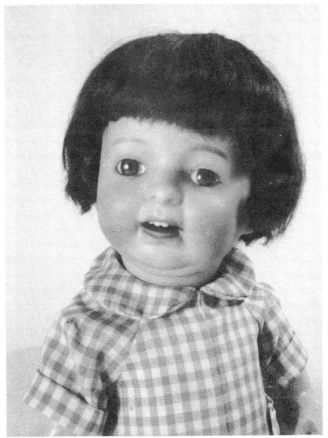

JAPA-5.

JAPA-5.

JAPA-3-1.

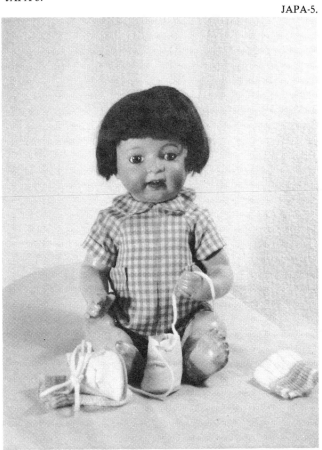

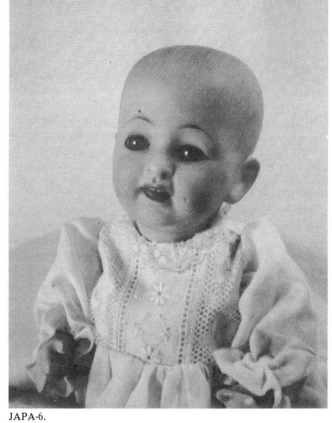

JAPA-6.

JAPA-6.

JAPA-7.

JAPA-7.

JAPA-8.

JAPA-9.

JAPA-10.

JAPA-6. 10" Baby. Bisque socket head, blue glass stationary eyes, brush stroke pale brown hair, painted lashes, dimples, open closed mouth, two painted, molded teeth. Composition, bent-leg baby body. Marks: **Nippon / B4.** *(Courtesy Phyllis Odell)*

JAPA-7. 9½" Lady with Parasol. A traditional doll, this is "Maiko", the name used for the young girl who takes minor rolls in Geisha dances. About 1952, by the Yoshitoku Company. *(Battagler collection)*

JAPA-8. 5½" Traditional Doll. Open mouth, stationary inset glass eyes. 1945. *(Battagler collection)*

JAPA-9. Japanese Wooden Dolls. Nodder heads, second from left is dressed in uniform of student, all clothes are painted on. Sizes are from 2¾" to 4¼". From Japan about 1952. *(Battagler collection)*

JAPA-10. 7½" All Bisque. Hawaiian souvenier doll, grass skirt, blue sleep eyes, marked **JAPAN** bottom of one foot. From Hawaii about 1945. *(Battagler collection)*

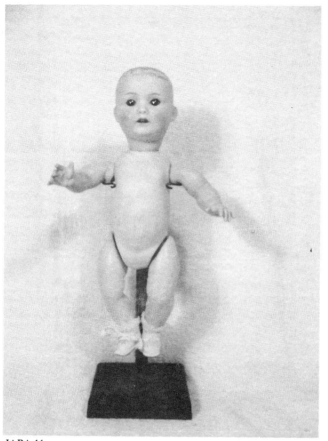

JAPA-11.

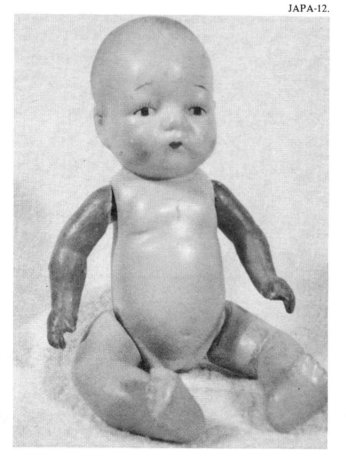

JAPA-12.

JAPA-11.

fig. JAPA-13

JAPA-11. 11" Baby. Bisque socket head, papier mache body, stationary brown glass eyes, open mouth, two teeth. Marks: **ISI** (in an oval) / **Nippon.** *(Author's collection)*

JAPA-12. 7½" Baby. All bisque, painted, with sprayed hair, heart-shape mouth, blue eyes. Marks: **MADE IN JAPAN** (around a circle with a symbol in it resembling a backward E.) *(Rebekka Anderton collection)*

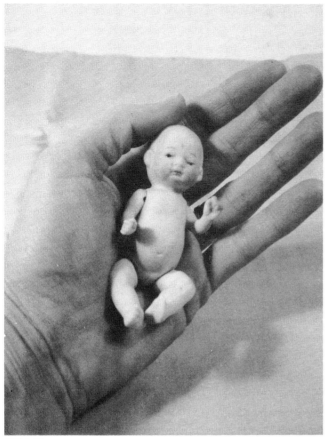

JAPA-13.

JAPA-14.

JOL-1.

JAPA-13. 4" Baby. All bisque, delicately tinted pink, blue painted eyes, well modeled hands. Marks: see fig. JAPA-13. *(Author's collection)*

JAPA-14. 7" Girl. Painted all-bisque, molded hair, closed mouth, jointed at shoulders, open crown covered with orange colored fabric to match painted hair, glass sleep eyes mounted on waxed rocker as in larger bisque-head dolls. Original pink dress and hairbow. Marks: **JAPAN** stamped in black on bottom of left foot. 1920's. *(Author's collection)*

JOL-1. 14" Imp. Plastic body, vinyl head, rooted tuft of hair, sleep eyes. Marks: **Jolly Toy Inc** / © **1960.** *(Author's collection)*

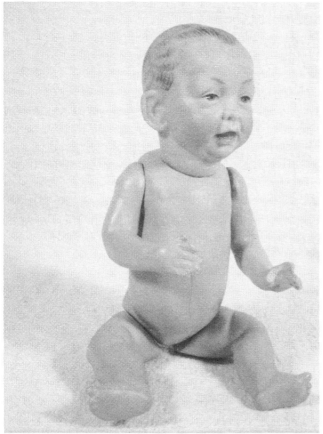

KR-1.

KR-1.

KR-1.

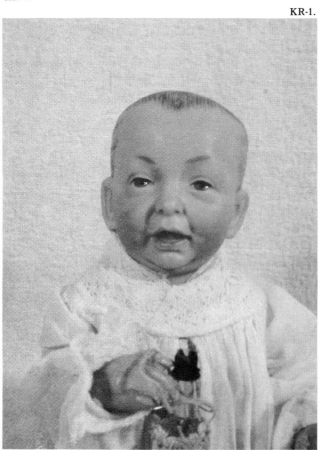

KR-1.

K

KAMMER & REINHARDT

This firm began production in the 1880's and specialized in character faces. Their *"Baby"* dates about 1910 and is one of a series of life-like children. Many celluloid heads are found with the **"K (STAR) R"** mark along with the turtle (or tortoise) mark of the Rheinische Gummi & Celluloid Fabrik Co. Dolls are also found with the **S & H** mark of Simon & Halbig, who made many of the bisque heads, combined with the **K (STAR) R.**

_____

KR-1. 10" Baby. Bisque socket head, brown painted eyes, open closed mouth, brush mark hair with bald spot at crown, composition baby body. Marks: **28 / K(Star)R / 100.** *(Author's collection)*

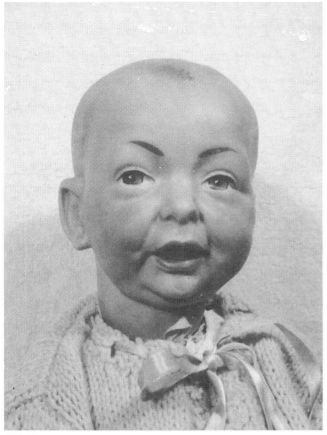

KR-2.

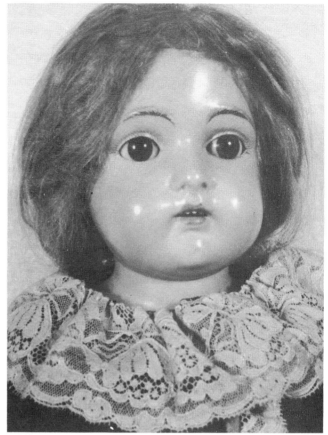

KR-3.

KR-4L.   KR-4R.

KR-2. 21" *Baby.* Bisque socket head, blue painted eyes, open closed mouth, painted brows and hair, composition baby body. Marks: **K(Star)R / 100 / 50.** The No. 100 *"Baby"* is often referred to as the *Kaizer Baby,* but it was shown in old advertiseements simply as *"Baby"*. *(Battagler collection)*

KR-3. 24" Celluloid Head. Kid body, leather feet with pointed, squared off toes, small, lady waist, pink bisque arms and hands glued into kid upper arms, open mouth, four teeth, molded brows, original blonde mohair wig. Marks: **K(Star)R / 255 / (Turtle Mark).** *(Battagler collection)*

KR-4. 17" Lady, 18" Man. Left, molded hair, painted blue eyes, open mouth, four teeth, kid body, celluloid lower arms and hands. Marks: **Turtle mark over No. 1** and some illegible numerals. Right, mohair wig, stationary brown glass eyes, kid body. Marks: **K(Star)R / 255 / (Turtle Mark).** *(Battagler collection)*

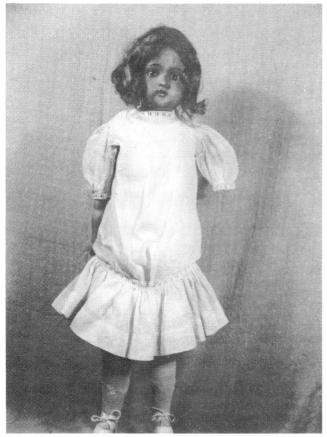

KR-6.

KR-5.

KR-6.

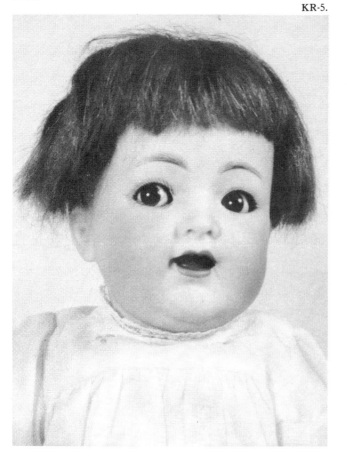

KR-5. 15" Baby. Bisque socket head, brown sleepy, flirty eyes, molded, painted brows. open mouth, two upper teeth, felt tongue, bent limb baby body, human hair wig. Marks: **K(Star)R / SIMON HALBIG / 126.** *(Battagler collection)*

KR-6. 28½" Celluloid Head. Shoulder head, blue sleep eyes, open mouth, teeth are missing, white bisque arms, pink cloth body, narrow waist, original blonde mohair wig. Doll was stored in an attic for last twenty years, head broke in many pieces when examined. With patience and care it was glued together in order to have a model for the original clothes which are still in good condition. One solid bisque arm was missing; knee joints have strips of hemmed cloth covering them. Marks: **K(Star)R / 255 /** (large heart painted in white with arrow piercing it) **/ 12** (incised). On body under shoulderhead is paper label with numerals **54.** *(Author's collection)*

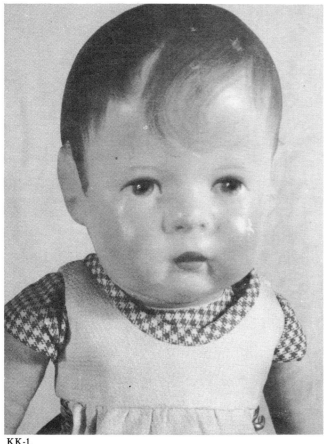

KK-1.

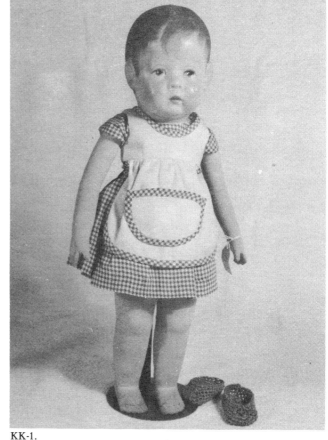

KK-1.

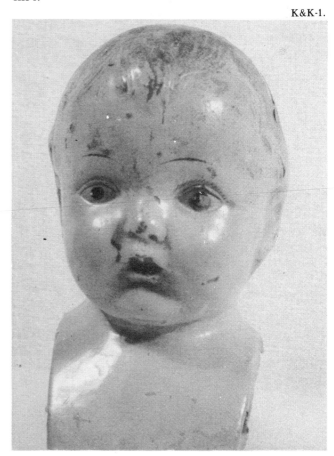

K&K-1.

K AND K

K&K-1. 7½" Composition Head. Blue painted eyes, open closed mouth, molded hair, evidence of wig. Marks: **K & K g.** Body is cloth stuffed with excelsior, arms and legs are composition. Purchased in 1924. *(Childhood doll of Margaret Anderton Lohrey)* Sears 1924 catalog shows K and K Mama Doll, 16½", white organdy and lace dress, sleep eyes, mohair wig, $3.89.

KATHE KRUSE PUPPEN

(See also Rag Dolls)

KK-1. 18" *Kathe Kruse Child* All fabric construction; head is reinforced, painted, molded. Doll is jointed hips and shoulders. Marks: **Made in Germany** on right foot, **94215** on left foot. All original. *(Zillner collection)*

KK-2.

KK-3.

KK-2.

KK-2. 15" *Kathe Kruse Boy.* All cloth construction, brown painted eyes, blond mohair wig, all original costume. Marks: **679** in red ink, **20** in black ink on right foot; a **triangular mark** on left foot. *(Wingfield collection)*

KK-3. 14", 18" *Jettchen.* Rooted or braided wig, from a 1969 Catalog illustration. Kathe Kruse.

KK-4.

KK-4. 14", 18" *Mimerle* and *Dorette*. Beautifully modeled and dressed, from a 1969 Catalog illustration. Kathe Kruse.

KK-5.

KK-5. 14", 18" *Helene* and *Riekchen*. Solemn little faces, pigtail braids. These are Hannah Kruse creations. From 1969 Kathe Kruse catalog.

KK-6.

KK-6. 10" *Kay* and *Jim*. Also Hannah Kruse creations in the Kathe Kruse tradition. From 1969 Kathe Kruse catalog.

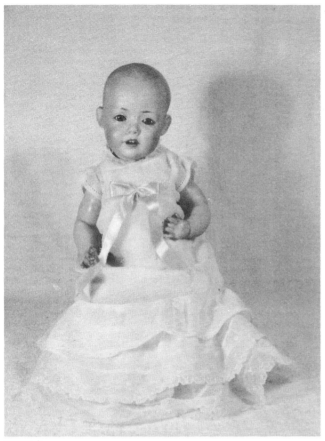

KEST-2.

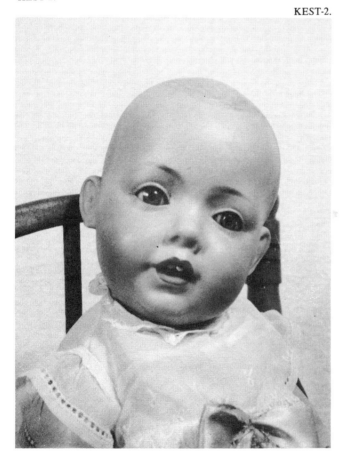

KEST-1.

KEST-2.

J. D. KESTNER DOLLS

The Kestner bisques are generally of a very fine grade material and the workmanship is excellent. This is another early company which continued production into this century. Many of the dolls were unmarked; some have been authenticated; others must be listed as *Kestner type*.

KEST-1. 14" Baby. Bisque socket head, bent limb papier mache body, blue stationary eyes, painted lashes, open mouth, five teeth. Marks: **made in / Germany / 10 / 16 / J.D.K. / 211.** *(Battagler collection)*

KEST-2. 16" Baby. Bisque socket head, bent limb baby body, blue sleep eyes, open mouth, two teeth, brush stroke hair. Marks: **J.D.K. / Gesgesch N1070 / Made in 12 Germany.** *(Battagler collection)*

KEST-4.

KEST-3a, -3b, -3d, 3-c.

KEST-3b.

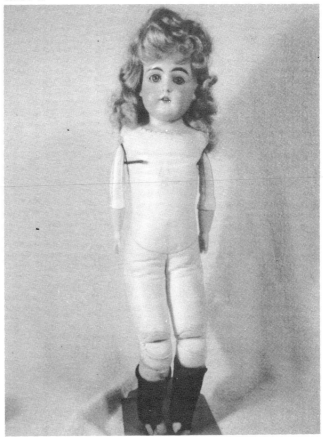

KEST-4.

KEST-3a. 4½" Girl. All bisque, brown sleep eyes, closed mouth, original mohair wig, molded, painted pink boots and sox with blue garters. Marks: **140 / 4 / 0** on head.

KEST-3b. 6" Girl. All bisque, brown sleep eyes, open mouth, four teeth, original blonde mohair wig, original clothes, molded, painted black shoes and pink sox. Marks: **150 / 11** on head. Original box label for **Biscuit Babies with Kestner crown mark** shown.

KEST-3c. 6" Soldier Boy. Bisque head, papier mache body, unpainted, stationary black eyes, open mouth, four teeth, dimples, original mohair wig, molded, painted shoes and sox. Wears original World War I army uniform, new hat. Marks: **I 17 / 0 11** on head.

KEST-3d. 2½" Monkey. Glass eyes, pink bow, very old. *All these dolls from Battagler collection.*

KEST-4. 18" Bisque Shoulder Head. Open mouth, four teeth, blue threaded sleep eyes, kid body, cloth feet, original brown knit stockings, new wig. Marks: **Made in Germany.** Probably Kestner; definitely Kestner **type.** *(Author's collection)*

KEST-5.

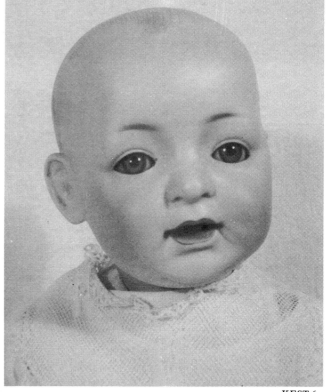

KEST-6.

KEST-7.

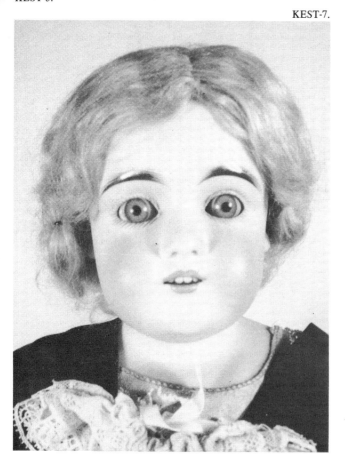

KEST-5. 15" Bisque with Fur Brows. Bisque shoulder head, blue sleep eyes, original mohair wig, open mouth, four upper teeth, kid body and feet, bisque hands. The Coleman Encyclopedia states these fur eyebrows were usually produced by Kestner; therefore, this doll earns a place in the "probably Kestner" category. Marks: **195 DEP 5** on top rim of head. **Made in Germany** on lower edge of shoulder. *(Battagler collection)*

KEST-6. 17" Baby. Bisque socket head, papier mache bent limb baby, blue sleep eyes, brush stroke hair. Marks: **J.D.K. / Made in 14 Germany.** *(Battagler collection)*

KEST-7. 21" Bisque Shoulder Head. Blue sleep eyes, painted lashes, painted, molded brows, open mouth, four teeth, kid body, ball-jointed arms, leather feet. Marks: **DEP / 154 / 9.** Definitely Kestner type. *(Battagler collection)*

KEST-8. 13" Baby. Bisque socket head, brown sleep eyes, open mouth, two teeth, molded tongue, papier mache and composition bent leg baby body, red lines between fingers and around nails, original mohair wig. Marks: **Made / in / Germany / 152 / 4.** *(Author's collection)*

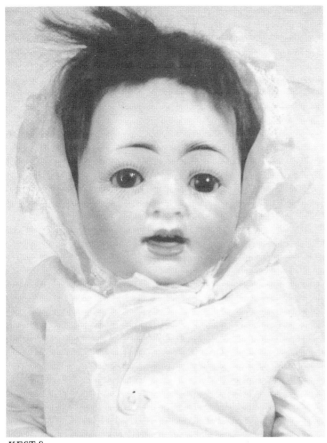

KEST-8.

fig. KEW-1

fig. KEW-2

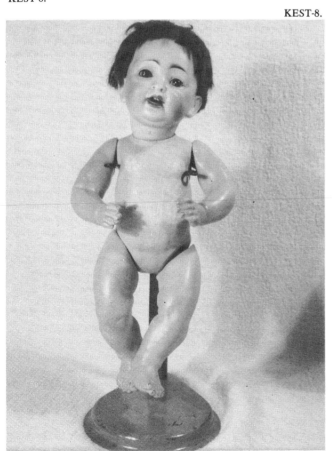

KEST-8.

KEWPIES©

A sampling of Sears catalog listings over the years gives a good cross section of the development of the *Kewpies* as dolls. In the 1919 catalog, 8½" *Kewpies* of composition with moveable arms are listed. They were sold "bare" for 98c, in apron and bonnet for $1.15, in flowered dress and bonnet for $1.29, or in knitted sweater and cap for $1.33. A *Kewpie* dressed in a costume of *point'd'esprit* net with large silk ribbon sash was $1.98, a price any *Kewpie* collector would willingly pay ten times over today. The author would never attempt a *Kewpie* **drawing,** but was brave enough to **sketch** these figures from the 1919 catalog, with apologies to Rose O'Neill and J. L. Kallus.

Returning to the pages of the Sears catalogs, we find all composition *Kewpies* in feathers in 1921. Also shown that year are *Kewpies* with composition heads and hands and jointed, stuffed bodies. These are in checked gingham dresses gathered at the neck, and retail for 98c. In 1928, new *Cuddle Kewpies* are listed as "Rose O'Neill's newest creation". They have painted, molded cloth (mask) faces, and kapok stuffed bodies of flannel, velvet, or crushed plush. In 1930 an 11½" *Cuddly Kewpie* of plush with mask face sold for $1.25.

Kewpie offerings continued through the years; a 1952 *Kewpie* of vinyl plastic, dressed in satin pantie costume was $1.79. A 25" *Kewpie* sold for $9.49 in 1960. All these dolls have been manufactured by Cameo Doll Products Company with rare exception. (See Cameo)

A real prize is a *Kewpie* talcum powder doll. This is a 7" composition *Kewpie* with painted eyes glancing to the right, little blue wings, red heart label on chest which reads **"Kewpie / Reg. U.S. / Pat. Off.",** and a metal cap for the powder at the crown of the head. On the back is a black and white label with **ROSE O'NEILL / © / 1913.** Label on original box reads: *"Kewpie Talcum makes me rosy, / Bright and cheery, cool and cosy."* The box illustration shows two *Kewpies,* one powdering the other, with the words: **KEWPIE TALCUM / 5028-182 / Copyright 1917 by Rose O'Neill.**

The *Kewpies* became so famous their image appeared on every imaginable type of merchandise from toy pianos and wallpaper to bottles and postcards. Here is a reproduction of a delightful Christmas Greeting, dated in the postmark *1921,* from the author's collection.

KEW-3.

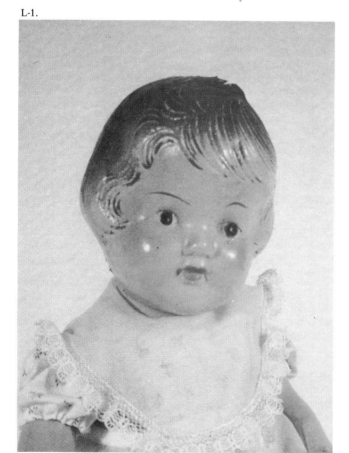

L-1.

L

L-1. 13" Girl. All composition, body and head one piece, dark brown molded hair, brown painted eyes. Marks: **A LIL SIS TOY PRODUCT.** 1920's. *(Wiseman collection)*

M-1.

M-2.

M-3.

M

M-1. 22" *Miss Marie.* Composition, soft body, sleep glass-like eyes, open mouth, teeth, human hair wig. Retailed at $2.79. One of a line of *Miss Marie* dolls from Sears. *1940 Catalog illustration courtesy Sears, Roebuck & Co.*

M-2. 21" *Miss Marie.* All composition, flirty sleep glass-like eyes, lashes, blonde mohair wig, **designer** clothes. Retailed at $2.98. *1940 Catalog illustration courtesy Sears, Roebuck & Co.*

M-3. 14", 18" *Baby Marie.* Composition, soft body, molded hair; 14" has glass-like sleep eyes, retails $1.98; 18" has flirty sleep eyes, lashes, retails $2.98. *1940 Catalog illustration courtesy Sears, Roebuck & Co.*

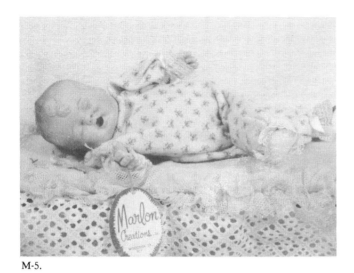

M-5.

M-4.

M-4.

M-4. 13" Australian Aborigine. Dark brown vinyl with soft matte finish, rooted Saran hair of dark red-brown, brown sleep eyes, red short skirt. Marks: **Metti / Australia** on doll; **bindi** on boomerang-shaped tag. *(Author's collection)*

This doll was produced by the House of Metti, Stepney, S.A., at the request of the Australian Plangon Club. Since no Australian-produced aborigine doll was available, the club wanted such a doll created to become their mascot. *"Bindi"* was the result and has since been joined by a small brother named *"Piccaninny"* (see MTCD). Both Mr. Metti, the company owner, and Mr. Hall, its director, are members of the club, which takes its name from the word *plangon,* an obscure Greek word for *"a girl made of wax"*.

M-5. 11" Musical Baby. Vinyl head, hands and feet, body is only a flannel cover for key-wind music box which plays Brahms' Lullabye. Tag reads: **MARLON Creations Inc.** *(Courtesy Kimport Dolls)*

M-6.

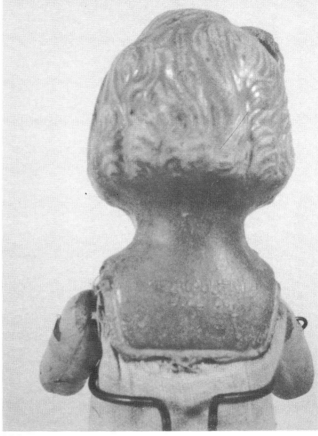

M-6.

M-7.

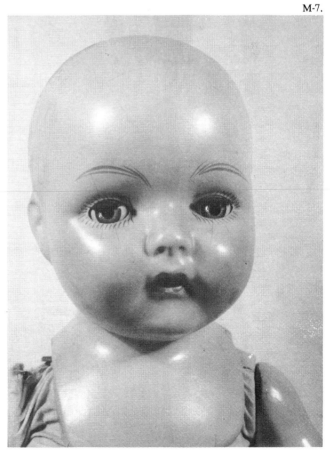

M-6. 15" Metropolitan Composition. Cloth body, stuffed with excelsior, cloth legs and feet, blue painted eyes, two painted teeth, molded hair-bow loop. Marks: **METRO-POLITAN / DOLL CO.** *(Spalding collection)*

M-7. 26" Mama Doll. Composition shoulder head, arms and legs, open mouth, two teeth, celluloid over tin sleep eyes, molded hair originally under a mohair wig, cloth body stuffed with excelsior. Marks: Faint **M** on front of shoulder plate. ca. 1928. *(Author's collection)*

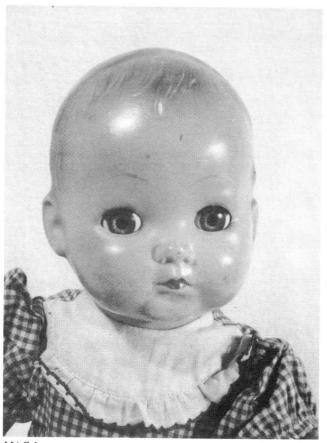

MAG-1.

M-7.

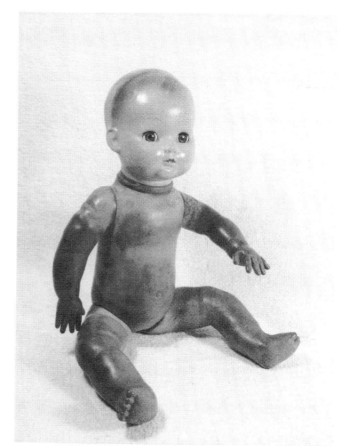

MAG-1.

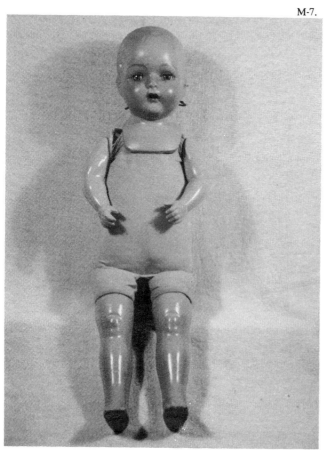

MAG-1. 18" *Magic Skin Baby.* Composition head, blue sleep eyes with whitest whites, hair lashes, closed mouth, molded and painted hair. Body is thin rubber "skin" stuffed with cotton and foam rubber, fingers are separate, toes are deeply indicated top and bottom, joints are pin and disc, doll is unmarked. Note discoloration and mottling of rubber. Original romper suit has matching bonnet. ca. 1940. *(Author's collection)* Note resemblance to F&B-36.

These dolls are sometimes found with flirty eyes and have hands with palms turned toward the body as in IDL-19. This writer feels these are the later versions of the doll since the improved attitude of the hands represents a more natural pose.

MARX-2.

MARX-1.

MARX-1. 11½" *Johnny West.* Solid plastic, intricately jointed, painted features. Horse measure 13" tall, 15" long. Equipment to outfit doll for "life on the Western range" includes cartridge belt with holster, pistol, derringer, coffee pot, coffee cup, frying pan, vest, neckerchief, sombrero, spurs, rifle, knife, sacks of *gold,* strong box, branding irons, canteen, and chaps. The horse is equipped with blanket, saddle, stirrups, bridle, reins, and saddle holster for rifle. Doll is marked **LOUIS MARX & CO. INC.** © **MCMLXV** (in a circle) on back. Horse marked same on left flank. *(Courtesy Joseph Richard Anderton II)*

MARX-2. 21" *Miss Toddler.* All plastic, moulded and painted, aqua dress, yellow hair, blue decal eyes. Note slide mechanism which links feet. Marks: **LOUIS MARX AND CO. INC.**/**MCMLXV**/**Patent Pending.** *(Courtesy Nita's House of Dolls)* Note: There is also a 15" *Baby Brother,* moulded in one piece of a thin, easily dented, celluloid-like plastic, also with decal eyes.

MATTEL, INC.

The company began as a partnership in a converted garage in 1945, and was incorporated in 1948. In seven short years it had passed the *five million dollar* net sales mark, and in 1960, operations were consolidated and headquartered at the present Hawthorne, California, site.

Mattel is now a publicly owned corporation whose sales in 1969 topped the $288 million mark. Acquisitions have included the Dee & Cee Toy Co., Ltd. of Canada, 1962; Standard Plastic Products, Inc., 1965; a major toy company in Hong Kong, 1966; a doll manufacturing plant in West Germany, also 1966; a new manufacturing plant in Taiwan, 1966; Rosebud Dolls, Ltd., a leading British doll company, 1967; a facility in Mexico, 1967; Monogram Models, Inc., 1968; joint venture with KBK, Japan, 1968; and many others. Mattell also entered into agreements to acquire *Ratti* and *Mebetoys* of Italy and EBIEX of Belgium, both in 1968.

From a garage to a world-wide manufacturing and distributing company of almost unbelievable magnitude in twenty-five years — an enviable accomplishment. *(Information courtesy Mattel, Inc.)*

MATT-1. MATT-2.

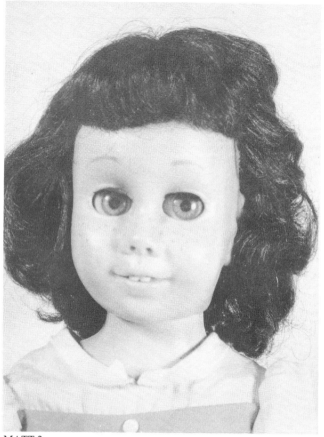

MATT-2.

MATT-3. MATT-4.

MATT-1. 20" *Chatty Cathy.* Strawberry blonde rooted Saran wig, light blue sleep eyes, curved right hand with pointing index finger, round, cloth-covered speaker. Plastic with soft vinyl head. Marks: (In a square): **CHATTY CATHY T.M. / PATENTS PENDING / © MCMLX / BY MATTEL, INC. / HAWTHORNE, CALIF.** Beneath square is circle with: **MATTEL INC / TOYMAKER.**

MATT-2. 20" *Chatty Cathy.* Dark brown rooted Saran wig, light blue sleep eyes, open right hand, rigid plastic head, six-sided speaker. Marks: Same as MATT-1, except without circle. *(Both dolls Author's collection)*

MATT-3. 20" *Chatty Cathy.* Long blonde rooted Saran hair, blue sleep eyes, open right hand, six-sided speaker with four holes spaced out below, says twenty-two phrases instead of standard eleven or eighteen. Clothes made from original patterns, shoes original wardrobe. Marks: (In a square): **CHATTY CATHY© / © 1960 / CHATTY BABY T.M. / © 1961 / BY MATTEL, INC. / U.S. PAT 3,017,187 / OTHER U.S. & / FOREIGN PATS. PEND'G. / PAT'D. IN CANADA 1962.**

MATT-4. 20" *Chatty Cathy.* Short dark brown rooted Saran wig, brown sleep eyes, pointing right hand, six-sided speaker, original dress and shoes. Marks: Same as MATT-1, except no circle. *(Both dolls Author's collection)*

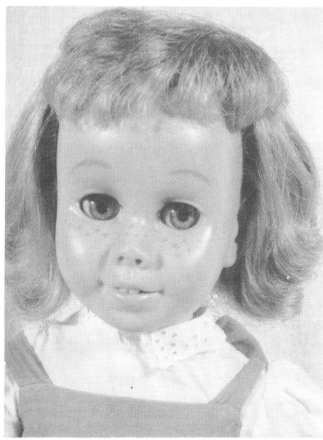

MATT-5.

MATT-6.

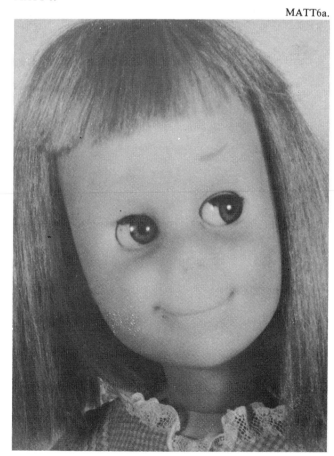

MATT6a.

MATT-5. 20" *Chatty Cathy.* Long blonde rooted Saran hair, blue sleep eyes, soft vinyl face, open right hand, round speaker, cloth covered. Marks: Same as MATT-1. *(Rebekka Anderton collection)*

MATT-6. 25" *Charmin' Chatty.* Plastic and vinyl, rooted Saran hair, side-glancing sleep eyes, lashes, closed mouth, original red, white and blue outfit, blue and white saddle shoes. Records fit in slot in side of doll; chatty ring to pull for voice. Records are "Proverbs and Poems" and "Get Acquainted" among others. Marks: (In a square): **CHARMIN' CHATTY / © 1961 MATTEL INC. / HAWTHORNE, CALIF. USA / U.S. PAT. / - PAT'D. IN CANADA / OTHER U.S. AND FOR- EIGN / PATENTS PENDING.** All this in less than a square inch. *(Author's collection)*

MATT-6a. 25" *Charmin' Chatty.* Long blonde rooted Saran hair, blue side-glancing sleep eyes, original blue and white checked dress. Doll had extensive wardrobe, available separately; birthday party dress, Cinderella costume, nightgown, etc., each with appropriate record. Marks: Same as MATT-6. *(Rebekka Anderton collection)*

MATT-7.   MATT-8.

MATT-9a.

MATT-9c.

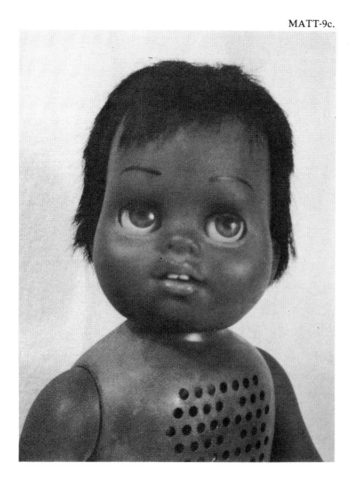

MATT-7. 18" *Matty Mattel.* Cloth with hard plastic turning head, painted features, glued-on yarn wig, original clothes, red and white shirt, black pants, tennis shoes are integral part of doll. Chatty ring; says eleven phrases. Marks: Tiny cloth tag sewn into side of doll: **MATTEL, INC.** Back of head: © **Mattel, Inc. / Hawthorne / Calif.** 1961. *(Childhood toy of Joseph Richard Anderton II)*

MATT-8. 18" *Sister Belle.* Same construction as MATT-7. Body, arms and legs are red cloth, shoes part of doll with separate straps and white buttons, blue and white ticking apron, red pockets, yellow yarn hair in ponytail. 1961. *(Childhood toy of Rebekka Suzanne Anderton)*

MATT-9a. 15" *Tiny Chatty Brother.* Vinyl and plastic, rooted hair, sleep eyes, chatty ring. *1963 Catalog illustration courtesy Sears, Roebuck & Co.*

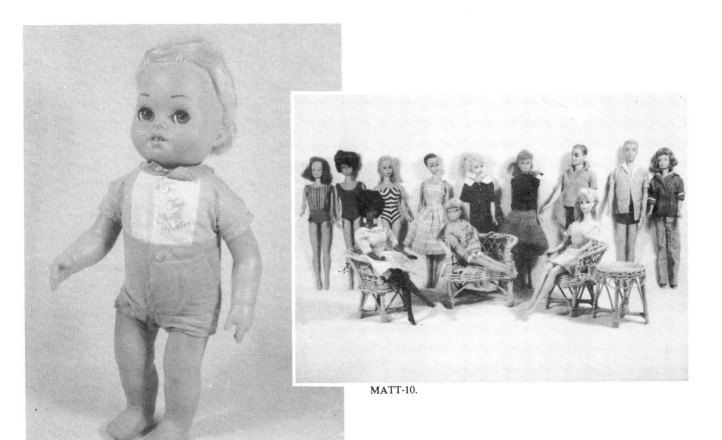

MATT-9b.

MATT-10.

MATT-11.

MATT-9b. 15" *Tiny Chatty Brother.* Original aqua cotton two-button romper suit. Marks: See MATT-22. *(Spalding collection)*

MATT-9c. 15" *Colored Tiny Chatty Brother.* Black rooted hair, brown sleep eyes, open mouth, two teeth. Marks: See MATT-22. *(Kirtley collection)*

MATT-10. *"Barbie* had a beach party and everyone came." Left to right, back row: *Midge, Midge, Barbie, Fashion Barbie, Barbie, Barbie, Ken, Ken,* and *Midge.* Seated, left to right: *Christie, Skipper,* and *Bendable Barbie. (Rebekka Anderton collection)*

MATT-11. 9¼" *Skooter* and *Ricky.* All vinyl, *Skooter* has rooted hair, *Rickey* has molded and painted hair, both have painted eyes. *1965 Catalog illustration courtesy Sears, Roebuck & Co.*

MATT-12.

MATT-13.

MATT-14.

MATT-15.

MATT-12. *Barbie* and *Skipper.* All vinyl, rooted hair, dressed in powder blue matching sweaters and slacks. *1965 Catalog illustration courtesy Sears, Roebuck & Co.*

MATT-13. *Barbie* and *Ken.* All vinyl, painted eyes, Barbie has rooted, bouffant hair-do, *Ken* has molded and painted hair. *1963 Catalog illustration courtesy Sears, Roebuck & Co.*

MATT-14. *Midge* and *Fashion Queen Barbie.* All vinyl, painted eyes, Midge has rooted hair, *Barbie* has molded and painted hair and several wigs to keep her in fashion. *1963 Catalog illustration courtesy Sears, Roebuck & Co.*

MATT-16.

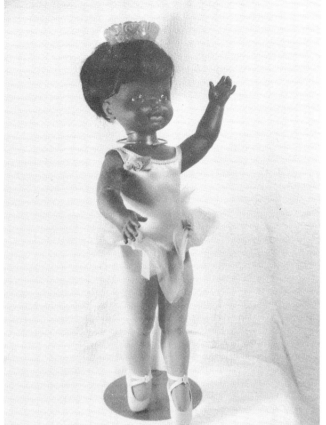

MATT-17.

MATT-17.

MATT-15. 20" *Scooba Doo*. Vinyl head, rooted hair, blue sleep eyes, black cloth body, pink cloth hands, talking mechanism, chatty ring, says "groovy" phrases. 1964. *(Kirtley collection)*

MATT-16. 19" *Sister Look 'n' Say.* Vinyl head and hands, rooted hair, eyes glance side to side and lips move as she talks, chatty ring, ten phrases such as "Lets stand on our heads and look at things upside down." Sears exclusive 1967, 1968, $11.99 retail. *1967 Catalog illustration courtesy Sears, Roebuck & Co.*

MATT-17. 24" *Dancerina*. Vinyl, rooted hair, painted eyes, control knob in magic tiara makes doll perform ballet steps. Battery operated. 1969. 11" *Baby Dancerina*, 1970. *(Kirtley collection)*

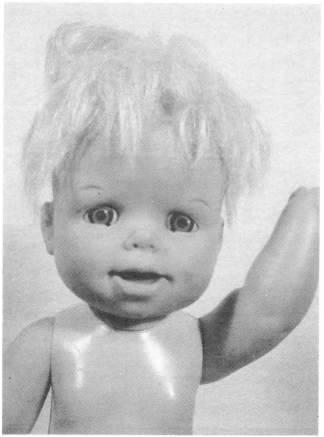

MATT-19.

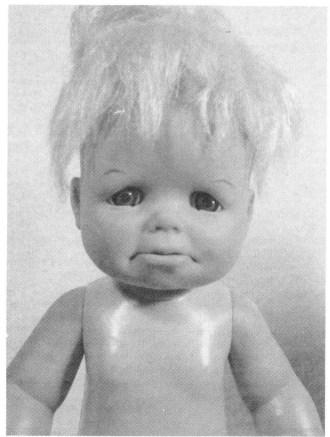

MATT-19.

MATT-18.

MATT-18. 11" *Cinderella.* All vinyl, rooted hair, talking ring, eight phrases, sixteen page storybook. Also *Goldilocks* and *Little Bo Peep,* 1969. *Snow White,* 1970. *1969 Catalog illustration courtesy Sears, Roebuck & Co.*

MATT-19. 13" *Cheerful Tearful.* Plastic and vinyl, painted eyes, rooted hair, left arm operates mechanism causing face to change from cheerful to tearful. Also *Tiny Cheerful Tearful,* 9". 1965. Marks: © **965 Mattel, Inc. / Hawthorne, Calif. / U.S. Patents / Pending / 3036-014-2.** *(Author's collection)*

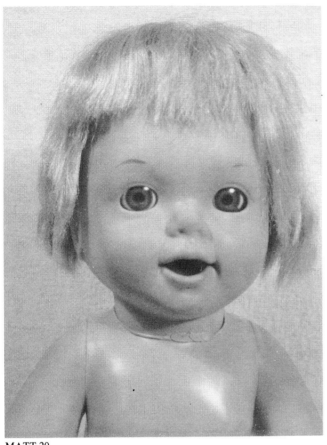

MATT-20.

MATT-20. MATT-21.

MATT-21.

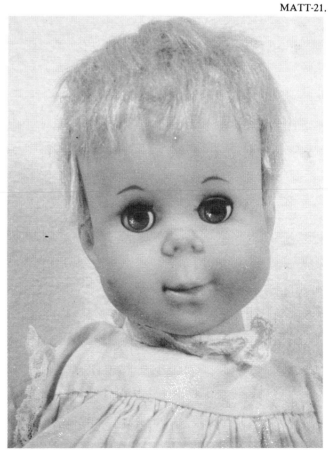

MATT-20. 16" *Baby's Hungry.* Vinyl plastic, battery operated, eyes roll, mouth chews, sucks on bottle, drink and wet feature. Marks: © **1960 MATTEL INC. / HAW-THORNE, CALIFORNIA / U.S. PAT PEND'G. MADE IN USA.** Doll has very pink "complexion". *(Author's collection)*

MATT-21. 18" *Baby Cheryl.* Vinyl head and limbs, cloth body, chatty talking ring. Cloth tag sewn into body reads: **QUALITY ORIGINALS BY / MATTEL® / BABY CHERYL T.M. / © 1964 MATTEL, INC. / HAW-THORNE, CALIF. USA-MADE IN USA / PATENTED IN USA / PATENTED IN CANADA / 1962. OTHER PATENTS PENDING.** Reverse of tag: (In a circle): **COMMONWEALTH OF PENNSYLVANIA DEPT. OF LABOR AND INDUSTRY SEAL OF APPROVAL;** and (In a circle): **MATTEL, INC. TOYMAKER.** Original pink dress. *(Author's collection)*

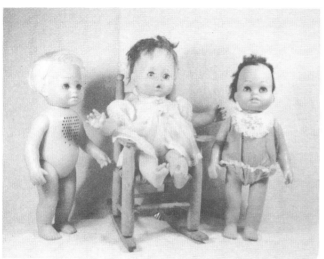

MATT-22a, -23, -22b.

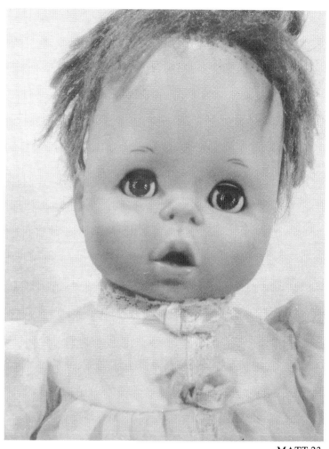

MATT-23.

MATT-22a.

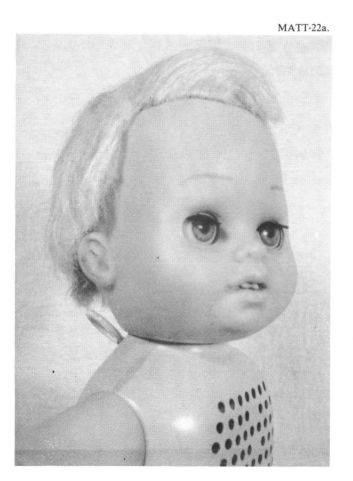

MATT-22a and b. 15" *Tiny Chatty Brother* and *Tiny Chatty Baby*. Vinyl and plastic, rooted hair, sleep eyes, talking mechanism, chatty ring. Marks: (In a square): **TINY CHATTY BABY / TINY CHATTY BROTHER / © 1962 MATTEL, INC. / HAWTHORNE, CALIF. USA / U.S. PAT 8,017,187 / OTHER U.S. AND FOREIGN / PATENTS PENDING / PATENTED IN CANADA.** *(Author's collection)*

MATT-23. 16" *Baby Pattaburp.* Vinyl head and limbs, cloth body containing "burping" mechanism similar in make-up to a cry box in other dolls. Note surprised expression of this baby. Original pink dress and matching panty. Marks: Cloth tag sewn into body reads: **QUALITY ORIGINALS BY / MATTEL / Baby Pattaburp TM / © 1963 Mattel, Inc. / Hawthorne, Calif. USA / U. S. PATENT PENDING / Made in U.S.A.** Reverse of tag same as MATT-21. *(Author's collection)*

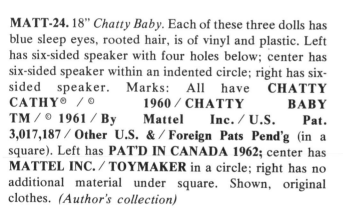

MATT-24a, -24b, -24c.

MATT-24.

MATT-25.

MATT-24. 18" *Chatty Baby.* Each of these three dolls has blue sleep eyes, rooted hair, is of vinyl and plastic. Left has six-sided speaker with four holes below; center has six-sided speaker within an indented circle; right has six-sided speaker. Marks: All have **CHATTY CATHY® / ©**   **1960 / CHATTY**   **BABY TM / © 1961 / By**   **Mattel**   **Inc. / U.S.**   **Pat. 3,017,187 / Other U.S. & / Foreign Pats Pend'g** (in a square). Left has **PAT'D IN CANADA 1962;** center has **MATTEL INC. / TOYMAKER** in a circle; right has no additional material under square. Shown, original clothes. *(Author's collection)*

MATT-25. 15" *Dee Dee.* Vinyl, rooted hair, painted eyes, original dress. *Dee Dee* is the "Cut'n'Button doll": "Make a wardrobe without sewing. Cut out, button together" a wardrobe for her. Marks: Sewn-in cloth label on dress: **Dee Dee TM / © 1964 / Mattel, Inc. Japan.** On doll: **Made in Japan / © 1964 Mattel, Inc. / Hawthorne, Calif. USA,** in a square. *(Author's collection)*

    Cut'n'button clothes included bathing suit, skimmer dress, nightie, and linen coat. Doll came in party dress.

MATT-28.

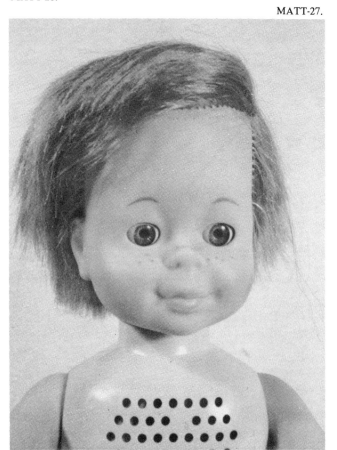

MATT-27.

MATT-26.

MATT-26. 18" *Baby Secret*. Vinyl head and hands, rooted hair, painted eyes, molded foam body covered with red flannel sleeper, chatty ring, mouth moves when she whispers "secrets"; "I know a secret, do you?", "Hold me close and whisper!", "I like to whisper in the dark!" and others. Marks: Cloth tag: **QUALITY ORIGINAL BY / MATTEL** ® / **Baby Secret TM** / © **1965 Mattel, Inc. / Hawthorne, Calif. / Pat'd in USA / Pat'd in Canada 1962 / Other Patents Pending / Made in Hong Kong.** *(Rebekka Anderton collection)*

MATT-27. 17" *Singin' Chatty*. Vinyl and plastic, rooted hair, sleep eyes, sings when you pull her chatty ring. Marks: (In a square): **SINGIN' CHATTY TM** / © **1964 Mattel, Inc. / Hawthorne, Calif. USA / PATENTED IN USA / PATENTED IN CANADA 1962 / OTHER PATENTS PENDING.** *(Author's collection)*

MATT-28. 12" *Captain Lazer*. Plastic and vinyl, painted features, silver colored accessories, blue uniform. Two pen-lite batteries operate "lazer" gun and light up eyes. Marks: © **1967 Mattel Inc. / Hawthorne, Calif. / Made in Mexico.** *(Courtesy James Phillip Holcombe)*

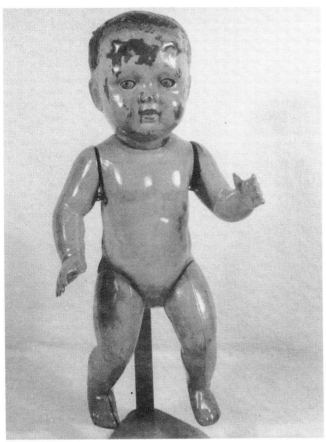

MET-1.

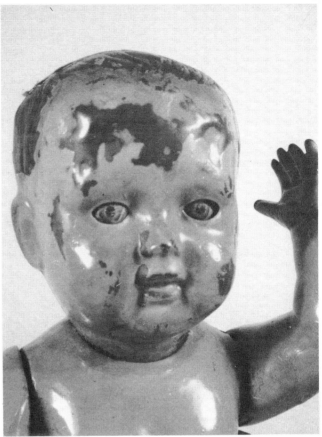

MET-1.

MET-1.

METAL DOLLS

Large quantities of metal dolls are not available. Although the material is quite durable, it does dent, chip and rust. Mrs. Lytle's doll is a perfect example; she tells how her brothers used her doll as a weapon in play. For every dent there is a corresponding chip in the paint. Metal dolls are easily repainted, but many collectors prefer the *original* state despite the often sad countenance presented.

———————

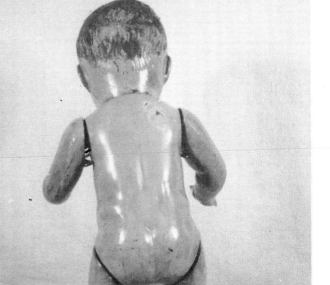

MET-1. 16" Baby. All metal, spring strung, molded hair, but had wig, center crown opening, blue tin sleep eyes, two molded teeth, open closed mouth. Unmarked. A birthday gift in 1920. *(Childhood doll of Mrs. Aurretta Lytle)*

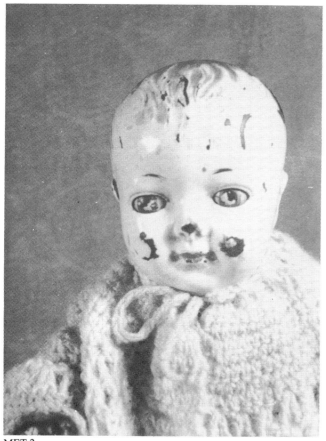

MET-2.

MET-3.

MET-4.

NOTE: ORIGINAL PRICES SHOWN
ARE NOT TODAY'S PRICES.

MET-2. 13" Baby. Metal shoulder head, cloth body, and legs, composition arms, tin sleep eyes. Marks: **Made in U.S.A.** on head. *(Zillner collection)*

MET-3. 4" *Minerva* Head. All metal shoulder head, blue stationary glass eyes, red dots at inner eye, blonde painted hair, nice rosey cheeks. Marks: *Minerva* across front. **Germany / 3** on back. *(Courtesy Kimport Dolls)* Featured in Sears 1915 catalog were Wearwell Brand dolls with metal *Minerva* heads. These were advertised as late as the 1934 catalog with fashionable modifications in style. *Minerva* metal heads were used on Sears' *"Violet"* in 1924 and 1925.

MET-4.

METRO-1.

METRO-1.

MET-4. 7½" *"Contortionist"*. Metal with composition head, hands and feet, intricately jointed; this doll is composed of parts which have been rolled, shaped, flanged, and pressed. The balls used are hollow, shaped metal. Original clothes, molded shoes with ties. Marks: **MADE IN / SWITZERLAND / PATENTS / APPLIED FOR** on stomach. This doll purchased for its present owner in 1916; many different characters were available. *(Courtesy Phyllis Odell)*

METRO-1. 17" Girl. Composition head, arms and legs to above knees; cloth body. Blue sleep flirty eyes, closed mouth, molded hairbow loop, molded and painted hair. Marks: **Metropolitan / Doll Co. / Pat. Pending** on shoulder plate. ca. 1921. *(Zillner collection)*

MULTIFACE DOLLS

MULTI-1.

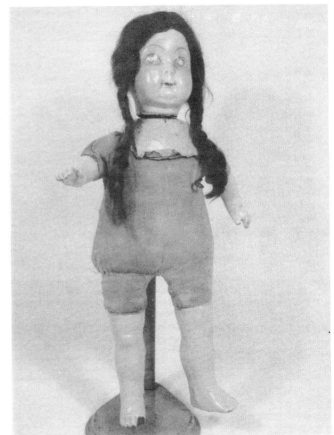

MULTI-3.

MULTI-2b.

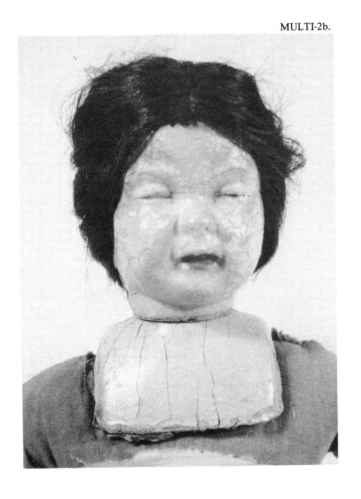

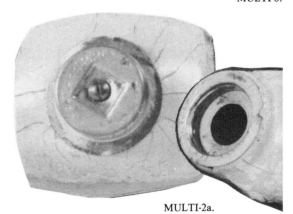

MULTI-2a.

MULTI-1. 16" *Famlee Doll.* "A Whole Family of Dolls in One", this doll had five different heads and costumes: Baby with white dress and bonnet; Athletic girl with wig and bloomer dress; Indian girl with long braid wig and fringed dress; Clown with face in white and colors and clown suit; and basic Mama doll with sleep eyes, mohair wig and little girl's dress. Other sets featured two and three heads; separate heads and costumes were available. Made by the Change-O-Doll Company. *1926 Catalog illustration courtesy Sears, Roebuck & Co.*

MULTI-2a. 16" *Famlee Doll.* Brass screw coupling; marks read: **Pat. Apr. 12, '21.**

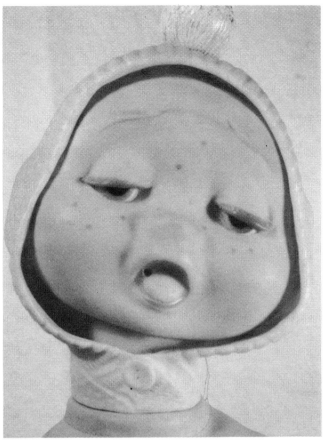

MULTI-4.

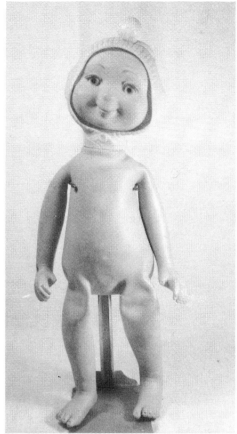

MULTI-4.

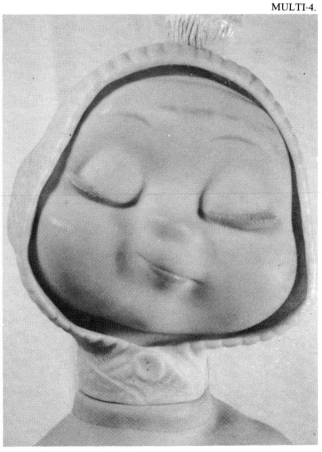

MULTI-4.

MULTI-2b. Head attached. This is sleeping face, replacement wig. *(Courtesy Dot & Joe's Browse Shop)*

MULTI-3. 16" *Famlee Doll.* These dolls are often found in poor condition. This may be because head was handled so much in changing from one head to another and partly because of inferior materials used. Note flaking, cracking and peeling. Paint worn off eyes probably from handling. Original mohair braided wig would appear to be "Indian girl" from catalog illustration MULTI-1. *(Kirtley collection)*

MULTI-4. 21" *Hedda Get Bedda,* Molded vinyl head, stuffed vinyl body and limbs. Three faces: "Poor Sick Hedda", "Sleepy Hedda", and "Happy, All Bedda Hedda". Turn pompom on top of nightcap to change faces. 1961, American Doll & Toy Co. *(American Character) (Kirtley collection)*

MULTI-5. 7" Three Face Doll. Vinyl, painted eyes, original clothes, turn knob to change face: crying, smiling, sleeping. Marks: On box: **My-Toy.** On doll: ®
1968 My-Toy Co. Inc. / Made in Hong Kong. *(Kirtley collection)*

MULTI-8.

MULTI-7.

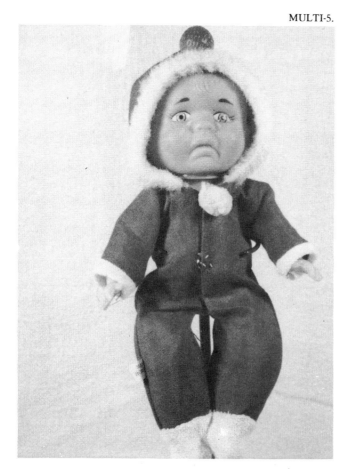

MULTI-5.

MULTI-6. 16" *Soozie Smiles, the Surprise Baby.* Painted eyes, composition with cloth body, two faces, two voices. *1923 Catalog illustration courtesy Sears, Roebuck & Co.* **Ideal Novelty & Toy Company** on tag attached to romper suit.

MULTI-7. 16" *Soozie Smiles.* Unmarked doll, original romper suit, cloth body stuffed with excelsior, blue painted eyes. Doll has been called *Baby Surprise* and *Surprise Baby* in ads and catalogs. Offered as a subscription premium with January, 1923, Needlecraft magazine. Apparently a very popular doll of the time; *Today's Housewife* magazine also offered the doll as a subscription premium in their ad appearing in the November, 1923, issue of *Modern Priscilla. (Battagler collection)*

MULTI-8. 16" "*Soozie Smiles,* The Doll That Made The Queen Smile". 1924 Catalog text reads: "Queen Mary of England had her picture taken holding Soozie Smiles because she liked the baby with two faces". Note change in costume from first year and that smiling face has sleep eyes. *Illustration courtesy Sears, Roebuck & Co.*

MULTI-9. 15½" *Trudy.* Composition head, cloth body and limbs, three faces, knob on top of head changes faces, original sleepers. Unmarked. 1946. Three-In-One Doll Corp. 1947 Catalogs show Trudy dressed in rayon fleece snowsuit; leggings, bolero and hood with curls attached. Sleepers on doll shown may actually be snowsuit. 1948 Catalog shows Trudy dressed in sheer cotton dress and bonnet; 1949 outfit is sheer cotton print dress and bonnet. Advertising calls faces "Sleepy, Weepy and Smiley". *(Zillner collection)*

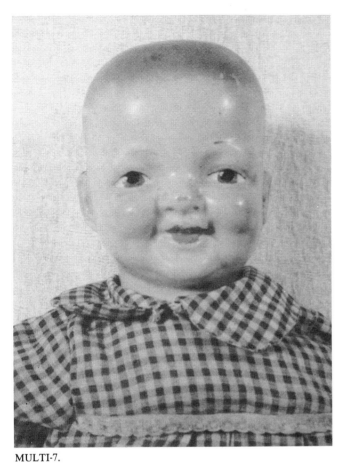

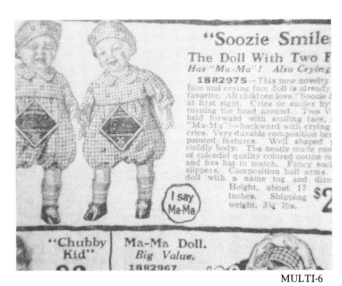

"Soozie Smile
The Doll With Two F
Has "Ma-Ma"! Also Crying

18R2975—This new novelty
face and crying face doll is already
favorite. All children love "Soozie
at first sight. Cries or smiles by
turning the head around. Two V
held forward with smiling face,
"Ma-Ma"!—backward with crying
cries. Very durable composition hea
painted features. Well shaped
cuddly body. The neatly made roo
of splendid quality colored cotton m
and has hat to match. Fancy sock
slippers. Composition half arms.
doll with a name tag and dire
Height, about 17 $2
inches. Shipping
weight, 3¼ lbs.

"Chubby | Ma-Ma Doll.
Kid" | *Big Value.*
          | 18R2967

MULTI-6

MULTI-7.

MULTI-9.

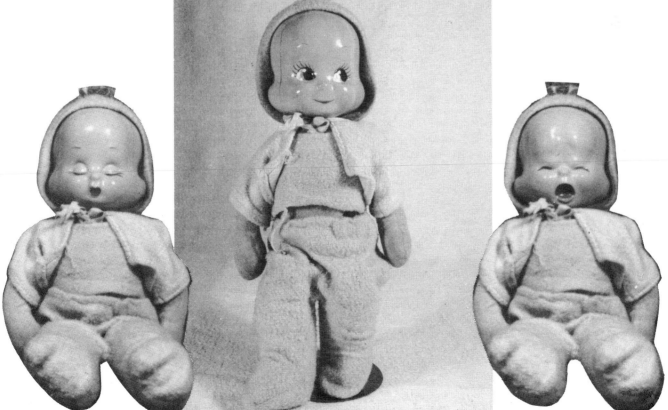

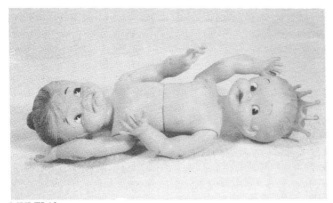

MULTI-10.

MULTI-11.

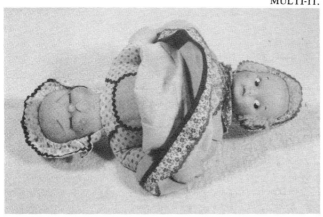

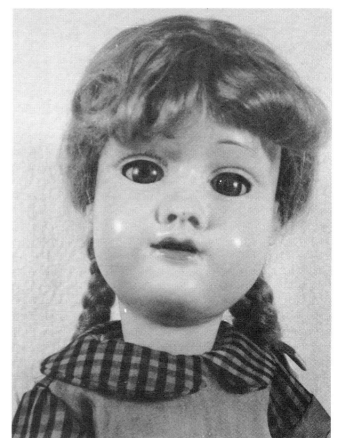

N-1.

N-2.

MULTI-10. 16" Double Doll. All vinyl, painted features and hair. 1960's, Knickerbocker. *(Kirtley collection)*

MULTI-11. 12" Double Doll. Vinyl mask faces, stuffed cloth bodies. 1960's, Knickerbocker. *(Kirtley collection)*

N   fig. N-1

N-1. 19" Composition. Ball-jointed, wood, papier mache and composition, open mouth, four teeth, celluloid over tin eyes. Heavy for size as is a Schoenhut. Composition socket head made from same mold as some bisque and celluloid heads. Marks: **19C** on back of neck. Fig. N-1 on body. National Joint-Limb Company. ca. 1917 to 1922. This company specialized in replicas of Kestner dolls. *(Wingfield collection)*

N-2. 15" Girl. Composition shoulder head and arms, cloth stuffed body and limbs, blue tin sleep eyes, open closed mouth, two painted teeth, molded hairbow loop. Marks: **NOVELTY / DOLL CO.** on shoulder. (Compare with Metropolitan head shown elsewhere). *(Courtesy Kimport Dolls)*

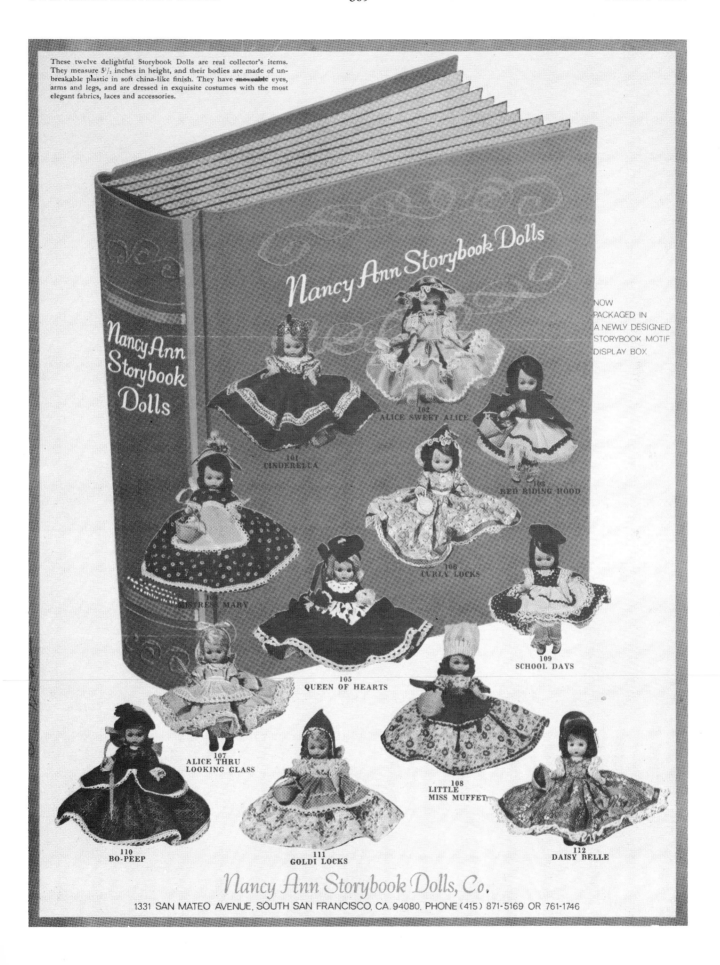

These twelve delightful Storybook Dolls are real collector's items. They measure 5½ inches in height, and their bodies are made of unbreakable plastic in soft china-like finish. They have moveable eyes, arms and legs, and are dressed in exquisite costumes with the most elegant fabrics, laces and accessories.

NOW PACKAGED IN A NEWLY DESIGNED STORYBOOK MOTIF DISPLAY BOX

Nancy Ann Storybook Dolls

101 CINDERELLA
102 ALICE SWEET ALICE
103 RED RIDING HOOD
104 CURLY LOCKS
MISTRESS MARY
105 QUEEN OF HEARTS
109 SCHOOL DAYS
107 ALICE THRU LOOKING GLASS
108 LITTLE MISS MUFFET
110 BO-PEEP
111 GOLDI LOCKS
112 DAISY BELLE

Nancy Ann Storybook Dolls, Co.
1331 SAN MATEO AVENUE, SOUTH SAN FRANCISCO, CA. 94080. PHONE (415) 871-5169 OR 761-1746

N-4. *Nancy Ann Storybook Dolls.* The Nancy Ann Storybook Dolls Company was founded in 1941. Early dolls were painted bisque or composition. From 1946 to 1952 dolls were made of plastic with stationary eyes. From 1952 to 1969 plastic dolls with glued-on wigs and sleep eyes were produced. Beginning in 1970 soft plastic dolls with rooted hair and painted eyes are available as shown in the advertising circular illustrated here. *(Courtesy Nancy Ann Storybook Dolls, Co.)* See also Bisque Dolls.

ROSE O'NEILL

When the name *Rose O'Neill* is mentioned, first thoughts are apt to be of *Kewpies* and such folk. Whie it is true that Rose O'Neill was famous as the creator of the *Kewpies,* it is equally true that she became world renowned as an illustrator, painter, poet, and sculptor. In her book, *The One Rose*[1], Rowena Godding Ruggles narrates the story of Rose O'Neill and her widely varied accomplishments. This biography should be required reading for any serious collector.

Mr. Joseph L. Kallus, long-time friend and co-worker of Rose O'Neill, has kindly provided a postcard for our enjoyment from his personal papers. The front of the card carries a photograph of Rose O'Neill with one of her best-known statues, *The Embrace of the Tree,* based on a legend from Greek mythology. The words in the lower left-hand corner were penned by Rose O'Neill and are not a part of the original card. The reverse of the postcard bears a message to Mr. Kallus concerning his recent (1937) Christmas card featuring his original painting, *"Portrait of an Old Man",* and a reference to a "gift of Scootleses".

[1] Ruggles, Rowena Godding, "The One Rose", Privately Published, Oakland, California, 1964.

"The Embrace of the Tree" and its mother

O'N-1.

O'N-1a.

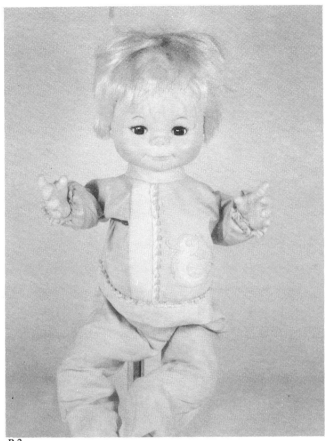

P-2.

P-1.

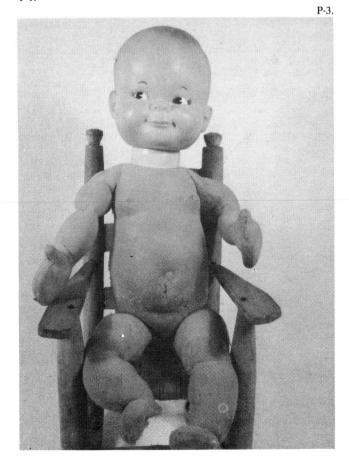

P-3.

The statue, *The Embrace of the Tree,* now stands in the grounds of the Shepherd of the Hills Museum in Branson, Missouri, where a room is set aside to display art work and personal treasures of *The One Rose.*

P

P-1. 17", 19", 22" *Plassie.* Hard plastic head, composition arms and legs, stuffed body, glass-like sleep eyes, cry voice. Note heavily painted lashes, typical of period. 1945-1949. See also Ideal. *1945 Catalog illustration courtesy Sears, Roebuck & Co.* Ideal TM appears to right of doll in catalog just out of our camera range.

P-2. 18" Baby. Foam and vinyl, black pupil-less sleep eyes, closed mouth, gauntlet molded vinyl hands and head, rooted synthetic hair, original suit. Apparently slightly more expensive and elaborate model of P-3. Marks: **Play Toys Inc.** on head. *(Spalding collection)*

P-3. 18" Baby. Molded vinyl head, molded foam body and limbs, over wire skeleton, painted side-glancing eyes, closed mouth. Note detailed molding of foam body. Marks: **AE 6 18 / 1** on head. *(Spalding collection)*

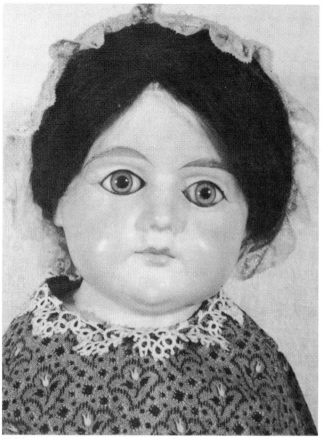

PM-1.

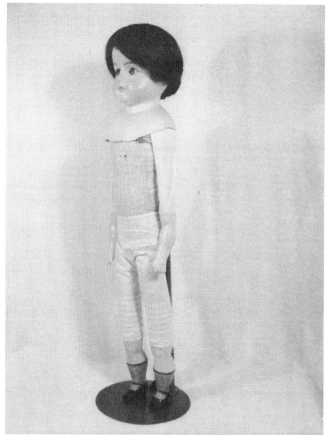

PM-1.

P-4.

P-4. *Princess of Doll Land.* Human hair, sleep eyes, lashes, open mouth, composition head and limbs, cloth stuffed body. One of a line of *Princess* dolls carried by Sears. *1929 Catalog illustration courtesy Sears, Roebuck & Co.* Compare with dolls in Unmarked Dolls section of this book.

PM-1. 30" Papier Mache. Composition lower arms, fastened to muslin empty-sleeve type upper arms, deep shoulder head of pepier mache, closed mouth, red dots in nostrils and inner eye, painted, brush stroke brows, inset glass eyes, solid crown, human hair original wig. Excelsior-stuffed cloth body, long straight lets, composition molded shoes and sox, knees molded, blue sox with darker blue edge, black strap slippers with tiny heel. Marks: Under wig at top, back of left ear is incised a large **X**. *(Battagler collection)*

This doll was purchased at a shop in Tennessee; the owner believes it to date prior to 1900, possibly as early as the 1880's. An identical example of this doll was also purchased in Tennessee and given to the mother of Mrs. C. J. Houston of Virginia on July 8, 1892, for her first birthday.

PERS-B2.

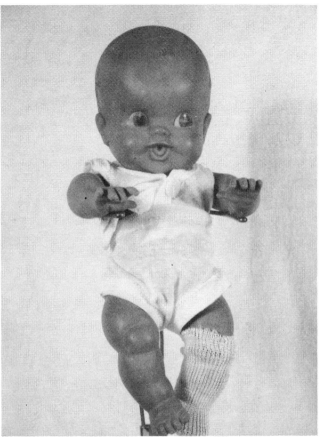

PERS-A1.

PERS-B1.

PERSONALITY DOLLS

Generally, a doll representing a famous personality will be issued at the height of that person's popularity and quickly discontinued at the slightest indication that the rage is over lest the doll manufacturer be caught with a large stock of unsaleable merchandise. The collector of popular personality dolls would do well to add new items to a collection as soon as they appear.

PERS-A1. 9½" *Amosandra.* All rubber, painted eyes, squeeker. Baby character from "old-time" radio program, "Amos and Andy". Marks: See fig. PERS-A1. *(Author's collection)*

PERS-B1. 20" *Baby Peggy* of the Movies. Composition head, arms and legs, stuffed cloth body, mama voice. 1923. There were also tiny bisque figures of *Baby Peggy. 1924 Catalog illustration courtesy Sears, Roebuck & Co. Baby Peggy* was Peggy Jean Montgomery, Century Comedies.

PERS-B2. 22" *Talking Mrs. Beasley.* Vinyl head and hands, stuffed cloth body and limbs, rooted hair, painted eyes, removeable apron, granny glasses. Says eleven phrases, talking ring. From television's "Family Affair". Mattel. © **1967** "A Family Affair". *1969 Catalog illustration courtesy Sears, Roebuck & Co.*

PERS-C1.

AMoSandRA
©
COLUMBIA BROADCASTING
SYSTEM, INC.

fig. PERS-A1.

PERS-B2a.

PERS-C2.

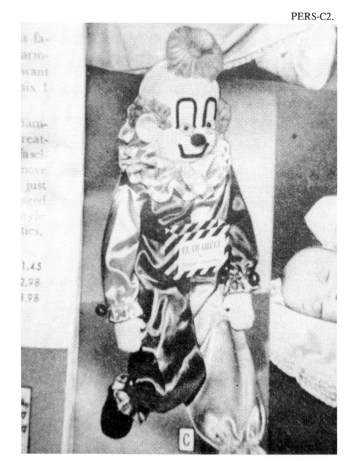

PERS-B2a. 6" *Buffy,* 3½" *Mrs. Beasley.* Vinyl heads, painted features, rooted wig. Buffy's body is vinyl with bendable wire reinforcement in limbs; Mrs. Beasley's body is stuffed cloth. Marks: © **1965 / Mattel Inc. / - Japan / 25** on Buffy's back; tag on her wrist reads: **BUFFY / © 1967 Family Affair Company.** Mrs. Beasley has cloth **Mattel** label sewn into her body seaming. *(Author's collection)*

PERS-C1. 5" Head, *Clarabelle the Clown.* Composition ventriloquist dummy head. Unmarked. Character is usually dressed in polka dot clown suit with large white ruff at neck. 1950's. *(Author's collection)*

PERS-C2. 19" *Clarabelle the Clown.* Television character from the Howdy Doody children's show. Mask face, floppy cotton stuffed body, felt features, two-tone rayon suit, velvet clown ruff. Retailed $4.79. Madame Alexander. *1951 Catalog illustration courtesy Sears, Roebuck & Co.*

PERS-D2.

PERS-E1.

PERS-D1.

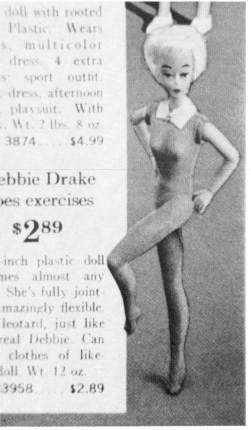

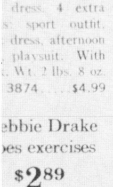

PERS-D1. 11½" *Debbie Drake.* Flexible plastic doll represents television personality who demonstrates figure exercises. *1963 Catalog illustration courtesy Sears, Roebuck & Co.*

PERS-D2. 12" *Patty Duke,* television and movies. Vinyl, rooted hair, painted eyes, poseable, original costume. 1965 Sears catalog shows pink top and white slacks outfit. Marks: **W / H** on head. Ideal. *(Zillner collection)*

PERS-E1. *Mr. Ed* Talking Hand Puppet. Plush "body", yarn mane, vinyl head, painted features, talking string, says "I'm a horse, of course", and other phrases. Represents the talking horse character, title role in television show "Mr. Ed". Marks: Tag reads: **MISTER ED / MR. ED © 1962 BY MR. ED CO.** Reverse of tag: **QUALITY ORIGINALS BY MATTEL / U.S. PAT 3017187 PAT'D IN CANADA 1962 / OTHER U.S. AND FOREIGN PATS. PEND'G.** *(Childhood toy of Rebekka Suzanne Anderton)*

PERS-E3.

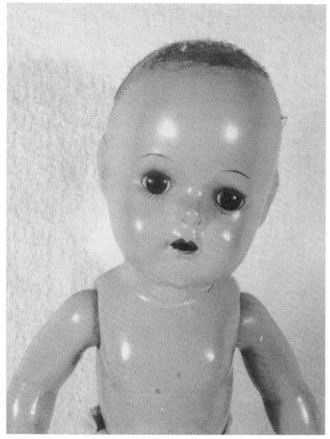

PERS-E2.

PERS-S4, -E3

PERS-E2. 15" *Princess Elizabeth.* All composition, brown sleep eyes, open mouth. Marks: **PRINCESS ELIZABETH / MADAME ALEXANDER CO.** 1938. *(Kirtley collection)*

PERS-E3. 18" *Princess Elizabeth.* Original blonde human hair wig, all composition, blue sleep eyes slightly crazed, original silk dress. Marks: Same as PERS-E 2 . Tag on dress: **PRINCESS ELIZABETH / MADAME ALEXANDER / NEW YORK N.Y. / ALL RIGHTS RESERVED.** *(Zillner collection)*

PERS-E4. 10" *Coronation Elizabeth.* Hard plastic, all original, sleep eyes, issued after the Coronation. 1950's. *(Zillner collection)*

PERS-F1. 12" *The Flying Nun.* All vinyl, jointed, brown painted eyes, rooted hair. Represents actress Sally Fields in title role of television show, "The Flying Nun". Cotton "habit", molded vinyl hat, black pantyhose, black molded vinyl shoes with tiny heels. Marks: © **1967** ® **/ HASBRO / HONG KONG** on back of doll. © **Screen Gems, Inc.** on box. *(Zillner collection)*

This doll is also found in an open mouth version.

PERS-E4.

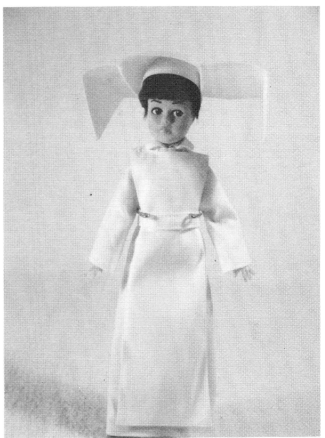

PERS-F1.

PERS-F3.

PERS-H1.

PERS-F2. Anne Francis as *"Honey West"* of television series of that name. For illustration see PERS-S1. Vinyl, rooted hair, painted eyes, dressed in original black leotard. 1960's. *(Zillner collection)*

PERS-F3. 9¾" *Fairy Tale Characters.* Composition, jointed hips and shoulders, tilting heads, dressed in character: *Little Red Riding Hood, Grandmother,* and the *Big Bad Wolf. 1934 Catalog illustration courtesy Sears, Roebuck & Co.*

PERS-H1. 8" *Mary Hartline.* Early hard plastic, sleep eyes, red dress. Sears 1952 catalog lists "Mary Hartline of circus fame. Blonde saran hair, red broadcloth dress and panties, white boots." Also available same catalog were television personalities, same type doll and size: Doctor Gale, a woman doctor, Togs Corbett, "25th Century Space Cadet"; Roy Rogers and Dale Evans in 1955. *(Zillner collection)*

PERS-H2.

PORT-L1.   PERS-H3.

PERS-M1.

PERS-H2. 16" *Mary Hartline.* Hard plastic, platinum glued-on saran hair, red dress, white boots, sleep eyes, lashes. Retail, $11.49. *1952 Catalog illustraation courtesy Sears, Roebuck & Co.* 1954 listing shows white dress trimmed in red; refers to Miss Hartline as "famous television star", wig is rooted saran. Also in 1954 there is a 4¼" diameter revolving stand fitted with Swiss music box, to which doll may be attached.

PERS-H3. 24" *Howdy Doody.* Hard plastic head, all original, soft body, sleep eyes, leather belt and boots. Marks: "Heart-shaped tag reads: *I am an EFFANBEE durable doll, the doll with the satin smooth skin.*" For close-up and description of Howdy's friend, see PORT-L1. *(Zillner collection)* In 1950 Ideal introduced 20" *Howdy Doody* with string in back which worked ventriloquist mechanism similar to those on *Charley McCarthy* and *W. C. Fields.* Ideal's *Howdy Doody* is shown in Sear's 1950 and 1951 catalogs, retailing at $5.69.

PERS-M1. 24" *Jerry Mahoney.* Composition head and gauntlet hands, red-brown painted hair, painted features. **PAT'D 1946 by Paul Winchell, New York.** *(Wiseman collection)* 1957 Sears catalog shows *Jerry* with hard plastic head, fiberboard torso, gabardine suit; 32" at $13.87; 24" at $5.87.

PERS-M2a.

PERS-M2.

PERS-M2.

NOTE: ORIGINAL PRICES SHOWN
ARE NOT TODAY'S PRICES.

PERS-M2. 14½" *Mary Martin.* Hard plastic washable lamb's wool wig styled as Miss Martin wore her hair for a starring role in the hit stage musical, "South Pacific". The script called for the character, Nellie Forbush to wash her hair and sing, "I'm gonna wash that man right out of my hair ..." from a Richard Rodgers song written for the musical. Doll is all original, has sleep eyes, is unmarked. Tag on clothes reads: **MARY MARTIN / OF SOUTH PACIFIC / MADAME ALEXANDER.** 1949. *(Zillner collection)*

PERS-M2a. Illustration from a Rayve Home Permanent advertisement in the August, 1950, Ladies' Home Journal.

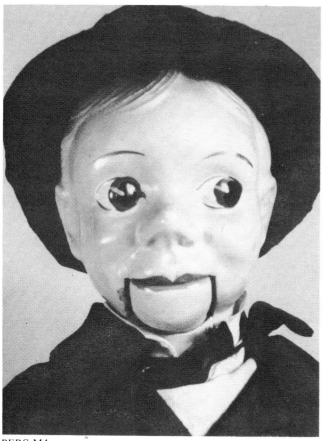

PERS-M4

PERS-M4

PERS-M3.

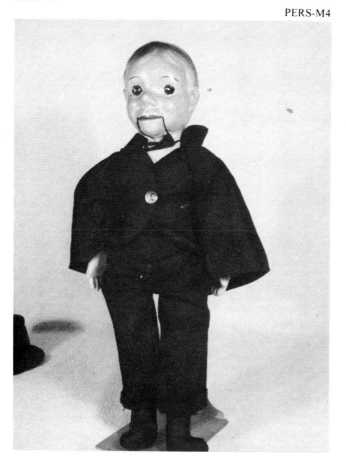

PERS-M3. 20½" *Charlie McCarthy.* Composition shoulder head, hands and feet, cloth body stuffed with cotton or kapok, painted features, ventriloquist string controls mouth. All original, dark blue double breasted coat, white buttons, original *Charlie McCarthy* button on lapel, white molded plastic shoes, white cotton trousers, white plisse shirt. Marks: **Edgar Bergen / Charlie McCarthy / AN / EFFANBEE PRODUCT / 1.** *(Courtesy Kimport Dolls)* Available as late as 1970 with vinyl head and cloth body and limbs.

PERS-M4. 16" *Charlie McCarthy.* Composition head and hands, cloth body and legs, control string for mouth, all original in his formal attire. Unmarked. Charlie was introduced as a doll in 1937 by EFFANBEE with composition head, hands and feet. This is probably an early example; certainly it pre-dates plastics. Charlie has been the friend of ventriloquist Edgar Bergen since the 1930's, was a regular on radio, and a frequent star in movies. 30" and 34" sizes also available. *(Zillner Collection)*

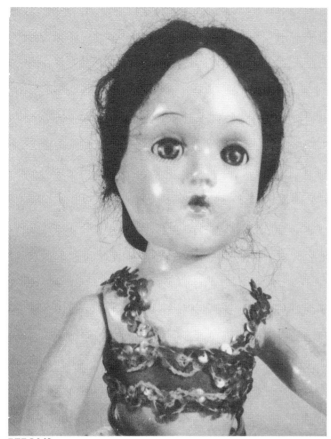

PERS-M5.

PERS-M5.

PERS-M6.

PERS-M6.

PERS-M7.

PERS-M8.

PERS-M5. 14" *"Carmen Miranda".* All composition, original mohair wig, sleep eyes, original costume. Marks: **Mme. Alexander** on head. Although this doll was not marketed as *Carmen Miranda,* the popularity of the movie star and singer have prompted collectors to attach her name to the doll dressed in a style she made famous. 1942. *(Zillner collection)*

PERS-M6. 21" *"Carmen Miranda".* All composition, blue sleep eyes, original black mohair wig arranged in bun at back of head, all original. Clothes: white satin skirt trimmed with red and green ric-rac, red satin bodice trimmed with gold sequins, black and gold cloth turban trimmed with fruit, feathers and flowers. This doll is completely unmarked; only when it was compared with Mrs. Zillner's (PERS-M5) was the true origin established, although it was firmly believed it was a Madame Alexander prior to that. Detective work often pays rewards. 1942. *(Author's collection)*

PERS-M7. 11" *Carmen Miranda* and Friend. All composition, inexpensive, unmarked dolls, painted features. Both dolls have original clothes; they are identical dolls except for costume. The *Carmen Miranda* costume helps date them as ca. 1942. These are *not* Madame Alexander dolls. *(Author's collection)*

PERS-M8. 21" *Herman Munster.* Abnormal green vinyl face, cloth body and limbs, talking ring, says ten phrases. Represents actor Fred Guinn who played role of Herman Munster on television series, "The Munsters", story about an unusual family of stereotype monsters who believe they are normal and everyone else is strange. Retail, $7.97. *1965 Catalog illustration courtesy Sears, Roebuck & Co.*

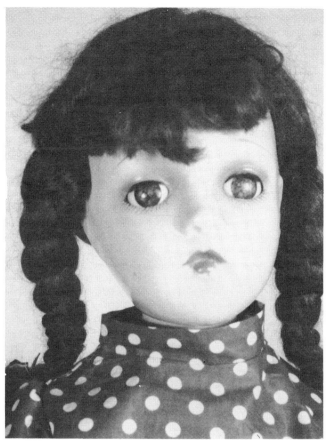

PERS-01.

PERS-02.

PERS-03.

PERS-01. 21" *Margaret O'Brien.* All composition, brown sleep eyes, original pigtail wig of mohair. Original dress with cloth label reading: **Madame Alexander / Margaret O'Brien.** 1946. *(Zillner collection)* According to catalog listings dolls came in 14½" at $7.79, 18" at $10.98, and 21" at $13.98, and were dressed in copies of original *Margaret O'Brien* costumes in assorted styles and colors. For full length view, see *Jane Withers.*

PERS-02. 12" *Our Gang Comedy Dancers.* All composition, dressed in characters of *Mary, Farina,* and *Fatty,* straight out of the "Our Gang" movies. Windup spring; twirl when released. *Mary* had bobbed wig; *Farina* and *Fatty* had painted hair. Retailed $1.23 each. (Distortion of photograph due to curve of catalog page.) *1926 Catalog illustration courtesy Sears, Roebuck & Co.*

These are probably the dolls made by Schoen & Yondorf Company *(Sayco)* in 1925 to represent the characters in the Hal Roach comedies.

PERS-03. 24", 30" *Danny O'Day.* Vinyl with cloth body and limbs, concealed strings in back of neck work "talking" mouth. Ventriloquist Jimmy Nelson is the voice behind "Danny O'Day" and several other characters seen on television. Available 1970.

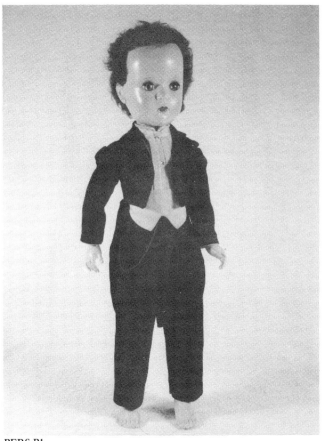

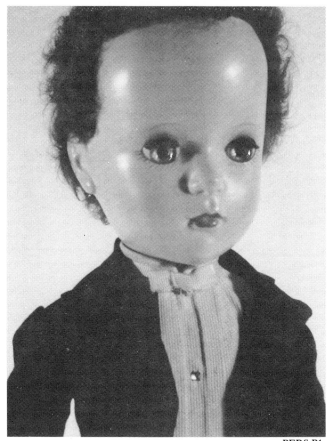

PERS-P1.

PERS-P1.

PERS-P2.

PERS-P1. 18" *Prince Phillip.* Hard plastic, lamb's wool wig glued on, green sleep eyes, all original. White shirt is sewn to trousers of tuxedo suit, gold chain, jacket has "tails". Clothes marked: **Madame Alexander.** 1953. *(Courtesy Camelot of Springfield, Missouri)* Also 1953 were Sir Winston and Lady Churchill; she is dressed in formal satin gown.

PERS-P2. 12" *Mary Poppins,* 8" *Jane* and *Michael.* Vinyl, rooted hair, painted eyes, all original. Marks: **H** on Mary's head; © **HORSMAN DOLLS INC. / 6681** on *Jane's* head; and © **9 / HORSMAN DOLLS INC. / 6682** on *Michael's* head. Dolls represent characters in Walt Disney movie, "Mary Poppins", based on story by P. L. Travers © 1934. Julie Andrews was *Mary Poppins;* Karen Dotrice was *Jane;* Matthew Garber was *Michael.* © 1964 Walt Disney Productions. *(Rebekka Anderton collection)*

Several dolls were produced representing *Mary Poppins.* Three-doll set as shown was listed in 1966 at $8.99 the set. In 1965 *Mary Poppins* and her wardrobe at $7.77 and *Mary Poppins* with umbrella and bag at $4.66 were offered. A 36" *Mary Poppins* set included striped

PERS-P3.

PERS-P-4.

PERS-P4.

Nanny dress and apron, white stockings, boots, carpet bag, umbrella, coat, bonnet, dress, high button shoes. Last outfit is nearly identical to one shown on smaller doll above. *Catalog information courtesy Sears, Roebuck & Co.*

PERS-P3. 31" *Pollyana*. Vinyl, rooted hair, sleep eyes, original dress. Doll represents character from 1960 Walt Disney movie of same name, played by actress, Hayley Mills. 31" sold from Sears at $14.88 in 1960; 10½", 17", and 32" were listed in 1961 Christmas Book. Marks: © WALT   DISNEY / PRODS. / MFD.   BY UNEEDA / N.F. *(Author's collection)* Note: Disney's 8" "Small World" dolls in national costumes (1965) have this same face.

PERS-P4. 17" *Pollyana*. Vinyl, rooted saran hair, open closed mouth, blue sleep eyes. All original: red and white checked dress and pantaloons, non-removeable molded shoes, knit permanently attached stockings. Marks: Same as PERS-P3. 1960. *(Zillner collection)*

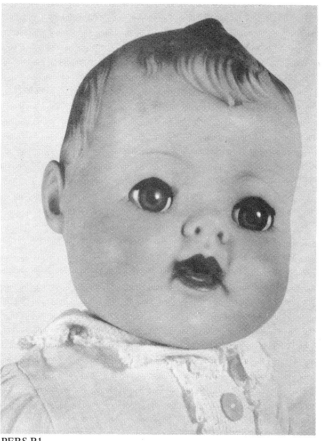

PERS-R1.

PERS-R1.

PERS-F2, -S1.

PERS-R1. 21" *Little Rickey (Rickey, Jr.).* All vinyl, molded hair, sleep eyes, original clothes. Marks: **American Character Doll Co.** on head. *Rickey, Jr.* on romper suit. *(Zillner collection)* Doll represents baby character of television show, "I Love Lucy", starring Lucille Ball and Dezi Arnaz. When Miss Ball became a mother in private life, the baby character was added to the television show. 1954 Catalogs shows a 17" vinyl baby, glassene sleep eyes, thick lashes, rooted hair "combed in a pompadour like his daddy's", retail $9.97. 1955 Catalog lists 13" and 17" all vinyl, molded hair, "can sit, stand, bend due to a wire inside his body". Wore corduroy overalls, cotton shirt, beanie, shoes and sox. *Catalog information courtesy Sears, Roebuck & Co.*

PERS-S1. 12" *Samantha the Witch.* Vinyl, painted eyes, rooted saran wig, all original, dressed in red. Doll represents character from television series "Bewitched", played by Elizabeth Montgomery. Ideal. 1966 Catalog mentions flexible arms and legs; doll retailed at $3.99. *Samantha's* friend is Anne Francis as *"Honey West";* see PERS-F2. *(Zillner collection)* A *"pos'n"* model of this doll was shown in the 1965 Speigel catalog.

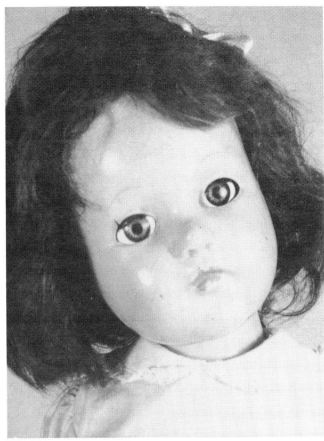

PERS-S4.

PERS-S2. PERS-S3.

PERS-S3.

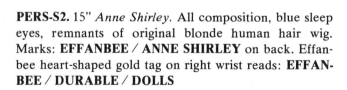

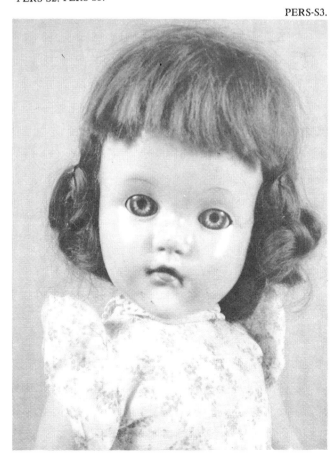

PERS-S2. 15" *Anne Shirley.* All composition, blue sleep eyes, remnants of original blonde human hair wig. Marks: **EFFANBEE / ANNE SHIRLEY** on back. Effanbee heart-shaped gold tag on right wrist reads: **EFFANBEE / DURABLE / DOLLS**

PERS-S3. 17" *Anne Shirley.* All composition, blue sleep eyes, replacement wig, old dress not original. Marks: **EFFANBEE / USA** on head and back. *(Author's collection)*

PERS-S4. 21" *Anne Shirley.* All composition, brown sleep eyes, original human hair wig, old but not original dress. Marks: **EFFANBEE / ANNE SHIRLEY** on back. *(Zillner collection)*

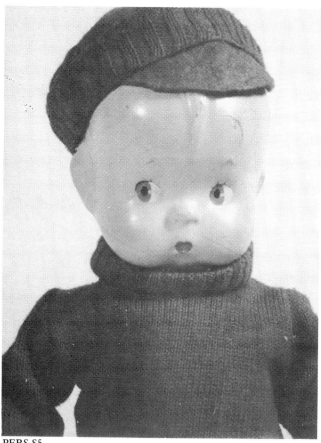

PERS-S5.

PERS-S5.

PERS-S6.

PERS-S5. 15" *Skippy*. All composition (has *Patsy*-style body), painted eyes and hair, re-dressed. Represents character portrayed by actor, Jackie Cooper, in the movies; originally *Skippy* was a comic strip by Percy L. Crosby. Marks: **EFFANBEE / SKIPPY /** © **. 1929.** *(Zillner collection)*

PERS-S6. 13½" *Skippy*. Composition swivel head, arms and legs (note method of attaching head), painted-on shoes and stockings, dark brown, painted eyes and hair, wears remnant of World War II army uniform with original medals. Marks: **EFFANBEE / SKIPPY /** © **/ P. L. CROSBY /** and another illegible line. *(Wiseman collection)*

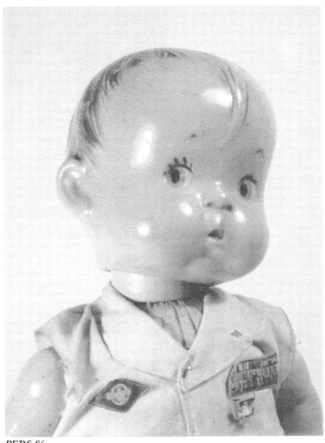

PERS-S6.

PORT-B3. PERS-S7.

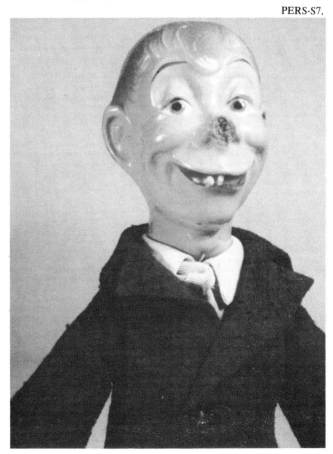

PERS-S7.

PERS-S7. 12½" *Mortimer Snerd.* Another "Flexy" doll. *Mortimer* is one of Edgar Bergen's character ventriloquist dummies, although this doll does not have the talking feature. For construction and full length view see PORT-B3. *(Zillner collection) Mortimer Snerd* ventriloquist dummy with vinyl head, cloth body and limbs is available as late as 1970 catalogs. Older dummies have composition head and extremities.

PERS-S8. 11" *Swing and Sway Doll, Bobbi-Mae.* All composition, head and body are balanced on rod mounted in feet. Cream or yellow dress trimmed in blue (her twin has a pink dress), painted side-glancing eyes and hair. Sammy Kaye, famous in what is now called "The Big Band Era" of the 1930's and 1940's, used a slogan, "Swing and Sway with Sammy Kaye". Marks: **BOBBI-MAE / SWING'N'SWAY DOLL / inspired by / SAMMY KAYE / Patent Pending / Manufactured by / WONDERCRAFT CO. / NEW YORK,** on paper label on bottom of feet. *(Kirtley collection. Label information Wingfield collection)*

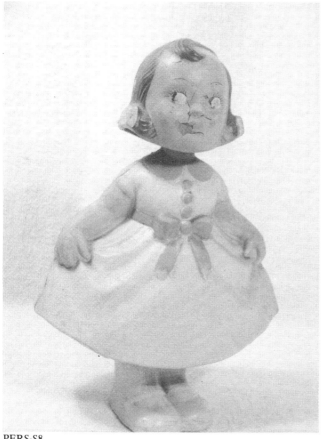

PERS-S9.

PERS-S8.

PERS-W1.

PERS-S9. *Judy Splinters.* 17" Ventriloquist doll representing character created by *Shirley Dinsdale* for television. Flexible vinyl head, ring on back of head controls facial movement, yarn wig, soft body stuffed with cotton and foam rubber, magic skin rubber limbs, dressed as on telelvision. 1950 Catalog illustration. *(Courtesy Sears, Roebuck & Co.)*

PERS-W1. 14" *Linda Williams.* Vinyl, blue-green sleep eyes, rooted synthetic hair, open closed mouth. Represents the character portrayed by actress Angela Cartwright in television series, "Make Room For Daddy", later titled, "The Danny Thomas Show". Doll and wardrobe were offered as mail-in premiums by General Foods about 1959. Marks: **LINDA WILLIAMS** on head. Body unmarked. *(Author's collection)* 15" size listed in Sears 1962 Christmas Book at $3.98.

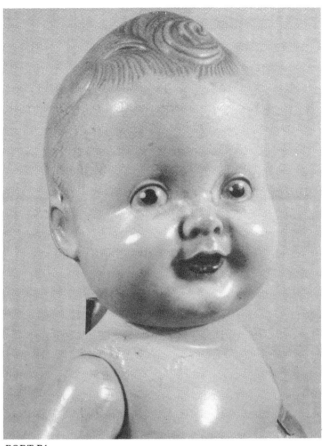

PORT-B1.

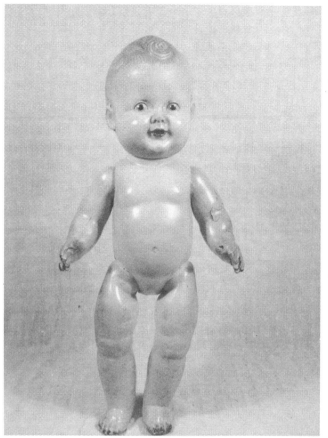

PORT-B1.

PORT-B2.

PORTRAIT DOLLS

Many celebrities and entertainment personalities have been "immortalized" in doll form. While a separate book would be required to cover this field thoroughly,[1] those presented here make up a good survey of what is available.

PORT-B1. 16" *"Baby Sandy" Henville,* movies, late 1930's, early 1940's. Dolls date from 1939. Early ones, as this one, had molded hair; some later ones had wigs. All composition, painted blue eyes with white high-light dot. Marks: **BABY SANDY** on head. *(Author's collection)*

PORT-B2. 12" *"Baby Sandy" Henville,* all composition, sleep eyes, re-dressed in duplicate of original boy's suit worn in movies in which she played boys' parts. Also available in 7" size. Marks: **BABY SANDY** on head. *(Zillner collection)*

[1] Burdick, Loraine, "Child Star Dolls and Toys", 1968, and "Shirley Dolls", 1966, 1968, Quest Books.

PORT-B3.

PORT-C2.

PORT-C1.

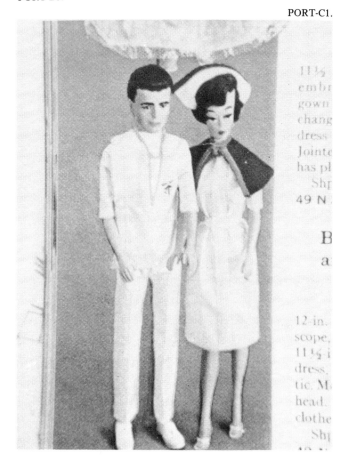

PORT-B3. 12½" *Fanny Brice,* comedienne, in her radio role of *Baby Snooks.* Doll is caricature of Miss Brice, has flexible wire "Flexy" body, composition head, hands, oversize feet, painted eyes. Original dress and pantalettes in red and white cotton print. Ideal. 1939. Shown with *Fanny* is another "Flexy" doll, *Mortimer Snerd,* which see. *(Zillner collection)*

PORT-C1. 12" *Ben Casey* and 11½" Nurse. *Dr. Ben Casey,* played by actor Vince Edwards, was popular television character of 1960's. Doll is recognizable likeness of actor, all vinyl, painted features, complete with stethoscope. 1963 catalog illustration. *(Courtesy Sears, Roebuck & Co.)*

PORT-C2. 14" *Charles Chaplain,* comedian, composition head and hands, rag body, all original. Hat missing. Tag sewed on tweed jacket reads: **"Charley Chaplain, World's Greatest Comedian, Made Exclusively by Louis Amberg, by Special Arrangements with Essanay Film Co."** On left side of rectangular cloth label is head of Indian complete with full feather head-dress. From 1915. *(Zillner collection)*

PORT-C2.

PORT-C3.

PORT-C4.

PORT-C3. 9½" *Prince Charles of England.* Vinyl doll, elaborately hand dressed, all original. Tag reads: "**Artistic / Copyright / is Claimed in Respect / of the Whole Range / of Coloured Costume / Dolls by / Peggy / Nisbet / Limited.**" Collectors Costume Dolls by Peggy Nisbet, made in England. *(Zillner collection)*

PORT-C4. 26" *Dick Clark,* host of popular televised dance show for teenagers. Autograph doll, cloth body and limbs, molded vinyl head and hands. All original suede saddle shoes, yellow vest, dark gray trousers, light gray jacket, white shirt, red plaid tie, and autograph pen. Marks: **JURO** on head. Original box labeled: **Juro Novelty Co., Inc., NYC, "ANOTHER JURO CELEBRITY DOLL."** From 1958, doll is listed in 1959 catalog at $7.49 retail. *(Author's collection)*

PORT-C5.

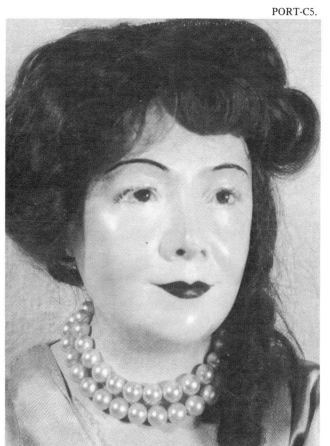

PORT-C5.

PORT-C5.

PORTRAIT SPECIALS

Having one's portrait done in doll form was a fashion of the 1920's. Fortunate, indeed, is the collector who chances upon an example of the type for they are usually considered heirlooms and remain with the family. Here is an excellent example of these dolls; she is in perfect condition, and is destined for a special niche in the Kansas City Museum. With that move the doll will have come *home;* the Kansas City Museum is housed in the beautiful mansion which belonged to the R. A. Long family of that city.

PORT-C5. 24" Portrait of *Loula Long Combs,* well-known Kansas City, Missouri, horsewoman who drove her sulky in American Royal Parades for years. Head is of a type of artists' composition, artist unknown, possibly made in Europe. Shoulder head is attached to typical bed doll body with composition hands and molded shoes. Wig is fashioned of subject's own hair. Original satin and lace dress is copy of one worn by Mrs. Combs. ca. 1928. *(Kirtley collection)*

PORT-C7.

PORT-C6.

PORT-C7.

NOTE: ORIGINAL PRICES SHOWN
ARE NOT TODAY'S PRICES.

PORT-C6. 13½" *Jackie Coogan*. Child star of movies, dressed as he appeared in role in movie, "The Kid". 1921, Horsman. *1924 Catalog illustration courtesy Sears, Roebuck & Co.*

PORT-C7. 21" *Hopalong Cassidy*. Vinyl head, stuffed cloth body and limbs, all original, excellent likeness of popular Western hero of television and movies. Doll is unmarked; badge reads: **HOPALONG CASSIDY** (curved around badge). 1949, Ideal. Also available is portrait of *Roy Rogers* made at same time and of same materials. *(Zillner collection)*

THE DIONNE QUINTUPLETS

The phenomenon of multiple birth always captures world attention. When this interest is stimulated by the efforts of public relations experts there seems no limit to which exploitation may extend. The *Dionne Quintuplets* were born May 28, 1934, in Callender, Ontario, Canada, and their first world-wide recognition was never allowed to abate. The names and faces of the five little girls, *Annette, Cecile, Emelie, Marie,* and *Yvonne,* were attached to hundreds of commercial items. Collectors wishing to specialize in this subject will find post-cards, spoons, ladies' fans, books, sheet music, toys of all kinds, dolls, paper dolls, magazine and newspaper articles and advertisements, and calendars with which to augment their collections.

The Madame Alexander Doll Company obtained sole rights to production of the dolls; however, dolls representing the Quints were produced both in Japan and Germany. A sewing outfit from Japan featured five small all-bisque dolls. Five tiny all-bisque babies, stamped *Germany,* in their original buntings and crocheted outfits, are marked with paper labels to indicate their identity. More figurine than doll, five nicely tinted composition babies in cute poses were sold as *"quints".* In addition, many mothers of the Depression years who could not afford the higher-priced genuine *Dionne* dolls, bought five identical dolls and dressed them as *quints* for eager little girls. This fact alone will account for many of the *"unmarked quintuplets"* being offered as authentic. These, too, may have a place in a comprehensive collection, so long as they are recognized for what they truly are.

PORT-D1.

PORT-D2, -2b.

PORT-D1. 11½ *Dionne* Toddler. All composition, brown sleep eyes, original human hair wig and dress. Marks: **DIONNE / ALEXANDER** on head. *(Wiseman collection)*

PORT-D2a. 10" *Dionne* Baby. All composition, brown sleep eyes, molded painted hair. Marks: **DIONNE / ALEXANDER** on head. *(Zillner collection)*

PORT-D2b. 20" *Dionne* Child. Composition swivel shoulder head on stuffed cloth body, composition arms and legs, brown sleep eyes, closed mouth, original human hair wig. Marks: **DIONNE / ALEXANDER** on head. *(Zillner collection)*

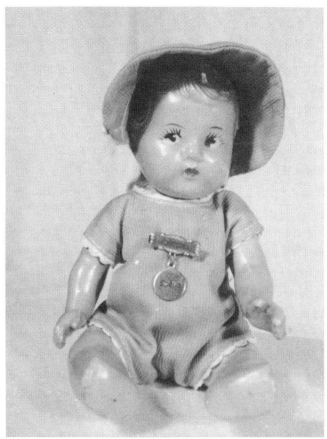

PORT-D3.

PORT-D4.

PORT-D2b.

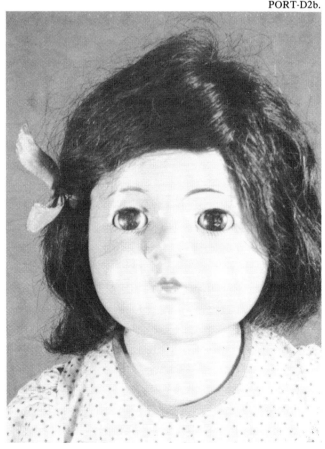

PORT-D3. 7½" *Dionne* Baby. Painted brown eyes and hair, all composition original sunsuit and bonnet. Each doll in set wears her "gold" name tag and different color clothes. These 7½" dolls available with two slightly different heads and straight legs. Marks: **DIONNE / ALEXANDER** on head. *(Zillner collection)*

PORT-D4. 8" *Dionne* Toddler. Red-brown mohair wig, brown painted eyes, original clothes, name pins, straight legs, all composition. Each doll has original folder attached showing all five Dionnes as babies. 1936 on tag. Dress tag same as PORT-D5. *(Wingfield collection)*

PORT-D4.

PORT-D5.

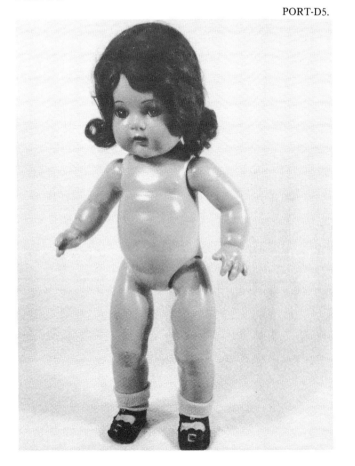

PORT-D5.

PORT-D5. 19" *Dionne* Toddler. All composition, brown sleep eyes, lashes, open mouth, four teeth, original human hair wig, all original clothes with golden dress pin *"Emelie".* Cloth tag on dress reads: **"GENUINE / DIONNE QUINTUPLET DOLLS / ALL RIGHTS RESERVED / MADAME ALEXANDER-N.Y."** Marked **ALEXANDER** on back of shoulders. Childhood doll of Gwen Odell Bower. *(Author's collection)*

PORT-D6. 7½" Baby. All composition, brown painted eyes, black painted molded hair, original pink organdy dress and bonnet trimmed with blue ric-rac, pink cotton undersuit. Unmarked. Sold to author as *"unmarked Dionne."* Compare with PORT-D3 and PORT-D4.

PORT-D6.

PORT-D7.

PORT-D8.

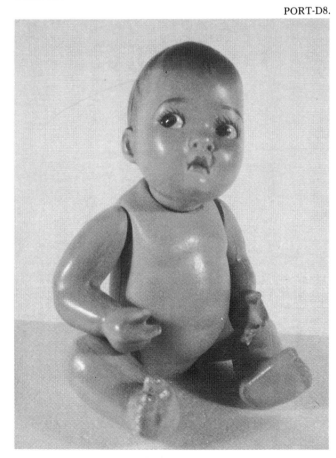

PORT-D7. 5" Babies. All composition, nicely painted, marked: **Made in Japan.** *(Kirtley collection)*

PORT-D8. 7½" Baby. All composition, painted brown side-glancing eyes, stamped in black **JAPAN** on back. Original clothes are nicely made white cotton baby dress, slip, and bonnet. Strong *Dionne* resemblance indicates they were made as competition for American-made *Dionnes. (Courtesy Camelot of Springfield, Missouri)*

PORT-D9. 1 3 / 8" Babies. All bisque, jointed hips and shoulders, original crocheted outfits, sewed into pink flannel bunting. Each doll has paper label with name. Marked **Germany** in red stamping ink on backs. These tiny dolls were found, in sets as shown, behind other stock in stationery store which was selling out. They had apparently fallen back and remained hidden since the 1930's. An orange card box stamped **Germany** held a quantity of these midget sets. *(Author's collection)*

PORT-D9-1. Illustration shows Karo Syrup advertisement from Better Homes and Gardens Magazine, February, 1937, inside front cover. *(Courtesy Mrs. Herman W. Mead)*

PORT-D9.

PORT-D9-1.

PORT-D10.   PORT-D11.

PORT-D10.

PORT-D11.

PORT-D10. 22" *Doctor Doolittle.* Title character from the movie, with actor Rex Harrison in the role. Cloth construction with molded vinyl head. Clothes are integral part of construction and not removeable. Doll bears striking resemblance to the actor. Talking mechanism with pull ring in left side. Says: "As a people doctor I was a total failure.", "I'd study elephant and eagle, buffalo and beagle . .", and "How do you do? I'm Doctor Doolittle.", several other phrases, all in the marvelous tones and accents of Rex Harrison. 1967. © **by Mattel and Twentieth Century-Fox Film Corporation, Apjac Productions, Inc.** *(Rebekka Anderton collection)*

PORT-D11. 6" *Doctor Dootlittle,* with his parrot, *Polynesia.* All vinyl with wires for bendability. Clothes are sewn on. 1967. Mattel. Copyright same as PORT-D10. Other animal characters from the movie have been made into talking toys. *(Author's collection)*

PORT-D13.

PORT-D13.

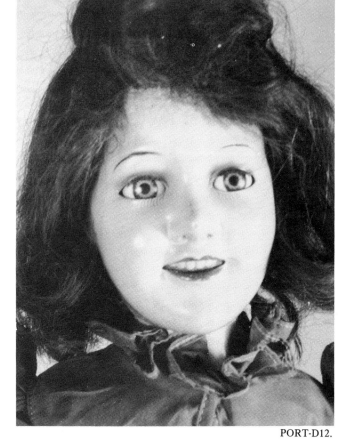

PORT-D12.

PORT-D12. 25" *Deanna Durbin.* All composition, old dress, possibly original, original human hair wig. Marks: **DEANNA DURBIN / IDEAL TOY CO.** on head. 1939. *(Zillner collection)*

PORT-D13. 21" *Deanna Durbin.* All composition, all original, human hair wig, green sleep eyes. Marks: **IDEAL DOLL** on back. **DEANNA DURBIN / IDEAL TOY CO.** on head. Sewn-in cloth dress tag reads: **GENUINE / DEANNA DURBIN / DOLL / IDEAL NOVELTY & TOY CO. / A UNIVERSAL STAR Made in U.S.A. Deanna Durbin** signature facsimile on bottoms of shoes. 1939. *(Author's collection)*

PORT-F1.

PORT-F1.

PORT-G1.

PORT-F1. 17½" *W. C. Fields,* actor-comedian. Cloth body, composition head, hands and molded shoes, blue painted eyes, ventriloquist dummy mechanism. All original: pearl gray beaver hat, red tie, black wool felt coat trimmed with light brown velvet, brown and white checked trousers, sleeveless shirt with dickey front. 1930. Marks: **W. C. FIELDS, AN EFFANBEE PRODUCT** on back of shoulder plate. *(Wiseman collection)*

PORT-G1. 18" *Judy Garland,* actress-singer. All composition, human hair wig, large brown sleep eyes, hair lashes, open mouth, six teeth, painted lower lashes. Clothes original but unmarked. Head unmarked. Doll definitely identified in Janet Johl's "Fascinating Story of Dolls", page 272. Loraine Burdick, in her "Child Star Dolls and Toys", states this doll originally had a tag on her wrist identifying the doll as **Judy Garland in the role of Dorothy in the M.G.M. film, "The Wizard of Oz".** 1939. Ideal. Doll shown has traces of *Shirley Temple* markings on the back, indicating Ideal used the same bodies for both dolls. *(Kirtley collection)*

PORT-G1.

PORT-G1.

PORT-H1.

PORT-H1. 15" *Sonja Henie,* actress-skater. All composition, blonde mohair wig, glass-like sleep eyes, long lashes, "real" figure skates. Ad states "only at Sears," appraently doll dressed in this red and white outfit was Sears exclusive. Doll retailed at $2.98, a markdown. 1941, Madame Alexander. Sears featured Sonja Henie ice skates in 1942 and 1943. *(Courtesy Sears, Roebuck & Co.)*

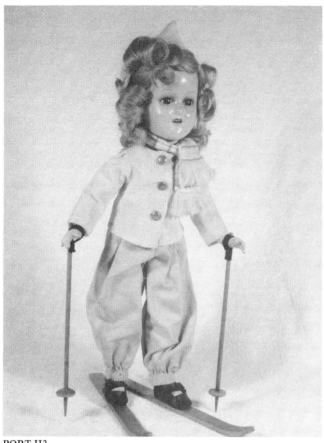

PORT-H3.

PORT-H3.

PORT-H2.   ALEX-14.

PORT-H2. 14" *Sonja Henie.* All composition, human hair wig, re-dressed. Marks: **Mme. Alexander.** Note difference in appearance with doll in PORT-H3; original paint job, condition of doll, costuming all contribute to apparent difference. Shape of face and dimples are two of doll's trademarks. *Sonja's* friend is Alexander's *"Alice". (Zillner collection)*

PORT-H3. 14" *Sonja Henie.* All composition, brown sleep eyes, blonde human hair wig, open mouth, teeth. Original ski suit of ecru corduroy, green, white, gray striped wool scarf, cap had white fur trim, only wisps of which remain. Marks: **SONJA HENIE** on head. Cloth tag on coat reads: **"Genuine Sonja Henie Doll / Madame Alexander N.Y. U.S.A. / All Rights Reserved."** Original skis, poles, and shoes. 1939-1940. *(Wiseman collection)*

PORT-J1.

PORT-T1.   PORT-J1.

PORT-J2.

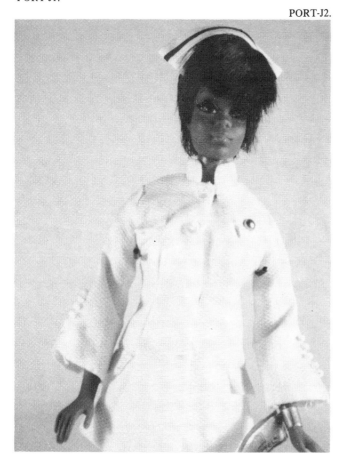

PORT-J1. 20" *Jeannie,* from television series, "I Dream of Jeannie." Doll is likeness of Barbara Eden, who starred in title role. All vinyl, all original, rooted synthetic wig, sleep eyes, lashes. ca. 1966. Libbey. Shown with *Jeannie* is "That Girl", *Marlow Thomas,* which see. Marks: **13 EYE 6 (c) 1966 LIBBY.** *(Zillner collection)*

PORT-J2. 11½" *Julia.* Actress Diahanne Carroll in title role of television series. Plastic and vinyl, rooted hair, painted eyes, hair lashes, twist 'n' turn waist, flexible legs. **1968, Mattel, Made in Japan.** © **Savannah Productions, Inc. / All Rights Reserved.** *(Zillner collection)*

PORT-K1.

PORT-J3.

PORT-K1.

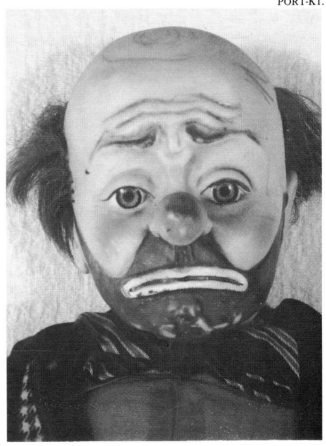

PORT-J3. 11½" *Julia.* Talking doll, chatty ring, Diahanne Carroll's voice and likeness as television's *"Julia".* Original clothes: lame jumpsuit. Plastic and vinyl, rooted hair, painted eyes, hair lashes, flexible legs. 1969 catalog illustration. *(Courtesy Sears, Roebuck & Co.)*

PORT-K1. 24" *Emmett Kelly* in his immortal act as *"Willie the Clown."* Vinyl head, set glassene eyes, rooted red synthetic hair, stuffed cloth body. Tag reads: **"Exclusive License / Baby Barry / Toy N.Y.C. / Emmett Kelly / Willie the Clown."** *(Kirtley collection)*

PORT-K2.

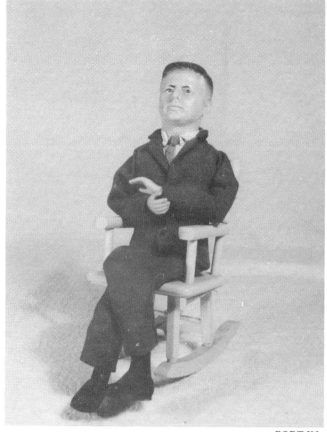

PORT-K3.

ADV.-P1. PORT-K2.

PORT-K2. 13½" *Emmett Kelly, Willie the Clown.*
Unjointed vinyl body, heavy for its size, molded-on hat,
redressed to duplicate original clothes. Marks: **B** on back
of head, probably Baby Barry Toy Co. A 15" size shown
in 1958 catalog, retailed at $2.79, described as cotton-
stuffed latex body, appears identical to doll above.
Shown with *"Willie"* is *"Johnny"* of Phillip Morris fame.
See *Johnny* in Advertising Dolls. *(Zillner collection)*

PORT-K3. 13½" *John F. Kennedy.* Excellent likeness of
the thirty-fifth President of the United States. Unmarked
doll has molded vinyl head, hands, shoes, and sox, wire
and card body and limbs which bend to allow him to sit
realistically in the rocking chair. ca. 1963. *(Zillner
collection)*

Original box marked: **KAMAR, INC., Los Angeles,
Made in Japan, 1963.** Head marked: **T.K.R.** in a flattened
triangle. Chair rocks as tune *"Happy Days are Here
Again"* plays. Brown chair with music box enclosed under
seat. Doll holds miniature *Herald Tribune* with picture of
John, Jackie, and Robert with words of song.

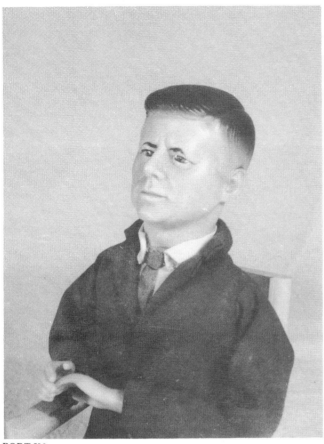

PORT-K3.

PORT-L2.

PORT-L1.

PORT-L1. 25" *Pinky Lee*, host of children's television show. All original, soft vinyl head and hands, stuffed cloth body and legs, talks with pull string. Label sewn on jacket reads: **"PINKY LEE NBC TV". JURO CELEBRITY PRODUCTS.** on back of neck. For full length view of this doll see *Howdy Doody*. 1960. *(Zillner collection)*

PORT-L2. 10" *Stan Laurel*, 8" *Oliver Hardy*, comic team. Wire, card, and cloth construction, vinyl heads. Sewn-in tag reads: **"Knickerbocker Toy Co. Inc. / - N.Y. / licensed by / Harmon Pic. Corp. Bend 'Em Doll TM."** Also available in this series is *Bozo the Clown, Pinocchio, Raggedy Ann,* and *Raggedy Andy. (Author's collection)*

PORT-L3.

PORT-M1.

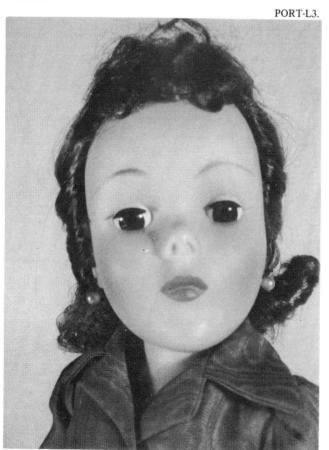

PORT-L3.

PORT-L3. 21" *Sherri Lewis,* television personality, children's programs. Plastic and vinyl, sleep eyes, rooted Saran hair, "high-heel" feet, lady body. Marks: **ALEXANDER** on head. Booklet reads: **"THE SHERRI LEWIS DOLL / The Sherri Lewis Doll made exclusively by Madame Alexander, bringing to little girls everywhere all the charm and beauty of the well-known and talented TV star. Alexander Doll Co. Inc., New York City, N.Y."** *(Zillner collection)*

PORT-M1. 16" *General Douglas MacArthur,* the "Man of the Hour" ca. 1942. All composition, molded-on hat, original uniform, and Sam Browne belt. Freundlich Novelty Corp., 1942. *(Zillner collection)*

PORT-M2. Illustration, Sears Christmas catalog, 1942, *General MacArthur* doll, retail at $1.98.

PORT-R1. 20" *Dianna Ross,* member of singing group, The Supremes. All vinyl, jointed doll, rooted black hair, large black sleep eyes, molded, painted mouth and teeth, lady body. © **1969, Ideal Toy Co.** *(Author's collection)*

PORT-M1.

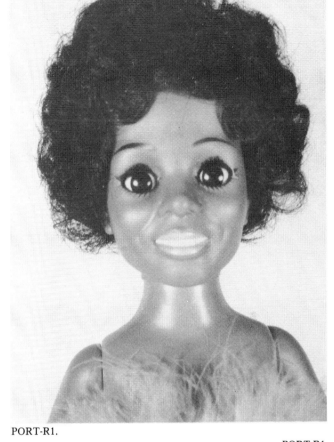

PORT-R1.

PORT-M2.

PORT-R1.

PORT-ST1. PORT-ST2.

PORT-ST2.

SHIRLEY TEMPLE DOLLS

"A Shirley Temple doll" — those words meant magic to millions of little girls during the 1930's when magic was a priceless commodity. As the country sank deeper into the Great Depression, the curls and dimples, the dancing feet, and the cheery little voice of this magic moppet were a bright focus in an often dreary world. *"Shirley Temple* hair-bows, dresses, and hats to make your own little girl look just like a movie star — send in your order today." *Shirley* frocks appeared in catalogs beginning in 1935, and, along with *Shirley* hats, were carried for several years. The last hats appeared in 1938. Other child stars endorsed hats and dresses: *Cora Sue Collins, Jane Withers* and *Marcia Mae Jones,* among others. But no one came through on those pages like Shirley Temple.

Ideal introduced the doll in 1934, and in their 1935 Fall and Winter catalog, Sears carried "The only original *Shirley Temple* doll," wearing the polka dot dress, copy of the dress worn in her first movie, *"Stand Up and Cheer."* Already in 1935 the child models in the catalog were wearing their hair in *Shirley Temple* curly styles. Mothers struggled to master the technique of producing such curls, topped off quite often with *Shirley Temple* hairbows, centered with cameo *Shirley* likenesses (fourteen cents each). Then the craze began to wane, and by 1938 the dolls were being offered with ever larger arrays of accessories. There is no *Shirley Temple* doll offered in the 1939 catalog. End of an era. Or *was* it?

Once again little girls sang *Shirley's* songs and mimicked her dances, for in 1957, television revived her movies and Ideal re-issued the doll, this time in hard plastic and vinyl. The new doll is not quite the doll the old one was and never achieved the popularity of the original. But vinyl or not, it is like a message from the past to those of us who remember *Shirley Temple.*

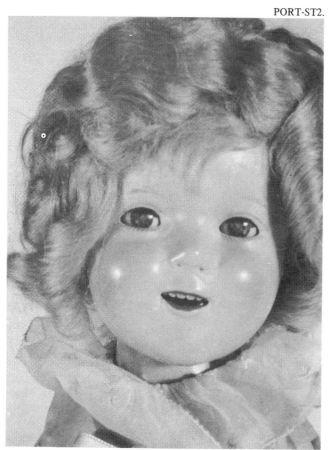

PORT-ST1. 29" *Shirley Temple.* All original, complete with picture badge. Eyes are example of age problem suffered by many *Shirley Temple* dolls. *(Zillner collection)*

PORT-ST2. 18" *Shirley Temple.* All original, complete with picture badge. Note differences in neckline and sleeve treatment of these otherwise identical pleated dresses. *(Zillner collection)*

PORT-ST3.

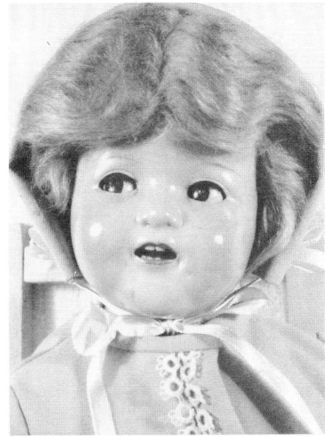

PORT-ST4.

PORT-ST4.

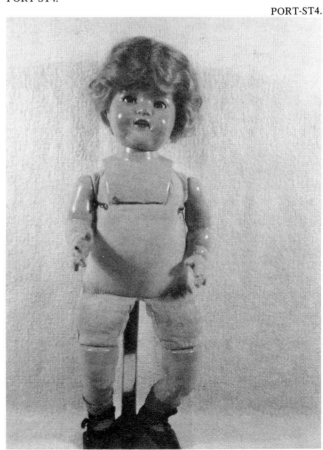

PORT-ST3. 27" *Shirley Temple.* Repainted, new dress and wig. Eyes in excellent condition. *(Kirtley collection)*

PORT-ST4. 19" *Shirley Temple Baby.* Composition swivel shoulder head, arms and legs, open mouth, four teeth below, two above, working cry voice, greenish flirty sleep eyes, may have been blue originally, new clothes, original blonde mohair wig. Marks: **SHIRLEY TEMPLE.** *(Wingfield collection)* Sears 1935 catalog listed: *Shirley Temple Baby,* 15½" at $2.89, 18" at $3.79, and 20" at $4.79. Doll had rubber arms, composition head and legs, kapok-stuffed cloth body, hazel glass eyes, pleated organdy dress and bonnet. *(Courtesy Sears, Roebuck & Co.)*

PORT-ST5.

PORT-ST6a, -ST6.

PORT-ST7.

SHIRLEY TEMPLE
Cop. IDEAL
N & Tᴄ   fig. PORT-ST5

SHIRLEY TEMPLE
18

fig. PORT-ST5

PORT-ST5. 18" *Shirley Temple.* All original, in costume from movie, "Wee Willie Winkie": red plaid kilt, tan gabardine jacket, tweedy stockings, black patent shoes, blue velvet and plaid hat. Marks: fig. PORT-ST5. *(Baume collection)*

PORT-ST6. 13" *Shirley Temple.* All composition, original mohair wig, light brown sleep eyes, open mouth, teeth. Marks: **SHIRLEY TEMPLE** on head. **SHIRLEY TEMPLE** (curved) with **13** beneath, on back of shoulders. *(Author's collection)*

PORT-ST6a. 13" Girl. All composition, same body and limbs as *Shirley Temple* doll on right. On back of shoulders is a smudged-out area of lettering which matches the **Shirley Temple** mark on other doll and a very clear number **13** beneath. Head is original to this body; author purchased doll from original owner. (See Ideal)

PORT-ST7a.

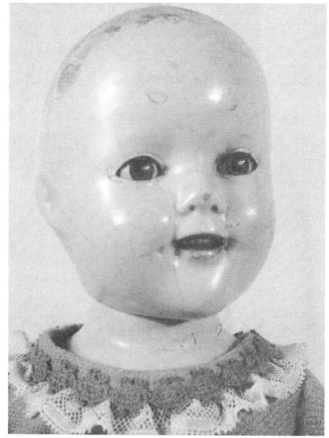

PORT-ST9.

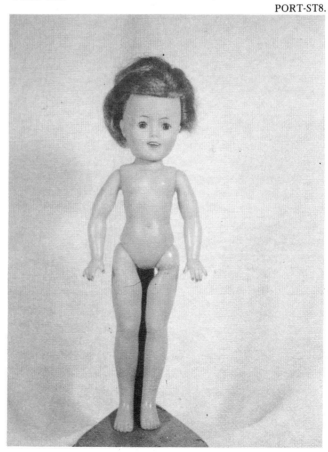

PORT-ST8.

PORT-ST7. 17" *Shirley Temple*. Plastic and vinyl, flirty sleep eyes, rooted Saran hair, dimples. Marks: **Ideal Doll / ST-17-1** on head. **Ideal Doll / ST-17** on back. (*Author's collection*)

PORT-ST7a. 1957 Catalog illustration, 17" and 19", $10.47 and $13.47 retail, respectively. Organdy dress with sewn-in half slip, fiberboard case with bobby pins and curlers. Also available same catalog, doll dressed in blue sleeveless top and knife-pleated striped skirt. (*Courtesy Sears, Roebuck & Co.*)

PORT-ST8. 12" *Shirley Temple*. Vinyl and plastic, sleep eyes, rooted hair, original red and white checked dress. Marks: **Ideal Doll / ST-12** on head. **ST-12-N** on shoulders. (*Author's collection*)

PORT-ST9. 18" *Shirley Temple*. Composition, sleep eyes, wig missing. Marks: Head marked as in fig. PORT-ST5. Body unmarked. (*Author's collection*)

PORT-ST8 ,-ST7,-ST10,-.ST9

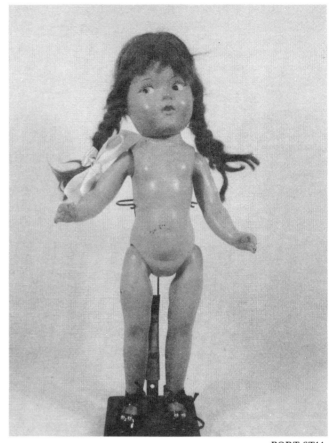

PORT-ST11.

PORT-ST10.

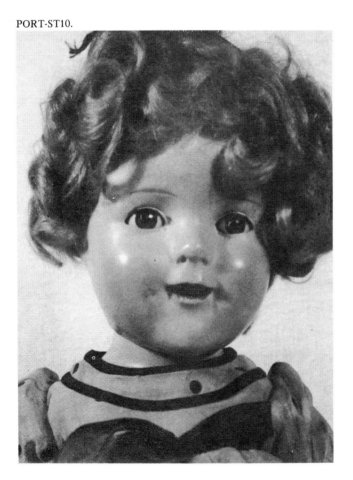

PORT-ST10. 18" *Shirley Temple.* Unmarked. Yes, there are such things. (See Ideal) Identical doll shown in 1935 catalogs wearing same red and white (or other colors) polka dot dress. Doll purchased from original owner in original box. An early doll. *(Author's collection)*

Some Shirley Temple dolls are found with only body marks, others have head marks, while still others have both. As finished parts moved down the assembly line these combinations occured. Occasionally two unmarked sections were joined, thus creating a *genuine* though *unmarked* Shirley Temple.

PORT-ST11. 15" Girl. All composition, **not** a *Shirley Temple* doll, but another Ideal doll using the *Shirley* body and limbs (see Ideal). Original mohair braids, painted features, side-glancing eyes. Unmarked. *(Spalding collection)*

PORT-ST12.

PORT-ST12,-ST6,-ST13.

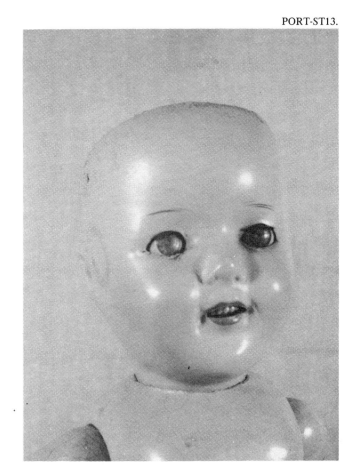

PORT-ST13.

PORT-ST12. 20" Toddler. New curly blonde wig enhances resemblance to *Shirley Temple* dolls, but doll is unmarked. Brown eyes, well modeled, good composition. *(Author's collection)*

PORT-ST13. 21" Walker. Bears strong resemblance to *Shirley Temple* dolls. Open crown allows access to walking mechanism. Unmarked. *(Author's collection)*

TERRI LEE DOLLS

An example of a non-celebrity portrait doll is the *Terri Lee* doll which is well known among collectors. The original *Terri Lee* dolls date from 1948; *Jerry Lee*, a boy with caracul wig, followed that same year. *Tiny Terri, Linda Lee* and *Baby Linda* were "born" in 1951, *Connie Lynn* came along in 1955, and *So Sleepy* was presented in 1957.

The dolls were first produced in Lincoln, Nebraska, then in 1952, after a disastrous fire, the doll manufacture was moved to Apple Valley, California. The Lincoln plant was rebuilt as a wardrobe factory; *Terri Lee* was one of the best dressed dolls in the world. Dancing dresses, playclothes, school clothes, hats, shoes, and even mink coats at $300.00 each were all available for this popular doll. *Terri Lee* could even sing and tell bedtime stories. This doll was touted as *"Terri Lee, The National Baby Sitter."* The doll was fitted with a speaker assembly and a receptacle in the back of the head to receive the jack. The kit included an adapter assembly which was to be installed in any available record player, and the jack with plugs at both ends, one to fit into the doll's receptacle and the other to fit into the jack adapter on the record player. Special instructions for this *Talking Terri* included three "don'ts": *"Don't wash my hair or take me swimming; don't use hair set or other liquids on my head or hair; and don't take me away from the phonograph without making sure I am unplugged".* Modern doll collectors may wish to take note of these first two "don'ts" especially.

The booklet which came with the *Talking Terri* reads:

"I am not a doll but a real little girl. My mommy made this likeness of me so I could be your playmate during the day and at night when I sleep with you. I will tell you stories and sing you songs. I will tell you of many wonderful things. My stories and songs are called "Terri Tales and Terri Tunes at Terri Time."

PORT-TL1.

PORT-TL1.

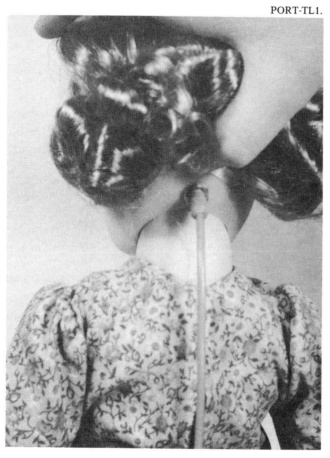

PORT-TL1. 16" *Talking Terri Lee*. Good quality hard plastic and vinyl, all original, painted eyes, synthetic, glued-on wig. A late doll. *(Kirtley collection)*

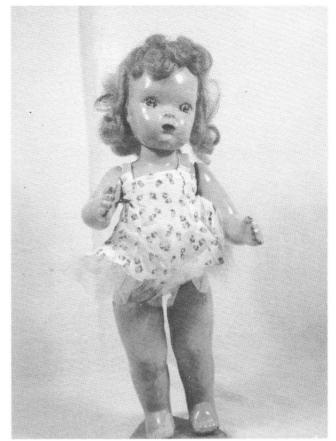

PORT-TL2.   PORT-TL2.

PORT-TL3.

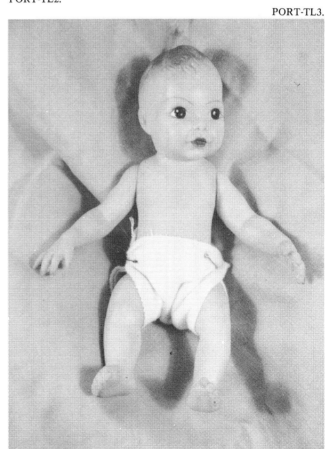

PORT-TL2. 16" *Terri Lee*. All composition, very early, marked only **PAT. PENDING** on back. Sunsuit is original *Terri Lee* wardrobe, but not original to this doll. *(Kirtley collection)*

PORT-TL3. 10" *Linda Baby,* a *Terri Lee* doll. All soft vinyl, painted features, separate fingers, jointed hips and shoulders, unmarked. 1951. *(Kirtley collection)*

PORT-TL5,-TL6.

PORT-TL7.

PORT-TL4.

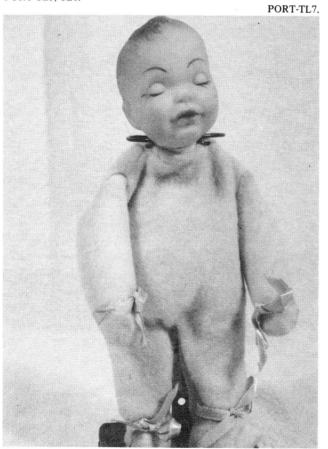

PORT-TL4. 18" *Connie Lynn, Terri Lee* Baby Doll. Good quality hard plastic, dark gray sleep eyes, extra long lashes, glued-on lamb's wool wig. 1955. Unmarked. *(Author's collection)*

PORT-TL5. 16" *Terri Lee.* All original, glued-on blonde mohair wig, nylon dress has white nylon sewn-in half-slip, painted eyes. Marks: **TERRI LEE** on back. *(Author's collection)*

PORT-TL6. 10" *Tiny Terri Lee.* All original, white nylon nurse uniform and cap, glued-on mohair wig. Marks: **TERRI LEE** on back. Cloth dress tag: **TERRI LEE.** Walker mechanism turns head as legs are moved. 1951. *(Author's collection)*

PORT-TL7. 9½" *So-Sleepy,* a *Terri Lee* Baby. Vinyl head, loosely stuffed body, sleepy, floppy baby effect. 1957. *(Kirtley collection)*

PORT-TL8.

PORT-T1.

PORT-TL8. *"Just between us Scouts, have you sold any cookies lately?"* Rebekka Anderton and *Terri Lee,* Girl Scouts. *(Kirtley collection)*

PORT-T2.

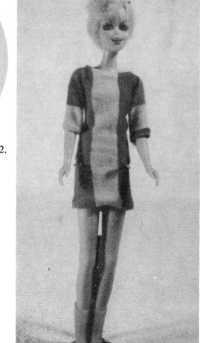

PORT-T1. 17" *Marlo Thomas,* actress. Hard plastic, soft vinyl head and arms, rooted hair, black pupil-less eyes. Issued in two original outfits; red velveteen formal gown shown here and two-tone jersey shift dress of blue and green with high-heel white boots. Marks: **ALEXANDER / 19© 66.** 1966 and 1967. Not true likeness but does resemble the actress. *(Zillner collection)* For full length see PORT-J1.

PORT-T2. 11½" *Twiggy,* the English fashion model. Vinyl and plastic, painted eyes, lashes, rooted hair, twist 'n' turn waist, bendable legs. Marks: © **1967 Minnow Co. Ltd. and Twiggy Enterprises Ltd.** Mattel. *(Zillner collection)*

PORT-W1.

PORT-W1.

PORT-V1.

PORT-V1.

PORT-V1. 25" *Dick Van Dyke,* actor, a caricature, as *Mr. Potts* in the Walt Disney movie, "Chitty Chitty Bang Bang". All cloth, flat features, chatty ring, speaks with actor's own voice. Marks: © **Mattel 1968** on cloth tag. *(Zillner collection)*

PORT-W1. 17" *Jane Withers,* actress. All composition, green sleep eyes, red-brown mohair wig, original clothes, tag on dress reads: **Jane Withers / ALL RIGHTS RESERVED / MADAME ALEXANDER, N.Y.** Good likeness of child star of the movies. 1936. *(Wiseman collection)*

PORT-W2. 20" *Jane Withers.* All composition, greenish-blue eyes, original red-brown mohair wig, original dress, tag sewn in, same as PORT-W1. Doll is unmarked. *(Zillner collection)*

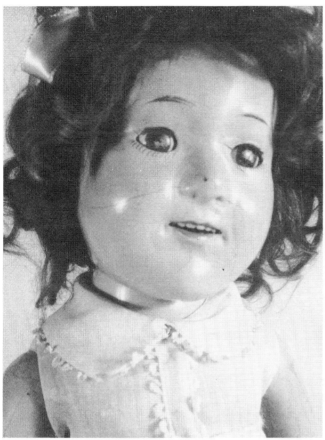

PORT-W2.

PERS-01, PORT-W2.

PUPP-1.

PUPPETS AND MARIONETTES

Puppets and marionettes have been called the *"magic dolls"* because of their quality of eliciting sympathetic response from young and old alike. Whether a finger puppet or a complicated marionette with *"talking"* face feature and intricate ankle movement, the dolls in this category do, indeed, appear to have a sort of magic *life* about them. Puppets and marionettes are among the most aged and ageless members of the *theatre*. They have been used not only in entertainment, but in educational and therapeutic applications as well. Television puppets have been successful in raising the experience level of underpriveleged children. Hand and finger puppets have evoked response in troubled children, allowing them to act out and often solve their problems. Evidence of the extent to which children identify with puppets and marionettes may be seen in the manner in which a child will carry on a conversation with a puppet "person". Truly these are the *magic* dolls.

PUPP-2.

PUPP-3.

PUPP-4.

PUPP-1. Famous Personality Hand Puppets. Vinylite plastic heads, cloth costumes. Radio, television and movies personalities: *Flub-a-Dub, Dilly Dally, Clarabelle Clown, Howdy Doody,* and *Roy Rogers. 1951 Catalog illustration courtesy Sears, Roebuck & Co.*

PUPP-2. Pelham Puppets. *Pinnochio.* Hand-crafted in England, fully jointed wooden marionettes dance, hop skip, wave arms as they are controlled by strings. *1965 Catalog illustration courtesy Sears, Roebuck & Co.*

PUPP-3. Pelham Puppets *Pop Singers.* With practice, operator can make this group "play" its instruments. *1965 Catalog illustration courtesy Sears, Roebuck & Co.*

PUPP-4. 11" Hand Puppet, *"The Monkees"* Singing Group. Talking hand puppet, each finger is one of the *Monkees,* Chatty ® ring, mod phrases, retailed $4.89. Mattel. *1967 Catalog illustration courtesy Sears, Roebuck & Co.*

HAZELLE, INC.

Hazelle, Inc. is Hazelle Hedges Rollins, founder and owner, artist and puppeteer. More than a million puppets have been produced by this firm in the past thirty-five years. *Bimbo* and *Teto*, two clowns, are the most popular of the marionettes. More than seventy-five characters are represented in the hand puppet line.

The company holds patents covering the mechanical construction of the body of the marionettes, the manipulation device called an *"airplane control"*, the *"talking"* mechanism of the marionette's mouth, and the life-like ankle movement. A patent is pending on the manner in which the finger puppets fit the finger of the operator without falling off.

Thousands of children visit the Kansas City puppet factory annually. Group tours usually include viewing an original puppet play as well as the opportunity for a glimpse into the world of *magic dolls*.

PUPP-6.

PUPP-5.

PUPP-5. *Hazelle Thimble Puppets.* Vinyl heads, painted features, cloth "bodies". Also: Family Set, Farm Animals, Feathered Friends, Fairy Tale Sets, and Friendly Animals. Special feature is "thimble" fit; puppets do not fall off fingers. This type has been used successfully in pre-schools, nursery schools, and Head-Start Programs. *(Photograph courtesy Hazelle, Inc.)*

PUPP-6. *Hazelle Hand Puppets.* Vinyl heads, painted features, cloth glove "bodies". Family and Community Worker sets are in black or white; also Fairy Tale sets and sets made up of characters from original playlets. "People" puppets and some animals have "hands" into which two of operator's fingers fit; others of animals have moveable mouths worked by thumb and fingers. *(Photograph courtesy Hazelle, Inc.)*

PUPP-7. *Hazelle Marionettes.* Vinyl or "Tenite" head, hands, and feet, mouth opens by touching string and closes automatically. Mohair or wool crepe wigs, well-made costumes, some have ankle movement. Sizes 15", 16", and 17". Large assortment of characters available including "Teto" the clown. The unique "airplane" control is a patented feature; simply tilt control back and forth to achieve action. *(Photograph courtesy Hazelle, Inc.)*

PUPP-7.

RAG DOLLS

One of the most successful and satisfactory materials ever used in the construction of dolls is that which is most readily available — cloth. The softness and warmth of rag dolls is appreciated by doll lovers of all ages. Many artists and manufacturers have produced cloth dolls, but the dolls most often visualized when someone says "rag doll" are the much-loved *Raggedy Ann* and *Raggedy Andy.* Two letters tell the story of *Raggedy Ann* and *Raggedy Andy* better than I could ever hope to:[1]

*Gainesville, Florida,
January 8, 1919*

Johnny Gruelle,
Care of P. F. Volland Company
Chicago, Ill.

Dear Johnny:

When I saw your Raggedy Ann books and dolls in a store near here, I went right in and bought one of each, and when I had read your introduction to "Raggedy Ann" I went right up to an old trunk in my own attic and brought down the doll I am sending you with this letter.

This doll belonged to my mother and she played with it when a little girl. She treasured it highly, I know, for she kept it until I came and then she gave it to me.

The fun that we two have had together I cannot begin to tell you, but often, like the little boy who went out into the garden to eat worms when all the world seemed blue and clouded, this doll and I went out under the arbor and had our little cry together. I can still feel it's soft rag arms (as I used to imagine) about me, and hear the words of comfort (also imaginary) that were whispered in my ear.

As you say in your Raggedy Ann book, "Fairyland must be filled with rag dolls, soft loppy rag dolls who go through all the beautiful adventures found there, nestling in the crook of a dimpled arm." I truly believe there is such a fairyland and that rag dolls were first made there, or how else could they bring so much sunshine into a child's life?

All the little girls of my acquaintance have your Raggedy Ann book and doll, and for the happiness you have brought to them let me give to you the doll of all my dolls, the doll I loved most dearly.

May it prove to you a gift from Fairyland, bringing with it all the "wish come true" that you may wish and, if possible, add to the sunshine in your life.

My mother called the doll Raggedy Andy and it was by this name that I have always known him. Is it any wonder that I was surprised when I saw the title of your book?

Introduce Raggedy Andy to Raggedy Ann, dear Johnny. Let him share in the happiness of your household.

*Sincerely yours,
Raggedy Andy's "Mama"*

———————

*Wilton, Connecticut
January 12, 1919*

Dear John:

Your letter brings many pleasant memories to my mind and takes me back to my childhood.

Living next door to us, when I was about four years old, was a little girl named Bessie; I cannot recall her last name. When my mother made Raggedy Ann for me, Bessie's mother made a rag doll for her, for we two always played together; as I recall, there was no fence between our two houses.

Bessie's doll was made a day or so after Raggedy Ann, I think, though I am not quite certain which of the two dolls was made first. However, Bessie's doll was given the name of Raggedy Andy, and one of the two dolls was named after the other, so that their names would sound alike.

We children played with the two rag dolls most of the time until Bessie's family moved away — when I was eight or nine years old. They had faces just alike; the mother who made the first doll probably painted both doll faces. I do not remember just how Raggedy Andy was dressed, but I know he often wore dresses over his boy clothes when Bessie and I decided that he and Raggedy Ann should be sisters for the day.

You will remember I told you about Raggedy Andy long ago, John.

Isn't it strange that the two old rag dolls should come together after all these years? I wish Raggedy Andy's "Mama" had signed her name, for I should like to write to her. Perhaps there may be some way of finding her out.

Anyway, it seems to me you have the subject for another rag doll book, for Raggedy Andy must have had some wonderful adventures in his long life.

Yours lovingly,

Mom

---

[1]From *RAGGEDY ANDY STORIES* by Johnny Gruelle, copyright © 1970, by the Bobbs-Merrill Company, Inc., reprinted by permission of the publishers.

PLATE IV

Raggedy Ann, with her floppy hat and her big shoe button eyes, was patented in 1915, and her smile has been winning the hearts of young and old ever since. These two were joined a little later by *Beloved Belindy,* a colored doll, who is illustrated along with them in catalogs of the 1920's.

Another rag doll familiar to children of the early Twentieth Century was *Dolly Dear* and her rag family. This doll was published by Saalfield Publishing Company as early as 1919 and was continuously offered in the catalogs through the 1920's and into the 1930's. There were three dolls lithographed on cloth, the largest of which was 25" tall when completed and wore real little girls clothes. The two smaller dolls were approximately 7" tall when completed and the piece of cloth 21" x 36" sold for from nineteen to twenty-five cents.

The *Chase* stockinette dolls, dating from the 1880's, were also available well into the Twentieth Century. These dolls have proved surprisingly durable with their washable, painted features and bodies. They are well jointed at shoulder, elbow, hip and knee, although later ones are usually found jointed only at hip and shoulder. They ranged in size from small 9" hand-dolls to big year-old child size. They were originated by Martha Jenks Chase, an artist who also conceived a group of large dolls to represent characters from "Alice in Wonderland."[1] Mrs. Chase is also noted for her life-size hospital training dolls.

The *Lenci* dolls from Italy were made of felt and often were dressed exclusively in felt costumes, although some of the dresses are a combination of felt and other fabrics such as organdy. They were patented in Turin, Italy, in 1921 by Di E. Scavinna(i) and were available in baby and child dolls as well as in many character representations. The colors of many of the dolls found today have faded out leaving them with a rather neutral appearance, but their original charm still shines through.

The near indestructibility of rag dolls is illustrated by the *Ella Smith* doll photographed here; however, it was rescued none too soon. The crate in which she lay was stored for twenty years in a basement where this "Alabama Baby" absorbed moisture, gathered dust, and possibly attracted insects. The doll in the picture belonged to Mrs. Kirtley's aunt who was seventy plus when she died in 1956. Fortunately the doll has been retrieved and is now on her way to rehabilitation. These dolls date from about 1904; some are found with patent marks of 1912 and, as here, 1919.

The doll business of Frau Kathe Kruse began almost by accident after she made a doll for her daughter *Mimerle* as a birthday gift. This soft, lovable type of doll with its painted features and lifelike appearance is most gratifying as a play doll for children of two to sixty-two. All the dolls have names; there has been a doll named for each of Frau Kruse's six children: *Mimerle, Fifi, Hannerle, Jockerle, Friedebalde,* and *Max,* the youngest.

After the death of Frau Kruse in 1968, the business was sold to the third daughter, Hannah, and her husband, Heinz Adler. They continue to operate as Kathe Kruse Puppen, although Hannah is designing some of the dolls in present production.

When questioned about the method used for marking the dolls, Mr. Gary Schild of Westbrook, Connecticut, the American representative for the firm, indicated early markings consisted of the Kathe Kruse trademark on the bottom of the foot. More recently, the date is being stamped on the other foot. What a boon for doll collectors if every manufacturer should follow this practice.

---

[1]See: Coleman, The Collector's Encyclopedia of Dolls, pp. 113-114 and Cooper, Dimples and Sawdust II, pp. 84-88.

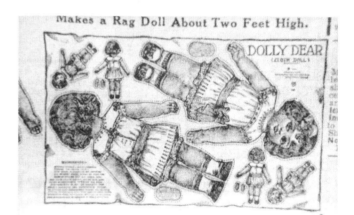

RAG-1.

RAG-1. *"Dolly Dear".* Printed flat for sewing on 21" by 36" piece of cloth, made 25" doll and two 7" dolls, price was 25c. Saalfield Publishing Company, sold as late as 1930's. *1919 Catalog illustration courtesy Sears, Roebuck & Co.*

RAG-2.

RAG-3.

RAG-4.

RAG-2. *"Shoebutton Sue"*. Billed as "The 1920 Doll Sensation", she was all cloth, painted features, shoebutton eyes, and had removeable clothes. "Guaranteed to take your mind off your troubles". Retailed at $1.19. A Jessie McCutcheon Raleigh doll. *1921 Catalog illustration courtesy Sears, Roebuck & Co.*

RAG-3. *Raggedy Ann* and *Raggedy Andy.* 1928 Catalog illustration courtesy *Sears, Roebuck & Co.*

RAG-4. *Beloved Belindy.* 1928 Catalog illustration courtesy *Sears, Roebuck & Co.*

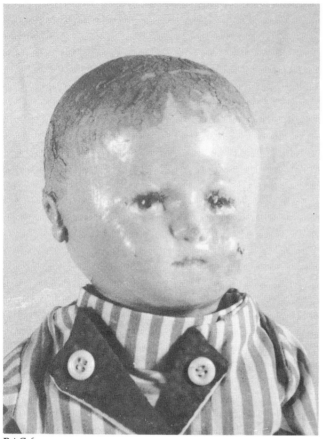

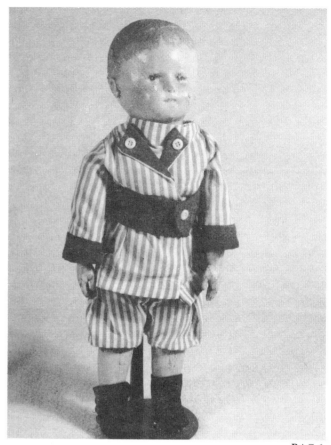

RAG-6.

RAG-5.

RAG-6.

RAG-5. *Raggedy Ann* and Friend. These two dolls were manufactured by the Knickerbocker Toy Company. Tag on black doll reads: **JOHNNY GRUELLE'S OWN RAGGEDY ANN AND ANDY DOLLS Copyright P.F. Volland Co., 1918, 1920 . . . 1945./GEORGENE NOVELTIES/NEW YORK CITY/EXCLUSIVE LICENSES MANUFACTURERS/MADE IN U.S.A.** *(Author's collection)*

RAG-6. 18" *Chase* Boy. Stockinette fabric, painted, molded features, blue eyes, applied ears, jointed shoulders and hips. Unmarked. *(Zillner collection)*

RAG-7.

RAG-7.

RAG-8.

RAG-7. 16" *Lenci*. All felt, all original, painted eyes, mohair wig, felt-trimmed dress, felt shoes, jointed shoulders and hips. Unmarked. *(Zillner collection)*

RAG-8. 1928 Catalog advertisement for *Lenci* dolls: 11" sold for $1.19, 15" was $1.95. Painted features, mohair wigs. Offered on same page were two felt dolls with composition heads, painted features, mohair wigs, apparently domestic. The 12" sold for 49c, the 15¾" was 95c.

RAG-9.

RAG-9.

RAG-10.

fig. RAG-9

RAG-9. 14" *Dean Rag Doll.* Mask face of molded stockinette, painted features (or printed), mohair curls sewn on in three places. Hooded coat is blue velvet with white "fur" trim and is removeable by taking out a few stitches. Panties are tacked on white muslin body, blue velvet legs match coat. Metal tag on one leg, see **fig. RAG-9.** Dean's Rag Book Company of London, England, was established in 1903. This doll ca. 1920. *(Author's collection)*

RAG-10. 17" Football Player. All cloth, yarn hair, felt ears. Marks: letter **K** in a blue circle and **TRADITIONAL / KRUGER / N.Y.C.** *(Kirtley collection)*

RAG-11.

RAG-13.

RAG-12.

RAG-11. 31" Topsy. All black cloth, felt features, cotton dress, jointed shoulders and hips. Has her own little black rag baby. Both dolls unmarked. 1950's. *(Kirtley collection)*

RAG-12. 14" *Norah Wellings Sailor.* All cloth, all original. Marks: **MADE IN ENGLAND / BY / NORAH WELLINGS,** on bottom of left foot. Clothes are integral part of body. *(Zillner collection)*

RAG-13. 13½" *Little Sister* and 15" *Big Sister.* Plastic-coated mask faces, painted features, cotton yarn curls, rubberized cloth legs, composition arms, stuffed bodies. These dolls appear in 1946 catalog and for several subsequent years. Dressed in typical baby doll fashions. Retailed at $2.79 and $3.59. *Catalog illustration courtesy Sears, Roebuck & Co.*

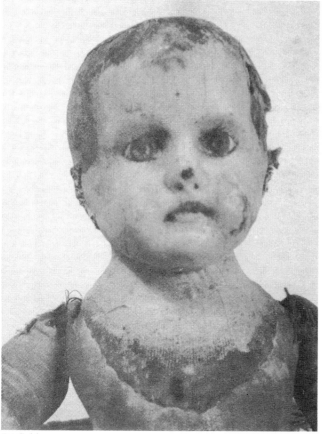

RAG-14.

RAG-15.

RAG-14.

RAG-14. 18" *Alabama Baby.* All cloth construction, painted on features, hair, shoes and stockings. Marks: Stamped on front of body: **THE ELLA SMITH / DOLL CO. MADE IN U.S.A. / THE ALABAMA IN-DESTRUCTIBLE DOLL / PAT. NOV. 1919.** *(Kirtley collection)*

RAG-15. 20" *Gramma©* . Rag, dressed in cotton print dress, apron, pantaloons. "She's fresh apple pie, a trip to the country, love and security all rolled into one". Created by Joyce Miller, sold only at Sears. Also available in 16" size and 19½" talking model, ten phrases, by Mattel. *1970 Catalog illustration courtesy Sears, Roebuck & Co.*

RAG-16. 21" *Captain Kangaroo©* . Rag, clothes are part of doll. Sears 1967 exclusive. Says 11 phrases, chatty ring, Mattel. "Do you remember to say thank you and please?" etc. *Catalog illustration courtesy Sears, Roebuck & Co.*

RAG-17. 20" Rag Clown. Mask face, removeable clothes, laughing voice. Cloth tag on clothes reads: **Gund Mfg. Co. / Swedlin, Inc. / New York City.** 1956. *(Childhood doll of Joseph Richard Anderton II)*

RAG-16.

RAG-17.

RAG-18.

RAG-19.

RAG-18. 15" *Gepetto.* One of three lithographed dolls sold flat for home sewing and stuffing. Back pocket is full of tools; vest and hat are red. Unmarked. The set included a 13" Pinnochio done in green and tan as well as Jiminy Cricket, DIS-8, shown on p. 166. Sold at J. C. Penney and other stores in 1960. *Gepetto* was the old woodcarver who yearned for a son of his own and carved *Pinocchio.* *(Courtesy Ralph's Antique Dolls)*

RAG-19. 14" *Muffin®* and 18" *Funny®* . *Muffin* has blue felt eyes, yellow wool yarn wig, flower print dress. *Funny* is entirely of checked gingham, blue chenille balls for eyes, yellow wool wig, big smile. *1970 catalog illustrations courtesy Alexander Doll Co., Inc.*

Christmas Dolls for the Kiddies

By Anne Wilson

I WISH I might take you with me to visit the home of Mrs. Jessie McCutcheon Raleigh, the mother of these dear little dolls, just so you can see for yourself the joy that goes into the fashioning of these little people so that they will carry happiness to all the little kiddies this Christmas. Mrs. Raleigh is a real Santa Claus and she has taken as her model for these dolls little American children. And the dresses she has made for them will delight big mothers, and little mothers as well. There are two kinds of dolls, those which open and close their eyes and those which do not.

The doll that walks is from Madam Georgine and the rag doll from Mrs. Denckla.

Mary-Quite-Contrary

Poppy

Big Mary

Doll-o'-My-Heart

This is Little Sherry

Dorothy and Fashionable Lucile are Good Friends

Little Lucile

Little Rabbit Lady

This is Miss Happy

A Darling Little Baby Who Toddles Along if You Hold its Hands

Here is a Rag Doll With Real Hair That Will Stand All Kinds of Rough Treatment

December, 1919   THE LADIES' HOME JOURNAL

| Goldilocks | Peeps | Mama's Angel Child | Red Riding Hood | Mary-Had-a-Lamb |

R-2 (upper section).

R-1. 13" *Johnny Hero, The All American Athlete.* Foam latex body, molded vinyl head, body reinforced with wire. Scaled for 6' 6" man; he wore all the major league baseball uniforms, as well as those of the NFL (National Football League) and the AFL (the former American Football League). Uniforms were available separately; basic doll was dressed as pictured. Rosko-Steele, Inc. *1965 Catalog illustration courtesy Sears, Roebuck & Co.* This doll was also marketed as *"Olympic Hero".* Boxes were so marked although doll and clothes were the same as *Johnny Hero.*

R-2. *Raleigh Dolls.* Composition heads and limbs, stuffed bodies, human hair, long curl wigs. Although Sears does not name the manufacturer of many dolls, there is ample evidence to indicate a number were Raleigh dolls. In 1920 several of the *"Sunshine"* line appear to be from this source, as well as a *"Goldilocks"* fairy story doll. The *"Miss Sunshine"* is shown again in 1921, this time listed as *"Charming Lucile".* It is the exact doll and costume called *"Little Lucile"* in the Ladies' Home Journal article by Anne Wilson, reprinted here from the author's copy of December, 1919, issue of that magazine.

The high quality composition used for the *Raleigh* dolls has been noted by other writers. Catalog listings checked by the author indicated the heads, arms and legs were of a "bisque-like composition". Costuming was also well done with much attention to detail.

Note the *"Madame Georgine"* (Georgene Averill Hendren) doll and the *"Mrs. Denckla"* rag doll also illustrated in the magazine article.

R-1.

REM-1.

REM-2.

REM-3.

REMCO

REM-1. *The Littlechap Family.* Left to right, Big sister, Judy, Lisa, Dr. John, and little sister, Libby. 1963, Remco. Illustration from a booklet packed with the dolls.

REM-2. 10½" *Libby,* 13¼" *Judy* of the Littlechap Family. All vinyl, rooted hair, painted eyes, these dolls had extensive wardrobes. Marks: Each doll has own name in relief on back of waist, with words: **Remco Industries © 1963,** in a circle. All clothes are fully marked with each doll's name and manufacturer's information, on cloth tag. *(Rebekka Anderton collection)*

REM-3. 15" *Dr. John Littlechap,* 14" *Lisa,* his wife. *Dr. John's* hair is molded and painted, touched with gray at temples and forelock; *Lisa* has fashionable gray streak in her rooted hair, painted eyes both dolls. Marks: Same as REM-2. *(Rebekka Anderton collection)* Available, in addition to large wardrobe, were a doctor's office, family room, and master bedroom, complete with punch-out, fold-up furniture and accessories. Each room folded up into a convenient carrying case which housed all accessories and dolls between playtimes. 1963. Remco Industries.

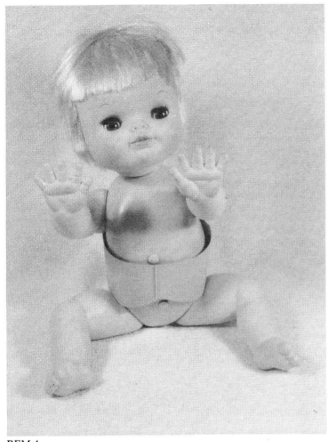

REM-4.

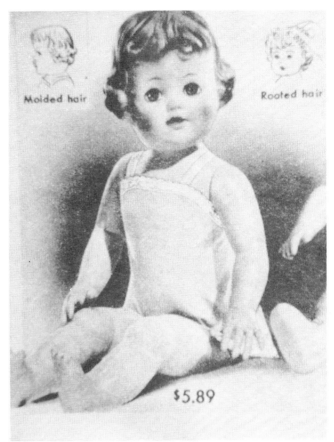

RUB-1.

RUB-2.

REM-4. 20" *Baby Craw-Along.* Plastic and vinyl, rooted hair, blue sleep eyes, head on ball socket, plastic sheath about waist protects mechanism, key wind. Marks: **REMCO / IND. / 17 EYE / New / 74 /** © **1967** on head. *(Spalding collection)*

RUBBER DOLLS

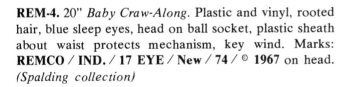

RUB-1. 26" Child. Soft vinyl head, molded hair, latex body, cotton stuffing, coos when cuddled, glassene sleep eyes. This doll is typical of many of the period. Retail $5.89. *1953 Catalog illustration courtesy Sears, Roebuck & Co.*

RUB-2. 11" *Sunbabe.* All rubber, painted eyes, drink and wet feature. Marks: **Mfd. by / The Sun Rubber Co. / Barberton, O., U.S.A. / Pat. 2118682 / Pat. 2160739.** Glass bottle, "ounces" marked on one side and picture of dog sitting up molded on other side, rubber nipple, marked with **B** in a circle, mark of Brockway Glass Co. ca. 1950. *(Author's collection)*

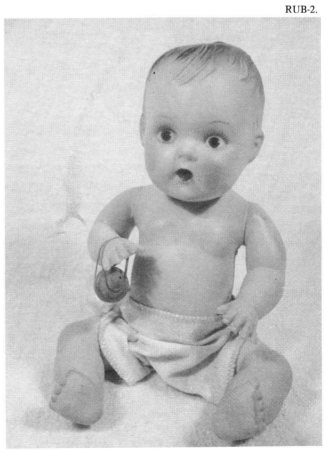

RUB-4.

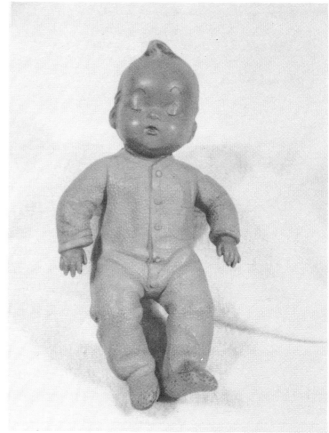

RUB-5.

RUB-3.

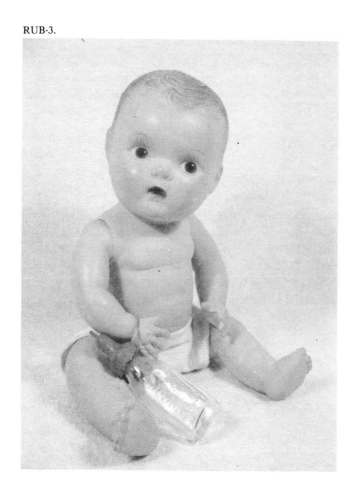

RUB-3. 13" *Sunbabe.* Same features as RUB-2, plus cry voice. Same markings. Note difference in modeling of hair. ca. 1950. *(Author's collection)*

RUB-4. 18" *Wendy* and *Billy Boy.* Molded heads, even the the braids, latex foam rubber and wire construction, bends to any position; dance, sit, kneel. Sleep eyes, separate clothes, rayon sox, separate molded plastic strap shoes. Retailed $7.55 each *1955 Catalog illustration courtesy Sears, Roebuck & Co.*

RUB-5. 10" Sleepy Baby. One piece all rubber, molded and painted pink sleepers with squeeker, closed mouth, painted features. Marks: **PAT PEND** on back. 1951. *(Author's collection)*

RUB-6. 1938 Montgomery Ward catalog illustrations. *(Courtesy Mrs. Herman W. Mead)*

Best Wetting Doll . . . Original Dy-Dee

There is only one genuine Dy-Dee and Wards is the only place you can buy it by mail. Patent EFFanBEE VALVE prevents water from running out as fast as she drinks . . . exclusive Dy-Dee feature. Only doll who blows soap bubbles, drinks from bottle, spoon, sleeps or stays awake sitting or lying down! Treated by chlorinization to seal pores. Hard rubber head turns, tilts, molded hair. Head, arms, legs held by strong rubber joints. Knit shirt, diaper, bottle, nipple, bubble pipe, spoon.

$2.49

11 in. Tall

48 C 2654—20 in. Tall. Ship. wt. 7 lbs. $8.50 Value... .$7.59
48 C 2655—14½ in. Tall. Ship. wt. 3 lbs. 12 oz. $5 Value 4.29
48 C 2656—11 in. Tall. Ship. wt. 2 lbs. 2 oz. $3 Value. 2.49

RUB-6.

Better - - - Wetting Doll, Layette

Best imitation of Dy-Dee Dolls. Made by Horsman. 10½ in. tall. Soft rubber body, jointed arms, legs. Molded hair, hard rubber turning head. Sleeping eyes, real lashes. Every time she drinks from bottle, she wets diaper. Pink Organdy dress, bonnet, White slip, 2 diapers; 4 clothes pins, 3 clothes hangers, bottle, nipple, 4 safety pins; soap, sponge. In hinged case.

$1.95

48 C 2619—Ship. wt. 3 lbs... $1.95

Good - - - Drinking - - - Wetting Doll

Best drinking--wetting Doll at this price. With 9-pc. outfit. Rubber body molded in 1 piece—no leaking at legs and arms. Dolls treated by chlorinization to seal pores, prevent dirt absorption . . . looks like real baby skin. Practically indestructible. Washable. 10½ in. tall. Painted features, swivel head. Jointed arms, legs. Bottle, 9-pc. outfit above. (Pillow not included.)

95c

48 C 2480—Ship. wt. 2 lbs.....95c

RUB-6.

Rubber Baby, Cries and Sleeps

11 in. tall, cry voice, sleeping eyes. Full jointed arms and legs that are movable. Her head turns, too. Made of fresh, new rubber, chlorinated to seal pores. Our finest low priced rubber doll.

79c

48 C 2483—Ship. wt. 1 lb. 6 oz.... 79c

Low Priced Rubber Doll—Same size and quality doll as above, but with pretty painted eyes. No cry voice.

48 C 2482—Ship. wt. 1 lb. 14 oz...45c

7-Piece Layette for Rubber Dolls. 50c Value! Layette for baby dolls above or any 10½ or 11-in. Rubber doll. More complete and better than most low priced layettes. Dress, lace trimmed slip and bonnet, in White Organdy. Pink booties, band, diaper and attractive White cotton sleeping suit. Safety pins.

48 C 2662—7-Pieces. Ship. wt. 6 oz........................37c

S

S-1.

S-1. 16", 18", 19½" *Dolly Sunshine.* One of a line of Sears *"Sunshine"* dolls. This one has straight legs, composition head and limbs, cloth stuffed body, sleep eyes, human hair wig, mama voice, and is dressed in silk taffeta dress and bonnet. *1929 Catalog illustration courtesy Sears, Roebuck & Co.*

The Sears 1930 Fall and Winter catalog lists *Baby Sunshine, Mary Sunshine, Dorothy Sunshine,* and *Dolly Sunshine,* all with Horsman labels.

S-3.

S-1a.

S-2.

S-1a. 14", 18", 23" *"Sunshine", the New Happy Baby.* Composition head and limbs, stuffed body, cry voice, painted, molded hair, open mouth, two teeth, sleep eyes, straight "kiddie" legs, stands alone. Prices were $2.98, $4.79 and $6.59. *1927 Catalog illustration courtesy Sears, Roebuck & Co.*

S-2. 18" *Miss Sunshine,* The Wardrobe Doll. Composition with cloth body, sleep eyes, human hair in pigtails, came with six outfits, retailed $1.98. *1940 Catalog illustration courtesy Sears, Roebuck & Co.*

S-3. 26" *Baby Sunshine.* This year a solemn-faced baby; previous years the laughing baby has been member of *Sunshine* line. Composition head and limbs, cotton stuffed body, glass-like sleep eyes, lashes, molded hair. *1940 Catalog illustration courtesy Sears, Roebuck & Co.*

S-4a.

S-4.

S-5.

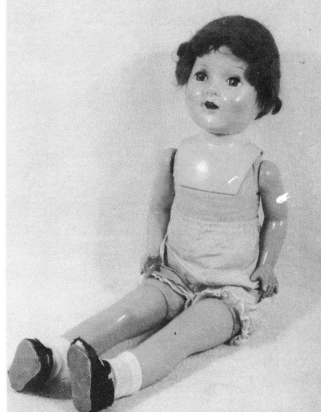

S-4. Shackman Toys. A selection of foreign-made reproductions of antique toys imported by Shackman of New York. *(Rebekka Anderton collection)*

S-4a. 9¼" Girl, 4¾" Baby. Composition heads, stuffed felt bodies and limbs, painted features, jointed hips and shoulders, wires in limbs, glued-on fibre wig. Paper label reads **COPYRIGHT / SHACKMAN / MADE IN JAPAN** on dress of larger doll. Presently available. *(Rebekka Anderton collection)*

S-6.

S-6.

S-5.

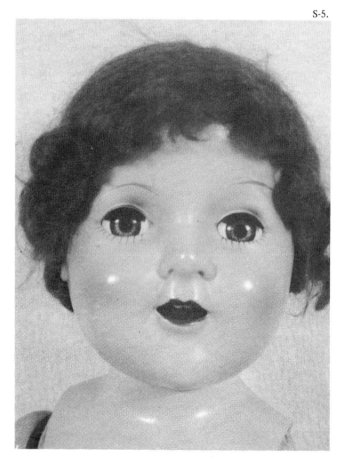

S-5.

S-5. 24½" Girl. Beautifully colored hard plastic head, mohair wig, glassene sleep eyes, lashes, composition arms and legs, stuffed cloth body. Unmarked. ca. 1949. Compare with *Miss Marie* M-2 or *Miss Sunshine* above; this may be a later version of these dolls. *(Author's collection)*

S-6. 18" Hard Plastic. Brown, glued-on synthetic wig, blue sleep eyes, nicely modeled hands, original pink dress with blue bows, wears girdle marked **Sarah Ann Dress.** 1950's. *(Wiseman collection)*

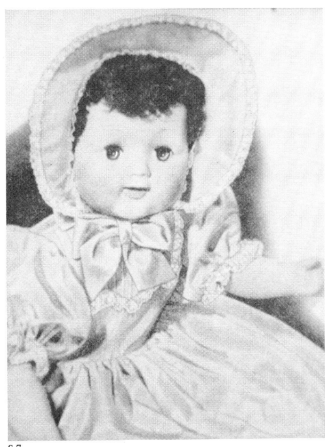

S-7.

S-8.

S-8.

S-7. 27" *Sweetie Pie.* Hard plastic, turning, tilting head, tousle wig of lamb's wool, open mouth, teeth, tongue, soft vinyl arms and legs, stuffed cloth body, rayon taffeta dress, bonnet, undies. Retailed $14.98; same with moulded hair retailed $12.98. *1951 Catalog illustration courtesy Sears, Roebuck & Co.* An EFFanBEE doll.

S-8. 26" Sayco Bed Doll. Plastic limbs, soft vinyl head, rooted hair, painted features, stuffed cloth body. Marks: © **Sayco Doll Corp.** *(Kirtley collection)* 1962 Catalog shows this doll dressed in full length rayon satin gown with tulle overskirt and high heels, $5.98. *(Courtesy Sears, Roebuck & Co.)*

S-9. 13" *Baby Janie* ™ . Black baby doll, all vinyl, rooted hair, sleep eyes. By Shindana Toys, Div. of Operation Bootstrap, Inc. *1970 Catalog illustration courtesy Sears, Roebuck & Co.* Also shown in 1969 catalogs. Sears exclusive.

S-10. 15" *Malaika.* Her name means "angel" in Swahili. Poseable vinyl body, rooted natural hair, wears Afro-print outfit. By Shindana Toys, Div. of Operation Bootstrap, Inc. *1970 Catalog illustration courtesy Sears, Roebuck & Co.*

S-10.

S-11.

S-11. 16" *Talking Tamu.* Her name means "sweet" in Swahili. Vinyl head and hands, rooted natural hairdo, cloth body and limbs, talk ring, eighteen phrases: "Can you dig it?", etc. By Shindana Toys, Div. of Operation Bootstrap, Inc. *1970 Catalog illustration courtesy Sears, Roebuck & Co.*

S-9.

S-12.

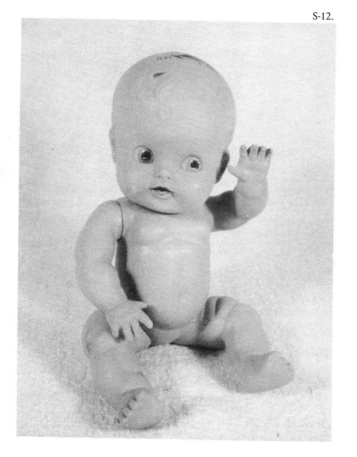

S-12.

S-12. *So-Wee.* All rubber, painted eyes and hair. Marks: SUNBABE / "SO-WEE" / © RUTH E. NEWTON / NEW YORK, N.Y. on head. **DESIGNED BY / RUTH E. NEWTON / MFD. BY / THE SUN RUBBER CO. / BARBERTON, O., U.S.A. / PAT. 2118682 / PAT. 2160739** on shoulders. This head may be found on several types of bodies as illustrated. ca. 1941. See also *Amosandra. (Author's collection)*

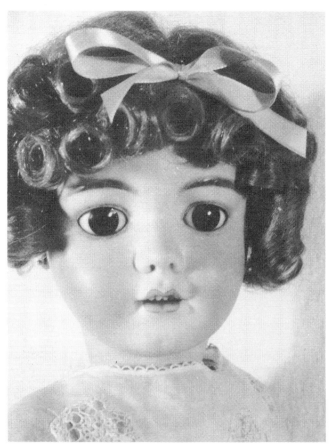

S&H-1.   S&H-2.

S&H-3.

S&H-2.

SIMON & HALBIG

This Nineteenth Century firm continued into the Twentieth Century, producing dolls heads for French makers as well as for such German companies as Kammer & Reinhardt.

S&H-1. 9" Child. Ball-jointed body, bisque head, brown stationary eyes, painted lashes, open mouth, four very tiny teeth, pierced-through ears, garnet earrings which appear to be original, redressed, original mohair wig. Marks: **1079 7 / 0 / Dep / S&H / Germany,** on head. *(Battagler collection)*

S&H-2. 16" Girl. Beautifully tinted bisque shoulder head, stationary brown glass eyes, painted lashes, open mouth, five teeth, human hair wig, kid body, white bisque fore-arms and hands, leather feet, new clothes. Marks: **S & H** at upper rim of head, **Germany** on lower part. *(Battagler collection)*

S&H-3. 34" *SANTA.* Bisque socket head, brown eyes, painted lashes, open mouth, four teeth, molded, painted brows, pierced-through ears, original mohair wig, ball-jointed body. Dressed in cut-down old baby dress, stockings hand woven in 1875, and size 3 baby shoes. *(Battagler collection)*

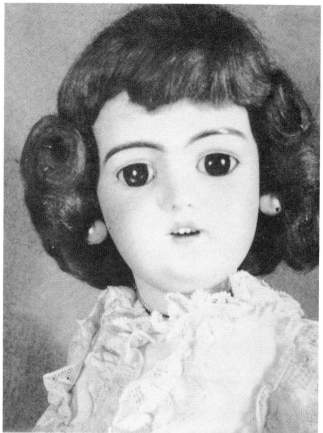

S&H-5.

S&H-5.

S&H-4.

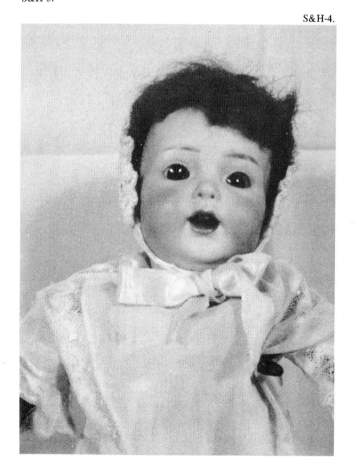

S&H-4. 11" Baby. Bisque socket head, stationary glass eyes, open mouth, two upper teeth, original mohair wig, bent-leg baby body. Marks: **SIMON HALBIG / 122 / 26.** *(Battagler collection)*

S&H-5. 19½" Child. Bisque socket head, stationary brown glass eyes, painted lashes, molded, painted brows, pierced-through ears, open mouth, four teeth, ball-jointed body. Dressed all original in yellow organza and lace dress printed with faint clusters of flowers in browns and gold, matching pantalettes, and white lace-trimmed slip. Marks: **S & H 1079 / DEP / Germany / 8.** *(Battagler collection)*

DOLL PRIMER:
The French Monopoly of "S.F.B.J."

A history could well be written called the "Franco-German Doll Wars." The contestants were little, but the rivalry was fierce, and the business of doll making rose or fell with the tides of empire! Again and again the Teutonic traits of patient labor, efficient production and aggressive selling was pitted against the artistry of the French, whose beauty of individual dolls seemed more important to them than meeting competition abroad on the basis of price or quantities by the hundred gross!

The Germans were first in the field and their dolls were in wide demand. Well before the time of factories they were producing by cottage craft great numbers of dolls. The trade aim was quantity at competitive prices, but many fine dolls were also made.

In the mid-19th century, French doll makers were capitalizing on their reputation for style. In miniature their costumes reflected the chic of Paris. They used some fine German heads in the earlier years, the extent of which has been earnestly debated. Bru never used any German heads; Jumeau after 1862 made his own dolls complete. The beautiful heads and great luminous eyes made their dolls distinctive. While the Germans were selling abroad the French found the world coming to their door. A score of gifted doll makers established their reputations in a few prosperous decades.

Then inexorably the machine overwhelmed the creative artist. One by one the French makers succumbed to German competition. Finally by 1899 only Jumeau remained strong and solvent. This company then set up a new corporation to take other companies under their wing and adopted the name "Societe Francaise de fabrication de Bebes et Jouets," — S.F.B.J. "French Society for the Manufacture of Dolls and Toys." Among the companies absorbed were Bru, Fleishmann & Bloedel, makers of "Eden-Bebe" and "Bebe Triompe;" Rayberry & Delphian, Pintel & Godchaux who made "Bebe Charmont;" also Danel Co., known for its "Paris Bebe" with Eiffel Tower trademark.

From 1899 on, the initials "S. F. B. J." were used on many of the dolls produced by members of the corporation. At the same time the name of the individual doll line, especially "Jumeau" would be included. Other words and initials are sometimes employed such as "S. G. D. G." "Sans Garant du Gouvernment," translated "Without Guarantee by the Government." Two other words often appear: "Depose" and "Brevete" or "Bte." It was the practice of the French Government to allow the doll makers to declare ownership (Depose) or register (Brevete-Bte.) a name.

The new corporation did well for a while and became the largest doll maker in France. But wars play havoc with dolls and men, and 1914 brought a halt to doll manufacture. There was some revival after the war but World War II completed the ruin.

"Doll Talk", Vol. 18, No. 9, Nov.-Dec. 1970. Reprinted by permission of Mr. Kim McKim.

TEDDY BEARS

The well-known story of the origin of the *Teddy Bear* seems always worth repeating. Imagine, if you are able, a world without *Teddy Bears*. Such was the condition of this globe in 1903 when President Theodore (Teddy) Roosevelt set off on one of his famous hunting trips, this time to the state of Mississippi. The states of Louisiana and Mississippi at this time were engaged in a border dispute of long standing. When the President refused to shoot a bear cub, political cartoonist Clifford Berryman drew a cartoon for the Washington Post entitled *"Drawing the Line in Mississippi"*. Teddy's bear was the talk of the country, and Morris Michtom, President of Ideal Toy Corporation, conceived the idea of *"Teddy's Bear"* as a toy. With the President's permission, Mr. Michtom designed and placed on the market the stuffed, plush creation which has occupied a place of importance in virtually every nursery in the land since.[1]

It would be impossible to list in this limited space the adventures of the *Teddy Bears* which have been produced all over the world. From the original plush *Teddy,* to the delightful *Winnie-The-Pooh,* and on into the present day of pink and blue and lavender bears, has marched a procession of much-loved and lovable descendants of *"Teddy's Bear".*

[1] Fraser, Antonia, "A History of Toys," Delacorte Press, 1966.

TED-3.

TED-1.

TED-2.

TED-1. 20" *Teddy Bear.* An early Teddy with glass bead eyes, stuffed with excelsior, belonged to an uncle born in 1896. Believed to date around 1904. *(Battagler collection)*

TED-2. 18" *Old Ted.* Golden brown, with velvet nose and beady eyes, his paws have been reinforced as a result of much loving. He dates about 1927. *(Author's collection)*

TED-3. *Teddy Bears.* Left: Mohair, 13" at $1.98 and 14½" at $2.69. Right: Short pile plush, 14", $1.00. *1928 Catalog illustration courtesy Sears, Roebuck & Co.*

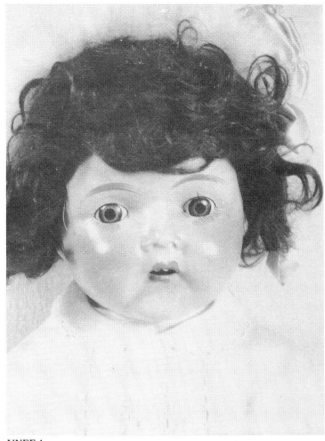

UNEE-1.

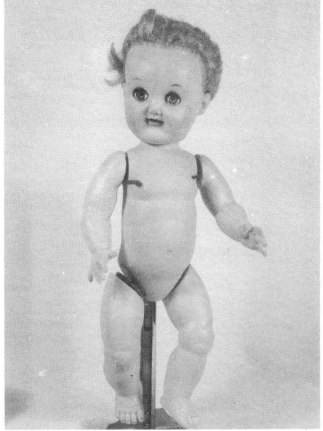

UNEE-2.

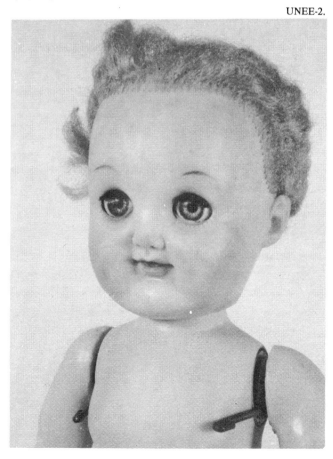

UNEE-2.

UNEEDA DOLLS

Uneeda is another Twentieth Century doll manufacturer "born" in the World War I period. A varied line of dolls includes personalities, babies, girls and toddlers, as well as lady types. Some of the early composition heads may have been used on certain of the specialty dolls such as the Coleman walking doll. Most of the dolls are well marked.

UNEE-1. 29" Mama Doll. Composition shoulder head, arms and legs, tin sleep eyes, open mouth, two teeth, cloth body. Marks: **UNEEDA** on head. Note resemblance to M-7. This doll is possibly earlier of the two. *(Spalding collection)*

UNEE-2. 16" Baby. Vinyl, blue sleep eyes, lashes, rooted hair, pin and disc joints, open mouth, drink and wet feature. Doll has mechanism in body; press tummy, head nods, feet kick. Marks: **UNEEDA** on head. 1950's. *(Spalding collection)*

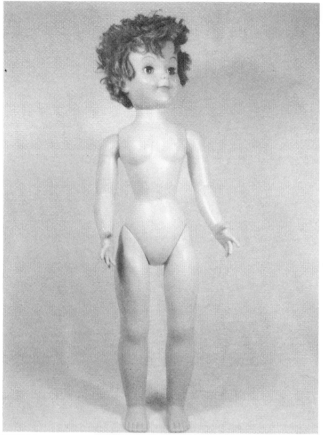

UNEE-3.

UNEE-3.

UNEE-4.

UNEE-3. 32" *Princess Doll.* Plastic vinyl, blue sleep eyes, rooted hair. Marks: **UNEEDA DOLL CO.** on head. (Note resemblance to *Pollyana* doll). 1961 Sears Christmas book lists this doll as "The Princess Doll from "Babes in Toyland", the Walt Disney movie, pink rayon satin gown, royal blue cape, silver color crown, blue sleep eyes, rooted **pink** acetate hair." Retailed, $15.88. In 1962 same doll was dressed as bride, $9.79, with natural hair colors.

UNEE-4. 32" *Freckles.* Same body as UNEE-3, with bright green eyes, orange rooted hair, open closed mouth with teeth showing, freckles. Marks: **UNEEDA/13** on head. Designed by Deet D'Andrade. *(Spalding collection)*

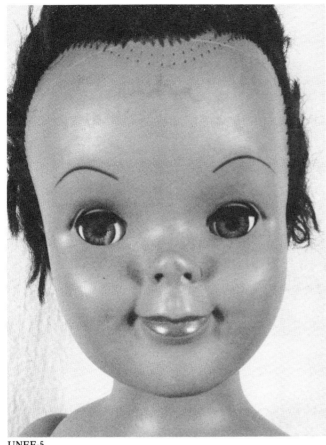

UNEE-5.

UNEE-6.

UNEE-6.

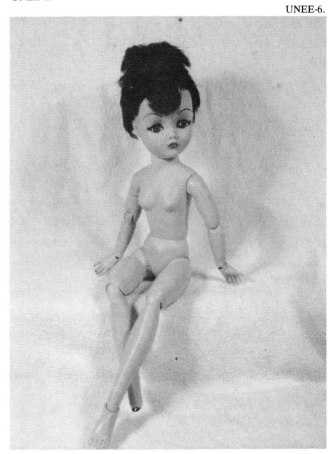

UNEE-5. 32" Colored Girl. Same body as UNEE-3, dots above forehead show line of stitching for rooted hair. Many UNEEDA dolls have this widow's peak hairline. Marks: **UNEEDA** on head. *(Kirtley collection)*

UNEE-6. 29" Dollikin. Hard plastic and vinyl, jet black rooted hair, blue sleep eyes, beautifully jointed adult body, separate fingers, pierced ears. Marks: **UNEEDA/25** on head. Early 1960's. *(Author's collection)*

UNEE-7.

UNEE-7.

UNEE-8.

UNEE-7. 16" *Coquette.* Vinyl, rooted hair, sleep eyes, original dress was short dark red velvet trimmed in lace. Re-dressed in 1968 in shocking pink velvet and white rabbit fur costume adapted from a Furga doll shown in Sears 1968 Christmas Book. Marks: **UNEEDA DOLL / CO. INC. / © 1963.** *(Childhood doll of Rebekka Suzanne Anderton)*

Objects often become so inter-related with events that we are never able to look at them without recalling vividly some particular experience. In 1968, Rebekka was seriously ill the entire month of December. To keep awake through the long nights, her mother sewed this new costume for her "best" doll. Perhaps it was "best" because it looked so much like Rebekka with its long, pale hair and charming face. At Christmas, when Rebekka was nearly well, the doll stood under the tree in all her new, handmade finery.

UNEE-8. 16" *Coquette.* Same doll as UNEE-7, with auburn hair, and numerals **28** beneath stated marks. *(Spalding collection)*

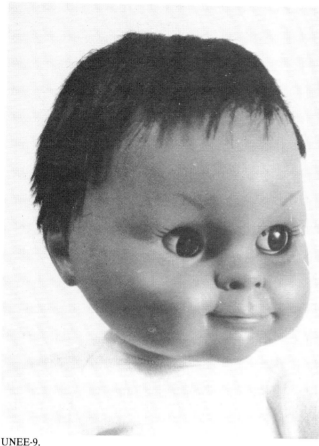

UNEE-9.

UNEE-10.

UNEE-11.

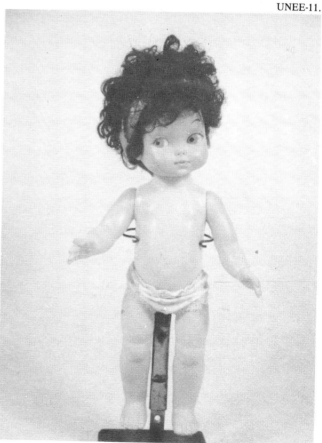

UNEE-9. 17" *Colored Pixie-type.* Foam body over wire, vinyl head with rooted hair and sleep eyes. Marks: © **UNEEDA / DOLL CO. / INC.** (in a circle) with **1964** beneath. **Posy Pixie** on soles of flannel pajamas. Early 1960's. *(Kirtley collection)*

UNEE-10. 17" *Posy Pixies.* Plastic foam bodies bend into many positions, molded vinyl heads and gauntlet hands, rooted hair. Retailed, $7.66. *1964 Catalog illustration courtesy Sears, Roebuck & Co.*

Here is an example of how a researcher may be led astray through extensive use of old catalogs. These dolls were actually made by Vogue Dolls, Inc. *Posy Pixie* was the first doll to have the complete body of foam and was designed by Deet D'Andrade. There never was a colored *Posy Pixie*; the doll shown in UNEE-9 was issued by Uneeda after the *Posy Pixie* was introduced. Although similar, it is not the same doll as shown in UNEE-9 and differs in many characteristics. It has, however, been dressed by someone in an original *Posy Pixie* pajama, further misleading the befuddled researcher. The author had the honor of having the record set straight by the designer herself!

UNEE-11. 11" Toddler. Vinyl and plastic, rooted synthetic hair, closed mouth, painted blue side-glancing eyes. Marks: © **UNEEDA / DOLL CO. / INC.** (in a circle) with **1966** beneath. *(Spalding collection)*

UNEE-12. 12½" *Pri-thilla.* Vinyl, rooted hair, glassene sleep eyes, blows up her own balloons. 1958, Uneeda. *Catalog illustration courtesy Sears, Roebuck & Co.* For *Popeye,* see COM-P5.

UNEE-12.

UNMKD-1.

UNMARKED DOLLS

Since many collectors give little or no consideration to the unmarked doll, here is a field ripe to the harvest. In some cases (refer to *Shirley Temple* dolls), unmarked dolls are actually *genuine* character or personality dolls. There are a variety of reasons why dolls were not marked.

According to Spinning Wheel Magazine (May, 1970, page 54), *"some dollmakers were elusive about themselves because they did not have outlets to sell dolls themselves but merely manufactured for the wholesale distributor who catered to the retail trade — from department stores to junk dealers. In this manner they could use one head and assembly but interchange marks or names to suit the fancy of their customers."* This is true as well in the world of old toys; the molds were sometimes unmarked and toys were undersold with little thought toward protecting jobbers.

Much of the joy of collecting is in the pursuit of knowledge. Comparison of unmarked dolls with well-marked ones of similar type often leads to exciting discoveries. (See also *"Carmen Miranda"*)

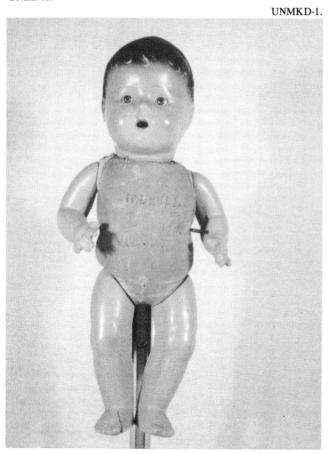

UNMKD-1. 13½" Baby. Composition swivel head and limbs, pink painted cloth body, kapok stuffed, brown tin sleep eyes, black painted, molded hair. Unmarked. Someone has written in ink on body: *"Mary Ada 1949. Made about 1919."* Metal tube from mouth inside body for drink and wet feature. *(Baume collection)*

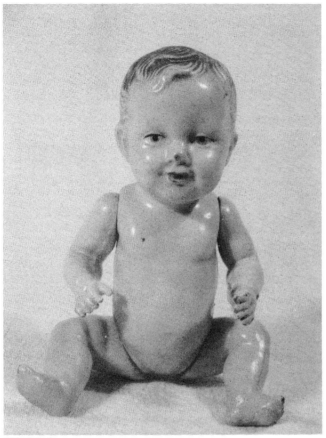

UNMKD-2.

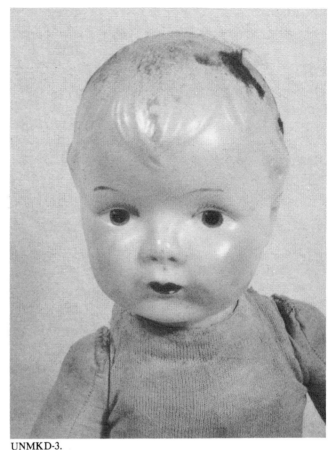

UNMKD-3.

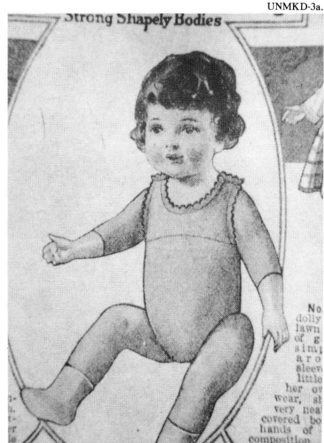

UNMKD-3a.

UNMKD-2. 11" Baby. All composition, blue painted eyes, one piece body and head, arms and legs attached with metal springs. 1910's. *(Wiseman collection)*

UNMKD-3. 18" Baby. Composition head and gauntlet hands, remainder cloth stuffed with mixture of excelsior and shredded cork. Pale tint composition of excellent finish is uncracked except where wig glue has ruined finish. Has almost a bisque-like quality. Molded hair under wisps of mohair wig; open crown for wig. Painted blue eyes, closed, painted mouth, pin and disc joints, knit undershirt is sewn to body. Note unusual shaping of legs which allows doll to sit solidly or to cross ankles naturally when lying on back. Can be positioned to "kick" realistically. 1910's. *(Author's collection)*

UNMKD-3a. Baby Doll. Same construction as UNMKD-3, mohair wig, natural baby-like figure. Came in five sizes: 12½" at 98c, 14½" at $1.39, 17" at $1.95, 20½" at $2.48, and 22¼" at $3.35. *1917 Catalog illustration courtesy Sears, Roebuck & Co.*

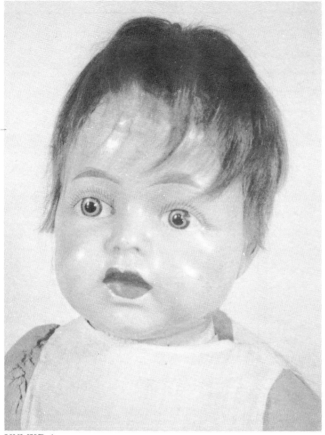

UNMKD-4.

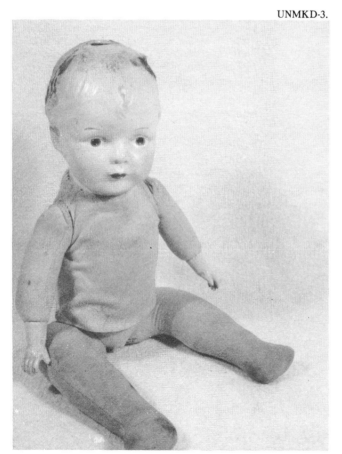

UNMKD-3.

UNMKD-3.

UNMKD-4. 21" Baby. Construction identical to UN-MKD-3. Original soft brown mohair wig, coloring of face is brighter than previous doll, painted upper and lower lashes, red dots nostrils and inner eyes. *(Baume collection)*

UNMKD-5.

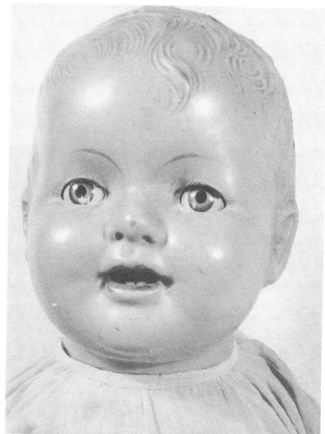

UNMKD-6.

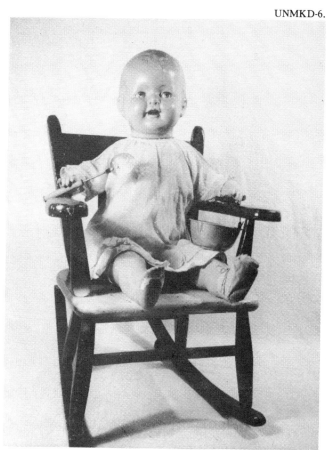

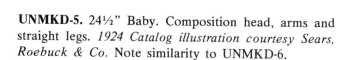

UNMKD-6.

UNMKD-5. 24½" Baby. Composition head, arms and straight legs. *1924 Catalog illustration courtesy Sears, Roebuck & Co.* Note similarity to UNMKD-6.

UNMKD-6. 25" Baby. Composition flange neck head, arms and straight legs, cotton stuffed cloth body, cry voice, celluloid over tin blue sleep eyes, open mouth, two upper and two lower teeth, molded, painted blonde hair, original pink organza dress and bonnet (not shown). Purchased in 1924. *(Charles Vandiver collection)*

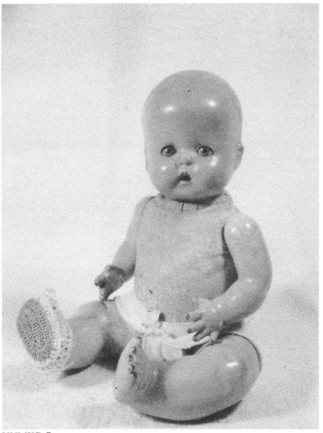

UNMKD-7.

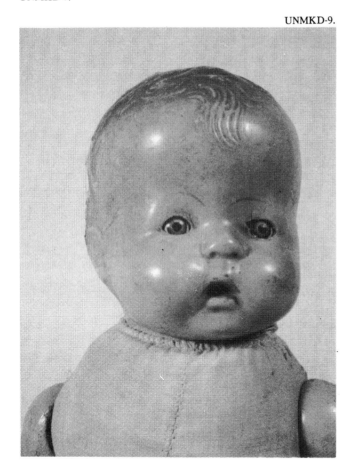

UNMKD-9.

UNMKD-8.

These three dolls, though differing in some respects, are very alike, indicating a style trend in representation of babies in doll form.

UNMKD-7. 13" Baby. Composition head and limbs, stuffed cloth body, bright blue tin sleep eyes. 1920's. *(Wiseman collection)*

UNMKD-8. 17" Baby. Composition head and limbs, cry voice, green tin stationary eyes, cloth body. 1920's. *(Spalding collection)*

UNMKD-9. 17" Baby. Composition head and limbs, stuffed cloth body, bent legs, blue-green tin eyes. 1920's. *(Wiseman collection)*

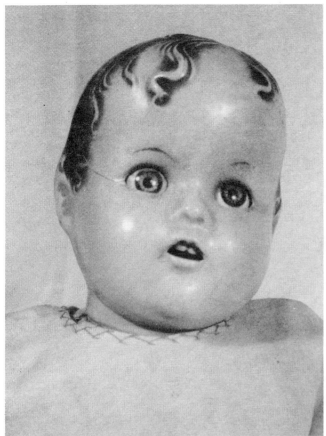

UNMKD-10.

UNMKD-11.

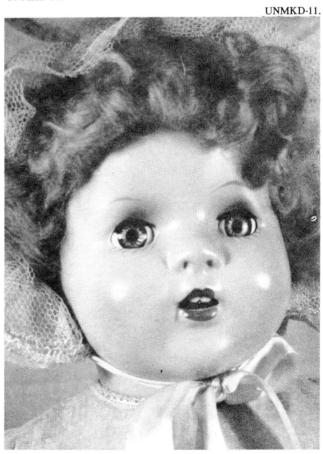

UNMKD-11.

UNMKD-10. 18" Baby. Composition head and limbs, cloth body, deeply molded hair. Found in original pink organdy dress and bonnet with lace trim, white lace-trimmed slip, socks, baby shoes. Note similarity to *"Momma-Poppa"* doll, which see. ca. 1940. *(Zillner collection)*

UNMKD-11. 21" Mama Doll. Composition head and limbs, stuffed cloth body, mama cry voice, mohair wig, bright blue sleep eyes. Original blue dotted Swiss dress and bonnet with pink ribbons, white lace, cheese cloth slip, panties, rayon sox, imitation leather shoes. Condition of composition, type of eyes and style of bonnet and dress indicate doll would date ca. 1940. *(Author's collection)*

UNMKD-13.

UNMKD-11.

UNMKD-12.

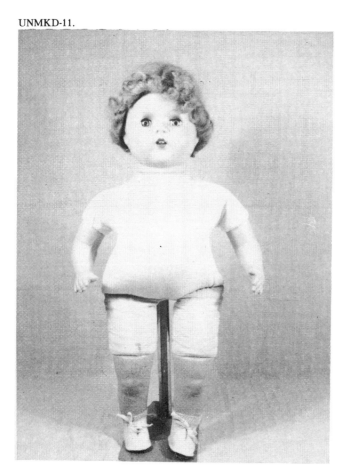

UNMKD-12. 10" Black *"Topsy"* Baby. All composition, head and body in one piece, painted eyes glance to right. 1944 Catalog illustration shows 9½" identical doll, dressed in checked romper, socks tied with ribbons about ankles, retail 54c. *(Kirtley collection)*

UNMKD-13. 9" Babies. All composition, head and body one piece, painted eyes. Center doll has drink and wet feature; composition shows the effects of such treatment. Doll on right has water putty mend on head, preparatory to repainting. These dolls were listed as early as 1924 at 43c each and as late as 1944 at 30c each. *(Author's collection)*

UNMKD-14. 14" Composition. Painted features, one piece head and body, has replacement Buddy Lee arms, molded hair under wisps of mohair wig. 1910's. May be a carnival doll or one of Sears' *Chubby Kids. (Kirtley collection)* Sears featured the *Chubby Kids* from 1915 into the 1930's.

UNMKD-16.

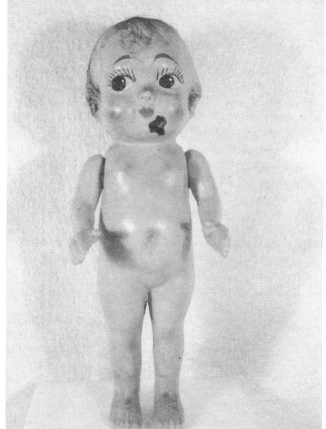

UNMKD-14.

UNMKD-15.

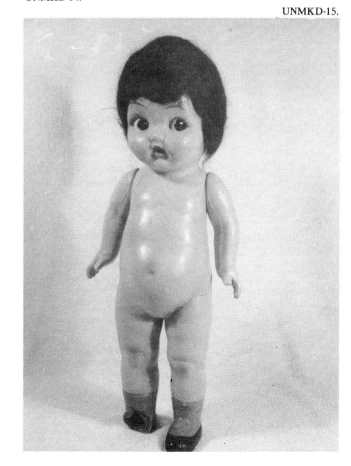

UNMKD-15. 18" *Chubby Kid*. All composition, original dark brown mohair wig, black painted eyes, green painted socks. Wig was originally "marcelled". Doll sold in 1920 for $1.95 with wig, $1.29 with painted hair. *(Wiseman collection)*

UNMKD-16. 8" *Chubby Kid*. All composition, this one is jointed at hips as well as shoulders, painted black eyes, black mohair wig is braided and fastened up with red ribbons. These *Chubby Kids* dolls were carried in Sears catalogs from 1920's into early 1940's. *(Spalding collection)*

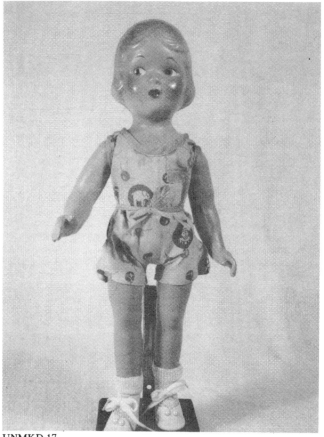

UNMKD-17.

UNMKD-17.

UNMKD-18.

UNMKD-17. 14" Girl. All composition, one piece head and body, blue painted eyes, original sunsuit. Note similarity to *Snow White,* which see. 1920's, 1930's. *(Wiseman collection)*

UNMKD-18. 14" Black Mama Doll. Composition shoulder head and gauntlet hands, dark brown cloth stuffed with cotton body and legs, mama voice box is large for size of doll, remnants of black mohair wig, original organza dress and bonnet. About 1919 a black mama doll such as this is shown in catalogs and referred to as *"Aunt Jemima";* this may be one of those dolls. *(Spalding collection)*

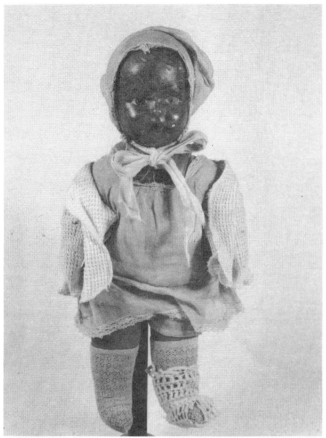

UNMKD-18.

UNMKD-19.

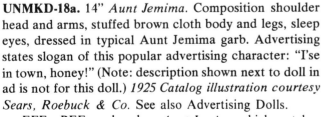

UNMKD-18a.

UNMKD-18a. 14" *Aunt Jemima.* Composition shoulder head and arms, stuffed brown cloth body and legs, sleep eyes, dressed in typical Aunt Jemima garb. Advertising states slogan of this popular advertising character: "I'se in town, honey!" (Note: description shown next to doll in ad is not for this doll.) *1925 Catalog illustration courtesy Sears, Roebuck & Co. See also Advertising Dolls.*

EFFanBEE produced an *Aunt Jemima* which matches this description. The EFFanBEE doll is more than likely the doll marketed by Sears and shown in this catalog illustration.

UNMKD-19. 10" Dutch Girl. Composition flange head and arms, cloth body and legs, painted eyes, original mohair wig, felt clothes and separate molded composition Dutch "wooden" shoes. Note Grace Drayton influence in style of features. *(Zillner collection)*

I SAY MA-MA

I SAY MA-MA I GO TO SLEEP

$1.49

18D2985

Shipping weight, 1¼ lbs. Neatly made 14-inch Doll with dainty bloomer style dress of colored cotton material; clever bonnet to match. Has mohair wig, moving eyes, Ma-Ma voice. Composition head, stuffed body and legs.

AUNT JEMIMA

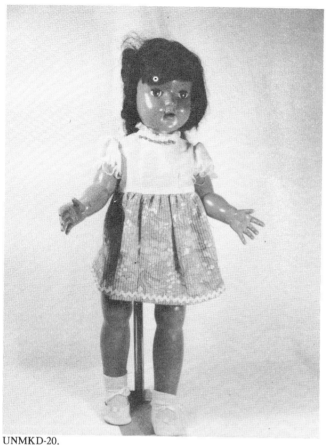

UNMKD-20.

UNMKD-22.

UNMKD-21.

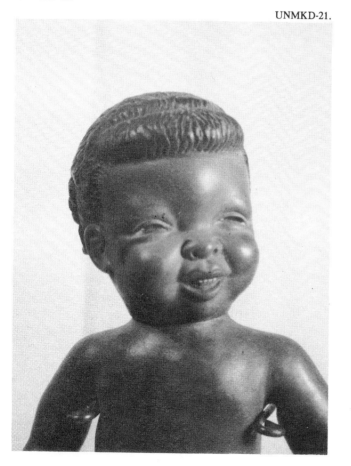

UNMKD-20. 27" Walker. Brown hard plastic, long, glued-on synthetic wig, brown glass-like eyes, open mouth, two upper teeth. Compare with EEGEE walkers. ca. 1953. *(Kirtley collection)*

UNMKD-21. 12" Colored Toddler. Stuffed vinyl one-piece body, stuffed vinyl head molded with deeply sculptured hair and tiny pig-tails. Charmingly modeled ethnic features; there is a boy doll to match. 1950's. *(Kirtley collection)*

UNMKD-22. 17" Boy. Composition flange neck head, open closed mouth, painted teeth, painted blue eyes, cloth body and limbs, excelsior stuffing. Real character face. 1910's. *(Wingfield collection)*

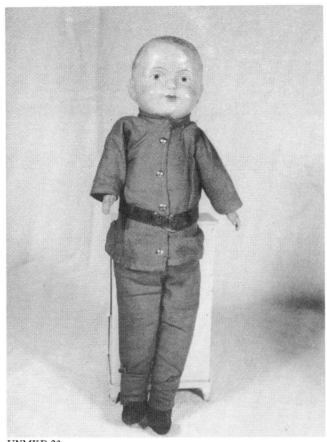

UNMKD-23.

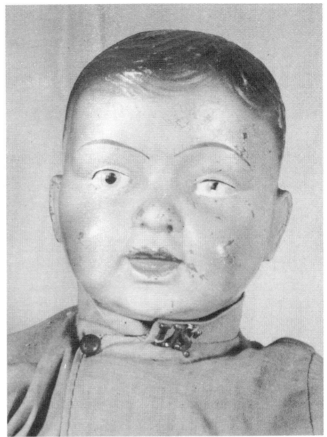

UNMKD-24.

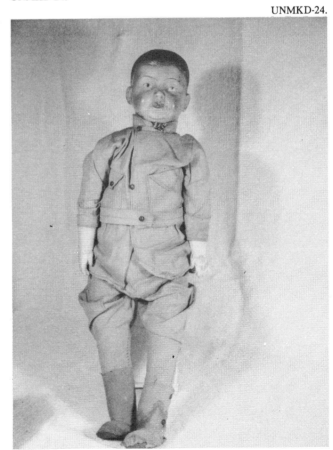

UNMKD-24.

UNMKD-23. 17" *Doughboy.* Composition head and gauntlet hands, cloth body and limbs, shoes are integral part of construction. Original World War I Doughboy uniform; note leggings. 1916-1918. *(Zillner collection)*

UNMKD-24. 29" *Doughboy.* Composition head and gauntlet hands, cloth body and limbs, blue painted eyes, red-brown painted hair. All original World War I Doughboy; note buttoned leggings and brass "US" insignia on collar. These "doughboy" dolls were made by several companies and were produced for a few years after the war. They are shown in catalogs as late as 1922. *(Zillner collection)*

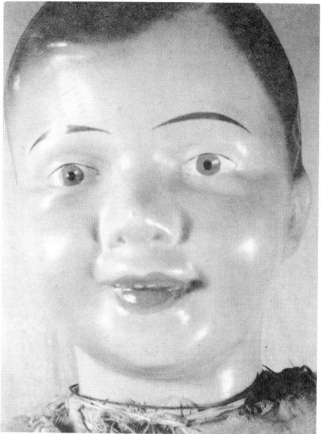

UNMKD-25.

UNMKD-26.

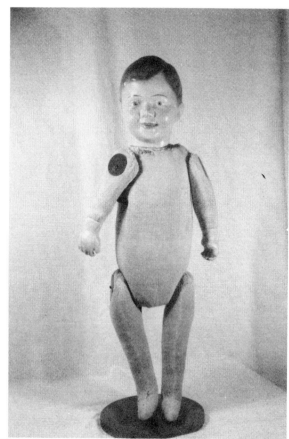

UNMKD-25.

UNMKD-25. 30" Boy. Similar to UNMKD-24, but not the same doll. Proportions are different and hands are larger. Cloth body is stuffed with excelsior. Note pin and disc joints on outside. The author has seen a girl doll which matches this boy. *(Kirtley collection)*

UNMKD-26. 10" Googly-Eyed Boy. Composition mask face, remainder stuffed cloth, fingers delineated by red thread, new wig replaces similar style original, glass set eyes, original clothes. 1910's. *(Wingfield collection)*

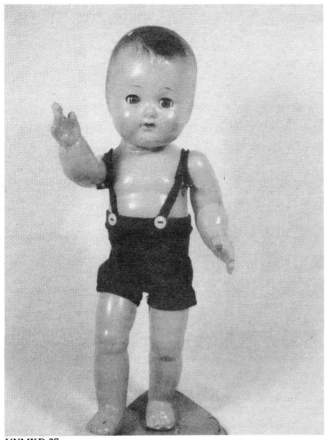

UNMKD-27.

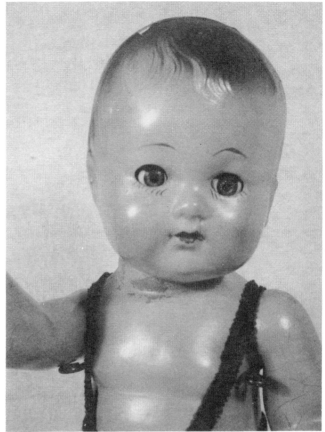

UNMKD-27.

UNMKD-28.

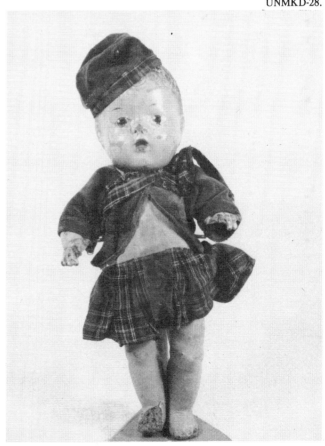

UNMKD-27. 15½" Chubby Boy. All composition, brown sleep eyes of type used in late 1930's, original knit suspender pants. Note husky modeling of limbs; he is all boy. *(Author's collection)*

UNMKD-28. 12" Boy. All composition, painted eyes and hair. All original red tartan kilt outfit. Doll was brought from Canada in 1942 for Mrs. Spalding's son, now deceased. *(Courtesy Lucy Spalding)* An identical doll has been found marked **Reliable Toy Co.** (Canada).

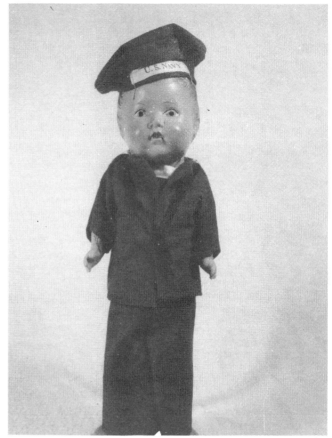

UNMKD-31.

UNMKD-30.

UNMKD-29.

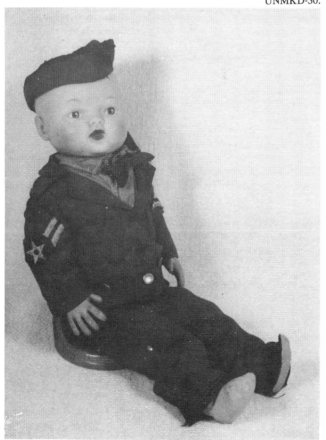

UNMKD-29. 15" Sailor Boy. Composition shoulder head, arms and legs, stuffed cloth body, painted blue eyes, molded, painted shoes. Original World War II Sailor uniform. *(Wiseman collection)*

UNMKD-30. 20" "Air Force Baby". Stuffed vinyl head, set glassene eyes, open closed mouth, magic skin type stuffed rubber body, separate fingers. World War II Air Force uniform is of rayon material and appears to be home-made. *(Author's collection)*

UNMKD-31.

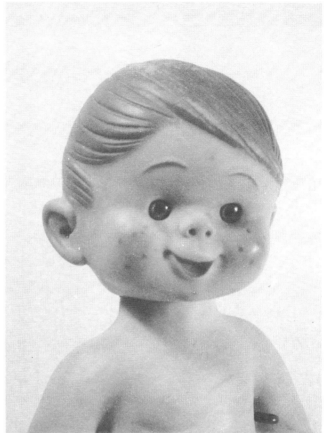

UNMKD-31-1.

UNMKD-32.

UNMKD-31. 20" Googly-Eyed Boy. Composition head, arms and legs above the knees, closed mouth, molded black hair, cloth body with squeeker. Eyes have unattached pupils which move freely. Also found in white version. 1945 Sears catalog shows 19" and 23", same head, attached to all stuffed cloth body and limbs of checked cloth to match checked dress and bonnet. *(Kirtley collection)*

UNMKD-31-1. 16" *Rusty*. Vinyl head with stationary inset eyes, open-closed mouth. Body and limbs are one piece, of stuffed vinyl; squeeker is mounted in neck, operates when head is squeezed. Marks: **RUSTY** on head and **A** on small of back. Late 1950's, early 1960's. *(Author's collection)*

UNMKD-32. 20" Girl. Pale composition shoulder head and lower arms, remainder stuffed cloth. Pin and disc joints, painted features, cobalt blue eyes, molded hair under human hair wig, straight legs, original clothes. Note resemblance to UNMKD-3. 1910's. *(Spalding collection)*

UNMKD-32.

UNMKD-33.

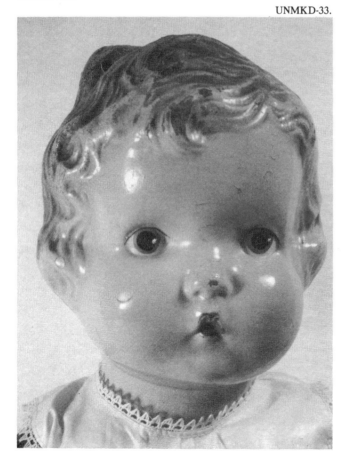

UNMKD-34.

UNMKD-33. 25" Girl. Composition shoulder head, arms and legs, cloth body stuffed with excelsior, blue painted eyes, painted, molded hair, molded hairbow loop. 1920's. *(Wiseman collection)*

UNMKD-34. 23½" Baby. Composition shoulder head and gauntlet hands, stuffed cloth body and legs. Doll is typical of many manufactured in 1910's and may well be a "War Baby" from World War I period when American manufacturers struggled to supply the market formerly dominated by German dollmakers. The type continued into the 1920's and one similar to this has been found with a cry box marked **Arthur A. Gerling / 1923.** The Gerling firm was a large supplier of voice boxes. *(Author's collection)*

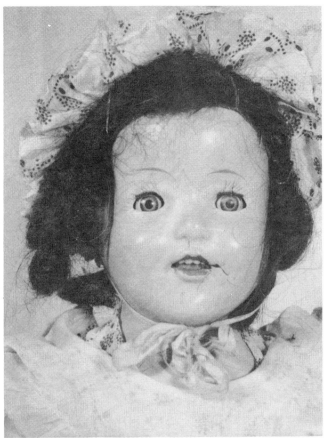

UNMKD-35.

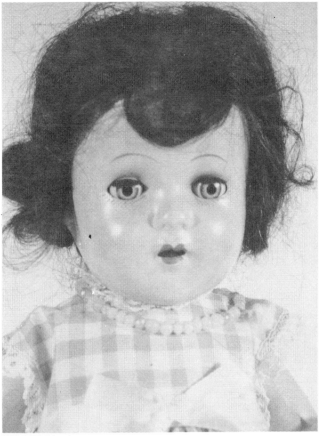

UNMKD-36.

UNMKD-37.

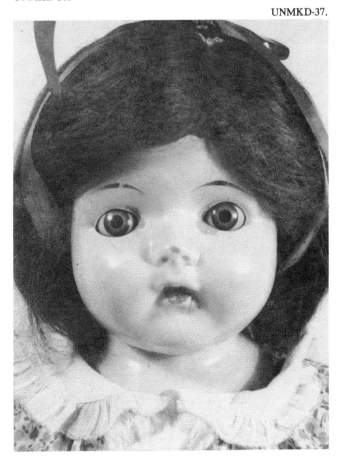

UNMKD-35. 23" Girl. Composition shoulder head, arms and legs, stuffed cloth body, blue-green decal sleep eyes, original dress and bonnet of green print lawn. ca. 1930. *(Zillner collection)*

UNMKD-36. 16" Girl. All composition, Patsy-type body, dark brown human hair wig, blue tin eyes. Note similarity to several of the 29" and 31" dolls. ca. 1928. *(Wiseman collection)*

UNMKD-37. 26" Girl. Pale composition swivel shoulder head, arms and legs, bulgy gray tin eyes, closed mouth, original human hair wig. ca. 1930. *(Wiseman collection)*

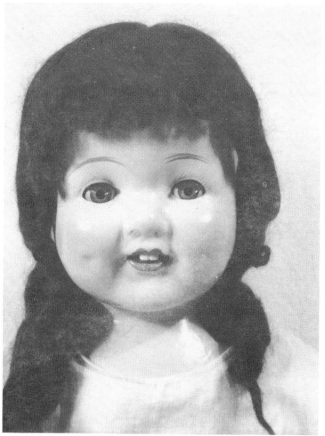

UNMKD-39.

UNMKD-40.

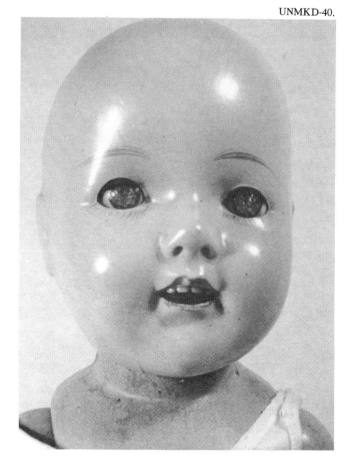

UNMKD-38.

UNMKD-38. 24" Girl. Composition swivel shoulder head, arms and legs, stuffed cloth body, open mouth, two teeth, green sleep eyes. 1930's. *(Wiseman collection)*

UNMKD-39. 27" Girl. Composition shoulder head, arms and legs, open mouth, two teeth, green tin eyes, original black mohair wig, cloth body. ca. 1928. *(Wiseman collection)*

UNMKD-40. 26" Girl. Composition head, open mouth, four teeth, green eyes of material used predominantly in 1930's. *(Wiseman collection)*

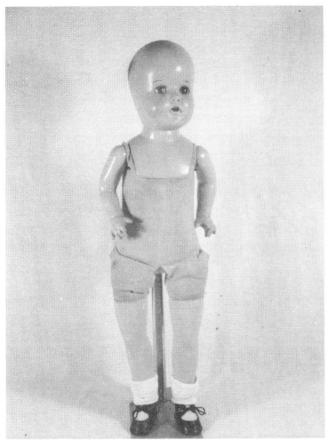

UNMKD-41.

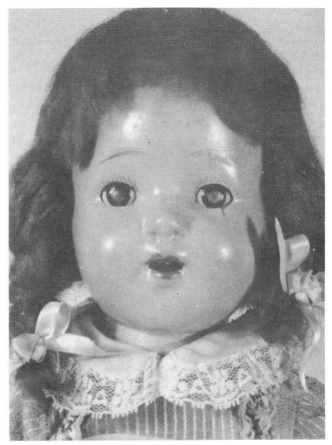

UNMKD-42.

UNMKD-41.

UNMKD-41. 24" Girl. Composition swivel shoulder head, arms and legs, stuffed cloth body, mama voice, brown sleep eyes; this doll is nearly identical to UN-MKD-40. Note this one has no *ears;* -40 has molded ears. Original pink cotton dress. *(Author's collection)*

UNMKD-42. 21" Girl. Same construction as two previous dolls, orange mohair wig and bright green eyes, molded ears, two teeth. *(Spalding collection)*

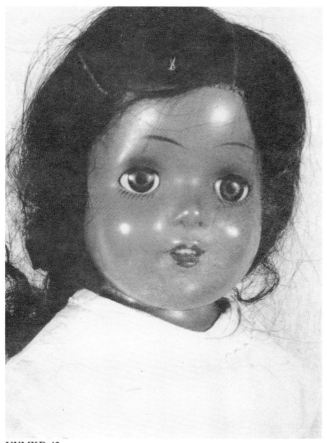

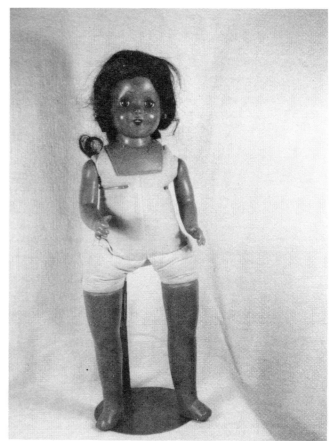

UNMKD-43.

UNMKD-43.

UNMKD-43.

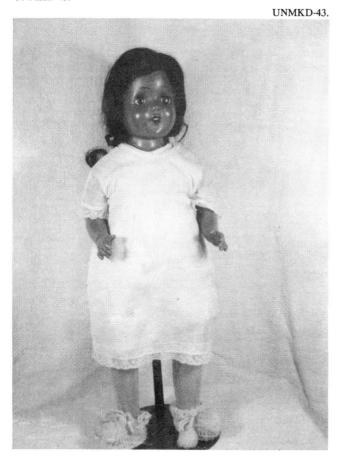

UNMKD-43. 22" Brown Girl. Brown sleep eyes, black human hair wig, open mouth, four teeth, no ears, just slight bumps. Note widely spaced hips. Purchased 1939 or 1940. All original. *(Childhood doll of Betty Kirtley)*

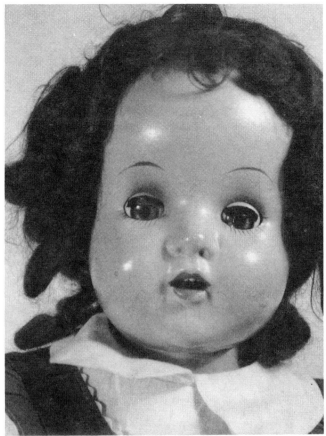

UNMKD-44.

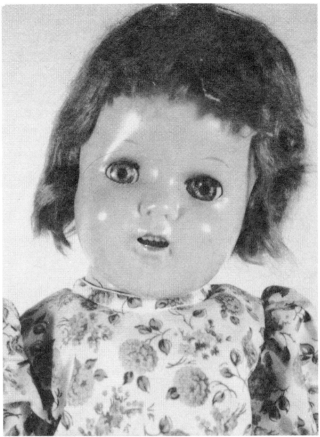

UNMKD-46.

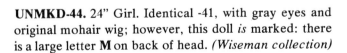

UNMKD-45.

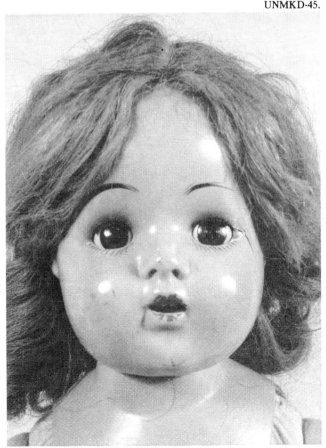

UNMKD-44. 24" Girl. Identical -41, with gray eyes and original mohair wig; however, this doll *is* marked: there is a large letter **M** on back of head. *(Wiseman collection)*

UNMKD-45. 25" Girl. Molded ears, blonde human hair wig, brown 1930's type eyes, open mouth, two teeth. *(Spalding collection)* Dolls of this type are offered in Sears catalogs from 1928 through 1931 as "Princess Dolls" and "Fairy Princess of 1931". They were standard mama styles of the period, dressed in rayon dresses and undies, lace trimmed, with snap fasteners, real hair with long double curls, silk ribbons, cloth body.

UNMKD-46. 18" Girl. All composition, light brown mohair wig, open mouth, six teeth, cornflower blue eyes. ca. 1936. *(Wiseman collection)*

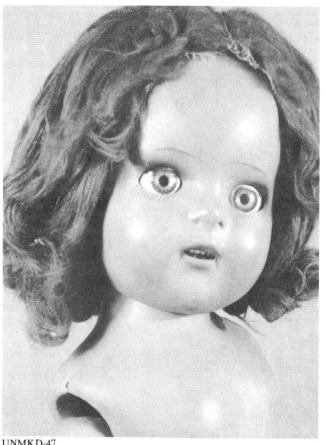

UNMKD-47.

UNMKD-48.

UNMKD-49.

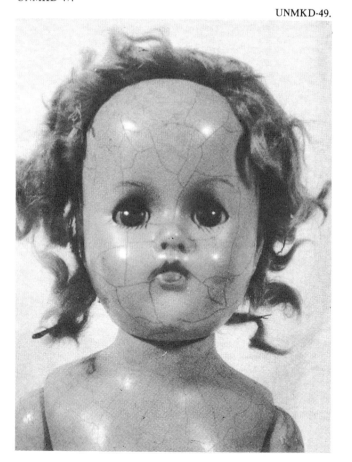

UNMKD-47. 20" Girl. All composition, highly tinted, open mouth, six teeth, original orange mohair wig, large, bright blue eyes, with whitest whites found in dolls beginning about 1939. Also found with brown eyes.

UNMKD-48. 20" Girl. All composition, brown sleep eyes of 1930's type, closed mouth, eye shadow, had stapled-on wig.

UNMKD-49. 20" Girl. All composition, blue-green sleep eyes, closed mouth, remnants of original blonde mohair wig. Note extensive crazing of paint surface. *(All three dolls from Author's collection)*

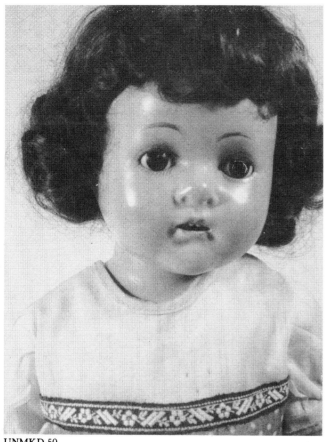

UNMKD-50.

UNMKD-47. -48,-49.

UNMKD-51.

UNMKD-50. 17" Child. Composition swivel shoulder head, arms and legs, cloth body. Brown sleep eyes, open mouth, two teeth, new wig. ca. 1936. *(Wiseman collection)*

UNMKD-51. 18" Girl. All composition, blue decal sleep eyes, eye shadow, original blonde mohair wig. Late 1930's, early 1940's. *(Spalding collection)*

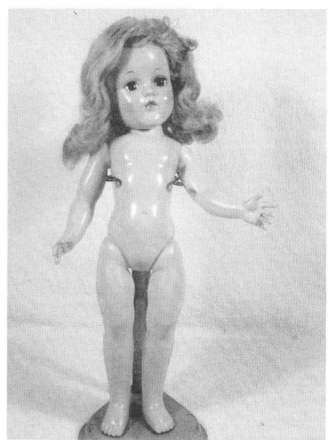

UNMKD-52.

UNMKD-51.

UNMKD-52.

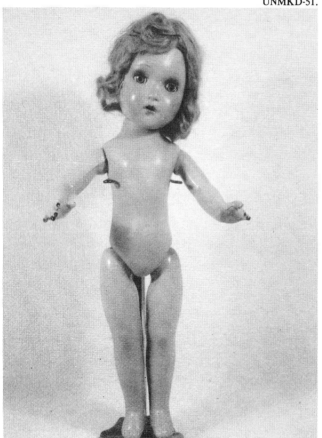

UNMKD-52. 15" Girl. Hard plastic, glued-on original synthetic wig, dark sleep eyes, closed mouth. ca. 1948. *(Author's collection)*

UNMKD-53. 16" Girl. All composition, sleep eyes, original mohair wig. For full length see R&B-5. ca. 1940. *(Author's collection)*

UNMKD-53.

UNMKD-54.

UNMKD-55.

UNMKD-54. 10" Chalk Cupids. Carnival dolls of painted chalk (plaster). Easily broken, many sidewalks have been decorated with their fragments. *(Kirtley collection)*

UNMKD-55. 27" Display Mannequin. All composition, coffee-with-cream color, black embroidery floss hair, painted-on silver high heel slippers, removeable arms. General style and construction dates it in 1940's. *(Kirtley collection)*

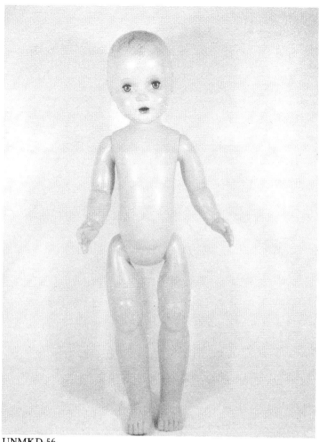

UNMKD-56.

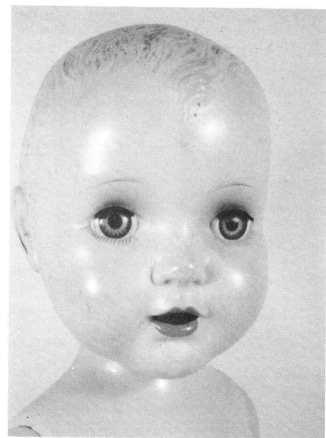

UNMKD-56.

UNMKD-55.

UNMKD-56. 28" Walker. Early hard plastic has bleached to a very pale tint, blue sleep eyes, open mouth. Molded hair under evidence of stapled-on wig. ca. 1955. *(Spalding collection)*

UNMKD-57.

UNMKD-57, -58.

UNMKD-58.

UNMKD-57. 19" Friend of the Bride. Plastic and vinyl, rooted Saran hair, blue sleep eyes, closed mouth. All original, dressed in pink plaid dress, nylons with seams, pink high-heeled shoes. Marks: **20** on head and **20 BALHH** on hip. *(Author's collection)*

UNMKD-58. 19" Bride. Plastic and vinyl, rooted poor quality synthetic hair, blue sleep eyes, Original white satin and net wedding dress. Both dolls ca. 1956. Marks: **14R / AE2006 / 16** on head, **20 5-SG** on shoulders. *(Author's collection)*

UNMKD-59.

UNMKD-59.

UNMKD-60.

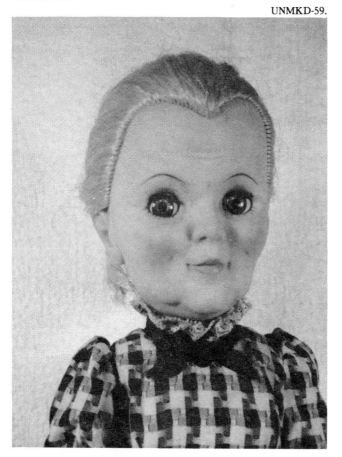

UNMKD-59. 19" Grandma. Vinyl, rooted gray hair tied back in bun with black ribbon, blue-gray eyes. Typical lady body of the period with defined bosom, separate fingers and high-heel feet. All original in red, gray and white checked dress. ca. 1964. *(Rebekka Anderton collection)* This doll is known to have been available as early as Christmas, 1960. Another example was dressed in high heels and long formal dress with sequins and was called *"The Modern Grandmother"*. Still another of these dolls was obtainable as an advertising premium for Ma Brown's Apple Butter and wore a checked dress and apron similar to that shown here.

UNMKD-60. 15½" *Gumdrop*. Vinyl and plastic, blue sleep eyes, rooted hair. Note resemblance to the Campbell Kids. Marks: © *1962*. These dolls are shown in 1963 and 1964 catalogs. *(Author's collection)*

UNMKD-60a. 16" *Gumdrop*. All vinyl and plastic, platinum or auburn hair, sleep eyes. *1965 Catalog illustration courtesy Sears, Roebuck & Co.*

Gumdrop is an EFFanBEE doll and was marketed by Speigels in 1965 as *"Honey"*. Marks: (**c**) **1962/EFFANBEE.**

UNMKD-60a.

VOG-1.

VOG-2.

VOGUE DOLLS, INC.

Mrs. Jennie Graves began making dolls clothes as a child, a hobby which served her well when she was left a widow and the sole support of two daughters in the 1930's. After nearly a decade of designing and producing dolls clothes for the Jordan Marsh Company in Boston, her company had grown to employ many of her neighbors as doll-clothes seamstresses.

Her company struggled through World War II shortages and in 1948 introduced the 8" *Ginny* doll. In 1951, *Ginny's* extensive wardrobe complete with jewelry and even furniture was offered. Developing the "doll family" concept, 8" Baby *Ginnette* (*Ginny's* baby sister), 10½" teenage *Jill* (*Ginny's* big sister), 12" *Jan* (*Jill's* girl friend) and 11½" *Jeff* (who served as a brother or boyfriend) were all placed on the market prior to 1955.

In 1960, Mrs. Graves introduced the floppy, life-like 18" *"Baby Dear"*, molded in the image of a real live one-month-old baby. Mrs. Graves retired that same year, and the business is continued by members of her family.

Vogue Dolls acquired the Arranbee Doll Company in 1958, discontinuing the use of that name and associated products in 1960.

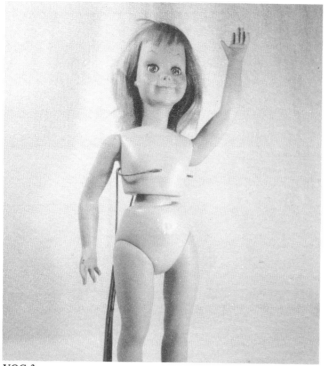

VOG-3.

VOG-3.

VOG-4.

VOG-1. 8" Skating girl, all composition, painted features, all original: red felt skirt, blond mohair braids. Marked: **Vogue,** back of head. Early. *(Kirtley collection)*

VOG-2. 13" WAC (Women's Army Corp World War II), all composition, painted features, all original: brown dress with attached underpants, brown socks and shoes, mohair wig. Marks: Gold paper label on coat, **Vogue** in circle. Body unmarked. *(Courtesy Janice Sanders)*

VOG-3. 22" *Brickett.* Hard plastic body and legs, soft vinyl head and arms, green eyes, orange rooted hair. Body unmarked. *(Kirtley collection)*

VOG-4. 19" *Brickett.* Similar to VOG-3, but unjointed at waist. *Brickett* was designed for Vogue by an Italian artist. *(Kirtley collection)*

VOG-5.

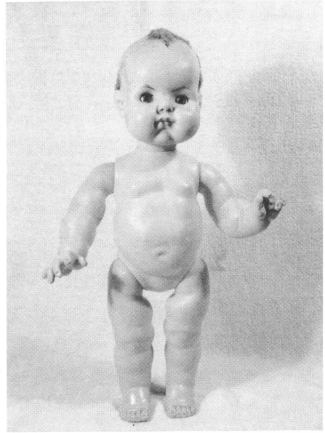

VOG-6.

VOG-7.

VOG-5. *Brickett.* From a 1960 catalog listing. Freckles, green eyes, polyethylene body, swivel waist, vinyl head and arms, dressed in cotton campus pajamas with black tights, candy stripe top, pompom slippers and night cap. In 16" and 22" sizes at $7.77 and $9.98. *(Courtesy Sears, Roebuck and Co.)*

VOG-6. 17" Husky Baby. All vinyl, with remains of rooted hair, blue sleep eyes, lashes. Note muscular modeling. Marked: © **1963 / E. WILKIN / VOGUE DOLL**, on head. *(Author's collection)*

VOG-7. 8" *Ginny.* All hard plastic, brown sleep eyes, solid, molded plastic lashes, jointed hip and shoulder, glued-on mohair wig. All original blue dress and underthings, pink hairbow, blue shoes. Marks: **GINNY / VOGUE DOLLS / INC / PAT. No. 2587594 / MADE IN U.S.A.** on back. *(Author's collection)*

W-1.

W-2.

W-1.

W

W-1. 18", Girl. All composition, bright glassene sleep eyes, original clothes, mohair wig. Bought at Montgomery Ward and Co. in 1947. Marked: **W,** on head. *(Childhood doll of Carolyn Battagler Sims)*

W-2. 20", Girl. All hard plastic, soft vinyl head, rooted synthetic hair, bright blue sleep eyes. Walker construction, jointed knees, voice box. Marked: **W. J. WILSON,** on head, and **190 / MADE IN U.S.A.,** on body. ca. 1950. *(Wiseman collection)*

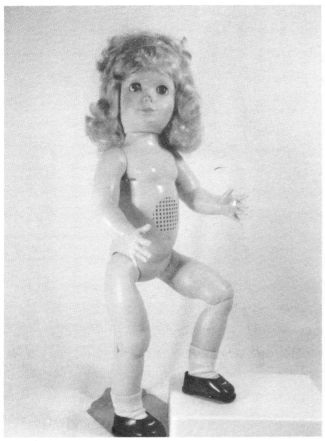

W-2.

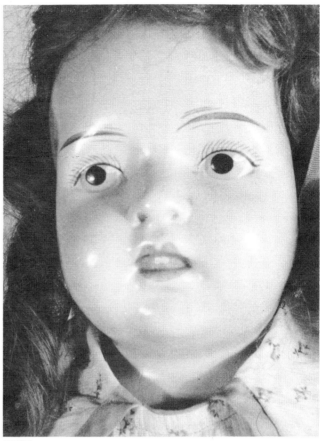

W-T-1.

W-T-1.

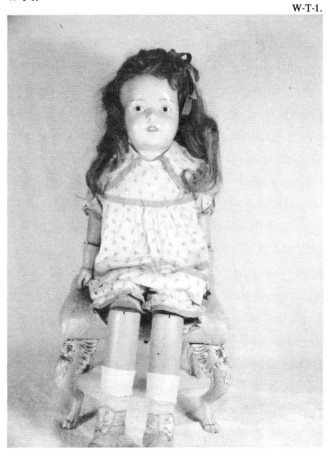

NOTE: ORIGINAL PRICES SHOWN
ARE NOT TODAY'S PRICES.

W-T-1. 29" *"Dolly Walker"*, Coleman walking doll.
Composition shoulder head, wooden limbs, legs jointed
at knees with ordinary hinges, crude carton body,
original human hair wig, painted features. Marks:
Stamped on back of shoulder plate: **"This is a Dolly
Walker / Patent Pending"**. Designed by Harry Coleman,
a ventriloquist, produced by Wood Toy Co., 1917. *(Zillner collection)*

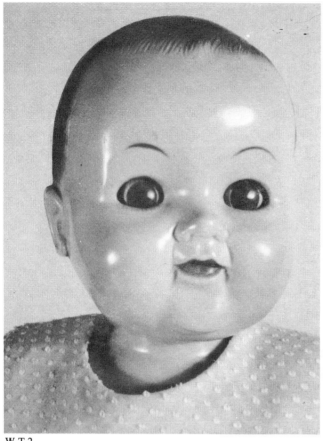

W-T-2.

W-T-2a.

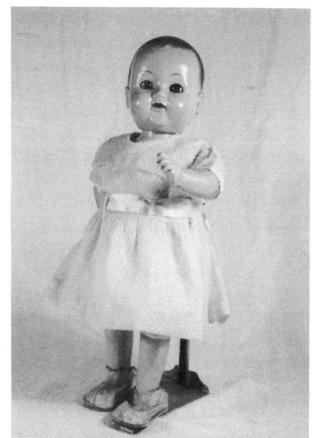

W-T-2.

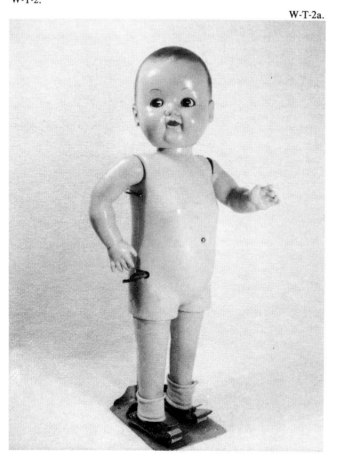

W-T-2. 21" *Walkalon doll.* All hard plastic with leather covering on foot mechanism, key wind on side, lever in back possibly acted as stabilizer when doll "walked". Marks: **Walkalon Mfg. Co. / Chicago, Ill.** ca. 1949. *(Zillner collection)*

W-T-2a. 20" Walkalon Walker. Three, possibly four, types of hard plastic were used in production of this doll. Covering has been removed to display roller-type walking mechanism on feet. Marks: **FOR SERVICE / SEND TO / WALKALON MFG. / CHICAGO 18** on back. *(Kirtley collection)*

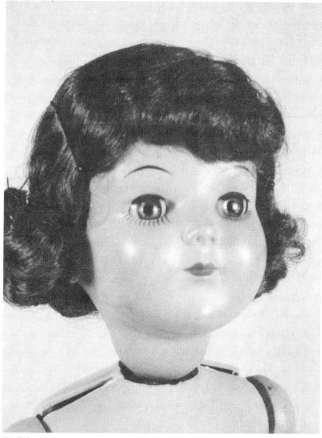

W-T-3.

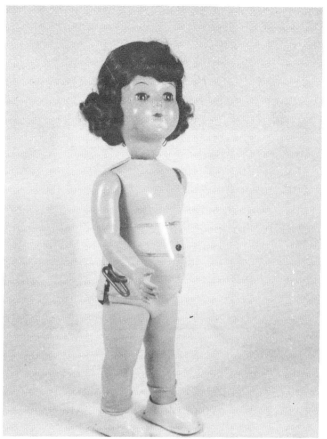

W-T-3.

W-T-4.

W-T-3. 18" *Wanda, The Walking Doll.* Several different types of plastic, molded shoes, rollers on bottom of shoes may be turned to change direction, blue-green sleep eyes, replacement wig. Note: key wind on side; arms raise, head turns back and forth as doll walks. About 1950. *(Spalding collection)*

W-T-4. 19" *Happi-Time Walker.* Hard plastic, blue sleep eyes, lashes, glued-on Saran wig, original clothes, shoes, socks. Head turns as she walks, holding her "mother's" hand. Purchased about 1947. Shown in 1953 catalog at $7.98 retail. *(Childhood doll of Carolyn Battagler Sims)*

W-T-4.

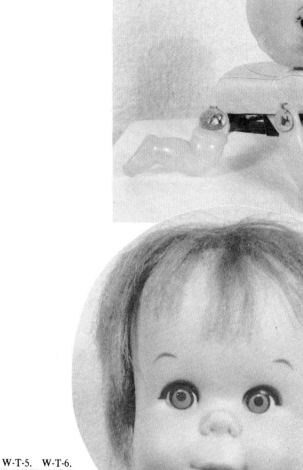

W-T-7.

W-T-5.   W-T-6.

W-T-5.

W-T-5. 18" *Baby Step*. Vinyl and plastic, rooted hair, painted eyes, molded white plastic baby shoes with knit socks inserted, walker treads on soles. Marked: © **1964 MATTEL, INC. / HAWTHORNE, CALIFORNIA / MADE IN U.S.A. / U.S. PATENTS PENDING.** *(Author's collection)* Sears 1967 catalog features *Baby Walk 'n' See*, 18" version with rolling eyes, open mouth, eyes roll as she walks or skates, curly rooted red hair.

W-T-6. 14½" *Baby Walk Alone*. Plastic and vinyl, rooted hair, sleep eyes, moulded shoes, walker wheels on soles. Marked: **624/REMCO INC./Copyright 1965,** on head. *(Author's collection)*

W-T-7. 6" Crawler, tin and vinyl, marked: **JAPAN.** *(Kirtley collection)* 1960's.

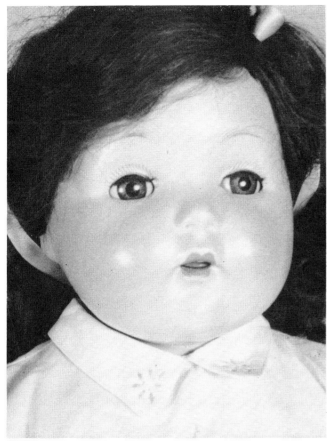

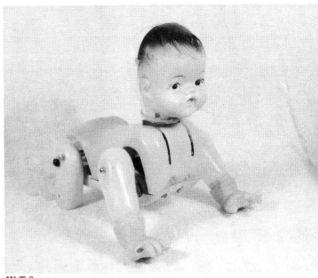

W-T-8.

W-T-9.

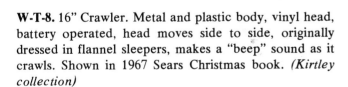

W-T-9.

W-T-8. 16" Crawler. Metal and plastic body, vinyl head, battery operated, head moves side to side, originally dressed in flannel sleepers, makes a "beep" sound as it crawls. Shown in 1967 Sears Christmas book. *(Kirtley collection)*

W-T-9. 28" *Mae Starr*. Construction is same as *Dolly Record* (See Averill), composition head and limbs, cloth body. Phonograph mechanism in body makes doll quite heavy. Record says: *"Hello, boys and girls! I'm a Mae Starr dolly and I can speak and sing for you! And, oh, yes, I can spell, too! D-O-G spells (groufff!). C-A-T spells (meeoow!) B-I-R-D spells (tweeet!)."* Sleep eyes, original human hair wig, wears size 3 child's dress. ca. 1930. Probably EFFANBEE. Doll and mechanism both unmarked, while author's identical doll is embossed **MAE/STARR/DOLL.** *(Zillner collection)*

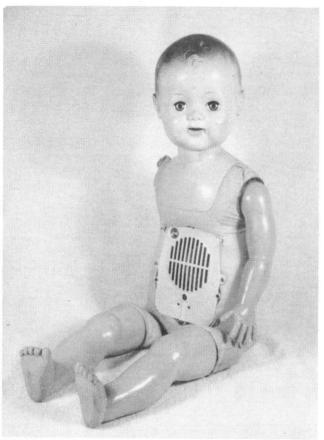

W-T-10.

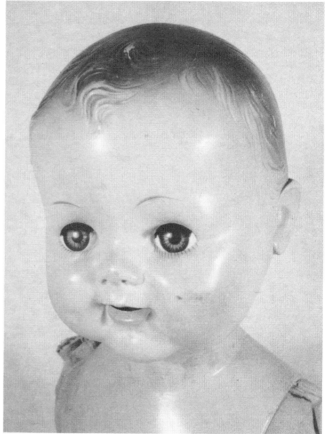

W-T-10.

W-T-10a.

W-T-10. 28" *Noma, Talking Doll.* Hard plastic swivel shoulder head, blue sleep eyes, lashes, open mouth, two teeth, tongue. Limbs are early soft plastic often mistaken for rubber. This material "weeps" and becomes quite sticky. Cotton body stuffed with cotton and reprocessed material. Talking mechanism uses two batteries. Record and speaker are visible through speaker grill. Mechanism marked: **NOMA ELECTRIC CORPORATION / NEW YORK, N.Y. / PATENT APPLIED FOR.** Head marked: **EFFANBEE.** 1950. *(Baume collection)* This doll was produced by EFFanBEE in 1949 as *Mommy's Baby.* Marks: **EFFANBEE** on back of head. *Noma* was created the following year when the company was owned for a brief period by the Noma Electric Light Company, at which time the talking mechanism was added.[1]

W-T-10a. *"Noma, New Electronic Talking Doll".* Touch buttons, she sings, talks, laughs, prays. Press button on chest to keep her talking. Off and on switch on back. Sleep eyes, molded hair, two batteries. 1950 and 1951 Christmas catalogs; $23.89 retail both years. *(Courtesy Sears, Roebuck & Co.)*

[1]Ellenburg, M. Kelly, "EFFanBEE, The Dolls With The Golden Hearts", The Trojan Press, Inc., North Kansas City, 1973.

W-T-13.

W-T-12.

W-T-11.

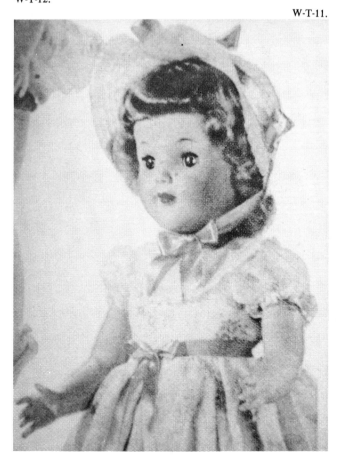

W-T-11. 30" *Melodie.* Walks, talks, sings, changeable records, two batteries. Press magic button, she recites rhymes, sings nursery ditties and prays. All plastic, jointed knees, sleep eyes, closed mouth, originally dressed in organdy dress, taffeta slip, straw bonnet. Song sheet for "mother". EFFanBEE. 1956. *(Courtesy Sears, Roebuck & Co.)*

W-T-12. 30" *Little Miss Echo.* Vinyl and plastic, knob control, continuous magnetic tape recorder, tape erases as you re-record, takes two D batteries, one 9-volt transistor battery. Sleep eyes, rooted hair. 1962. *(Courtesy Sear, Roebuck & Co.)*

W-T-13. 30" *Little Miss Echo.* Vinyl and plastic, 1965 version of W-T-12, retails at $14.99. *(Courtesy Sears, Roebuck & Co.)*

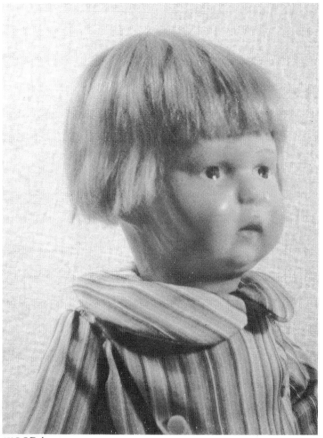

WOOD-1.

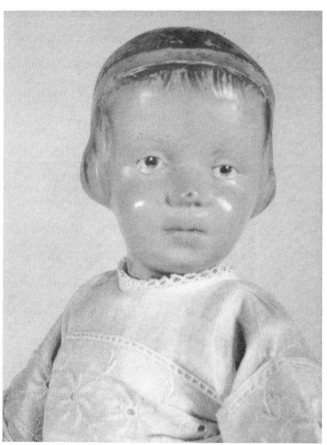

WOOD-2.

WOOD-3.

WOODEN DOLLS

A doll of wood may be carved, turned, glued, sanded, painted, or chiseled. Wooden dolls have been fashioned from spoons, bedposts, tree limbs, and other bits of lumber. Nut dolls may even qualify as wooden dolls. Many wooden dolls came from the forest areas of Germany where ample wood supplies and cheap labor combined to center a huge industry which shipped dolls all over the world. Here in the United States, a German named Albert Schoenhut continued his family's tradition to perfection in the creation of his famous dolls and toys.

WOOD-1. 16" *Schoenhut* Boy. Original blond mohair wig, straight toddler legs. *(Wingfield collection)*

WOOD-2. 14" *Schoenhut* Girl. Mold-carved hair, ribbon, painted eyes, new dress. *(Zillner collection)*

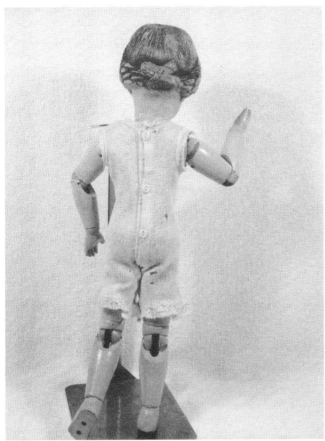

WOOD-3.

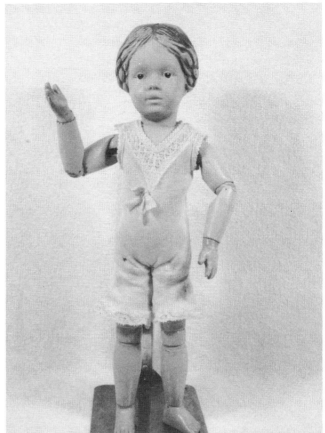

WOOD-3.

WOOD-4.

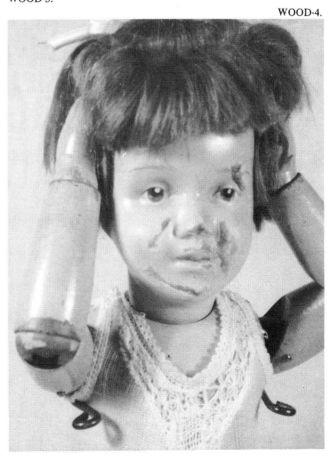

WOOD-3. 16" *Schoenhut* Girl. Mold-carved hair, brown, braided, pink bow in back (some have blue bows), original fine-knit cotton undies, lace-trimmed with three buttons down back. *(Wingfield collection)*

WOOD-4. 16" *Schoenhut* Girl. Original mohair wig has rusted wig nails, intaglio painted brown eyes, original undies. Marked: **SCHOENHUT DOLL / PAT. JAN. 17, '11, U.S.A. / & FOREIGN COUNTRIES.** Note scarred paint; this doll has been much-loved. *(Author's collection)*

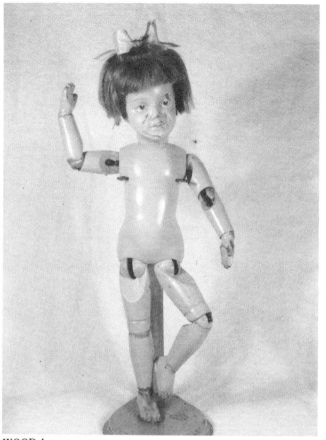

WOOD-4.

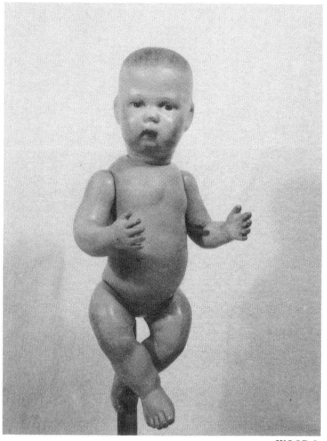

WOOD-5.

WOOD-4.

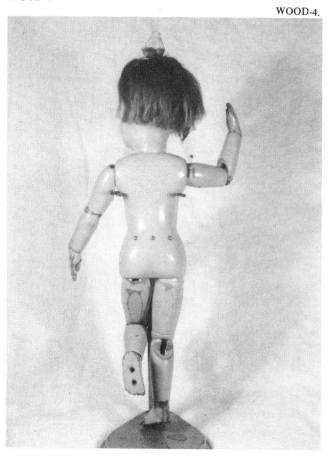

fig. WOOD-5

fig. WOOD-5

WOOD-5. 12½" *Schoenhut* Baby. Blue painted eyes, sprayed and brush-stroked hair, pink-painted fingernails and toenails. Marked: Head and shoulders, see fig. WOOD-5. *(Battagler collection)*

WOOD-6. *Schoenhut* Piano. "All carefully tuned so child may play melodies and learn rudiments of music." Also available were 12-key at $1.98 and 8-key at $1.10, plus a baby grand and an 18-key "high grade" at $4.98. 1926 Catalog illustration. *Courtesy Sears, Roebuck & Co.*

WOOD-7. *Schoenhut* Circus. "The Greatest Show on Earth". 1926 Catalog illustration *Courtesy Sears, Roebuck & Co.*

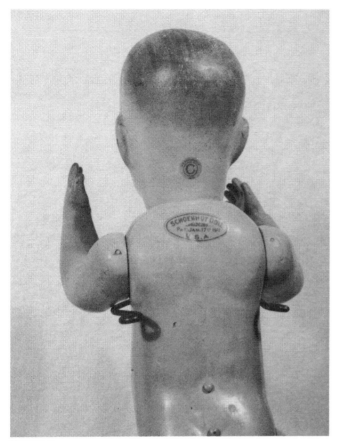

WOOD-5.

WOOD-6.

SCHOENHUT TOYS

All the skill and knowledge of the master German wood carver was brought to bear in the creation of these wonderful bits of childhood joy. Many of the pianos are still playable today and the tiny circuses remain bright and colorful in spite of many hours of play by other-year's children.

WOOD-7.

WOOD-7.

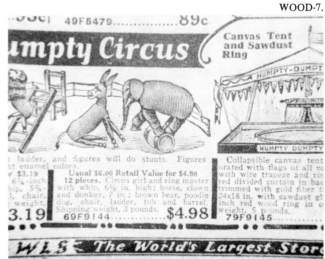

WOOD-8a.

WOOD-8b.

WOOD-8c.

WOOD-8. Remaining figures from a *Schoenhut Humpty-Dumpty Circus* which Mrs. Baume purchased at a thrift shop in 1948 for 25¢ — for the entire box. As her daughter played with the set over the years, broken pieces were discarded. Survivors are a 10" x 7" horse, 8" x 5" bear, 8" x 6" goat, 9" x 6" donkey, 8" x 5" elephant, 7" clown, 9¼" colored performer, 8½" lady performer, and a 4½" chair. These one-time residents of the toy box now occupy important places on a collector's shelf. *(Baume collection)*

WOOD-9.

WOOD-10.

WOOD-11.

WOOD-9. 7" *Pinnochio.* Jointed shoulders and hips, painted features, dressed in stockinette. Marks: **Made in Poland.** *(Kirtley collection)*

WOOD-10. 5" All wood. Painted features, unmarked. Metal lever in back pulls hair down into center of open-domed head to make doll appear frightened. *(Vandiver collection)*

WOOD-11. 10" *Mr. Muscles.* All wood, spring strung, painted features. Came from a Chicago warehouse where stored for forty years. Marked: **Pkd. & Inspected / by Ill. Industries / for Blind—1310 S. Newberry Ave. / Chi., Ill.** *(Spalding collection)*

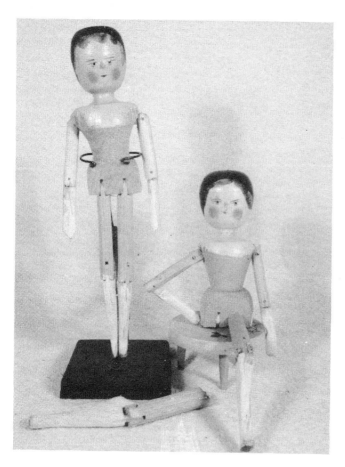

XYZ

WOOD-12. 11½" "Dutch" dolls. Hand-carved and hand-painted. Note differences in faces; different artists contributed their "personalities". Doll on right has fallen victim to common malady of these poorly made dolls; the right leg has broken off just below the pivot joint because of improper construction of the joint. *(Author's collection)*

The author welcomes your letters; she regrets, however, her inability to acknowledge all correspondence. Neither is she able to make appraisals or bids. If writing about your dolls, send *complete* descriptions and clear, well-lighted black and white photographs if available. Marks, if any, should be carefully copied; sizes should be accurately measured.

— The Editors

THE VALUE OF DOLLS

"What are my dolls worth?"

The author is often asked this question by dealer and collector alike. The answer is not a simple one. Aside from the market value, *ie,* the price at which a doll may easily be disposed of in today's antique market, dolls often carry *sentimental* value which clouds the judgment of the owner. A woman whose doll dates back several generations in her family may feel her doll is worth several hundred dollars when, in fact, it is a rather common type of German bisque worth only fifty to sixty dollars *in a shop.*

Age is certainly a factor in consideration of value; however, *condition* of the doll is rather more important. Dollar for dollar investment in a 1920 doll of mint condition, with its original dress and in its original box, makes more sense than buying an 1890's bisque with cracked head and leaking leather parts or a chipped china with a replacement body.

Another factor which must be considered is the cost of repairs required to restore the doll to collectible or saleable condition. A saving may be realized if the collector or dealer is able to make minor repairs, is willing to spend the time, and has the patience. Labor costs are high in doll repair as in other areas. Extensive repairs should be considered in detail before investing in a derelict doll of questionable value. Wigs, eyes, stringing elastic, and all the other paraphernalia required for proper repair of dolls may increase the outlay for a doll to a price above that of a mint doll of the same type purchased from a reliable dealer.

Costuming the doll is an added expense although many skillful collectors take great delight and pride in outfitting their dolls and prefer to buy them undressed. If a doll dressmaker must be engaged to provide needed clothing such costs should be taken into consideration in determining the value of a doll. Tiny garments often take as much time and skill as full-size fashions. If a doll wears an original outfit, its value is greatly increased, of course.

Finally, there is a price rule which collectors should remember: *There are several prices for any antique or collectible.* First, there is the price a dealer pays another dealer. Yes, dealers do buy from one another, often with particular customers in mind. Dealers usually sell to one another at a small discount to allow for a reasonable mark-up. Second, there is the price a dealer would expect to pay in buying a group or *lot* from an auction, estate, or individual picker. This price is based on the picker's cost plus a small mark-up for his time and trouble, or in the case of an auction or estate, it is based on a reasonable, appraised price set by a dealer or other qualified person. Another price base is indicated when one collector buys from another collector; this price is usually set much lower than *shop price.* Finally, there is the *lucky* price one may pay at a garage sale, flea market or thrift shop, although these last two categories may constitute a separate and higher category with increased awareness of values among proprietors of such establishments.

Each doll must be priced as an individual with full recognition of all these factors. The collector should examine the doll closely for imperfections, gauge its approximate age and needed repairs, check for original clothes, wig, eyes, etc., and finally ask that all-important question, *"Do I want this doll enough to pay the price?"*

BIBLIOGRAPHY

BOOKS

Angione, Genevieve, "All-Bisque & Half-Bisque Dolls", Camden, N. J., Thomas Nelson, 1969.

Bateman, Thelma, "Delightful Dolls Antique and Otherwise", Washington, D. C., Hobby House Press, 1966.

Burdick, Loraine, "Child Star Dolls and Toys", Puyallup, Washington, Quest Books, 1968.

Burdick, Loraine, "Shirley Dolls and Related Delights", Puyallup, Washington, Quest Books, 1968.

Coleman, Dorothy S., E. A., and E. J., "The Collector's Encyclopedia of Dolls", New York, Crown Publishers, Inc., 1968.

Cooper, Marlowe, "Dimples and Sawdust, Volume 2", Privately Published, 1968.

Cooper, Marlowe, "Doll Home Library Series, Volume Three, Grace Drayton Collectibles", Privately Published, 1970.

Culff, Robert, "The World of Toys", London, The Hamlyn Publishing Group Limited, 1969.

Ellenburg, M. Kelly, "Effanbee—The Dolls With The Golden Hearts", North Kansas City, Missouri, The Trojan Press, Inc., 1973.

Fawcett, Clara Hallard, "Dolls, A Guide for Collectors", New York, H. L. Lindquist Publications, 1947.

Fawcett, Clara Hallard, "Dolls, A New Guide for Collectors", Boston, Charles T. Branford Co., 1964.

Frazer, Antonia, "A History of Toys", Delacorte Press, 1966.

Gruelle, John, "Raggedy Andy Stories", New York, Bobbs-Merrill Co., Inc., 1960.

Hart, Luella, "Directory of United States Doll Trademarks 1888-1968", Privately Published, 1968.

Hertz, Louis H., "The Toy Collector", New York, Funk & Wagnalls, 1969.

Hillier, Mary, "Dolls and Dollmakers", New York, G. P. Putnam's Sons, 1968.

Marquette, Arthur F., "Brands, Trademarks, and Good Will", New York, Mc-Graw-Hill, 1967.

Noble, John, "Dolls", Toronto, Ryerson Press, 1967.

Ruggles, Rowena Godding, "The One Rose", Privately Published, 1964.

Young, Helen, "The Complete Book of Doll Collecting", New York, G. P. Putnam's Sons, 1967.

PERIODICALS

Alumni Magazine, University of Kansas at Lawrence, May, 1968.

Pen Woman, Official Publication, The National League of American Pen Women, Inc., Rosenberg, Ruby Holland, Washington, D. C., Dec., 1970.

Spinning Wheel Magazine, Hanover, Pa., Jan.-Feb., 1969.

NUMERICAL MARKS INDEX

Doll Mark	Page Number
0—81, 85-87, 108, 111-113, 222-224, 257, 281, 387	
0½—88	
1—81, 275, 311	
2—27, 82, 112, 222-224	
2¼—220	
2½—219	
3—27, 85, 86, 109, 110, 241	
4—86, 87, 106, 145, 162, 239, 262, 264, 271, 281, 282	
5—85, 108, 282, 423	
5½—87	
6—85, 103, 108, 111, 162, 225, 311	
6½—85, 219	
7—89, 223, 237, 387	
8—87, 113, 240, 241, 388	
8½—113	
9—81, 88, 108, 147, 162, 282, 324	
10—106, 111, 280	
011—281	
11—104, 105, 107, 109, 110, 219, 222, 223, 240, 263, 281, 437	
12—27, 97, 224, 276, 280, 355	
13—354	
14—83, 222, 241, 282, 423	
15—224	
16—263, 280, 423	
17—112, 257, 263, 264, 355, 379, 437	
18—222, 239, 262-264, 311, 430	
VT18—40	
19—42, 241, 308	
19C—308	
20—423	
21—161, 248, 260	
22—240, 260	
23—241	
25—239, 241, 314, 393	
26—96, 388	
28—274	
30—106	
34—138	
40—105	
48—87	
49—224, 236	
50—275	
54—242, 276	
60—223	
62—109, 110	
63—162	
65—162	
66—109, 148, 237	
67—162	
73—112	
74—19, 379	
76—224	
87—223	
P-90—34, 42	
P-92—42	

Doll Mark	Page Number
92—113	
96—239	
100—237, 274, 275	
101—110	
109—219	
112—113	
117—280, 281	
122—388	
126—276	
127—112	
128—222	
136—108	
140—280, 281	
144—241	
150—162, 210, 280, 281	
152—282	
154—282	
170—111	
185—222	
189—224	
190—428, 429	
195—282	
210—89	
211—280	
229—162	
240—112	
255—275, 276	
275—111	
320—222	
327—81	
341—82	
351—83	
351.14—83	
352—84	
370—85	
390—85-87	
399—224	
461—104	
624—432	
631—167	
758—115	
818M—97	
965—296	
971—86	
1070—280	
1079—387, 388	
1235—103	
1272—105	
1310—441	
1894—88	
1899-5—108	
1909—225	
1913—284	
1914—113	
1917—284	
1919—374	
1922—151	
1923—412	

Doll Mark	Page Number
1924—112, 151, 181, 182	
1925—149	
1932—157	
1937—232, 233	
1946—318	
1951—159	
1952—156	
1958—59	
1959—20, 192	
1960—273, 290, 297	
1961—18, 62, 63, 239, 240, 290, 291, 299	
1962—33, 297-300, 315	
1963—162, 240, 290, 298, 427	
1964—76, 162, 221, 297, 299, 300, 395, 432	
1965—27, 64, 160, 221, 262, 296, 300, 314, 432	
1966—160, 161, 263, 361, 395	
1967—64, 200, 241, 242, 300, 313, 314, 316, 361, 379	
1968—150, 158, 263, 305, 346, 362	
1969—36, 156, 264, 350	
2006—423	
2202—150	
2580—241	
2700—241	
3512½—142	
4129—264	
5667—200	
6099—145	
6611—165	
6681—324	
6682—324	
7845—223	
9493—147	
1283558—186, 191	
1355525—96	
30441—115	
43580—122	
67191—242	
94215—277	
1357936—96	
2118682—30, 379, 386	
2160739—30, 379, 386	
2587594—427	
2620061—164	
2675644—75	
2728947—130	
2728948—130	
2728980—130	
3017187—290, 299, 315	
3036014-2—296	
3162976—264	
3277602—221	
5028182—284	
8017187—298	

A

A, 411

A.B.C., 17

ABC, 113

Aborigine, 286

Active dolls, 12

Active Miss, 58

ADC, 17

Advertising, 20-39, 156, 214, 220, 238

AE, 311, 423

Affectionately Peanut, 131

African Baby, 224

Air Force Baby, 410

Airplane control, 365

"Alabama Baby", 368, 374

Alaskan, 204, 205

Albert Alligator, 156

Alexander Doll Co., 44-69, 158, 314, 316, 319, 323, 324, 336-340, 344-346, 350, 351, 362, 375, 377

Alice in Wonderland, 45, 46, 51, 67, 150, 345, 368

All American Athlete, 377

Alphabet, 113

Alter, 18

Amberg, 18, 44, 112, 332-3

Am Doll, 18

American Beauty, 19, 242

American Character, 13, 25, 34, 35, 43 70-80

American Children, 196

American Doll Mfg. Co., 18

American Doll & Toy, 305

American-Made, 10

Amosandra, 313

Amos and Andy, 313

Andrews, Julie, 324

Angel Child, 377

Animals, Circus, 438-440

Annette, 174, 336-340

A(crown)P,G, 224

Armand Marseille, 81-89, 108

Arnaz, Desi, 326

Arranbee, 12, 90-95, 425

Arrow Novelty, 201

Arrow Plastic, 19, 20

AS, 103, 107

Athlete, 377

Aunt Jemima, 20, 21, 404, 405

Aunt Jenny, 215

Australian Aborigine, 286

Averill, 96-99, 370, 376, 377, 433

Ayer, Harriet Hubbard, 22

B

B, 223

BB, 115

B.G., 268, 269

Babes in Toyland, 392, 393

Babette, 174, 175

Babs, 55

"Baby", 16, 274

Baby Aire, 230, 231

Baby "B", 71

Baby, Bannister, 100

Baby Barry Toy Co., 347, 348

Baby Betty, 88

Baby, Bi-Bye, 234, 235

Baby Big Eyes, 256

Baby Bo-Kaye, 126

Baby Bright Eyes, 196, 197

Baby Bud, 33

Baby Bumps, 226

Baby Carrie, 173

Baby Cheryl, 297

Baby Coos, 254

Baby Crawl-Along, 379

Baby Dainty, 176

Baby Dancerina, 295

Baby Dear, 425

Baby Dimples, 12, 230, 231

Baby Effanbee, 178

Baby First Step, 432

Baby Giggles, 263

Baby Ginnette, 425

Baby Grumpy, 177

Baby Hungerford, 214

Baby Janie, 385, 386

Baby Linda, 359

Baby Linda, see also Linda Baby

Baby Lu, 263

Baby Magic, 161

Baby Marie, 285

Baby Mine, 132, 133

Baby Pattaburp, 298

Baby Peggy, 313

Baby Ruth, 99

Baby Sandy, 12, 331

Baby Secret, 300

Baby Shirley Temple, 353

Baby Smiles, 243

Baby Snooks, 332

Baby Step, 432

Baby Sunshine, 12, 381, 382

Baby Surprise, 306, 307

Baby Tweaks, 242

Baby Weems, 129

Baby's Hungry, 297

Ball, Lucille, 326

Ballerina, 56, 58, 59, 61, 62

Bannister Baby, 100

Barbie, 293, 294

Baseball player, 377

Beautiful Crissy, 264

Beauregard Hound, 156

Beasley, Mrs., 313, 314

Bebe Charmont, 389

Bed Doll, 100, 102, 206, 207

Bed Doll, see also Flapper

Beloved Belindy, 368, 369

Bend 'Em Doll, 349

Betsy Wetsy, 242, 246, 247, 258, 264

Bergen, Edgar, 320, 329

Bertha, 144

Berryman, Clifford, 389

Betty Boop, 128

Bewitched, 326

Bi-Bye Baby, 234, 235

Big Baby, 399

Big Bad Wolf, 168, 317

Big Eyes, 256

Big Huggums, 64, 65

Big Mary, 376

Big Sister, 373

Billiken, 225

Billy Boy, 211, 212, 380

Bimbo, 365

Biscuit Babies, 281

Bisque, 103-115, 387, 388
    see also company listings

Blessed Event, 252

Blind, Industries for, 441

Blonde China, 144, 146

Blossom, Auntie, 151

Blossom, Mrs., 151

Bobbi-Mae, 329, 330

Bonnie Blue Bell, 212

Bonnie Braids, 159

Bonomi, 266

Borgfeldt, Geo. Co., 116, 126, 127

Bottletot, 71

Brahm's Lullaby, 241, 286

Brevete, 389

Brice, Fanny, 332

Brickett, 426, 427

Bride, 54, 55, 216, 423

Bridesmaid, 54

Brockway Glass, 379, 380

Brookglad, 211

Brother, 8, 9, 197, 233

Brother Coos, 237, 238

Brown, Buster, 22, 23

Brown, Charlie, 148

Bru, 389

Bte., 389

Bubbles, 12, 181, 182

Buddy Lee, 16, 32, 33, 402, 403

Bundle of Joy, 174

Bunny-Baby, 57

Buttercup, 12, 231, 148

Butterick, 41

Bye-lo Baby, 11, 116-119, 229

Cahill, W. F., 27

Cameo, 120-134, 157

Camilla, 173

Campbell Kids, 23-26, 225, 424

Canadian, 409

Candy Kid, 195

Can't Break 'Em, 24, 226

Captain Kangaroo, 374, 375

Captain Lazer, 300

Carmen Miranda, 13, 16, 321, 322

Carol, 173

Caroline, 62, 63

Carroll, Diahanne, 346, 347

Cartwright, Angela, 330

Casey, Dr. Ben, 332

Cassidy, Hopalong, 335

Cassini, Oleg, 135

Cathy, Chatty, 290, 291

Cecile, 336-340

Celebrity Doll, 333, 349

Celluloid, 9, 12, 135-136, 143, 275, 276

Century, 13

Chadwick-Miller, 221

Chalk dolls, 421

Champ, 130

Change-O-Doll Co., 304, 305

Charles, Prince of England, 333

Charmin' Chatty, 2, 291

Charming Lucile, 376, 377

Charmont, Bebe, 389

Chase Bag Co., 29

Chase, Martha Jenks, 368, 370

Chatterbox, 62

Chatty Baby, 13, 299

Chatty Brother, 13, 299

Chatty Cathy, 13, 290, 291

Chatty, Charmin', 291

Checkerboard Squarecrow, 39

Cheerful Tearful, 296

Chef, 27

Chein, J. & Co., 157

China, 11, 12, 144, 147

Chinese, 202, 203

Chinese Baby, 204, 205

Crissy, 264

Christie, 293

Christmas Cards, 284

Christopher Robin, 165, 166

Churchill, Sir Winston and Lady, 324

Churchy La Femme, 156

Chubby Baby, 234, 235

Chubby Boy, 179, 409

Chubby Kids, 33, 402, 403

Cinderella, 56, 68, 296

Cinders, Ella, 148

Cigarette smoker, 28, 29, 206, 207

Circus, Humpty-Dumpty, 438-440

Cissy, 58

Clairol, 27

Clara Ann, 243

Clarabelle Clown, 314, 363, 364

Clark, Dick, 333

Clicquot Club Eskimo, 27

Clodrey, 208

Clown, 304, 314, 347, 348, 374, 375

Cochran, Dewees, 13, 196

Coke delivery man, 32, 33

Coleman, Harry, 429

Coleman Walking Doll, 429

Collecting, 13

Collins, Cora Sue, 352

Colored Baby, 253

Columbia Toy Products, 149

Combs, Loula Long, 334

Comic, 148-160

Composition, 11, 12

Connie Lynn, 360

Contortionist, 302, 303

Coogan, Jackie, 335

Cooper, Jackie, 328, 329

Cop, 98

Coquette, 394

Corry, Grace, 136, 137

Cowboy, 32, 98

Crackels, 39

Crackerjack, 28

Crackle, 31

Crawling Baby, 241, 379, 433

Cream of Wheat Chef, 27

Cream Puff, 258

Creech, Sarah Lee, 253

Cricket, 79

Crissy, 264

Crosby, P. L., 328, 329

Crown mark, 281

Crying baby, 236

Cubeb, 28, 29

Cuddle Kewpie, 283

Cuddles, 37, 245

Cuddly Kewpie, 283

Cupids, 421

Cut 'n' Button, 299

Cynthia, 58

D, 224

D., 163

Dad, 259

Dagwood, 149

Dainty Dorothy, 191

Daisy mark, 223

Dakin, R. Co., 150

Dancerina, 295

Dancing Doll, 36

D'Andrade, Deet, 221

Dean Rag Doll, 372

Dean's Rag Book Co., 372

Deanna Durbin, 16, 342

DebuTeen, 90

Dee & Cee Toy Co., Ltd., 289

Dee Dee, 299

Degas Girl, 68

Deluxe Reading, 161-163

Dencla, 376, 377

Dennis the Menace, 149-150

Depose, 389

Depression, 12

Dick Tracy, 159-160

Di E. Scavinna(i), 368, 371

Dilly Dally, 363, 364

Dimples, 230

Dinah, 20

Dinsdale, Shirley, 330

Dionne, Emelie, 16

Dionne Quintuplets, 336-340

Disney, Walt, 164-168, 245, 247, 324
     325, 375, 377, 392, 393

Display doll, 421, 422

Doctor, 332

Doctor Doolittle, 341

Doll-o'-My-Heart, 376

Dollar Princess, 110

Dollikin, 393

Dolly Dear, 368

Dolly Dingle, 25

Dolly Dumpling, 178

Dolly Record, 96

Dolly Rosebud, 229

Dolly Sunshine, 381, 382

Dolly Walker, 429

Donald Duck, 164

Doolittle, Dr., 341

Dopey, 165

Dorette, 279

Dorothy, 376

Dorothy Sunshine, 381

Dotrice, Karen, 324

Double Doll, 308

Doughboy, 11, 38, 407

Dr. Ben Casey, 332

Dr. John, 378

Drake, Debbie, 314, 315

Drayton, Grace, 23, 25, 405

Dream Baby, 11, 82-84, 95

Dresser Dolls, 145

Drink and wet, 12, 381

Ducky, 244

Duke, Patty, 315

Dumbo, 129, 167

Durbin, Deanna, 12, 342

Dutch dolls, 442

Dutch girl, 405

Dy-Dee Baby, 197-201

Dy-Dee Bunting Twins, 200

Dy-Dee Darlin', 198, 199

Dy-Dee-Ette, 197
Dy-Dee-Kin, 197

Dy-Dee-Lou, 197

Dy-Dee-Wee, 197

Dyp-a-Baby, 130

E

EBIEX, 289

Echo, 435

Ed, Mr., 315

Eden, Barbara, 346

Edwards, Vince, 332

EEGEE, 169, 406

Effanbee, 12, 13, 27, 176-201, 288, 289, 318, 320, 327-329, 343, 385, 405, 424, 433

E.G., 169

E. Goldberger, 169

E.I.H., see Horsman

Electronic doll, 434

Elise, 61, 62

Elizabeth, coronation, 316, 317

Elizabeth, Princess, 49, 50, 316

Elizabeth, Queen, 218

Eloise, 159

Embrace of the Tree, 310, 311

Emelie, 336-340

Engineer, 32

Eskimo, 27, 29

Eskimo Pie Boy, 29

Ethnic dolls, 201-205

Eugenia, 168

F

F&B, 343

F&B, see Effanbee

Fairy Princess, 417

Fairy Queen, 55, 56
Fairy Tale Characters, 317

Familee, see Famlee

Family Affair, 313, 314

Famlee, 304, 305

Fashion Barbie, 293, 294

Fashion, Little Lady of, 135

Fashion Queen Barbie, 294

Farina, 323

Fatty, 323

F.D.P.Co., 206

Federal Doll Prod. Co., 206

Felix, 151, 168

Felt dolls, 371

Fethalite, 142

Field, Rachel, 217

Fields, W. C., 343

Fifi, 368

Fisher, Ham, 156

Flapper, 206, 207

Flea markets, 13

Fleischaker & Baum, see Effanbee

Fleishmann & Bloedel, 389

Flexy, 329, 332

Flexy soldier, 250, 251

Flintstones, 150

Flora McFlimsey, 48, 49

Florodora, 16, 88, 89, 111

Flossie Flirt, 30, 31, 243, 244

Flower girl, 54

Flowerkins, 174, 175

Flub-a-Dub, 363, 364

Fluffy, 193

Fly-lo Baby, 118

Flying Nun, 316, 317

Football player, 372, 377

Francis, Anne, 317, 326

French Dandy, 100

French dolls, 208-210, 389

French Societe de Bebes et Jouets, 389

Fresh-up Freddie, 41

Freundlich Novelty Corp., 350, 351

Friedebalde, 368

F.S. & Co., 105

Fudd, Elmer, 150, 158

Funny, 375

Fur brows, 282

Fur wig, 243

Furga, 265, 266, 394

G

Garber, Matthew, 324

Garland, Judy, 12, 16, 248, 249, 343
    344

Gasoline Alley, 151

Gbr.K., 111

Geisha, 270, 271

Gem, 13, 211, 213

General Electric, 33

General Foods, 330

Georgene Novelties, see Averill

Gepetto, 375

Gerber Baby, 30, 214

Gerling, Arthur A., 412

German Bisques, 11, 13, 103-115, 387,
    388
German Bisques, see also company
    names

German composition, 210, 212

Gesgesch, 280

Get Well Doll, 59, 60

GH, 223

GI Joe, 221

Giggles, 126, 128, 263

Ginny, 425, 427

Girl, 12

Girl Scout, 200, 361

Glamour Misty, 27

Glaubach, Stanley, 31

Gold Medal Baby, 231

Goldberger, 169-175

Goldilocks, 377

Goody Two-Shoes, 262

Google-Eye, 408, 411

Grace, 243

Gramma, 374

Grandma, 424

Grandma Jane, 68

Grandmother, 317

Grant, Helen Oakes, 243

Graves, Mrs. Jennie, 425

Great Depression, 12

Green Giant, 31

Green, Nancy, 20

Gruelle, John, 366-368

Grumpy, 164, 177

Guatamalean, 204

Gumdrop, 424, 425

Guinn, Fred, 322

Gund, 167, 374-377

H

Half-doll, 145, 147

Half Pint, 200

Hand puppets, 30, 31, 43, 365

Handmade dolls, 214-218

Handwerck, 109, 219, 220

Handwerck, Heinrich, 219
Hanes Baby, 238

Hannerle, 368

Hansel & Gretel, 210

Happi-Time Walker, 431, 432

Happy, 65

Happy Baby, 382

Happy Flossie, 243

Happytot, 72

Hard plastic, 12, 253, 254

Hardy, Oliver, 349

Harmon Pic. Corp., 349

Harrison, Rex, 341

Hartline, Mary, 29, 317, 318

Hasbro, 221, 222

Hassenfeld Bros., see Hasbro

Hawaiian, 271

Hazelle, Inc., 365

HEbee-SHEbee, 228

Hedda Get Bedda, 305

Heidi, 67

Heinz Baby, 214

Helene, 279

Hendren, 96-99, 376, 377

Henie, Sonja, 344, 345

Henry, 150

Henville, Baby Sandy, 331

Herman Munster, 322

Heubach, 222-224

Heubach-Koppelsdorf, 111

History, 10-12

Hitty, 217

HKO, 109

HO-HO, 128

Hollywood Doll, 143, 212, 213

Honey Bee, 37

Honey Moon, 160

Honey Walker, 197, 198

Honey West, 326

Honeysuckle, 244, 245

Hopalong Cassidy, 335

Horse, 288

Horsman, 8, 9, 12, 13, 24, 25, 211, 225-242,
335, 381

Horsman Bye-lo, 229

Hospital dolls, 370

Howdy Doody, 318, 363, 364

Howland Owl, 156

Hoyer, Mary, 213

H.St., 113

Huck Finn, 215

Huggums, 64, 65

Hula Girl, 202, 203

Hummel, 214

Humpty-Dumpty Circus, 438-440

Hungerford, 214

Husky Baby, 427

Hygeinic Toys, 372

I

Ice Skater, 55

Ideal, 12, 13, 26-28, 30, 31, 34, 35, 37,
40-42, 70, 156, 159, 160, 234, 242-
265, 306, 307, 311, 315, 332, 335,
342, 343, 352, 353-357, 389

I Dream of Jeannie, 346

Indian, 201, 202, 304, 305

Industries for the Blind, 441

Irvin Wallace, 216

Irwin Plastics, 143

ISI, 272

Italian, 11

Italian Moderns, 265

italiocremona, 266

J

Jackie Kennedy, 239

Jacqueline, 63

Jan, 425

Jane, 324

Japanese, 267-273

Japanese Baby, 201, 202

JDK, 280-283

Jean, 151

Jeannie, 346

Jeannie Walker, 53

Jeff, 425

Jenny Lind, 68

Jettchen, 278

Jill, 425

Jim, 279

Jiminy Cricket, 166-168

JK, 239

Joan, 243

Jockerle, 368

Joey, 150

Johnny, 38, 348

Johnny Hero, 377

Johnny West, 288

JO-JO, 232

Jolly green Giant, 31

Jolly Toy, 273

Jones, Marcia Mae, 352

Jordan Marsh Co., 425

Judy, 378

Judy Splinters, 330

Julia, 346, 347

Juro, 333, 349

Jutta, 113

K

K, 374

K and K, 117, 277

"Kaizer Baby", 16, 274, 275

Kallus, J. L., 120-134, 283

Kammer & Reinhardt, 274-276

Kangaroo, Capt., 374, 375

Kathe Kruse, 11, 277-279, 368

Kay, 279

KBK, 289

Kellogg, 30, 31

Kelly, Emmett, 347, 348

Ken, 293, 294

Kennedy, Caroline, 239

Kennedy, Jacqueline, 63, 239

Kennedy, Pres. John F., 348, 349

Kestner, 280-283

Ketcham, Hank, 149, 150

Kewpie Kin, 240

Kewpies, 2, 120, 124, 283, 284, 310

K., Gbr., 111

Kid, The, 335

Kiddie Joy, 81

King, Frank, 11, 151

Kiss Me, 252

Kissing Pink, 40

Kissy, 260, 261

Kissy Baby, 261

Kitten, 59, 60, 62, 63

K&K, 117, 277

Knickerbocker Plastic Co., 142, 308, 349

Knoch, Gebruder, 111

Kodak, 31

Koppelsdorf, see Heubach

Korean, 204, 205

K(star)R, 100, 16, 226, 274, 275

Krauss, Gebruder, 111

Kruger, 372

Kruse, Hannah, 277-279, 370

Kruse, Kathe, 11, 277-279, 368

Kuhnlenz, Gebruder, 111

L

Lamour, Dorothy, 255

Lastic Plastic, 236

Laurel and Hardy, 349

Laurel, Stan, 349

Lee, Buddy, 32, 33

Lee, H. D. Co., 32, 33

Lee, Pinky, 318, 349

Lenci, 368, 371

Leslie, 64

Lewis, Sherri, 350

Libbey, 346, 378

Lil Sis, 284

Lil Sweetie, 200

Linda Baby, 16, 359

Linda Williams, 330

Linus, 152

Lipfert, Bernard, 253

Lisa, 378

Little Annie Rooney, 126, 127

Little Bo Peep, 45, 46

Little Hans, 36

Little Huggums, 64, 65

Little Lady, 195

Little Lady of Fashion, 135

Little Lost Baby, 263

Little Lucile, 376, 377

Little Lulu, 152

Little Miss Echo, 435

Little Miss No Name, 221

Little Orphan Annie, 44, 153, 154

Little Miss Revlon, 40

Little Rabbit Lady, 376

Little Red Riding Hood, 317

Little Rickey, 326

Little Sherry, 376

Little Sister, 373

Little Women, 44

Littlechap Family, 378

Louise, 243

Lovums, 186, 187, 190, 191

Lucinda, 66

Lullabye Baby, 241, 286

M

M, 287, 288, 417

M E, 212

MacArthur, Gen. Douglas, 350, 351

Madame Doll, 67

Madame Georgene, see Averill

Madame Hendren, see Averill

Madame Pompadour, 145

Mademoiselle Dolls, 241

Mae Starr, 433

Magic Lips, 257

Magic Skin Baby, 12, 242, 249-251, 288, 330

Magoo, Mr., 33

Mahoney, Jerry, 318

Majorette, 195

Make-up doll, 22

Malaika, 385

Mama's Angel Child, 377

Mammy, 218

Mannequin, 9, 35, 41, 421, 422

Manufacturers, 13

Margaret, 150

Margie, 131, 132, 168

Margot Ballerina, 58

Marie, 285, 336-340

Marilee, 12, 185

Marionettes, 363-365

Marks, 13

Marlon, 286

Marvel Tot, 72

Marx, 289

Mary, 323

Mary Ann, 12, 194

Mary Cassatt Baby, 65

Mary Had a Lamb, 377

Mary Hartline, 317, 318

Mary Hoyer, 213

Mary Jane, 12, 176, 177

Mary Martin, 319

Mary Poppins, 324

Mary-Quite-Contrary, 376

Mary Sunshine, 381

Marybel, 59, 60

Mattel, 13, 289, 313, 314, 341, 346, 347 362, 364, 376, 432

McOwan, Mrs. Clarence, 215

Mebetoys, 289

Melitta, 109

Melodie, 435

Merrichild, 238

Metal dolls, 301-303

Metropolitan, 287, 303

Metti, 286

Mexican, 201

Michael, 324

Michtom, Benjamin, 242

Michtom, Morris, 242, 389

Mickey, 198, 199

Mickey Mouse, 167

Middie, 226

Midge, 293, 294

Mighty Mouse, 155

Matty Mattel, 292

Max, 368

McAboy, Mary, 201

McCall, 34, 35

McCall, Betsy, 34, 35, 79

McCall, Peggy, 35

McCarthy, Charlie, 320

McFlimsey, Flora, 48, 49

McGuffey Ana, 47, 48, 59, 60

Miller, Joyce, 374

Mills, Hayley, 325

Mimerle, 279, 368

Minerva, 302

Minnie Mouse, 166, 167

Minnow Co., 361

Miranda, Carmen, 321

Miss Century, 135

Miss Clairol, 27

Miss Columbia, 88

Miss Curity, 29

Miss Echo, 435

Miss Happy, 376

Miss Ideal, 258

Miss Marie, 285, 384

Miss No Name, 221

Miss Peep, 132

Miss Revlon, 40

Miss Sunshine, 377, 384

Mister Ed, 315

Mister Wilson, 150

Mr. Magoo, 33

Mr. Muscles, 441

Mr. Peanut, 38

Mrs. Dencla, 376, 377

Mobley, Edw. Co., 20

Modern Priscilla, 33

Modern Toy Co., 148

Mom, 259

Momma-Poppa, 401

Monkees, 364

Monkey, 281

Monogram Models, 289

Montgomery, Elizabeth, 326

Montgomery, Peggy Jean, 313

Moon Maid, 160

Morimura Bros., 268, 269

Mortimer Snerd, 329

Mouseketeer, 167

Movie stars, 12

My-Toy, 305

Muffin, 375

Multiface, 263, 304-308

Munster, Herman, 322

Murray, Arthur, 36

Music Box, 19

Musical Baby, 286

Mutual Doll Co., 120

N

NAJO(Natl. Joint-Limb Doll Co.), 308

Nancy, 92

Nancy Ann, 113, 309, 310

Nancy Ann Story Book Dolls, 113

Nancy Lee, 246

Nancy Nurse, 162

Nast, Thomas, 268, 269

National Joint-Limb Doll Co., 308

Navajo Indian, 202

Nestle's Chocolate, 36

New Born Babe, 112

Newton, Ruth E., see So-Wee

NF, 37

Nickerson Farms, 37

Nilsen, Margit, 43

Nina, 56

Nippon, 268-272

Nisbet, Peggy, 333

Nize Baby, 12, 155

Noma Elec. Corp., 434

Noma Talking Doll, 434

Norah Wellings, 373

Novelty Doll Co., 308

NS, 103

Nun, 316, 317

Nurse, 11, 226, 332

Nurse, GI Joe Action, 222

O

O'Brien, Margaret, 323, 362, 363

O'Day, Danny, 323

O'Hara, Scarlett, 47, 48

OK, 142

Olive Oyl, 155

Olympic Hero, 377

O'Neill, Rose, 10, 11, 120-126, 128, 283 284, 310, 311

Original, 13, 14

Operation Bootstrap, 385, 386

Orphan Annie, see Little Orphan Annie

Our Gang, 323

Overall Doll, 17, 32

Ozark Woman, 215

P

Page, Polly, 215

Palooka, Joan, 156

Papier mache, 312

Parrot, 341

Parsons-Jackson Celluloid Collar Co., 140

Pat-o-Pat, 185, 186

Pat. Pend., 237

Patsy, 12, 13, 192

Patsy Ann, 187, 188, 192, 193

Patsy-Baby, 189

Patsy-Baby-ette, 187, 188

Patsy-Joan, 12, 191

Patsy Lou, 12, 188, 189

Patsy-Mae, 190, 191

Patsy Ruth, 190, 191

Patsy type, 191, 192, 413

Patsyette, 16, 188, 189

P.E., 268, 269

Peanut, 131

Pearl, see Poor Pitiful Pearl

Ped-a-Dolls, 218

Peeps, 377

Peg wooden, see Dutch Dolls

Peggy, Baby, 313

Pelham Puppets, 364

Penny Brite, 162

Penney, J. C. Co., 230

Penny woodens, see Dutch Dolls

Pepper, 260

Perfect Beauty, 72

Perfect doll, 13

Personality dolls, 12, 13, 313-330

Pete and His Pony, 260

Pete and Repete, 255

Peter Pan, 68, 69

Peterle, 214

Petite, 13, 25, 26, 70-80

Pettitcollin, 210

Phillip Morris, 38, 348

Phonograph doll, 433

Piano, 438, 439

Pillsbury, 38

Pinkie, 129

Pinocchio, 167, 168, 245, 364, 375, 441

Pioneer woman, 216

Pitiful Pearl, see Poor Pitiful Pearl

Pixie, 395

Plangon Club, 286

Plassie, 242, 251, 311

Play Toys Inc., 311

Pogo and Friends, 156

Pogo Possum, 156

Poland, 441

Polly Pigtails, 56

Pollyana, 325, 392, 393

Polynesia, 341

Poor Pitiful Pearl, 211

Pop, 31

Popeye, 12, 157, 396

Popin' Fresh Doughboy, 38

Poppins, Mary, 324

Poppa-Momma, 234, 248

Poppy, 376

Porky Pig, 158

Porky Pine, 156

Portrait, 331-363

Portrait Children, 68

Portrait of an Old Man, 310

Posie, 256

Posie Playmate, 174

Pos'n Misty, 27

Posy Pixie, 395

Postcard, 284

Pretty Baby, 80

Prices, 13

Prince Charles, 333

Prince Phillip, 324

Princess dolls, 392, 393, 417

Princess Elizabeth, 49, 50, 316

Princess line, 312

Princess of Doll Land, 312

Pri-thilla, 396

P.Sch., 108

Puddin', 65

Pumpkin, 64, 65

Puppets, 30, 31, 43, 363, 364

Puppetrina, 174, 175

Purina, 39

Purpose dolls, 242

Pussycat, 66

Putnam, Grace Story, 11, 116-119

Put-togethers, 13

Q

Quaker Crackels Boy, 39

Queen Elizabeth, 218, 316, 317

R

RA, 112

R&B, see Arranbee

Rabbit, stuffed, 42

Rabbit Lady, Little, 376

Rachel, 151

Rag dolls, 11, 12, 366-375

Raggedy Andy, 366-372

Raggedy Ann, 366-372

Ragsy-Kewpie, 124, 125

Railroad King, 17

Raleigh dolls, 371, 376, 377

Raleigh, Jessie McCutcheon, 366, 367, 371

Rastus, 27

Ratti, 265, 289

Raynal, 208

Rebecca, 67

Red Riding Hood, 377

Remco, 378, 379, 432

Renoir Girl, 68

Revlon, 40

Rex Doll Co., 120

Rheinische, Gummi, 11

Rickey, 293

Rickey, Jr., 326

Riekchen, 279

Rock-a-Bye Baby, 98

Roddy, 168

Rogers, Roy, 335, 363, 364

Rookie, 226

Roosevelt, Pres. Theodore, 389

Rooted wigs, 12

Rosco-Steele, Inc., 377

Rose, 214

Rosebud, 87, 225, 228, 229

Rosebud Dolls, Ltd., 289

Rosemary, 183, 184

Ross, Dianna, 16, 350, 351

Rubber, 12, 214, 379, 380

Rusty, 411

Ruth, 144

S

S&H, 104

S&Q, 110

Saalfield Publishing, 370

Sad Eyes, 221

Sad Sack, 158

Sally, 12, 71, 191

Sailor, 28, 97, 98, 373, 410

Sailor boy, 226

Samantha, 326

Sammy Kaye, 329, 330

Sandy, 153, 331

Santa, 387

Sara Lee, 253

Sarah Ann, 384

Saucy Walker, 255, 256

Savannah Prod., 346

Sayco Doll Corp., 323, 385

Scarecrow, 39

Schmidt, Paul, 108

Schild, Gary, 370

Schoenhut, 151, 436-440

Schoenhut-Circus, 438-440

Schoenhut-Piano, 438-439

Scooba Doo, 294, 295

Scooter, 293

Scootles, 124, 125

Sears Specials, 13

Semco, Ltd., 155

Seven Dwarfs, 164, 165

Seven-Up, 41

Sewing kits, 35

S.F.B.J., 11, 13, 106, 389

S.G.D.G., 389

SH, 104

Shackman toys, 383

Shepherd of the Hills Museum, 311

Shindana, 385, 386

Shirley, Anne, 13, 196, 316, 327

Shoebutton Sue, 369

Shoemaker, 375

Shoen & Yondorf Co., 323

Shoofly Rocker, 263

Simon & Halbig, 220, 276, 387, 388

Sims, Carolyn, 216

Singer Mannikin, 41

Singin' Chatty, 300

Singing doll, 433

Sioux Indian, 202, 203

Sister, 197, 233

Sister Belle, 292

Sister, Big and Little, 373

Sister Look'n'Say, 295

Skater, 425, 426

Skeezix, 151

Skipper, 293, 294

Skippy, 151, 328, 329

Skookum, 201

Sleepy, 164, 238, 239

Sleepy Baby, 380

Sleepy-Time Twins, 251

Sleepy, Weepy, & Smiley, 306, 307

Sleeping Beauty, 61

Slumbermate, 57

Slogans, 11

Smith, Ella, 368, 374

Smith, Sherman E., 217

Smith, W., Ind., 41

Smokey the Bear, 41

Smoking doll, 28, 29, 206, 207

Snap, Crackle & Pop, 31

Snerd, Mortimer, 329

Snoozie, 245, 252

Snow Crop, 43

Snow White, 247, 404

Snyder, Charles M., 23

So Big, 64

Softina, 174, 175

Soft vinyl, 12

Soldier, 11, 226, 251, 281, 407

Soozie Smiles, 306, 307

So-Sleepy, 360

Sound of Music, 44, 68, 69

"South Pacific", 319

Souvenier doll, 271

So-Wee, 386

Spanish lady, 217

Sparkle Plenty, 160, 242

Special, 110

Splinters, Judy, 330

Squalling baby, 236

Squarecrow, 39

Standard Plas. Prod., 289

Starr, Brenda, 158

Starr, Mae, 433

Steig, Wm., 211

Steiner, Hermann, 113

Stockinette, Chase, 370, 372

Stork Mark, 140

Story Book Dolls, 113, 309, 310
Successful Farming Magazine, 230

Suck-a-Thumb, 245

Sugar Kandi, 172

Sun Rubber Co., 30, 313, 379, 380, 386

Sunbabe, 379, 380

Sunny Girl, 99

Sunshine, 377, 381, 382

Surprise Baby, 306, 307

Susan Stroller, 170

Suzanne, 195

Suzy, 67

Suzy Cute, 162, 163

Suzy Homemaker, 161

Swedlin, 167, 204, 205, 374, 375

Sweet Sue, 78

Sweetie, 33

Sweetie Pie, 197, 385

Swing and Sway, 329, 330

Switzerland, 302, 303

Synthetic rubber, 12

T

Talcum, 284

Talking doll, 221, 386

Talking dolls, see Mattel and other companies by name

Talking Terri Lee, 358

Tammen Mfg., 201

Tammy and Family, 259, 260

Tamu, 386

Ted, 259

Teddy Bear, 242, 389, 390

Teddy Snow Crop, 43

Tee Wee, 230

Teen Star, 248, 249

Teenie Weenie, 80

Teeny Tiny Tears, 13

Teeny Weeny Tiny Tears, 13

Temple, Shirley, 8, 9, 12, 13, 16, 169, 196, 242, 245, 352-357

Terri Lee, 358-361

Terry Twist, 258

Teto, 365

That Girl!, 346, 361

The Kid, 335

Thomas, Danny, 330

Thomas, Marlow, 346, 361

Three Little Pigs, 168

Thrift shops, 13

Thumbelina, 262

Thumbs Up, 43

Tickletoes, 243, 244, 252

Ticklette, 243

Timothy Mouse, 129

Tinker Bell, 166

Tintair, 44

Tiny Chatty Baby, 298

Tiny Chatty Brother, 292, 293, 298

Tiny Tears, 13, 75, 77

Toddler, 406

Toddle-Tot, 72

Toni, 42, 43, 242

Toodles, 73-75

Toots and Casper, 148

Topper Toys, see Deluxe Reading

Topsy, 373, 403

Tortoise mark, see Turtle mark

Traditional, 372

Traditional construction, 267-269

Traditional dolls, 270, 271

Tressy, 79, 264

Trudy, 306, 307

True life toys, 242

Truflesh, 244

Turtle mark, 138-141, 275, 276

Twelvetrees, Charles, 225

Twiggy, 361

Twins, 251, 255

Tynie Baby, 225, 229

U

Uncle Mose, 20

Uncle Pink, 215

Uncle Walt, 151

Uneeda, 160, 325, 391-396

Unmarked Dolls, 8, 9, 14, 396-424

V

Van Dyke, Dick, 362

Vanity Flossie, 243

Vanta Baby, 44

Velvet, 264, 265

Ventriloquist dummies, 318, 320, 323, 329, 343

Victoria, 66

Victory doll, 43

Vinyl, 12

Violet, 57, 58, 302

Virginia Mae, 216

Vogue Dolls, 425-427

Voice boxes, 412

W

W, 220, 428

W-K/IN, 207

WAC, 425, 426

Wade, 20

Walker, 171, 255, 256, 262, 289, 357 406, 422, 428-431

Walker, Dolly, 429

Walker, Honey, 197

Walker, Jeannie, 53

Walker, Toni, 42

Walker, Wanda, 431

Walkalon Doll, 430

Walkalon Mfg. Co., 430

Walking dolls, see Walker

Walking-Talking Dolls, 429-435

Wanda Walker, 431

War Baby, 412

Wardrobe, 13

Wardrobe doll, 382

Wearwell Brand, 302

Weatherbird Shoes, 18

Wedding Party, 54

Wee Willie Winkie, 354

Weiderseim, Grace, 23

Wellings, Norah, 373

Wendy, 380

Wendy-Ann, 50, 51

West, Honey, 317, 326

West, Johnny, 289

Wetting doll, 381

WG (superimposed), 224

Whimsies, 80

Whipple, Billie, 22

Whistler, 97, 98

Whistling Boy, 222

Wilkin, E., 427

Williams, Linda, 330

Willie the Clown, 347, 348

Wilson, W. J., 428, 429

Winchell, Paul, 318

Winnie, 245

Winnie-The-Pooh, 389

Withers, Jane, 12, 352, 362, 363

Wondercraft Co., 329-330

Wood Toy Co., 429

Wooden dolls, 271, 436-442

Women's Army Corp., 425, 426

World War I soldier, 11, 12, 281, 407, 412

World War II, 11, 410

X, 312

YANOCO, 143

Yes-No, 193, 237

Yoshitoku, 271

Yvonne, 336-340

Young, Helen, 218

Zest coffee, 220

"HEAR MY DOLLIES' PRAYER"

O LORD, I pray Thee, hear my dollies' prayer,
  And teach them how to ask for what is right,
But if it's going to give You extra care,
  Then You might skip MY blessings for to
    night.
Please make them all more loving and polite ;
  I pray Thee not to let their covers tear,
But keep their sawdust stuffings out of sight,

AND please help Anne to grow a head of
  hair.
I wish poor Bella's knees were made to bend,
  I truly am as sorry as can be.
I hope that You won't mind, and that You'll send
  The blessings that each dolly asks of Thee.
And, Lord, I pray that You will just pertend
  This is my dollies talking, 'stead of me.

PINOCCHIO